# CITIZEN HOBO

TODD DEPASTINO

# CITIZEN HOBO

## HOW A CENTURY OF HOMELESSNESS SHAPED AMERICA

THE UNIVERSITY OF CHICAGO PRESS
CHICAGO AND LONDON

Todd DePastino is an independent scholar who teaches history at Waynesburg College and Penn State Beaver. He lives in Pittsburgh, Pennsylvania.

The University of Chicago Press, Chicago 60637
The University of Chicago Press, Ltd., London

12 11 10 09 08 07 06 05 04 03     1 2 3 4 5
ISBN: 0-226-14378-3

Library of Congress Cataloging-in-Publication Data
DePastino, Todd.
    Citizen hobo : how a century of homelessness shaped America / Todd DePastino.
        p. cm.
Includes index.
    ISBN 0-226-14378-3 (alk. paper)
    1. Tramps—United States—History.   2. Homelessness—United States—History.
3. Marginality, Social—United States—History.   4. Subculture—United States—History.
I. Title.
HV4504 D47 2003
305.5′68—dc21

                                                          2002154907

⊗ The paper used in this publication meets the minimum requirements of the American National Standard for Information Sciences—Permanence of Paper for Printed Library Materials, ANSI Z39.48-1992.

*For Steph, Ellie, and Libbie*

# CONTENTS

# PART IV
## THE ENDURING LEGACY:
## HOMELESSNESS AND AMERICAN CULTURE SINCE 1980

## 9
### *Rediscovering Homelessness* 247

# ILLUSTRATIONS

# ACKNOWLEDGMENTS

This book was long in the making and would never have been possible without the help and support of many people. It is my privilege to thank some of them here.

This book began as a dissertation at Yale University, where, I am ashamed to say, I drew upon the expertise and kind offices of friends, colleagues, and professors in grossly unequal proportion to the amount I returned. From the moment I walked into his office, announced my dissertation topic, and asked him to advise it, Jean-Christophe Agnew has given indispensable direction, encouragement, and support through every step of my career. Offering guidance with his characteristic humor and insight, he has profoundly deepened my basic understanding of the historian's craft. This book's scholarly contribution is largely the result of Jean-Christophe's constant but gentle prodding to get me to expand the scope of my argument and recognize the larger significance of my material.

I am also deeply grateful to David Brion Davis, whose high standards of scholarship, devotion to his students, and strong moral vision not only greatly improved this book, but also continue to inspire me as a scholar and teacher. Ann Fabian guided me out of the murkiness that characterized the early stages of this study, and also, incidentally, provided the wonderful company that helped make graduate study at Yale collegial and pleasurable. Like countless others who have come before me, I thank David Montgomery for sharing his invaluable advice and encyclopedic knowledge and for first inspiring my interest in working-class history. I appreciate his patience through my early missteps as much as I do his voluminous and painstaking commentary on every draft I sent his way. Finally, I must confess my long-standing debt to three scholars and teachers at Boston College—Paul Breines, Alan Lawson, and Mark O'Connor—

who taught me about writing, history, and critical thinking long before this book was conceived.

So many friends and colleagues contributed to this book that I can only mention those who commented upon all or large parts of the manuscript. With his characteristic intellectual generosity and enthusiasm, James E. Mooney emboldened me to address larger themes. Robert Sherry not only read drafts and listened patiently as I tried to make sense of this topic, but also helped me to work through the strains of writing. His guidance has meant more to me than he could know. As a friend and confidant, Kevin Rozario read virtually every sentence—fragments and run-ons included— produced during this writing process, subjecting each to his exacting critical review. With his gentle humor, sharp wit, and humane approach to scholarship and life, Kevin has shaped this book in immeasurable ways. Lane Hall-Witt lent his truly rare intellect to early chapters, offering extensive and imaginative written commentaries that forced me to rethink and revise the very questions I was posing. Louis Warren provided many kinds of support and advice, not least of which was suggesting its very topic in the first place. Finally, my old friend Paul Allen Anderson devoted his prodigious intellectual, scholarly, and literary skills to a thorough critique of the entire manuscript that reoriented the study as a whole. I can only hope that the final product repays his efforts, if only in part.

At the University of Chicago Press, Doug Mitchell provided enthusiastic support and encouragement past many deadlines and over many hurdles. When I felt like the chips were down, Doug offered a stunningly erudite, and overly flattering, précis of the book that guided my final revisions. Two anonymous readers at the Press also contributed to these revisions, saving me from making several blunders, though perhaps not as many as they would have liked. On short notice, Douglas Harper generously extended his expertise, critical eye, and literary gifts to a thorough reading of the entire manuscript, contributing greatly to some final improvements. Robert Devens and Timothy McGovern supplied their own expertise as I prepared the final manuscript. No one read this work more closely than Erin DeWitt, who lived up to her billing as the best manuscript editor in the business.

In my search for sources, I have been assisted by the knowledge and energies of many persons. The reference librarians and archivists at Yale University, the University of Illinois at Chicago, the University of Pittsburgh, the New York Public Library for the Performing Arts, the Chicago Historical Society, the State Historical Society of Iowa, the Library of Congress, the Rockefeller Archives Center (where Thomas Rosenbaum was particularly helpful), and the National Archives were indispensable. I would especially like to thank Pat Groeller, Polly Inge, and Carol Pistachio at Penn State Beaver for cheerfully putting up with my weekly stacks of arcane interlibrary loan requests. Marie Steenlage and George Horton of Iowa offered both their hospitality and access to their wonderful collections of tramp and hobo ephemera.

Financial support for research and writing came from many sources, including a John F. Enders Grant and an Andrew W. Mellon Fellowship at Yale University, an American Historical Association Albert J. Beveridge Award, a Rockefeller Archives Center Grant, and a National Endowment for the Humanities Fellowship and summer stipend. Parts of chapters 3 and 4 appeared in *Community in the American West,* a Halcyon imprint published by the Nevada Humanities Committee. I thank them for their permission to reprint.

Finally, no study of homelessness would be complete without acknowledging the manifold gifts of home. My parents, Allan and Bernice De-Pastino, shall always have my undying gratitude for the sacrifices they have made on my behalf, the love they have shown, and the example they have set. These and the many other gifts they have given will be a part of me always. My brother, Blake DePastino, offered insights and inspiration in his own inimitable style, forcing me to admit to myself, though never to him, that he is the better writer. Jennifer and Drew Haberberger have offered unflagging encouragement, support, love, and understanding throughout this project. Their daughters, my nieces Rosaleigh and Annabel, have enriched my life beyond anything I could ever have imagined.

This book is dedicated especially to the three persons with whom I most closely share my life. My wife, Stephanie Ross, has lived with this book far longer than was promised. She has supported and nourished this effort often to the detriment of her own work and dreams. Her love and respect have set a high standard for our marriage, and although I know my debt to her can never be repaid, I nonetheless hope that over our long life together I will find an appropriate way to say thank you. My daughters, Eleanor and Elizabeth, were not here when I started this study and were of not much help when I finished it. They read no drafts, provided no insights, and offered no support or encouragement. Indeed, apart from keeping up their nap schedules, Ellie and Libbie constantly distracted me and hampered my best efforts to keep my life focused on research and writing. For this, I thank them.

# INTRODUCTION

"Warren," she said, "he has come home to die:
You needn't be afraid he'll leave you this time."

"Home," he mocked gently.

    "Yes, what else but home?
It all depends on what you mean by home.
Of course he's nothing to us, any more
Than was the hound that came a stranger to us
Out of the woods, worn out upon the trail."

"Home is the place where, when you have to go there,
They have to take you in."

      "I should have called it
Something you somehow haven't to deserve."
—Robert Frost, "The Death of the Hired Man" (1914)

Perhaps no category of human experience exerts more ideological power than that of home. Fundamental and universal, home nonetheless defies simple definition, for it exists in memory and imagination as much as it does in brick and mortar. More than mere shelter or the means of social reproduction, home provides a well of identity and belonging, "a place in the world." In exchange, home demands subordination to prescribed roles and routines, exercising a tyranny over its members and a vigilant defense against the encroachments of outsiders. A castle for some, a prison house for others, home structures and regulates human activity in ways that model and articulate the social relations governing the larger community. Societies riddled with persons deemed "homeless" are, by definition, societies in crisis.[1]

In 1914, when Robert Frost crafted his poetical meditation on the meaning of home, the United States was in the grip of such a crisis. Ever since the Civil War, a veritable army of homeless men, predominantly white and native-born, had occupied the nation, growing virtually unabated year by year until it had become such a permanent fixture on the American landscape that few thought it could ever be resettled. For these men, commonly referred to as "tramps" and "hoboes," homelessness was not so much a shelter condition, but a distinct way of life characterized by casual lodging, temporary labor, and frequent migration. As both products and agents of corporate capitalist expansion, hoboes pressed everywhere on the eyes and minds of a nation struggling to match nineteenth-century domestic ideals with the new realities of urban industrial life. Challenging home's status as a central place of being and building block of social order, hoboes put their own ideals of "homelessness" on prominent display, especially as they gathered along the "main stem" of the industrial city. By the time Frost published his poem about the final journey and unwelcomed claims of a "Hired Man," they had forged a swaggering counterculture known as "hobohemia" that defied, unsettled, and eventually transformed everything Americans meant by home.

Thus, while Frost's poem offers a timeless allegory of a universal human alienation, it also captures a particular historical moment when white male homelessness cast such an ominous shadow over American nationhood and citizenship that it called into question the very status of home in a democratic polity. In the poem, a once-fractious and inconstant Hired Man appears at the door of his former employer in an exhausted and ailing condition. Having once flaunted, and now barely weathering, the hard freedoms afforded by the wage contract, the Hired Man triggers a crisis in the farmhouse, compelling the farmer and his wife to deliberate over the meaning of home, to negotiate its boundaries and define its rules of access and exclusion. Whereas the farmer's definition emphasizes the social power, and hence the obligations, of the householder, his wife's rejoinder focuses on the relative powerlessness, and hence the inalienable rights, of the dispossessed. All the while, the question of what constitutes a home remains open, as do the terms and conditions under which the Hired Man will be "taken in." "It all depends," as the farmer's wife reminds her husband, "on what you mean by home."

*Citizen Hobo* examines what Americans have meant by home—and, by extension, its absence—since modern homelessness first emerged in the late nineteenth century. It argues, in essence, that the specter of white male homelessness so haunted the American body politic between the end of the Civil War and the onset of the Cold War that it prompted the creation of an entirely new social order and political economy. Over these decades, the Hired Man took on many forms—the "tramp" of the Gilded Age, the "hobohemian" of the Progressive Era, the "transient" and "migrant" of the Great Depression, and the skid row "bum" of the postwar period—but each time he appeared at the threshold, he signaled a crisis of home that was always also one of nationhood and citizenship, race and gender. Each crisis, in turn, reinvigorated efforts to resettle the hobo army and reintegrate the white male "floater" back into the American polity. By the middle of the twentieth century, these efforts had yielded not only in the welfare state and corporate liberal economy, but also in the modern American home itself, with all it entails for class formation, gender order, and racial identity.

As this argument suggests, *Citizen Hobo* is not a comprehensive history of American homelessness. Neither does it offer a sustained structural analysis, nor even an exhaustive ethnography of hobo subculture, although both the structural and ethnographic approaches form key components of the study. Rather, this book traces the history of homelessness as a category of culture as well as economy, focusing especially on how its racialized and gendered meanings shaped the entitlements and exclusions of "social citizenship" in modern America.[2]

In so doing, it draws upon a rich body of previous scholarship in the history of race, poverty, gender, sexuality, social welfare, migratory labor, and urban culture. Indeed, the subject of American homelessness brings together a great many discrete historiographies, from the social and institutional histories of tramping and poor relief to the now-crowded fields of "whiteness studies" and gender and social policy. While social, urban, and public policy historians have documented the changing experiences, social composition, institutional contexts, and physical spaces of homelessness, feminist and political scholars have demonstrated the racialized and gendered dimensions of social citizenship, as well as the ways in which social policy constitutes racial, gender, and class difference.[3] These studies have supplied the departure points for my own investigation, one that explores how culturally defined crises of homelessness have both reflected and shaped larger changes in the political economy and culture of America since the late nineteenth century.

The first step of such an investigation is to narrate the rise, fall, and indelible legacy of hobohemia, plotting the boundaries, recapturing the culture, and analyzing the politics of a way of life largely forgotten by historians and obscured by contemporary assumptions and concerns. As part of the larger homeless world to which the Hired Man belonged, hobohemia constituted a distinct white male counterculture with its own rules of membership, codes of behavior, and notions of the good life. Rejecting the range of manners, morals, and habits associated with middle-class domesticity, hobohemia fostered a powerful sense of collective identity among its members, an identity reinforced by the numerous advocacy groups that arose to promote hoboes' interests. By World War I, virtually every main stem in America hosted a local of the Industrial Workers of the World (IWW) or some other formal organization intent on mobilizing the subculture for the larger purposes of social change. Through their pamphlets, newspapers, and songbooks, these organizations also disseminated a powerful set of hobo myths that enhanced group definition and celebrated hobohemia as a revolutionary vanguard.

But while the IWW touted migratory homeless men as the "real proletarians," hoboes almost always defined their world in terms not only of class, but also of race, ethnicity, gender, and region. Jealously guarding the road as the preserve of white men, hoboes also, from time to time, staked compelling claims to the polity on the basis of white male privilege. These claims carried particular weight when registered in the form of a disenfranchised hobo "army," a figure that evoked not only the size, sway, mobility, militancy, and camaraderie of the subculture, but also the spectacle of an aggrieved "National Manhood." These armies occupied real spaces—not just discursive ones—most conspicuously when rail-riding protesters in old military garb swept down on the nation's capital to dramatize the burdens they had borne for the state and to demand the compensating entitlements. The Industrial Armies of 1894 and the Bonus Army of 1932 proved particularly effective in offering up powerful models of nationhood, as well as working-class white manhood, during times of severe economic crisis. Coupled with the everyday claims that hoboes made on railroads, employers, householders, local officials, and urban space itself, these protests suggested to many Americans that the "imagined fraternity of white men" that had historically constituted American nationhood needed to be domesticated.[4] On the road too long and enchanted by its romance of perfect freedom and brotherhood, the hobo had to be "taken in," reminded of his "paternalist" duties, and resettled as a family breadwinner.

In tracing the various campaigns to recover and resettle the homeless man, this book examines the diverse and conflicted meanings that hobohemia held for Americans, from the investigators who first charted the problem of homelessness to the poets, performers, songwriters, filmmakers, labor organizers, and various other commentators who saw both perils and possibilities in the hobo life. Of special consequence, of course, was the attention that hobohemia attracted from politicians, policy makers, businesspersons, and reformers of all stripes. Over time and through a sweeping series of interventions in labor, housing, and transportation markets, these activists eventually managed to dismantle hobohemia and demobilize the roving army of hobo labor. Through their struggle with a population they deemed homeless, they created, in effect, the modern American home, redistributing its benefits as well as its burdens.

When homelessness first emerged as a widespread social problem after the Civil War, most Americans still clung to patriarchal ideals of home as productive property, a shop or farm that harbored the labor of dependent families and granted its owner the full privileges of citizenship. By the turn of the twentieth century, these old ideals had succumbed to the new realities of industrial wage earning, which stripped home of its central economic purpose and its civic status. Amidst Progressive and New Era experiments with "welfare capitalism," and working-class housing arose a new vision of suburban homeownership, a vision that emphasized the aesthetic and spiritual values of rootedness, place, and familial belonging.

While this vision effectively recast the problem of homelessness in the modern terms of alienation and estrangement, it was not until the New Deal of the 1930s when mass suburban homeownership became an explicitly political goal, a way of restoring the bonds of community and nationhood during a time of unparalleled homelessness. After World War II, when the discharge of millions of soldiers and sailors once again threatened to unleash a homeless army upon the nation, this political goal was finally achieved. With the help of the GI Bill, the suburban home became the centerpiece of a new corporate liberal order that promoted masculine breadwinning, feminine child rearing, and the steady consumption of durable goods within the context of the nuclear family. By extending the family-wage pact and the suburban ideal of single-family homeownership to a broad segment of the white working class, the corporate liberal state effectively solved the modern problem of homelessness and infused the home with new meanings for democratic citizenship.

As a solution to the vexing problem of white male homelessness, the "postwar settlement" redefined the privileges of whiteness by failing to extend the full social benefits of citizenship to those who had historically been barred from hobohemia. This failure ensured that when the corporate liberal order faltered in the 1970s, a new homeless army would arise bearing the marks not of white manhood, but of a feminized and racialized "underclass."

Cast adrift by the very political economy of home that recovered the

Hired Man, the so-called "new homeless" have once again fractured our unified domestic visions and triggered a new round of debate over what we mean by home. The homeless men, women, and children of postmodern America also bear witness to the unresolved issues of nationhood and citizenship that struggles over home have historically entailed. Almost one hundred years after "The Death of the Hired Man," we find ourselves asking the same questions posed by Frost's farm couple: What are the rules governing access to and exclusion from settled society? How are the dispossessed and disenfranchised to be "taken in" as full members of the polity and economy? Is home truly "something you somehow haven't to deserve," or is it a privilege reserved for the worthy? Although, as a work of history, this book cannot presume to answer these questions in any definitive or programmatic way, it can provide a new context for thinking through the vexing problems of poverty, inequality, and alienation. Like the proverbial traveler who arrives where she started and knows that place for the first time, we explore what we mean by homelessness in order to understand better the rules, privileges, and exclusions by which we claim our homes.

Because this book tells a story, it proceeds in chronological order with each chapter highlighting a particular event or turning point in the history of modern American homelessness. To signpost the overarching narrative, the chapters are organized into four parts that together chart the rise and decline of hobohemia and track its legacy down to the present day. In addition to plotting change over time, this book also analyzes in depth key topics and themes—especially those relating to race, ethnicity, class, gender, sexuality, nationhood, and citizenship—that emerged and accumulated during each stage of the long crisis.

Chapter 1 traces the roots of the crisis to the depressions of the Gilded Age, when a "great army of tramps"—departing dramatically in size, scope, and composition from previous generations of vagrants and vagabonds—let loose upon the land, conjuring up widespread fears of gender disorder, class warfare, and a masculine regression to "savagery." Chapter 2 turns to working-class observers and victims of the crisis who, like Walt Whitman, often idealized the "Open Road," but also valued "home" as the property necessary for free, independent "manhood."

Opening with an analysis of the Industrial Army movement's unprecedented March on Washington in 1894, chapter 3 tracks the emergence of hobo subculture, including its peculiar sexual code, through the bunkhouses, boxcars, "jungle" camps, and main stems of the western "wageworkers' frontier." Chapter 4 then examines how the IWW and other radicals infused hobohemia with new political meanings, crafting an enduring canon of hobo folklore that drew upon frontier romances of virile white manhood.

From the romances of the open road, chapter 5 turns to the mysteries of the great city, exploring how, in the context of Progressive efforts to reform the main stem, the "tramp crisis" became known as the "problem of homelessness." The new language figuratively linked the hobo to the larger urban "hotel spirit," which, reformers argued, bureaucratized and commodified "home," reducing it to the functions of "housing." While the "hotel spirit" received a ringing endorsement from the likes of Upton Sinclair, Charlotte Perkins Gilman, and the outrageously popular comic tramps of vaudeville, a coalition of activists worked to dismantle "hotel civilization" and reengineer the American home in the suburbs.

While housing activists advanced new suburban ideals as antidotes to a broadly defined moral crisis of homelessness, employers and industrial relations experts after World War I, as chapter 6 demonstrates, worked to curtail hobohemia through long-term changes in the migratory labor market and the political economy of unemployment. As hobohemia slipped into the past, a cultural struggle over its memory pitted radicals like John Dos Passos on the Left against popular folklorists on the Right. These debates not only reflected the realities of New Era capitalism, but also shaped popular and official responses to the mass homelessness of the 1930s, a decade haunted by the specter of hobohemia.

This specter acquired flesh and blood in 1932, when, as chapter 7 argues, the Bonus Army's March on Washington sparked a new crisis of nationhood that eventually prompted President Franklin Roosevelt to make the recovery of the "Forgotten Man" the priority of his New Deal. In response to stinging criticism that FDR's various "armies" of recovery merely replicated the fraternalist camp camaraderie of hobohemia, the second New Deal shifted its emphasis to bolstering men's breadwinning roles. While the hobo endured as a populist folk figure, he competed with diverse new folklores of homelessness featuring those never counted among the Forgotten Men, namely, women and nonwhites.

The Forgotten Man's recovery became complete only after World War II, when, as chapter 8 explains, returning veterans took to the suburbs rather than the streets. Meanwhile, blighted skid row districts served as embarrassing reminders of past grievances as well as living laboratories for the study of "disaffiliation," the diagnosis given to those single white men who stubbornly refused their entitlements to breadwinning and homeowning. While the postwar Beat counterculture tried to revive the spirit of the old main stem, the road took on very different meanings with the countercultural upheavals of the late 1960s, by which time most skid row districts had met the wrecking ball.

Chapter 9 traces the emergence and persistence of a new homelessness crisis during the 1980s and 1990s, when a population largely bereft of the romance, the housing, and the racial and gender privileges of its hobo forebearers appeared on the streets. Betokening a renewed cultural crisis of "home," as well as an economic crisis of shelter, the "new homeless" fell victim to the same racialized and gendered politics of the nuclear family imperative that had recovered the hobo. Like their predecessors, however, America's homeless continue to forge their own communities and chafe against family breadwinning ideals. Imprecise and ideologically loaded as it is, the category of homelessness persists not only as the most visible symptom of larger racial, class, and gender inequalities, but also as an immanent frame of reference for their analysis.

A final word on terminology is in order, especially for those readers who are already frustrated with the imprecise and shifting use of the word "homelessness" in this book. As the ironizing quotation marks suggest, "homelessness" is a term whose meaning depends entirely on the specific historical conditions of its use. It has therefore denoted different things to different people at different times. Sometimes its meaning is quite narrow, as in contemporary references to shelterlessness. At other times, the term has signified the dispossession of particular kinds of property, the estrangement of men from the feminine realm of nurture, or the condition of alienation associated with the rise of modernity. The following chapters will signpost these shifts in meaning, paying careful attention to the larger claims implied by the term's use.

While "homelessness" serves as a rich and useful metaphor and a wonderful heuristic device for charting larger changes in ideology and social structure over the twentieth century, it works very poorly as an objective measure of poverty and inequality. Despite the arresting sight of a family waiting for shelter or persons sleeping on a steam grate or huddled under a bridge, those we call homeless differ very little, if at all, from the laboring poor in general. As a symptom of poverty, the dramatic loss of home is rarely permanent, and the resort to the streets largely episodic. In their effort to gain a margin of social power and define the terms of their own situations, the dislocated stake new claims to space and place, squatting, resettling, and otherwise improvising new homes in alien environments. While prevailing notions of home often cast these domestic improvisations as "homelessness," such struggles really concern the normative conditions, meanings, and forms of "home" themselves. One of the goals of this study is to examine our own habitual uses of these keywords, to recover the unacknowledged assumptions, fears, and desires buried within our seemingly objective concepts and definitions. This is not to say that such public encounters with the dispossessed should not prompt concern, outrage, or action on our part. Like the Hired Man at the door, the visible presence of homelessness reminds even those of us who are comfortably housed that no home is purely private and no place in the world is always guaranteed.

# PART I

## THE RISE
## OF HOBOHEMIA,
## 1870–1920

# 1

# "THE GREAT ARMY OF TRAMPS"

Long before he became famous as a pioneering photojournalist and slum reformer, Jacob Riis was a tramp. Riis first arrived to America in the spring of 1870, a twenty-one-year-old Danish immigrant with empty pockets but great ambition. For the next three and a half years, Riis walked and rode over thirty-five hundred miles in search of work, traveling back and forth between the metropolitan areas of New York, Buffalo, Pittsburgh, Philadelphia, and Chicago. While on the move, Riis improvised shelter—"rarely the same for two nights together"—stealing sleep in hay wagons, sheds, barns, open fields, and graveyards (because "brownstone keeps warm long after the sun has set"). While in the city, Riis lodged day-to-day when he could, taking to doorways, parks, and, in at least two instances, police station lodging when money ran out. For food, Riis scavenged and begged, searching out "windfall apples," knocking on back doors, and even, on occasion, hunting rabbits and squirrels, in order to eat the meat and sell the pelts. Of course, Riis also sold his labor. By the time he launched his career as a Bowery beat reporter, Riis had worked as a carpenter, coal miner, farmhand, railroad tracklayer, dockworker, steamship sailor, sawmill hand, factory operative, drummer, peddler, brick maker, telegrapher, and house servant. Not one of his jobs lasted for more than six weeks; most lasted for only a few days. "The love of change belongs to youth," Riis explains in his autobiography, "and I meant to take a hand in things as they came along."[1]

Whether from the love of change or the pinch of hunger, Jacob Riis had joined a growing body of young male workers who, in the years following the Civil War, traveled far and often in search of wage labor. In 1870, when Riis entered this migratory labor stream, most Americans were unaware of what Riis called "the great army of tramps" flocking to American highways. It would take a Wall Street crash in September 1873 and five subsequent years of bankruptcies, wage cuts, layoffs, strikes, and mass unemployment—the first international "great depression"—to thrust the tramp army to the fore of public consciousness. With thousands, perhaps millions, on the road, newspaper editors, charity workers, and government officials across the nation asked the question "What shall we do with our tramps?"[2] "There is perhaps no problem in social science that is just now more pressing," declared the *New York Times* in 1875, "than what to do with the great and increasing army of mendicants who . . . from their mode of life, have gained the name of 'tramp.'"[3]

In responding to this problem, America's opinion and policy makers were not generous. Rather than offer charity, they called for mass arrests, workhouses, and chain gangs. Some advocated more creative solutions. On July 12, 1877, the *Chicago Tribune* advised "putting a little strychnine or arsenic in the meat and other supplies furnished to tramps" as "a warning to other tramps to keep out of the neighborhood."[4] Another paper proposed flooding poorhouses with six feet of water so that tramps would "be compelled to bail" or drown.[5] Justifying such extreme measures was the dean of Yale Law School, Francis Wayland, who delivered a widely circulated paper on tramps before the American Social Science Association in September 1877. "As we utter the word *Tramp*," Wayland declared at the outset of his address, "there arises straightway before us the spectacle of a lazy, shiftless, sauntering or swaggering, ill-conditioned, irreclaimable, incorrigible, cowardly, utterly depraved savage."[6]

Although revealing little about actual tramps themselves, such expressions of fear and loathing tell us much about middle-class perceptions of crisis in the Gilded Age. Tramps stood at the center of a swirling vortex of concerns about the new corporate industrial order coming into being after the Civil War. Americans in these years saw the rise of large-scale manufacturing and mass production, the spread of railroads and continental markets, and the creation of strict workplace hierarchies based on a universal system of wage labor. As the pace of industrialization quickened and economic power became concentrated in fewer hands, pitched battles erupted between capital and labor over not only the fruits of production, but the very destiny of industrial civilization itself. Tramps were both victims and agents of the new economic system, itinerant laborers clinging beneath the speeding freight train of industrial capitalist expansion. Because they seemed strange and placeless—"here to-day and gone tomorrow"—tramps served as convenient screens onto which middle-class Americans projected their insecurities, anxieties, and fantasies about urban industrial life.[7]

Tramps, of course, wrestled with their own insecurities, though middle-class descriptions of tramp life hardly mentioned them. Tramping was an expression of the new social and economic relationships coming to dominate American life in the Gilded Age. Increasingly dependent upon wages and decreasingly secure in their jobs, working people the nation over faced the threat of poverty, dislocation, and the shattering of their customary patterns of life. In the face of these changes, some workers took to the road and, in so doing, collectively gave rise to a new modern problem of homelessness that would command the attention of private and public officials for generations to come.

Because the alarm raised by the tramp crisis of the 1870s reverberated halfway into the twentieth century, charting the emergence of this first tramp army is crucial to understanding the subsequent history of American homelessness. What exactly was new about the great army of tramps? How did Gilded Age tramps differ from previous generations of homeless vagrants? Where and how did they travel? Why did some poor Americans hit the road while others stayed put? And how did tramps get by once they found themselves, as Jacob Riis did, "on the tow-path looking for a job"?[8]

As for the larger culture, what was its response to this new tramp army? How did middle-class observers explain its rather sudden appearance? What logic, conscious or not, governed middle-class nightmares about "savage" tramps? And why did the tramp crisis become such a flashpoint in the larger struggle over the destiny and meaning of the new industrial America?

## THE MAKING OF AMERICA'S TRAMP ARMY

In what one commentator called "a happy innovation of language," Americans in 1873 coined the word "tramp" to describe the legion of men traveling the nation "with no visible means of support."[9] Previously, the noun had denoted "an invigorating walking expedition" or, during the Civil War, "a long, tiring, or toilsome walk or march."[10] Stressing mobility, the new usage also signified a sense of novelty, as if older terms such as "vagrant" or "vagabond" were somehow inappropriate to the moment.

But despite the innovation of language, neither homeless migration nor the fearful responses to it were new to American life in the Gilded Age. Long before the tramp crisis of the 1870s, poor men and women traveled in search of work and relief, often encountering fear and hostility instead. Indeed, court records from the earliest English settlements in America abound with references to the "strolling" or "wandering" poor. Seventeenth-century English colonists had left a country that itself was awash with "vagabonds" and "masterless men": displaced laborers drifting in and out of urban centers. A flourishing literature of "roguery" that purported to catalog the various deceits and depredations of these wayfarers kept the sense of crisis alive, while new draconian penalties for vagabondage—whipping, branding, and hanging among them—set the standard for cruelty. The problem was so urgent that propagandists for colonization such as Richard Hakluyt even urged the establishment of English settlements in America in order to relieve the mother country of its vagrant and "surplus" population. British America, in a sense, was founded as a refuge from, and solution to, the homelessness crisis of Tudor and Stuart England.[11]

A highly mobile people themselves, seventeenth- and eighteenth-century Americans harbored the Old World's suspicions of wandering strangers and took vigorous measures to suppress the transient poor. "Masterlessness" remained a major problem in the New World as the vagabond population swelled with escaped slaves, runaway servants and apprentices, and a host of others recently released from bondage. Those with skills or money usually gained residency or "settlement" when they moved to a new town, while indigent migrants were often "warned out" and physically removed beyond town limits. Settlement laws, which remained in effect until well into the twentieth century, protected towns not only from the responsibilities of poor relief, but also from the exotic and unwanted cultural influences that often accompanied wandering strangers. The tightly regulated towns of colonial New England, for example, frequently banned newcomers who carried religious convictions, political ideas, or moral standards that departed from community norms. Transients judged to be particularly dangerous, in either the criminal or cultural senses, could be deemed "vagabonds" and subjected to the grisly punishments customary in England. Pillorying, branding, flogging, or ear cropping often awaited those migrants who could not give "a good and satisfactory account of their wandering up and down."[12] Like the laws of settlement, vagrancy statutes legitimized and facilitated the mobility of better-off transients while discouraging and criminalizing the movement of the poor.

These laws, strict as they were, proved ineffective in the face of the market and transportation revolutions of the 1820s and 1830s, which unleashed new streams of poor migrants throughout the country. Some of these migrants sought the new employment opportunities afforded by the Jacksonian economy. Young single men poured into and out of such inland boomtowns as Rochester, New York, for example, finding seasonal work along the Erie Canal. These unattached and highly mobile workers made up 71 percent of Rochester's adult male workforce, filling the city's burgeoning workshops, boardinghouses, barrooms, and streets. The rowdy subculture they created alarmed Rochester's more stable middle-class residents. Caught up in the religious revivals of the Second Great Awakening, reform-minded citizens launched temperance crusades and other organizations to impose moral order on this floating army of workers.[13]

While the commercial revolution set new groups of migrants in pursuit of opportunity, it also dislocated those farmers and artisans bankrupted by the new wildly competitive economy. Rural families scrambling for cash to pay rents, debts, or taxes swarmed into urban centers such as Philadelphia and NewYork on the promise of wage labor. Testifying to the frequent failure of these cities to make good on that promise was a newly refurbished urban institution: the almshouse. No longer able merely to "pass on" or "warn out" shelterless paupers, antebellum civic leaders sought to control and rehabilitate the vagrant poor in regimented caretaking institutions.[14]

The vast majority of those we might now call homeless, however, managed to avoid whatever care the almshouse afforded by earning their subsistence in the economy of the streets. Indeed, when antebellum commentators talked of the "vagrant mode of life," they denoted not homelessness per se, but the casual labor that poor city dwellers increasingly pursued. Peddling, scavenging, begging, prostitution, petty thievery, gambling, and any other "disorderly" public activity that threatened or "injured" the moneymaking potential of urban real estate all fell under the legal purview of vagrancy. By 1860 entire neighborhoods of the propertyless poor, like NewYork City's notorious Five Points in lower Manhattan, became known as "vagrant" districts not only because of their degraded housing conditions, but also because of their illegal street economies. That relatively settled neighborhood residents could be deemed vagrants attests to the enduring and multifaceted nature of vagrancy in nineteenth-century America.[15]

As these historical precedents suggest, the tramp crisis of 1873–78, while eclipsing everything that had come before in its breadth and intensity, was not entirely, as one journalist claimed in 1877, like "a thunderburst from a clear sky."[16] Indeed, the great army of tramps was in many ways merely another variation on the old, if ever-changing, theme of American homelessness stretching back to the days of colonization. Gilded Age tramps, like their homeless predecessors, took to the road because of dislocation and unemployment or because of new opportunities resulting from economic expansion. Just as propertyless migrants in the early nineteenth century encountered an array of law enforcement and charity officials bent on punishing, incarcerating, or rehabilitating them, so, too, did late-nineteenth-century tramps. Indeed, tramps of the 1870s inspired a whole new generation of vagrancy laws and workhouse disciplines. But, also like earlier vagrants, most tramps found temporary refuges of their own in working-class neighborhoods and the casual labor economy.

Middle-class perceptions of crisis in the Gilded Age also mirrored earlier panics over vagrancy. The factors generating concern about the "vagrant mode of life" in the antebellum period also fueled the tramp scare of the 1870s: the struggles between the propertied and unpropertied over the uses of public space, fears about the growth of a propertyless proletariat, and anxieties about the loss of traditional social controls in American cities. Viewed from one perspective, the rise of America's great tramp army in the 1870s proves nothing more than the biblical adage "the poor you have with you always."

But, to borrow again from Scripture, American homelessness was a house of many mansions, and the great army of tramps possessed numerous features distinguishing it from previous groups of the migrant poor. As the term "tramp" suggests, what struck Gilded Age Americans most about the new homeless army was its stunning mobility. Jacob Riis's constant shifting back and forth between and within metropolitan regions was not unusual. Unemployed men of the 1870s routinely traveled hundreds of miles at a stretch. Even in a nation where over half the population changed residences every ten years, such extreme mobility caused alarm.

The primary reason for this new mobility was the vast expansion of the nation's railroad network in the years following the Civil War. A loose collection of tracks in the antebellum period, railroad lines expanded into a tightly connected web by the 1870s, adding as much as 7,379 miles in a single year and attaining a total mileage of 93,000 by 1880.[17] With a continental network of transportation and communication in place, the consequences of industrial life—beneficial and unsavory alike—penetrated every corner of the land. Created to deliver commodities to a great national market, railroads now also transported, often without remuneration, an increasingly footloose working class that circulated throughout industrial America after the Civil War. No longer were the problems of vagrancy and floating workers contained within metropolitan regions. Almshouses that had previously served local paupers now swelled with nonlocal tramps who could not claim residency anywhere.[18] America, it seemed to many, was overrun with wandering strangers. To make matters worse, those who wandered most tended also to be the poorest.

What was it about the post–Civil War years that put the poor in motion? Elite observers often attributed Gilded Age migrations to a certain "roving disposition" among the poor.[19] Jacob Riis, however, revealed the predominant cause while describing his arrival in New York City from New Brunswick, New Jersey, where he had previously worked in a brickyard:

> It was now late in the fall. The brick-making season was over. The city was full of idle men. My last hope, a promise of employment in a human hair factory, failed, and, homeless and penniless, I joined the great army of tramps, wandering about the streets in the daytime with the one aim of somehow stilling the hunger that gnawed at my vitals, and fighting at night with vagrant curs or outcasts as miserable as myself for the protection of some sheltering ash-bin or doorway.[20]

Jacob Riis's dependence on wages had made him vulnerable to seasonal shifts in the demand for labor, a vulnerability that compelled him to scavenge for the food and shelter he could not purchase on the market. In other words, Jacob Riis, like millions of other Americans, had discovered firsthand the problem of unemployment.

Although the problem of unemployment might seem as old as time, it is actually a fairly recent phenomenon. In fact, the word "unemployment" did not even appear in print in America until 1887.[21] The experience of joblessness, of course, predated the term, as any Jacksonian-era laborer standing outside the shuttered doors of his former workshop could have attested. But unemployment did not become a widespread problem until roughly the eve of the Civil War, when, for the first time, a solid majority of Americans in the industrializing North worked for others. In the first half of the nineteenth century, most northern heads of households were self-employed, either as farmers, artisans, or tradesmen who owned the property they used to make a living. Although they all faced periods of "forced idleness," self-employed property owners possessed precious "shelters against unemployment" that allowed them to subsist during slack periods. Farmers and shop owners controlled the pace of their labors and prepared for intervals of inactivity. In addition to growing their own food, farming families also manufactured at home important necessities—such as clothing, soap, and candles—that wage-earning people had to buy on the market. Finally, for those Americans who did work for others, the customary intimacy of the small farm and workshop often generated personal bonds between employers and their workers that protected employees from being laid off during economic downturns.[22]

Through the course of the nineteenth century, the ever-encroaching tide of commercial exchange steadily eroded these protections. By the 1870s they had diminished to the vanishing point. Most northerners were now wage earners who did not own productive property and who encountered their employers in relations of the market rather than paternalist authority. In such cases, the seasonal inactivity such as Jacob Riis experienced precipitated not a routine shifting of productive activity, but rather a desperate search for the cash income one needed to survive.

Seasonal inactivity marked virtually every field of occupation, from agriculture to industry. Outdoor labor—harvesting, dock work, canal digging, and building of all sorts, for example—had to be done in temperate months, leaving many unemployed during the winter, a season when poorhouse populations swelled.[23] Indoor labor in factories and workshops also had their idle periods, usually corresponding to the cycles of consumer demand. These slack periods—coupled with local, regional, and national business cycles—made for highly volatile employment patterns. One scholar estimates that between 20 and 25 percent of all northern wage earners spent at least three months jobless during the average year in the late nineteenth century, with both figures rising sharply during depressions.[24]

Once jobless, many wage earners had little choice but to move. Housing, which earlier in the century had provided a resource for subsisting through idle periods, was now a cash drain that required the constant transfer of wages into rent.[25] "I'll give you one instance out of a hundred how workingmen manage to live in these hard times," explained one worker in the 1870s. "A man moved eighteen times in two years without paying his rent."[26] The lack of cheap public transportation meant that most workers had to live within walking distance of their workplaces. Since each neighborhood supported only a limited amount of wage labor, losing one's job quite often required changing one's residence. Under these circumstances shelter was anything but permanent, and being caught, like Riis, without lodging or the means to pay for it became a routine hazard of working-class life.

Just how far and in what direction jobless migrants traveled once on the road depended largely upon their point of origin and the skill level they expected from their jobs. Most migration involved cities, either as departure points or destinations. Cities with diverse employment opportunities sustained comparatively higher and more stable employment rates than smaller communities dominated by fewer industries and trades.[27] Rather than pursue random itineraries, then, jobless migrants everywhere traveled predictable routes to urban centers, expecting with reason that cities would offer good chances for employment. As Riis found in New York

City, however, moving to a metropolis was not a guarantee of finding work. Whether or not an urban job search succeeded, migration to a city exposed the tramping worker to a greater variety of subsequent migration options. The larger transportation networks available to urban migrants—such as carriage roads, water routes, and especially railroads—broadened the choice of travel methods and destinations, as Riis demonstrated when he tramped, ferried, and hitched freight trains to Philadelphia after his traumatic experiences on the streets of New York.[28] Cities also served as information centers on labor market conditions elsewhere, enabling migrants to determine with greater precision what travel routes would likely lead them to jobs. Twenty years before urban lodging-house districts provided institutional frameworks for disseminating such information, Jacob Riis and other transient men of the 1870s gathered reports from the job front in the streets, parks, and saloons surrounding cheap boarding-houses.

Whether into or out of metropolises, short migrations, such as Riis's trip from New Brunswick to New York City, were more common than longer ones, especially among "casual" workers who circulated around fixed and familiar territories. Most tramping workers, especially unskilled day laborers, headed for the closest cities and towns where they thought they might find work. Skilled workers tended to tramp farther than their less skilled cohorts, taking advantage of the Gilded Age's rapidly expanding railroad networks to plot more elaborate travel routes.[29] Jacob Riis's longer migrations, such as his direct trips back and forth between Pittsburgh, Buffalo, and New York City, generally corresponded with stints as a carpenter, furniture maker, and journalist. Once these highly skilled jobs ended, Riis often then traveled shorter distances to surrounding towns or villages, picking up whatever work he could, usually casual labor in a factory, lumber camp, or on a farm. Skilled workers were also more likely to pursue wage opportunities in rapidly growing communities of the Midwest and West. These places especially attracted large numbers of workers in building trades who followed construction booms only to depart when demand inevitably slackened. Jacob Riis's very first migration in the United States was to build housing for coal miners in what soon became the industrial town of East Brady, Pennsylvania. After "some temporary slackness in the building trade," Riis then tried mining ("one day was enough for me") and various kinds of casual labor before pawning his clothes for a trip back to New York.[30]

Unlike previous generations of jobless migrants, the tramp army of the 1870s contained large numbers of skilled workers like Riis.[31] Some of these workers benefited from formal "tramping systems" sponsored by unions of printers, carpenters, cigar makers, iron molders, and miners to control and accommodate the mobility of their notoriously footloose members.[32] The vast majority of "tramping artisans," however, migrated without the aid of union-sponsored traveling cards, relief funds, and lodgings. Especially during depressions, most skilled workers stole freight train rides, begged meals, competed for common labor, and faced vagrancy arrest right alongside their less skilled compatriots. By the time Jacob Riis found himself among the great army of tramps, occupational skill provided precious little buffer against the hazards of seasonal unemployment.

In addition to finding work, another ongoing task a jobless migrant faced when in a new district was securing shelter. By the turn of the century, virtually every American city contained lodging house neighborhoods that offered transient workers a wide array of cheap lodging options, from full private rooms in furnished hotels to dry spaces on saloon floors. In the 1870s, however, the temporary lodging market was still in its infancy, and most tramping workers roomed in private homes or in small boardinghouses. The most affordable boarding arrangements in the 1870s were in tenements, which were already overcrowded and offered few amenities that could not be scavenged elsewhere. Finding himself "crowded out of the tenements of the Bend by their utter nastiness," the destitute Jacob Riis turned to the doorways of Chatham Square, which, in dry weather, provided a cheaper (and perhaps better) opportunity for sleeping, despite periodic roustings by police officers.[33] Outside of larger cities, cheap boarding options were scarce, leaving transients like Riis to inhabit barns, wagons, and sheds, often even when employed.

Another shelter alternative for migrants both in small towns and large cities was the public lodging provided by poorhouses and police stations. Even if, as Jacob Riis testified, public lodging was a last resort for "honest" homeless men, it was nonetheless an increasingly common recourse for the migratory poor during the 1870s. Overnight lodging was one of the first functions performed by the newly organized urban police departments of the 1850s. Nineteenth-century police departments often fed and lodged more persons than they arrested, although during seasons of slack labor demand, an otherwise homeless "lodger" could be locked up as a criminal vagrant. By the 1870s police stations had replaced poorhouses as the primary public lodging for indigent working-age males. Conditions of police station lodging varied, but most provided only temporary shelter on bare floors for a few days or hours, leaving lodgers to shift for themselves once released. By the end of the century, a growing chorus of social reformers led by Jacob Riis would condemn the short-term, unsupervised relief offered by police stations as an encouragement to tramping. By that time, however, cheap private lodging houses had begun to replace police stations as the poor man's last resort. Before then, approximately one adult male in twenty-three slept in a police station at some point in his life, and between 10 and 20 percent of American families contained a member who had lodged. In the late nineteenth century, police station lodging was a familiar and even routine experience for many poor Americans.[34]

The rise of police station lodging signaled major changes in the social composition of the migratory homeless. Whereas previous populations of vagrants exhibited considerable ethnic, gender, and even racial diversity, those who gained admission to police stations in the 1870s were a remarkably homogenous group. Bordering as it was on incarceration, admission to police station lodging hardly seems a privilege. But given the importance of police stations in underwriting the mobility of tramps, denial of admission could effectively bar a poor person from conducting a migratory job search at all. As a result, only a narrow segment of the laboring population could respond to their job insecurity through the extreme and deliberate transiency of a Jacob Riis.

Poor women, for example, were excluded from police station lodging, one reason they were not counted among the great army of tramps. Homeless women have always existed, but in the late nineteenth century their presence so disrupted settled notions of dependent womanhood that they were quickly rendered "invisible," either by being placed in protective custody or by being recruited into the army of female "tramps," that is, prostitutes, that occupied nineteenth-century urban centers.[35] Subsisting through an economy of sex, rather than itinerant labor, was indeed one of the few options available to indigent women. While female wage opportunities in manufacturing and domestic services improved during the nineteenth century, the kind of extensive migrations often required to maintain employment were exceedingly difficult for female workers. On the road, women faced frequent harassment, violence, as well as exclusion from such public services as police station lodging. In order to prevent women from hitting the road in the first place, charitable organizations founded unprecedented numbers of caretaking institutions for poor women that housed and often put the indigent to work before they could even begin their job searches. Thus, only a little over 6 percent of all jobless migrants who applied for public aid in New York State in the winter of 1874 and 1875 were female; of these, over half were accompanied by husbands.[36] In Philadelphia the proportion of women vagrants incarcerated in the city's House of Correction dropped dramatically between the antebellum period and the 1870s, from about half to a quarter or fewer. Accounting for this decline was the extreme underrepresentation of women among the increasing numbers of transient poor. The rise of "mothers' pensions" and other protectionist measures in the early twentieth century ensured that tramping, as it emerged in the 1870s, remained an experience defined almost exclusively by men.[37]

In addition to sex, race also played a large role in determining the social composition of America's tramp army in the 1870s. African Americans had long idealized geographic mobility as a crucial component of freedom, both before and after the end of slavery. For slaves, self-emancipation often involved long, arduous journeys, whether escaping individually or in mass during the Civil War. After the war black migration continued as former slaves took to the road for diverse reasons: to search for family members, to establish independent livelihoods, and, as Peter Kolchin so aptly puts it, simply "to affirm their freedom."[38]

Infusing this ideal of free movement with even greater urgency was the coordinated campaign on the part of white planters and their political allies in the South to coerce black workers to stay put. Southern power brokers after the Civil War sought to secure their rural labor force by restricting mobility through debt peonage, draconian vagrancy ordinances, and a uniform structure of low wages. Without the right to move on their own terms, African Americans were effectively barred from the privileges of tramping. Southern homelessness, therefore, tended to be a white, urban, and relatively infrequent experience, a product of the same patterns of wage employment that created larger-scale homelessness in the North.[39]

Homelessness among African Americans in the North was even rarer proportionately than in the South. Late-nineteenth-century surveys of public lodgers report consistently low rates of black admission; only 2.3 percent of New York State's homeless aid recipients during 1874 and 1875, for example, were African American.[40] Nonlocal black paupers became especially rare, for few poor African Americans dared to step foot on the road. The black aversion to tramping is attributable not only to outright racial discrimination in public assistance, but also to the hostility and violence that blacks could expect to encounter on the road itself. Simply put, black migrants could not count on the already haphazard kindness of strangers—not to mention railroads, missions, and municipal authorities—upon which the transient homeless so often depended.

Tramps often threw up barriers of their own to black migration. The large number of Irish immigrants in America's tramp army suggests that the road itself may have served as a critical racial proving ground for poor white men. Notorious for their particularly virulent brand of white supremacy, Irish immigrants accounted for almost one-half of police station lodgers and vagrants.[41] Jacob Riis's disdain for his fellow tramps stemmed in part from his dislike of the "Irishmen" with whom he was forced to share the road. While German-, English-, and native-born men all found their places in the great army of tramps, the Irish wayfarer became a common Gilded Age stereotype, one that gained strength and currency toward the turn of the century. Indeed, as new waves of immigrants from southern and eastern Europe poured into the country, the equation of Irishness and tramping became even more pronounced as the newcomers failed to take their places in the tramp army. By the 1890s the sons of older immigrants and native-born Americans were replenishing the army's ranks, while the new immigrants followed their own distinct patterns of group migration.

Regardless of nativity or nationality, Gilded Age tramps, like their foot-loose forebearers, were overwhelmingly young. Tramping was a young man's pursuit, a virtual stage in the working-class life cycle. Age figures culled from police and relief records document a median age for tramps in the mid- to late twenties, with the vast majority being under forty and unmarried.[42] Old age, of course, did not preclude poverty. But age did discourage many of the elderly poor from exercising the migration options so often seized by the young, a fact that explains why local poorhouses of the period increasingly took on characteristics of old-age homes. One forty-eight-year-old tramping worker told an investigator in 1893 that although he had "tramped and roamed about more in my life than any man of my age" and had experienced "all the vicisitudes [sic] and hardships it is possible for a human to stand," he still remained "Hale and Harty [sic]" and tramped when jobless instead of taking refuge in almshouses.[43] Although being single contributed to this older migrant's continued transiency, two important attributes of youth—health and hardiness—also certainly permitted him to pursue the migratory existence he thought preferable to institutionalization.

In contrast to this persistent vagabond, the vast majority of Gilded Age vagrants did not make a career out of tramping, roaming about for months or years on end. For most homeless wanderers, the road represented a brief stage of poverty, an episodic experience rather than a permanent condition. Almost 90 percent of those migrants who applied for public aid in New York State in 1874–75 had been on the road for less than one month. Fewer than 5 percent of police station lodgers surveyed in 1891–92 had been tramping for more than one year. Vagrancy arrest records from the period reveal low rates of recidivism, with three-quarters of incarcerated vagrants having committed no previous offense. Far from a stable population, America's Gilded Age tramp army relied on high turnover rates and fresh recruits to maintain its muster rolls.[44]

As a variation on an old theme, the rise of the Gilded Age tramp army signaled the triumph of an industrial capitalist order that had been generations in the making. But that army's unique features—its mobility and its preponderance of white men—also reflected the transitional character of the 1870s. Having completed its long march toward dominance, the wage labor system now conferred upon the country, and the laboring classes in particular, a crisis of home and work that would endure for the next three-quarters of a century. Faced with the diminishing use value of home as productive property and an increasing dependence on wages, working people responded in various ways, from scavenging, taking in boarders, and going into debt to the more extreme recourses of institutional relief. For the young (or at least hale and hardy), white, male members of the northern working class, moving about from place to place and doing without the luxury of "home" was an additional possibility. One can even consider life on the road as something of an option, albeit a dire and life-threatening one, among competing strategies of survival. Homeless men would certainly have recognized their own feelings in labor leader Terence Powderly's recollection of his "painful experience as a tramp" in 1874 when he was uniformly "unsuccessful, footsore, heart-sick and hungry."[45] But, weighing their options, many must have also considered the road to be the most agreeable way to endure their poverty. Those who pursued this option joined an already overstocked mobile labor force that the nation's rapidly expanding industrial economy required.

However, by the fall of 1873, when Jacob Riis quit his migratory habits by finding a secure employment niche in New York City journalism, the great army of tramps had yet to emerge as a topic of widespread concern. When tramps did make their dramatic appearance on the American landscape, their presence provoked strong reactions from a culture that had long promoted free labor as a national system. Beholding the spectacle of ragged, road-weary nomads tramping up and down the country, middle-class observers questioned each other about the origins of these grim travelers. Some recognized their colonial, even Old World, provenance. Others saw the tramp army as an entirely novel phenomenon. In developing their various explanations, legislators, journalists, clergymen, and social commentators of all stripes formulated imaginative origin myths of tramping that disclose much more about the concerns of the dominant culture than they do about tramps themselves. By addressing the problem of the tramp, civic leaders grappled with new problems of labor discipline and class conflict, as well as with broad cultural crises of nation, community, and family that the triumph of corporate capitalism had precipitated. In the vision of a rising tramp army, the middle classes saw a force alien and hostile to all they had worked so hard to achieve: "the deadly foe," as one writer put it, "to civilization, thrift, and property."[46]

## TASTING OF THE "FOUNTAIN OF INDOLENCE": ORIGIN MYTHS OF TRAMPING

Given the coincidence of industrial depression and mass joblessness with the rise of tramps in the 1870s, one might expect the most learned commentators on the tramp crisis to have recognized its roots in the problem of unemployment. Such, however, was not the case. Surprising as it seems, a preponderance of official opinion rejected out of hand any contention, usually proffered by labor tribunes, that members of the tramp army were involuntary conscripts. Like the American Social Science Association president Francis Wayland, most pundits considered tramps to be flouting the primal curse: "By the sweat of thy brow shall thou eat bread."[47] The litany of adjectives used to describe tramps invariably began with "lazy" and "shiftless" before winding its way to "sauntering" and "savage." Consequently, few experts who approached the matter from the perspective of charity administration or social science blamed the tramp crisis on the depression. Echoing the mass of expert opinion, the *New York Times* argued in 1877 that "if the tramp nuisance is ever brought to an end in this country, it will not be by a return of prosperous times." "Good times," the paper concluded, "will only make things easier for him."[48]

The charge of laziness only begged the question of what had caused this epidemic of indolence in the first place. Those who took up this question offered various theories. Almost all noted American habits of "indiscriminate charity" that discouraged the "able-bodied poor" from working. Others pointed to the flood of poor immigrants from Ireland, unschooled in the habits of thrift and industry and perhaps irreclaimable in their degeneration. Inspired by the burgeoning pseudoscience of eugenics, some theorized tramps to be the issue of degenerate immigrants who reproduced at higher rates than the racially "purified."[49]

One further theory about the origins of the "tramp nuisance" recurs so frequently in the 1870s that one might fairly call it one of the period's prevailing explanations for why men tramp. Time and again, the literature on tramping returns to "the lazy habits of camp-life" acquired by the millions of men who served in the Union army during the Civil War.[50] "This tramp system is undoubtedly an outgrowth of the war," stated one Massachusetts police official in 1878. "The bummers of our armies," he continued, "could not give up their habits of roving and marauding, and settle down to the honest and industrious duties of the citizen." Another charities official in 1877 explained that the war had taught "to a large number of laboring men, the methods of the bivouac." Having learned how to travel quickly, find temporary shelter, forage for food, and otherwise "trust to-morrow to take care of to-morrow," the Civil War veteran, according to this theory, possessed the skills necessary to live without working.[51]

Renowned private detective and Union army spy Allan Pinkerton also had no doubt that "our late war created thousands of tramps." Having spent part of his youth as a tramping barrel maker in Scotland, Pinkerton had a great fondness for army "camp-life," but admitted that the only habits it fostered were "to play social guerilla and forage."[52] Similarly, the first novel about tramping, Lee O. Harris's *The Man Who Tramps: A Story of To-day*, explains the rise of tramping with reference to the Civil War. In telling his story about villainous tramps who "stir up strife between capital and labor," Harris digresses to describe how the war lured many of the "manufacturing and producing classes" into the thralls of trampdom. "The reckless, free life of the army had given them a taste for wandering and a distaste for every species of labor," Harris explains. Once discharged, old soldiers recruited others into the habits of the bivouac, which offered "so many fascinations, so much change and adventure." "Once having tasted of the fountain of indolence," Harris writes, these men "lost all wish to labor" and consequently became "professional tramps."[53]

For Gilded Age Americans, then, the phrase "tramp army" was more than a mere metaphor for the assembled masses on the road. It was also a literal explanation for why men tramped. The Civil War did indeed shape the contours of the tramp crisis. The very term "tramp" gained currency during the war to denote the kind of exhausting marches to which virtually all combatants were subjected. More importantly, the war had also spurred railroad construction in the North to facilitate the rapid movement of troops. The first men to clamber aboard a boxcar were not homeless job seekers, but soldiers headed toward or away from battle lines. Scattered accounts also suggest that the trauma of war itself created a population of the walking wounded, those afflicted by an "acute mania" that prevented them from settling down or adjusting to domestic life. Prisons of the late 1860s swelled with demobilized veterans, many of whom had hitched freight rides home after being mustered out of the army. Memories of the terrors and thrills of combat, as well as the camaraderie of camp life, caused more than a few veterans to chafe against what one soldier called the "monotonous quiet of home" and to turn to a life of unfocused wandering.[54]

While the Civil War certainly ruptured patterns of everyday life and perhaps set some men tramping, it did not in itself create the tramp army. Rather, the causal explanation of the war possessed a deeper symbolic meaning for Americans in the 1870s. By linking tramps and war, commentators figuratively connected the tramp crisis to the larger struggles taking place in Gilded Age America, especially that over the very meaning of America itself.

No other Gilded Age institution signified American nationhood more than the Union army, whose struggle to redeem the Republic from slavery was still a vivid memory. Having conquered the Confederacy in the name of free labor, this army, now a bedraggled assortment of tramps, seemed to be turning against the whole principle of free labor, the "new birth of freedom" that Abraham Lincoln so famously proclaimed in the Gettysburg Address. According to Lincoln, American freedom meant, above all, the freedom to profit from one's own labor, at first from wages and then as an independent businessman. The ideal of America for which so many millions of northerners fought was one where the "producing classes"— laborers and capitalists alike—reaped the wealth they created, rather than see it siphoned off by social "parasites," such as speculators, bankers, rich planters, or vagabonds "unwilling to work."[55]

The unemployment crisis of the 1870s undermined the free labor ideal by exposing the fundamental rift between employers and employees. While the depression destroyed many capitalists, it also served to concentrate markets, production, and therefore wealth into the hands of fewer corporations. For workers, the depression precipitated a desperate struggle merely to maintain wage employment, a struggle that mocked any dreams of independent ownership. While Americans never agreed on what precisely the term meant, the notion of the "producing classes" lent a coherent sense of partnership to capital and labor. Now that partnership seemed torn. Instead of a unified nation of diverse producers working together to create wealth, the United States seemed divided, as the Populists would so memorably put it years later, into "two great classes—tramps and millionaires."[56] By the end of the depression of the 1870s, violent conflict would unmistakably confirm this sense of growing social cleavage.

Given the centrality of free labor to the meaning of post–Civil War America, the battles that erupted between capital and labor during the Gilded Age also raged on the cultural ground of national identity. As a figure of speech, the phrase "tramp army" derived its power from the way it symbolically drew together the diverse challenges to reigning concepts of nationhood in the 1870s. To elite observers, the great army of tramps represented a rebuke not only to the pre–Civil War ideal of free labor, but also to the ideals of home and family that, in conjunction with free labor, defined America as a harmonious, yet dynamic, nation of producers.

The very triumph of free labor as a national system after the Civil War had given rise to the problem of how to handle those workers who "abused" their freedom by refusing to work. Unlike earlier systems of servitude, apprenticeship, and other forms of bound labor, wage labor allowed workers to change employers at will and, in theory at least, to quit work altogether. Quitting work altogether, of course, was never really an option for anyone, except the very rich, despite whatever lessons of the bivouac had been learned in the army. But workers the nation over did take advantage of any opportunities they had to escape dependence upon wages, whether it be through squatting on unused land, poaching wild game, or bartering stolen goods in the streets.[57]

In the South, agricultural employers struggled to reestablish a plantation labor force out of newly emancipated slaves who overwhelmingly desired to live on small plots of their own outside the plantation system. For postwar plantation owners, the goal was to force open southern blacks' tenacious grip on whatever economic autonomy they had through innovations in contract law and new forms of labor compulsion. Vagrancy legislation played a crucial role in the conversion of the South to free labor by serving as a coercive stick to balance the carrot of market choice.[58] African Americans in the South possessed a margin of freedom to choose certain terms of employment. But no propertyless person was free *not* to sign a labor contract.

The rise of the tramp army in the North redirected the debate over labor compulsion toward white, especially Irish, industrial workers. These workers, employers and legislators feared, seemed as indolent and determined to flout the wage system as their black counterparts in the South. By raising the specter of the "professional tramp" who was, as one state legislative committee put it, "bound to live without work," the tramp crisis conjured fears that the Civil War's "new birth of freedom" had shaded into an anarchic rebellion against wage labor.[59] As a tramp "Boss" profiled in the *New York Times* made clear, free labor meant the right not to work. "Wurruck," says the tramp in a thick Irish brogue after removing a "villainous-looking clay pipe" from his lips, "was made for niggers. I'm a white man born free."[60] Basing his own racialized sense of freedom on the subordination of African Americans, this media caricature captures at once prevailing stereotypes about "savage" Celtic racial traits and the actual Irish ethnic strategy for claiming the privileges of whiteness. For the Irish, preserving the road as a domain of white men was one of these key privileges, even if it confirmed among elites that the Irish were a race apart, sharing the same vagrant characteristics as African Americans (fig. 1.1).[61]

[155]

December 9, 1876

The Ignorant Vote—Honors Are Easy.

Figure 1.1: As Thomas Nast's cartoon from *Harper's Weekly* suggests, prevailing white opinion placed the "Celt" on par with the "Negro," not only in terms of social position, but actual physiognomy. Drawn in 1876 during the height of the tramp scare and toward the end of Reconstruction, this cartoon racially debases both groups even as it laughingly recognizes the racist antipathy that the Irish hold for African Americans. With their well-known disposition for tramping, the Irish raised fears about the breakdown of labor discipline and social order similar to those evoked by emancipated slaves in the American South. Freshly minted "tramp acts" targeted Irish "rovers" in the North, just as draconian vagrancy laws applied almost exclusively to African Americans in the South. For many Irish workers, however, tramping evolved into a jealously guarded bastion of white privilege that blacks entered only at their peril. (*Harper's Weekly*, December 9, 1876)

To address this rebellion against wage labor, every state legislature in the industrial North retooled centuries-old vagrancy laws, now termed "tramp acts," and engineered new mechanisms for enforcement. Beginning with New Jersey in April 1876, a rapid succession of states, numbering forty by the 1890s, adopted legislation that subtly shifted the focus of vagrancy from begging and "disorderly" street activities to wandering without work. These acts also increased the hazards of tramping by converting misdemeanor offenses into felonies when committed by tramps and by assigning to state governments the costs of vagrancy incarceration.[62] Local governments, which had never consistently enforced vagrancy statutes, continued to administer the tramp acts haphazardly. Contradictory policies that provided for the relief and lodging of homeless men also persistently compromised the tramp acts at the local level. Nevertheless, some towns and cities vigorously prosecuted offenders of the new laws, which generally called for the arrest and confinement of "all persons [usually men over seventeen years of age] who rove about from place to place, begging or living without labor or visible means of support."[63] By specifically requiring workers to accept the prevailing wages of local labor markets and forbidding them from obtaining "a living without labor," the tramp acts attempted to foreclose whatever stopping-off points remained on the road to a universal wage system.

Related to the sudden flurry of legislative activity was the renewed effort on the part of philanthropic groups to abolish "outdoor relief" and "indiscriminate charity," which, elite charity officials argued, served as "stimulants to vagrancy."[64] The long campaign to eradicate "outdoor relief"—the government provision of money, coal, food, and other supplies to the poor—achieved its greatest success in the 1870s. With the tramp crisis raging, two prominent private agencies, the Association for Improving the Condition of the Poor (AICP) and the Charity Organization Society (COS), convinced New York City officials to stop all donations to the indigent in order to force them "indoors" to regimented poorhouses. Rushing into the backwash left by the halting of municipal relief, churches, labor assemblies, fraternal organizations, and other community groups opened soup kitchens and began dispensing coal to the poor, frustrating the AICP's and COS's efforts to restrict aid.[65] The established charities also faced the more intransigent problem of informal neighborhood networks dispensing aid to the needy. As private citizens continued to donate food, lodging, clothing, and other essentials to the local and nonlocal poor alike, Edward Hale despaired that "the reckless generosity and hospitality of the people" would forever prevent the tramp army from disbanding.[66]

The campaign to abolish "reckless generosity" and restrict relief was part and parcel of the larger effort to increase workers' dependence upon wage labor. Contradictory as it may seem, private and public agencies played crucial roles in enforcing the dictates of the free labor market. Since the days of enclosures in sixteenth-century England, proponents of the wage system had sought to "give the poor an interest in toiling" by abolishing common lands and other sources of subsistence that existed outside of the wage contract.[67] In Gilded Age America, a major obstacle to workers' absolute dependence upon employers was the custom of mutual aid embedded in working-class life. For the industrial working class, poor relief was not "charity," but a "right," won by virtue of democratic citizenship and community membership. The money, provisions, and odd jobs channeled to the unemployed were also expressions of self-interest on the part of the givers: municipal officials seeking reelection and better-off neighbors eager to maintain their community standing.[68] Interpreting such relief practices as "corruption," elite charity administrators of the 1870s feared for the moral and economic health of the Republic. The will of a "foraging" tramp army "bound to live without labor" seemed to be prevailing over a free labor ideal where all wealth rightly goes only to those who produce it.

Far more fearsome than the consequences of "reckless generosity" was the prospect of tramps demanding not just handouts, but social and political power as well. To the genteel ear, the phrase "tramp army" rang with connotations of violence. As Lee O. Harris puts it in *The Man Who Tramps*, Americans shivered with "the thrill of horror" at the vision of tramps "combining in one great organization" to seize the Republic by force.[69] The symbolic power of this vision arose from the real militancy that workers increasingly exhibited in their confrontations with employers during the Gilded Age. Class violence was not an isolated phenomenon, but a persistent theme throughout the working-class protests and demonstrations of the period. As corporations and state governments created new armed forces to meet growing civil unrest, workers themselves formed their own militias, drilling, marching, and parading under both republican and socialist banners.[70]

Posed before this smoldering background of violence, the tramp assumed a menacing profile. When a nationwide strike, the first ever in American history, gripped the country in July 1877, middle-class anxiety over tramps exploded into outright panic. The strike began with a seemingly isolated job action among workers on the Baltimore and Ohio Railroad in the small town of Martinsburg, West Virginia. Even as President Rutherford B. Hayes dispatched troops to regain control of the B & O, the strike spread rapidly across the land, encompassing not only the nation's railroad workers, but also farmers, coal miners, steelworkers, the unemployed, and myriad other groups. By the end of July, towns and cities stretching from Philadelphia to San Francisco became engulfed in a bloody labor conflict. One hundred thousand workers across the nation walked off their jobs. The entire cities of St. Louis, Pittsburgh, and Chicago shut down. In the fighting that ensued between workers and the various armed forces sent to quell the insurrection, millions of dollars worth of property went up in flames. By August over one hundred people lay dead and thousands more injured.[71]

Tramps emerged from the ashes of 1877 as the primary scapegoats for the uprising. Francis Wayland attributed "the inner history of the recent disgraceful and disastrous riots in some of our principal cities" to the "large detachments of our great standing army of professional tramps."[72] By fingering tramps for blame, observers such as Wayland explained away not only the strike's unusual levels of violence but also its extraordinary geographic breadth. As a worker cut loose from any one locality, the tramp transcended parochial attachments and suggested the formation of a larger national community of men on the move. Lee O. Harris subtitled *The Man Who Tramps* "a story of to-day" precisely because he sought to explain the singular strike wave of 1877 as a product of this larger mobile community. Unfolding along the timeline of the strike, the novel's plot reaches its climax on July 21, 1877, when "hundreds of tramps from all parts of the country" descend upon Pittsburgh to commandeer the city's strike. Having recruited the "irresponsible floating populace" on its way, the revolutionary tramp brotherhood arrives in Pittsburgh dreaming of the day "when we will be no longer vagrants, but rulers in this land." The tramps proceed to make "inflammatory appeals to the passions of the crowd" and send the city up in smoke. Inevitably, however, the tramp leaders die in their own conflagration, and troops restore order to Pittsburgh.[73]

With their perceived ability to lure other unemployed workers into their ranks and steal train rides to distant destinations, America's tramp army played the villain in most accounts of the strike. But, in fact, tramps were noticeably absent from virtually all the sites of conflict during July 1877. The crowds that assembled in and above the railroad yards of Pittsburgh, for example, were made up largely of local men and women who walked from their homes and workplaces. While the new networks of transportation and communication had indeed made the general uprising of 1877 possible, they did so not because railroads and telegraphs directed opportunistic tramps to the sites of rebellion. Rather, these networks had linked working people to each other across a vast geographic terrain, making the recognition of common identities and interests, and the class action based on that recognition, ever more likely.

Despite the facts of the matter, one month after the strike wave subsided, Francis Wayland proclaimed to an agreeing audience of charity officials that tramps were "at war with society and all social institutions."[74] While the strikes had indeed left little doubt that the institution of free wage labor was under siege, the voluminous commentary on tramps appearing after the strike also focused attention on another endangered American institution: the family. Tramp bivouacs represented an escape not only from work, but also from home. Just as army camp life had raised concerns over labor discipline, so, too, did it inspire fears of gender disorder. Armed service removed men from their customary positions at home as well as work, placing them in regimented, mobile, all-male environments. In re-creating the male camaraderie of camp life after the Civil War, the great army of tramps seemed in rebellion against domestic life.

Unlike today's homeless, tramps in the late nineteenth century were seen not so much as lacking permanent shelter, for as numerous mobility studies have shown, few Americans of the period enjoyed anything resembling a permanent home. Rather, the tramp's "homelessness" denoted a broader-based moral crisis of domesticity, a crisis of men, as one religious journal put it, "let loose from all the habits of domestic life, wandering about without aim or home."[75]

In the 1870s the prospect of a "homeless" man threatened the delicate balance between workplace and home, public and private, men and women, that the middle class had long considered crucial to a healthy social order. As far back as the early nineteenth century, Americans had so valued the balancing functions of home that a "cult of domesticity" had emerged to inundate the nation with advice manuals, song sheets, and prints of genre scenes celebrating family life. Promoted largely by the clergy and the popular press, this passion for domestic harmony and happiness advanced in lockstep with the commercial revolution of the antebellum period. As wage labor and mass markets eroded the traditional economic functions of farming and artisanal households, families once bound together by productive activities now had to reinvent domestic life. With the sphere of work increasingly divorced from that of the household, new familial relationships developed to foster and regulate individual pursuits outside the home. Meanwhile, the home itself, which had once been the center of productive activity, increasingly became a sphere of "culture," infused with the abstract qualities of virtue, nurture, and "civilization." Women guarded and presided over these domestic qualities while men enjoyed the home as a private refuge from the public strife and striving of democratic politics and the competitive workplace. According to this doctrine of "separate spheres," distinct gender roles preserved the dynamism of American life while curtailing the centrifugal forces of free market democracy.[76]

If the home, as one Gilded Age writer put it, was "the crystal of society and the nucleus of national character," then the rise of a homeless army signaled a breakdown in domestic relations that endangered the nation as a whole.[77] One popular origin myth of tramping served as a warning to the country to get its homes in order. In *The Man Who Tramps*, Lee O. Harris explains the rise of tramps both through "the reckless, free life of the army" and the lack of nurturing motherhood. The protagonist of the novel, sixteen-year-old Harry Lawson, grows up in the tenements of New York City until the death of his parents leads him by orphan train to an Indiana farm family. The pastoral promise of farm life, however, is betrayed by an adoptive mother with a "tyrannical disposition" who incites Harry to run away. Although determined not to become a tramp, Harry falls in with "Black Flynn"—an Irishman, a communist, and a tramp "Boss" who masterminds the July 1877 uprising in Pittsburgh.[78]

Those women who fail to exercise their redemptive powers of nurture, argues *The Man Who Tramps*, drive men from their feminine influence and thereby imperil the Republic. This severing of men from the civilizing and restraining realm of home was, from one perspective, the essence of the tramp crisis. In assessing the peculiar hazards of America's tramp army, Francis Wayland echoed the common nineteenth-century faith in the sentimental home's restorative powers and raised new fears of a growing population of men cut loose entirely from the woman's sphere:

> The strength and sacredness of family ties, the love of mother or wife, or child, have often restrained, and sometimes reclaimed a hardened criminal, to whom the idea of home was still a present reality. But this possible refuge of respectability is wanting to the tramp. He has no home, no family ties. He has cut himself off from all influences which can minister to his improvement or elevation.

The home, as Wayland made clear, functioned in the nineteenth-century doctrine of separate spheres as an important check on man's natural aggression. Living outside the home—that is, outside the range of feminine influence—the tramp operated on pure instinct, "inspired by no motive except a momentary impulse of gain, or lust, or revenge."[79]

A masculine impulse frequently identified with tramps, as well as with the restraining influence of home, was sexual desire. For centuries religious doctrine legitimated and contained the unruly passions associated with human sexuality by defining it almost exclusively in terms of procreation. With the emergence of the private nuclear family in the nineteenth century, the intimate pleasures of nonprocreative sex gradually gained legitimacy. As a result, ministers, physicians, and moral advisers of all sorts struggled to place new boundaries on sexual expression. Ideologies of domesticity invested women with what John D'Emilio and Estelle B. Freedman describe as "an elaborate ideal of femininity [that] emphasized innate sexual purity as a means of controlling male excess."[80] According to the domestic ideal, wives contained husbands' "explosive" sexuality in order to preserve and concentrate men's powers for success in the marketplace.

With no such sexual constraints, homeless tramps of middle-class commentary not only eschewed the disciplines of productive labor; they also attacked the very moral foundations of the sentimental home itself (fig. 1.2). Francis Wayland led a chorus of opinion associating tramps with rape. Tramps, according to Wayland, preyed upon "the innocent maiden on her way to school" or "the farmer's wife busied about her household cares" in order to commit an "outrage worse than murder."[81] Lee O. Harris put the matter in even more strident terms. "The homes of the pioneers, surrounded by a wilderness, harboring ravenous wolves and skulking savages," Harris claims, "were not more unsafe than our homes of to-day."[82]

According to the dominant origin myths of tramping, "savage" homeless men lacked the sexual self-government and moral incentives that all men needed to compel them to labor. Therefore, tramping workers drifted into a purely masculine life of self-directed indolence. In a sense, the tramp symbolically took the nineteenth century's cult of self-made manhood to its logical extreme by abandoning the home in favor of purely acquisitive pursuits. But whereas the undomesticated capitalist augered the unruly extremes of acquisitive individualism, the homeless tramp raised the specter of collective aggression. Although the line of causation seems bizarre, the cultural logic of the Gilded Age tramp crisis identified tramping as a first step toward rape, "professional" indolence, and revolutionary communism.

The same cultural logic that steered pundits away from unemployment as an explanation of the tramp crisis generated imaginative origin myths of tramping that symbolically captured the epoch's intersecting crises of family, community, and nation. The image of a foraging, pillaging great army of tramps symbolically reversed the harmonious world of free labor

Figure 1.2: A tramp with a beseeching air threatens to invade and defile a sentimental home in this illustration from *Harper's Weekly*. Although the picture leaves the ragged wayfarer's intentions ambiguous, the accompanying article states that the engraving faithfully depicts "the alarm and danger to which women and children are frequently subjected by these vagabonds." Such a peaceful country cottage, the editors add, is "usually the spot selected by the tramp as the scene of his depredations." "Fortunately in this case," they note, "rescue is at hand; for the tramps, who are only valorous when they have to contend with weakness, never fail to assume the humility of a suffering mendicant when confronted by the muscles of a sturdy yeoman." (*Harper's Weekly*, September 2, 1876)

and sentimental domesticity vouchsafed to the nation by a bloody Civil War. Gilded Age problems of labor discipline, class conflict, and gender disorder all found rich cultural expression in the expansive literature on tramping, especially after 1877.

Even though learned and popular commentary seemed to speak with one voice on the tramp terror, the terms of panic did not remain frozen in the fearsome moment of July 1877. Indeed, the very qualities attributed to tramps in the 1870s—indolence, violence, and undomesticated primitivism—were susceptible to opposite valuations. Those approaching the tramp crisis from the bottom up, for example, might consider what Francis Wayland called indolence to be an idyllic escape from the drudgery of wage labor. Similarly, to working-class readers fantasizing about the end of the wage system altogether, Lee O. Harris's graphic account of tramp insurrection might inspire "oppositional readings" where the "rioting" tramps are the heroes and the troops dispatched to "restore order" to Pittsburgh are the villains. Finally, to those middle- or working-class men chafing under the constraints of feminine "civilization," the tramp's life on the road might have romantic appeal as a masculine liberation from the rarefied realm of home.

Each of these reevaluations began to surface in the literature on tramping even before the nation climbed out of its great depression in 1878. While the return to prosperity softened the edges of panic, it did not resettle the tramp army. Neither did the economic upswing solve the problems of wage insecurity or geographic drift faced by the working class. As depression gripped the United States once more in the 1880s and again in the 1890s, the nation's common discourse on tramps approached the realm of high theory. Origin myths of tramping born in the 1870s matured into greater sophistication and complexity as new voices entered the debate over why men tramp. Some of these new voices came from labor tribunes and working-class pamphleteers eager to challenge the terms of middle-class panic. Others came from the middle class itself as a new generation of social investigators took to the road in order to gain firsthand knowledge of tramp life. The new media also carried the voices of tramps themselves, who, for the first time, sought to define the terms of their own situation. By the 1890s those labeled tramps no longer passively accepted the meanings attached to them by others. The great army of tramps was now ready to develop it own means of expression.

# THE OTHER SIDE
# OF THE ROAD

I n 1879 a sixty-year-old Walt Whitman gathered notes for a lecture on "the tramp and strike questions," the "two grim and spec-
tral dangers" that the poet saw as most threatening to the Republic.
Remarking that the "American Revolution of 1776 was simply a great
strike," Whitman expressed doubt as to that Revolution's lasting success:

> If the United States, like the countries of the OldWorld, are also to grow vast
> crops of poor, desperate, dissatisfied, nomadic, miserably-waged popula-
> tions, such as we see looming upon us of late years—steadily, even if slowly,
> eating into them like a cancer of lungs or stomach—then our republican ex-
> periment, notwithstanding all its surface-successes, is at heart an unhealthy
> failure.

Having diagnosed this cancer on the body politic, Whitman, unlike his
contemporary Francis Wayland, did not prescribe new law enforcement
measures or the strengthening of "family ties." Rather, Whitman saw the
problem in terms of "social and economic organization, the treatment of
working-people by employers, and all that goes along with it—not only
the wages-payment part, but a certain spirit and principle."[1] According to
Whitman, capital had abandoned both the spirit of cooperation between
the "producing classes" and the principle of free labor, thereby becoming
"a sort of anti-democratic disease and monstrosity."[2]
 Two decades before the tramp crisis, Whitman had celebrated the
"Open Road" as a place where diverse travelers could encounter each other
as equals, "loos'd of limits and imaginary lines." Unlike the three tramps
Whitman observed in February 1879, "plodding along, their eyes cast
down, spying for scraps, rags, bones, etc.," the wayfarer of "Song of the

Open Road" is "light-hearted," "strong and content," the very embodiment of "good-fortune":

> Going where I list, my own master total and absolute,
> Listening to others, considering well what they say,
> Pausing, searching, receiving, contemplating,
> Gently, but with undeniable will, divesting myself of the holds that
> would hold me.[3]

Whitman offered his "Open Road" as a manly challenge to the antebellum middle class, which had regressed into the feminine bosom of home. Leaving sheltered ports and calm waters for the "pathless and wild seas," Whitman's traveler called upon Americans to extend the reach of human possibility and consciousness. "What beckonings of love you receive you shall only answer with / passionate kisses of partings."[4] Embracing the nation's growing bustle of human commerce, Whitman proposed a public, dynamic, and unfinished "Open Road," rather than the private, staid, and refined sentimental home, as the idealized model of American democratic culture.

Driven to the open road by poverty, rather than by the thought of "heroic deeds . . . all conceiv'd in the open air," the Gilded Age tramp army mocked Whitman's democratic vision, just as it challenged middle-class notions of domestic and national harmony.[5] Like many Americans, Whitman saw the tramp crisis as a betrayal of the free labor ideals forged in the Revolution and tempered in the crucible of the Civil War. But from Whitman's side of the road, a side shared by the working class generally, the crisis of homelessness appeared not as a loss of feminine nurture and refinement, but as a threat to free, independent "manhood." The vision of the "Open Road," as Whitman came to realize, depended upon "a more universal ownership of property, general homesteads, general comfort—a vast intertwining reticulation of wealth."[6] To travel freely as one's own master was an American birthright, as Whitman saw it, granted to white men and underwritten by a broad access to independent property ownership. The "real culmination" of America, Whitman wrote in the 1870s, would be the "establishment of millions of comfortable city homesteads and moderate-sized farms, healthy and independent, single separate ownership, fee simple, life in them complete but cheap, within reach of all."[7]

This republican dream of reclaiming independent homesteads carried wage earners through their Gilded Age struggles with unemployment and poverty. Those knocked down from Whitman's "Open Road" to the low road of wage dependence framed the tramp crisis in terms of a betrayed republican legacy. Through the labor press and cheap dime literature, workers articulated their side of the tramp debate, a side that not only critiqued middle-class notions of free wage labor, but also depicted the tramp as a militant agent of social change. But could the tramp army reclaim the heights of Whitman's "Open Road" without casting the Republic to ruins? By 1894, during the third, final, and most devastating depression of the Gilded Age, the labor movement's struggle with the tramp crisis had reached an impasse. Hanging in the balance was America's cherished Revolutionary legacy, a legacy that had guided the working class through the nineteenth century.

### "THE BROKEN HOME CIRCLE"

In 1877, as the Gilded Age panic over tramps reached its peak, a correspondent to the *Labor Standard* by the name of John McIntosh submitted a satirical poem mimicking the dismay and bewilderment of the commercial press:

> Oh! what will be done with the tramp—the scamp!
>> The curse of our Yankee nation
>> A nuisance is he,
>> And a mystery,
>> Defying interrogation . . .
> O, what shall be done with the tramp—the scamp!
>> Our national poor relation?
>> A riddle is he,
>> And perplexity
>> Defiant of legislation . . . [8]

Although rarely expressed with the biting humor of John McIntosh, pointed criticisms of mainstream newspapers for sensationalizing the tramp crisis were part of the labor press's cautious response to the problem. Labor tribunes generally joined with the *Journal of United Labor* in complaining that "what has been said hitherto [about tramps] has all been on one side."[9] Presenting the other side of the tramp debate was a primary concern of newspapers such as the *National Labor Tribune*, which argued that "society is a criminal and tramps are its victims."[10] By giving readers this other side, labor journalists challenged the strident rhetoric of Francis Wayland and the *New York Times* and anticipated the larger culture's "discovery of unemployment."[11]

At the same time that the labor press ran sympathetic accounts of unemployed workingmen, it followed the time-honored customs of vagrancy law by harshly condemning those tramps who could not "give a good account of themselves." Indeed, the *National Labor Tribune* itself sounded remarkably similar to opponents of outdoor relief when it attempted "to draw the line between the honest laborer in misfortune, and the idle, improvident, vicious vagrant."[12] In 1876 the *Workingman's Advocate* also drew such a line, imploring enforcers of the new tramp acts to distinguish "honest and industrious men" on the road from those "scamps who are prowling about the country, refusing to work, but neglecting no opportunity to steal and commit other crimes."[13] "Our tramp," explained the *Iron Molders' Journal* in a similar vein, is not the "bummer, the periodical inmate of our work-houses and county jails," but rather "the hard-fisted mechanic or laborer to whom work would be a blessing."[14]

As these remarks suggest, the labor press's strategy in the face of the tramp crisis was not simply to lay bare the problem of unemployment as the underlying cause of tramping. Nor did labor journals merely expose the prejudices and ideological biases behind the dominant culture's hostility toward tramps.[15] Instead, Gilded Age labor newspapers incorporated prevailing stereotypes of tramps into their own analyses of the crisis. To some measure, labor's jaundiced view of tramps reflected customary working-class concerns about the wandering poor. Desperate job seekers who accepted any wage just to keep body and soul together threatened the delicate balances of mutualism and craft prerogative upon which trade unions depended for their power. The appearance of even a small reserve army of the unemployed in a laboring community could irreparably damage union bargaining leverage and disrupt the painstaking negotiations of price that determined local wage standards. Workers who dared to disturb jealously guarded wage equilibriums were deemed "unmanly" for failing to put the common good above personal self-interest. The unprecedented size and mobility of the Gilded Age tramp army, then, raised fears that the roving jobless would depress wages everywhere. As the era's persistent wage deflation proved, those fears were entirely justified.

In addition to reflecting such practical concerns as wages, the tension in the labor press regarding tramps also betokened a larger ideological crisis in working-class culture, a crisis that the rise of the tramp army had, in part, precipitated. For American workers, the tramp army tainted the shining ideals of free labor that the patriotic ardor of the Civil War had burnished. Like the mainstream press, labor newspapers frequently invoked the heroic sacrifices of the late war as they searched the crisis for meaning. "Tens of thousands of men are wandering listlessly, hopelessly, in search of work," announced the *National Labor Tribune* in 1875. " . . . Was it for this we fought?"[16] The more radical *John Swinton's Paper* printed a letter in 1885 from "an old soldier on the tramp" who claimed to have fought "from Bull's Run to Chickamauga, Lookout Mountain, Mission Ridge, and others." After describing the mass unemployment in his Indiana hometown, the old soldier expressed his resolve to "rig me up some kind of an outfit, take to the country, and forage." "It is enough to make a man damn himself," the writer concluded, "for coming to the rescue of such a Government that allows its soldiers to starve."[17]

This Civil War imagery derived from a common language of republicanism that pervaded the era's discourse of nationhood. But the meanings trade unionists gave to such terms as "free labor," like the meanings they gave to tramping, differed dramatically from those held by their better-off compatriots. For the propertied classes, the triumph of wage labor and feminine domesticity represented the fulfillment of free labor republicanism. But for the working class, these same developments spelled the doom of the republican ideals that had informed the labor movement for generations.

Since the Revolution, workers had viewed the American Republic as a collection of independent citizens possessing rights not only to the polity, but also to the commonwealth of "producers" who secured their livelihoods through the productive use of privately owned property. Racial and gender discrimination effectively barred African Americans and women from the realm of citizen-producers, thus further enhancing the status of white men as inheritors of the Revolution's cherished legacy. While the spread of wage labor in the antebellum period seriously compromised the viability of this republican legacy, the rapid concentration of industrial capital after the Civil War relegated that legacy to the realm of anachronism. Despite the republican vision's increasing distance from the realities of working-class life, the ideal of a producer's commonwealth persisted in working-class culture through the Gilded Age. The ideological baggage of free labor republicanism encumbered the labor press's response to the tramp crisis, even as that response itself marked the erosion of republicanism's credibility.

A case in point was the labor press's attempt to draw a line between "common tramps" and "honest workingmen." Such a strategy was consistent with the nineteenth-century republican practice of splitting the population not into distinct classes, but rather into the categories of producers and nonproducers. The dependent poor and idle rich, two groups long associated with social "parasitism" on the body of productive labor, found their Gilded Age analogues in tramps and millionaires, a coupling that the *Journal of the Knights of Labor* colorfully described as "dregs and scum from the same social fermentation."[18] By discriminating between "forced idlers," who traveled in searched of work, and "common tramps," who wandered out of indolence and depravity, the labor press expressed justifiable outrage at noxious vagrancy legislation that branded all men on the road as criminals. To highlight the injustice, labor journalists reshuffled age-old republican categories in order to define the unemployed as "producers" worthy of their rights to free labor.

But while "common tramps" could be used figuratively to bolster a besieged ideology of free labor, the effort to widen the boundaries of the "producing classes" to include destitute wayfarers represented a subtle degradation of the free labor ideal. Before the Civil War, it was a worker's skills, control over the labor process, and especially property that determined his status as a republican producer. In the tramp commentary of the Gilded Age labor press, however, these criteria are replaced by the single standard of a "willingness to work." In privileging a "willingness to work" as the primary criterion in evaluating tramps, labor tribunes silently conceded the "visible means of support" to the narrowing ranks of the propertied classes. The labor press figuratively exchanged the visible, public, and material realm of social position—property—for the hidden, private, and intangible domain of individual intentions—"a willingness to work." In doing so, papers like the *National Labor Tribune* demonstrated that for the working class, homelessness represented far more than a mere crisis of shelter. It was also a crisis of citizenship and identity. For, without a home—that is, productive property—workers had no visible claim upon the polity and even risked arrest as "common tramps."

In its coverage of the tramp crisis, the labor press lamented the passing of the traditional republican household as a patriarchal domain and site of productive activity. Whereas the emerging middle class had never mourned this loss and, in fact, had figuratively saturated the home with intangible "feminine" associations of nurture and refinement, the working class explicitly rejected feminine domesticity in favor of older proprietary ideals. Although the household economies of the nineteenth-century working class amounted to little more than the exchange of wages into rent, workers nonetheless retained hopes that their alienation from the land would somehow be healed and traditional domestic arrangements restored.

The domestic traditions so nostalgically invoked by the labor movement were, in fact, anything but egalitarian. Republican proprietorship had entitled male heads of households not only to land, tools, and housing, but also to the labor of those residing within the household as dependents. While wives, children, and servants created valuable goods and services, household patriarchs, or "producers," appropriated that labor value, thereby gaining exclusive control and profit from the household economy.[19]

The exploitations of this system notwithstanding, Gilded Age workers recognized their own crowded and precarious housing arrangements as part of a larger despoiling wage system that had broken faith with the free labor ideal. Thus, while the likes of Francis Wayland saw domesticity in terms of the "strength and sacredness of family ties," working-class interpretations of these "family ties," sentimental as they often were, hinged on an entirely different definition of home altogether. For white workingmen, the ideal home was not only a haven of familial love in a world of exploitative work, but also productive property that harbored the labor of dependent families.

The sentimental language used by the labor press to describe the homelessness crisis often evoked the sense of eroding patriarchal barriers that protected otherwise vulnerable women and children. "How many of the vast army are kind fathers, who have homes behind them, a wife and children full of grief and dread, and pinched with hunger?" asked the *National Labor Tribune* in May 1876. "What are the thoughts of children when they see father gone, mother in distress? . . . What anguish fills the hearts of wives when they see the broken home circle? . . . Homes are broken, desolate. Hearts are crushed."[20]

Often this language also betrayed a patriarchal ideal of protecting wives and children from the wage labor market and preserving the productive value of dependent labor for the household. "Without the right to employment, whereby he may live honestly," wrote one correspondent telling his "tale of a tramp" to readers of the *National Labor Tribune* in 1877, "what other right has a poor man? His right to the children of his loins, the wife of his bosom—his right to their lives, or even his own—do not exist."[21] As conveyed in this correspondent's proprietary language, working-class men's dependence on wages jeopardized their right to their families' "lives." Wage labor had dethroned the household patriarch by reducing the productive capacity of the household economy and by requiring that other family members work outside the home to supplement family incomes. While the patriarchal ideal minimized women's social connections, resources, and wage opportunities beyond the home, it did establish "family ties" as those of labor as well as love, a component of domesticity that middle-class sentimentality denied.

The dream of recovering the patriarchal home also informed the Gilded Age's numerous popular movements that focused their ire on landlords as well as employers. The most prominent of these, Henry George's Single Tax campaign, proposed abolishing the real estate market altogether through a single confiscatory tax on rent. An economist who had also spent time on the road as an itinerant typographer, George was alarmed by the "tramp problem" and explicitly directed his critiques of Gilded Age capitalism toward explaining it. Tramps, George argued, were the result of "the barriers that fence labor off from land," namely, private property. If real estate were freed from private ownership, persons "from all the various occupations would betake themselves to the land to relieve any pressure for employment."[22] Fittingly, a Gilded Age utopian novel based on Henry George's theories chose as its title *A Tramp in Society*. In this story, a homeless apostle of the single tax founds a colony of squatters who collectively own the market value of their land. By its shining example, this colony of former tramps leads the nation down the redemptive path of the single tax.[23]

The Gilded Age's most prominent labor organization, the Knights of Labor (which Henry George joined in 1883), also interpreted the tramp crisis in terms of workers' alienation from productive property. "Complaint is made," commented one reporter for the *Journal of the Knights of Labor* in November 1893, "that the tramps intrude into the parks. To my mind, it is a greater cause for complaint that the tramp's counterpart, the millionaire, has grabbed so much of the land that men who would gladly be farmers are forced to tramp." Alluding to Jacob Coxey's Good Roads Bill, which proposed public works to relieve unemployment, this journalist argued that the solution to tramping was to restore the productive value of home, rather than create more wage labor. "As an effectual remedy for tramps—and millionaires—I'm inclined to think that improving American homes would be better than macadamizing American roads."[24] Throughout the Gilded Age, then, it was the promise of recovering productive property, rather than a broadly diffused "belief in the rural ethic," that inspired working people to turn toward the land for solutions to homelessness.[25]

In addition to housing as productive property, the connotations of "home" in working-class tramp commentary also included the local allegiances and community-based relationships that sustained laborers through hard times and everyday struggles alike. Unlike most tramps, residentially stable workers maintained crucial networks of support that included kin, shopkeepers, churches, social clubs, unions, political parties, and relief agencies. Moving beyond even the boundaries of neighborhood was a hazardous enterprise, for it often meant forfeiting the social protections that community membership provided. Commenting on how tramp legislation as a matter of course persecuted poor workers away from familiar surroundings, Elbert Hubbard wrote that "a man in a town where he is unknown, be he chaste as ice and pure as snow, if he has no money, cannot 'give good account of himself.' He cannot telegraph to distant friends, his word is not accepted, he can produce no witnesses to testify to his good character."[26]

Bereft of "visible means of support," tramps relied solely on their ability to demonstrate "good character." The stakes of this confidence game were high, entailing not only handouts and odd jobs, but the basic rights of democratic citizenship. A tramp unable to "give a good account of himself" in Francis Wayland's home state of Connecticut, for example, faced possible confinement and hard labor for up to three years.[27] No longer citizen-producers with ready claims to the household economy and republican polity, tramping workers were now undeniably full-fledged proletarians, even outlaws, with nothing to sell but their labor and "good character." In the face of this crisis, newspapers wedded to free labor republicanism vainly attempted to vouch for "honest workingmen" by raising archaic distinctions between producers and nonproducers. At the same time, their hope remained ardent that the labor movement would somehow repair the "broken home circle" by returning the "great army of tramps" to the land.

But what if the tramp army refused to demobilize and go home? What if the descent from "honest workingman" to "common tramp" proved so widespread and so complete among American workers that the distinction lost all meaning? This possibility, and its consequences for the Republic, pervaded the working-class literature of tramping, especially the "tales of the tramp" found in poems, cheap dime novels, and reports submitted to labor newspapers from roving correspondents. Offering imaginative accounts of the road, these narratives all documented the loss of a visible patriarchal identity grounded in home and work. Some of these tales of descent, however, were also stories of liberation. As they dramatized the peculiar freedoms of the tramp, these stories reveal ambivalence toward the prospect of tramps being, as genteel author Lee O. Harris so fearfully puts it, "no longer vagrants, but rulers in this land."

## FROM PATRIARCH TO PARIAH

Because nineteenth-century workers defined themselves primarily as producers, their tales of tramping recounted, first and foremost, a profound loss of identity. Although the vast majority of tramping workers were young and unmarried, working-class dime novels and newspapers depicted them as middle-aged and married, unemployed patriarchs forced to leave their dependent families. In these narratives, the patriarch steps foot on the road and begins immediately to shed his former identity. Soon the tramp enters what Victor Turner calls a "liminal" realm, "betwixt and between the positions assigned and arrayed by law, custom, convention, and ceremonial."[28] Floating between the worlds of the criminal and the "honest workingman," the tramp becomes a man without a home or identity, a negation often portrayed allegorically as death. In "Only a Tramp," a poem published in the *Locomotive Engineers Journal* in 1876, for example, an unemployed worker leaves his wife and children in the care of "a kind-hearted neighbor," while he tramps about looking for work. Starving and sick, cut loose from his sources of support and identity, the tramp finally dies, his identity known only to "a merciful God."[29]

For those tramps who lived to tell their tale, the loss of identity proceeded in stages, beginning with the struggle to represent "good character." A poem published in the *Iron Molders' Journal* in 1878, for example, tells the story of a man "knocking about from town to town" in search of work but meeting only "with here a sneer and there a frown." Unknown, distrusted, and in a world bereft of mutuality, the speaker describes himself as "dying by inches, for there is no one to care . . . no one watching to see how I fare." Moreover, despite being "willing to work for board and bread," the tramp is nonetheless "set down as a felon and thief . . . For a few old rags and shattered health / Is all I boast of worldly wealth."[30] Without "visible means of support," the poem's speaker implies, winning the confidence of employers and law enforcement officials is impossible.

In many narratives, tramping becomes a confidence game where a "willingness to work" gets expressed through carefully chosen words, gestures, and apparel. On the road, it was the clothes that often made the man. One tramp, who spent the depression of the 1890s selling scavenged wares throughout the Midwest, put the matter succinctly. "We soon learned," he wrote, "that if a person looked as though he needed to sell his goods it was very hard to do so."[31] Accordingly, Gilded Age tales of the tramp make frequent reference to "roaming in rags all tattered and torn" and to "tatterdemalion attire," signifying not only poverty and the loss of identity, but also the problem of representing oneself to strangers.[32] These stories also describe elaborate rituals of laundering and bathing that mark the early stages of the homeless job hunt. Failing in his effort to win an employer's confidence, the job hunter sometimes quits the confidence game altogether to embrace a more authentic, if dangerous, freedom from social convention.

Such a personal transformation provides the drama of *A Tight Squeeze*, a cheap dime novel published in 1879 that tells the story of a wealthy young man who temporarily "turns tramp" on a wager. Describing the newly homeless protagonist as "feeling as he has never felt in his life—A TRAMP," the narrator asks in an aside: "Reader, were you ever 'broke'? . . . Perchance you have been 'broke' more than once. Several times it may be. . . . Do you dread it? No. It has lost its horrors." The narrator then summarizes the process of release: "Rags become familiar to you. . . . And, withal, there is a sort of freedom in the situation that is agreeable. The conventionalities of society have no claim upon you." In time, the tramp becomes as "free as the winds to come and go, to work or play, sing or howl—in fact, to do as you please!" This freedom from restraint, explains the narrator, often entails "wild promptings to some desperate act":

> You were an Ishmaelite, and there was a savage satisfaction in feeling that all the world had its hand raised against you, and yours against the world. Indeed, to tell the truth, you were not far from desperate deeds. The step from poverty to crime is a short one—if poverty, *itself*, be not a crime. A man without money feels an ownership in every one else's property. An ownership where Might becomes an agent of Possession.[33]

In *A Tight Squeeze,* a millionaire turned tramp fulfills every genteel property holder's nightmare about homeless men flagrantly violating the rules of work, propriety, and property. But for working-class readers, the story demonstrated the thin line between crime and poverty, producers and nonproducers, strikers and rioters, "honest workingmen" and "common tramps." As a cautionary tale about the great army of tramps, *A Tight Squeeze* warns that if the dispossessed are not returned to the land, then the Republic, already shaken by the events of July 1877, will be forced to combat a growing subculture of nonproducers who feel "an ownership in every one else's property."

Working-class narratives of tramping are replete with such republican tales of caution, tales that often end with the propertyless tramp army seizing its rightful inheritance. When labor commentators invoked the martial motif of the tramp army, they did so not only to suggest the betrayal of the free labor ideals that launched Lincoln's Grand Army, but also to augment the sense of danger and approaching cataclysm. "Beware ye money bags; beware ye political leeches; beware ye cormorants of society," warned the usually circumspect *National Labor Tribune* in 1875. "The tramps you now despise will some day become tigers, and . . . rise like an army and suddenly wrest your ill-gotten gains from your grasp [and] appropriate them to their rightful owners."[34] Two years later, in the aftermath of the national strike wave, the same paper commented further on the dangerous and militant force that the "grand industrial army" represented:

> Two millions of men are wandering about in idleness, not knowing where their next meal of victuals is to come from. . . . How and where will these men live? Their numbers are increasing. Secretary Stanton feared the effect of the disbandment of a million soldiers at the close of the war. But what is that to the disbandment of the grand industrial army that has for years been building up the wealth and creating the strength of this great nation? There is danger from this vast unemployed mass. They will not tamely die of starvation. Their brothers who still have a little to live on will not allow them to be dispersed like banditti, for none knows how soon they may add to the ranks of that army.[35]

When Henry George posed his question "What is the tramp?" in his 1883 text, *Social Problems*, he, too, associated the tramp army with revolutionary violence. "Known as he is from the Atlantic to the Pacific," George writes, the tramp constitutes "an appearance more menacing to the Republic than that of hostile armies or fleets bent on destruction." Just as the vast bulk of an iceberg rests below the water's surface, George explains, so did a deeper significance reside beneath "this terrible phenomenon, the tramp." For George, the unemployed workingman's degeneration into "a vagabond and an outcast—a poisonous pariah" served as a reminder "that in civilized man still lurks the savage" poised to emerge wherever men were alienated from property. "Not in desert and forest, but city slums and country roadsides are nursing the barbarians who may be to the new what Hun and Vandal were to the old."[36]

Such suggestions of cataclysmic social change derived not only from traditional republican concerns about the growth of a propertyless proletariat, but also from what Herbert Gutman calls the "pessimistic premillennialism" that informed much of Gilded Age plebian culture.[37] Premillennialism was the grim Christian faith in a coming Apocalypse that was to burn away corrupt human institutions and usher in the golden age of Christ's rule. To the middle classes, wedded to beliefs in progress and the gradual improvement of human life, such apocalyptic traditions amounted to superstitious nonsense. Bourgeois evangelicalism embraced a *post*millennialist faith in the power of human agency to achieve a thousand-year golden age before the Apocalypse's arrival. For impoverished workers assailed by the onrush of commercial "progress," however, the great army of tramps seemed to auger cataclysmic delivery from a corrupting wage system. "Christianity was ushered into existence by tramps," argued the *National Labor Tribune* in 1876. "The new civilization whose grey dawn glimmers over the Eastern horizon will no doubt be ushered in by tramps too. Great movements come from the bottom layer of society, who possess the truest instincts and the noblest impulses. Our tramps are but the beginning of the end of a worn-out system."[38]

Often likening the lonely struggles of the tramp to Christ's passion, labor prose and poetry strained to put the travails of the industrial age into a larger transhistorical framework.[39] One poem published in the *Journal of United Labor* in 1883 invoked such a broad perspective in comparing tramps with both the "ten Hebrew tribes / leaving slavery's galling chains" and those "from every strand / where despotic wrongs despoils."[40] For working-class readers, tramps served figuratively as agents of redemption. "How much longer shall we wait and suffer?" asked the *National Labor Tribune* in 1876 in a column on "The Army of Tramps." "Can we summon the courage to meet the issue and conquer? Or shall we tremble and hide from the pelting storm? No. Let us be men even in our poverty. We are yet free men. Still sovereigns. This nation is ours."[41]

An imaginative story that draws together these plebian themes of republican betrayal, apocalyptic change, and redemption is *The Tramp: His Tricks, Tallies and Tell-Tales,* an elaborately illustrated pamphlet novel published in 1878. Claiming no author (but illustrated and "edited" by Frank Bellew), this cheap novel tells the tale of an unemployed journeyman printer who "became a Tramp" after failing in his search for steady work. The tramp narrates his descent from "honest workingman" and then guides the reader through the dangerous and radical subculture of homeless men he encounters on the road. Located deep in the forests of north-central Pennsylvania, this revolutionary "Brotherhood" initiates the tramp into its cabal and formulates a plan "to hurl their power at the throat of organized authority."[42]

This dime novel's tale of descent resembles Lee O. Harris's *The Man Who Tramps,* a melodramatic novel about an innocent farm boy lured into a revolutionary tramp bivouac on the eve of the strikes of 1877. But unlike Harris's novel, *The Tramp* tells its story in what Michael Denning calls "mechanic accents."[43] That is, where Harris's novel is explicitly didactic and aims to educate its working-class audience in the free labor values of the middle class, *The Tramp* adopts the language of its working-class audience to articulate that audience's own concerns and perspectives. In other words, *The Man Who Tramps* speaks *to* its readers, while *The Tramp* speaks *for* its readers. Like the labor press, *The Tramp* purports to represent the other side of the road, the side denied by Lee O. Harris and the big-city dailies.

In giving this other side, the novel replicates the labor press's strategy of separating and excluding tramps from "honest workingmen," identifying the narrator as a formerly "respectable member of society" who happens to fall in with "tatterdemalion vagabonds." But *The Tramp* also departs dramatically from this convention, as well as from those of middle-class melodrama, by raising the following question: Which is more corrupt, "the central camp of Tramps" or "respectable society"?[44]

Following the convention of the labor press, *The Tramp*'s narrator opens his story by describing how he was "thrown out of work" during "dull times," encountered "much rum and many misfortunes," and consequently became "a ragged, dirty, unwholesome Tramp" (5). Once homeless, he finds "swarms of Tramps on the road," but little work, and notices quickly that "poverty seems to arouse [others'] anger and hatred, instead of kindness and compassion" (6). Consistent with the working-class preoccupation with appearance, as well as with age-old pollution taboos, the narrator describes himself as "tried, foot-sore, and dirty. Oh, so dirty! I felt as though the filth had entered my very heart and veins, and even soiled my moral character."[45] In response to this problem of appearance and soiled character, the narrator takes refuge in the "sweet, fresh air, the song of the birds, and the glory of the rising sun," things that cannot be taken away, "even from a Tramp" (7).

For a while the tramp roams in a "syndicate," a cooperative network dedicated to "sharing their beggings, and findings, and stealings together." Resolving to rejoin respectable society, the tramp quits the syndicate and looks for work. But he soon discovers that he cannot support himself alone and again seeks the company of other homeless men. This is when he encounters the "promised land" of the tramp bivouac, an encampment located in "a wild, uninhabited region, where bears and rattlesnakes abide" (13). Fortunately, however, "game and fish were also plenty there," making the site "an admirable retreat for men of our class" (14). "The Ragged Red Rovers," as the bivouacking gang calls itself, initiates the tramp into its subculture and demonstrates the harsh punishment that awaits those members who transgress the rules of loyalty and collective ownership. Despite the Brotherhood's brutality, the narrator describes the gang as a "pretty amiable lot of vagabonds," possessing a colorful array of character defects and dialects (19). The camp is also a haven of "kindness and charity" where those willing to "work when they can" (the "Bees") coexist peacefully with the "constitutionally tired" (the "Butterflies"). After amassing collective earnings and plunder, the tramps periodically rise up in carnivalesque celebration of their freedom (19). "Indeed," the narrator explains, "we lived in grand style, going so far, frequently, as to give large dinner parties to 'the rank, fashion, and beauty of Roverglen'" (28). Anticipating the "Big Rock Candy Mountain" of hobo lore, the tramps "rioted in all the delicacies of the season for two or three days together," a practice that encouraged the narrator to look "with a certain admiration on organized Tramp life as it appeared to me" (28, 26). As a new member of this organization, the narrator hones his skills at foraging, pilfering, and swindling unsuspecting rural folk out of their worldly goods.

As refugees from the wage system, the residents of Roverglen also harbor greater ambitions than petty theft. After a while the narrator learns that his camp is but part of a larger "Tramp organization" that is "political and revolutionary" (20). He learns also that the organization's membership includes thousands of ordinary workingmen, "good honest fellows, who would rejoice at obtaining employment," but who, failing to find work, are now "only looking forward with longing eyes to some grand national smash-up, when there should be a glorious scramble for the prizes" (20, 23). "Our sufferings and hardships are educating us up to be soldiers," explains the "Perfessor," one of the architects of the tramp Brotherhood. Sounding remarkably like those genteel commentators who believed that tramping had its roots in the "reckless, free life of the army," the Perfessor expounds on tramps' superior military skills. The tramp, the Perfessor tells his recruits, possesses the ability to "outmarch any other body of men," to "concentrate at any given point quicker than his adversaries," and to "live off less food, and rough it better in the field." When the tramps mobilize, the Perfessor concludes, "let those twaddlers who prate about *things regulating themselves,* and about the holy capitalists, as though they were another race of beings—let them see whether it would not have been better to regulate things a little, rather than to have left them to regulate themselves with lamp-posts and lead pills" (23).

The narrative tension of this short pamphlet novel hinges on the dilemma faced by the narrator. Should he choose the life of an honest, if poor and despised, casual laborer? Or should he follow the path of a carefree, if revolutionary, member of the tramp Brotherhood? *The Tramp* resolves this conflict ambiguously through an improbable third option, that of being domesticated as "a respectable member of society" through betrothal to a prosperous farmer's daughter.

Just how this conclusion comes about adds further to the ambiguity, for the tramp wins the confidence of his prospective father-in-law only by deceptively manipulating his appearance. Having pilfered a diamond breast-pin, gold watch, expensive suit of clothes, and some money from "two sporting gentlemen" who were out for a swim, the narrator returns to a farm where he had previously worked dressed in his new finery (29). Keen on marrying the farmer's daughter, the tramp conceals his identity as "a common thief and vagabond" and projects instead "the appearance of prosperity." This appearance wins over the farmer, who grants the tramp not only the hand of his daughter, but also his homestead. In the end, the narrator considers his booty the rightful "spoils of war—plunder of the past," as well as "the lever which was to pry me out of the mire" (31).

Just as the ill-gotten attire compromises the tramp's claims to property and respectability, so, too, does the protagonist's deception undermine the conventions of sentimental literature. Instead of winning his matrimonial and patriarchal bliss through a purity of intentions and motives, the tramp of this cheap dime novel achieves his reentry into respectable society through the cunning manipulation of surface appearances. The novel ends with a searing critique of a social system that, in essence, is nothing more than a confidence game:

> I had tried honestly and frequently to obtain work, and failed. I had been treated with scorn, because I was in need. All mortals who are suffering and without power are hated by their fellow creatures; . . . I had rebelled against this hoggish insolence of the prosperous, and wrested by cunning and force what they had denied to me on fair terms—a living. . . . I used to hate all the world, and would have contemplated any general calamity with a certain fiendish delight. I would picture to myself the city burning, and the rich rushing from their homes poor and helpless as myself, and revel in the spectacle; famine, pestilence, war, would each furnish me with material for tableaux to delight the eye of my imagination. This feeling I resolved to set myself to work to battle against, and in its place to cultivate a more rational and humane spirit. (31)

Unlike Lee O. Harris's *The Man Who Tramps,* this cheap dime novel refuses to disperse the tramp army and keeps the Brotherhood intact as a lingering menace to the Republic. Meanwhile, the narrator's apocalyptic revenge fantasies remain stilled, for the moment, beneath the surface of a prosperous front. In a supreme irony that negates any distinction between "producers" and "nonproducers," the tramp does not earn his newly won productive property as an "honest workingman." Rather, it is the skills he acquires on the tramp, the skills of the confidence man, that lead him back to the patriarchal household.

In resolving its plot through the success of a confidence game, *The Tramp* invokes one of nineteenth-century America's most potent figures of social danger. Long before the Gilded Age, the confidence man had symbolized the moral hazards faced by men and women in a dynamic commercial society governed by contracts and cash transactions. As market relations spilled beyond the boundaries of a circumscribed market-place to permeate nearly all aspects of life, Americans increasingly encountered each other as buyers and sellers in the placeless market. The commercial revolution also set people in motion toward large cities, where anonymity, rather than face-to-face familiarity, was the rule. Feeling at home in a world of strangers required high standards of trust, or confidence, in personal motives and intentions. So, at the same time as Americans indulged in the self-defeating game of projecting a sincere appearance, they also desperately searched each other for clues of deception and fraud. Confidence, it seemed, was more highly valued than ever, but more elusive too. The figure of the professional confidence man, then, embodied what Walt Whitman called "the terrible doubt of appearances."[46] In a society so heavily invested in artifice, no one, especially those conspicuously displaying "good character," escaped suspicion.[47] For select critics of American commercial life, the national confidence game raised the possibility that "good character" and stable identities simply did not exist.[48]

Lacking property and thus utterly dependent on his ability to project "good character," the tramp quickly took his place among the ranks of suspected confidence men, which already included itinerant actors, doctors, peddlers, evangelists, and a host of other traveling tradesmen.[49] Just as magicians possess the power to expose the tricks of their trade, so, too, did the confidence man figuratively threaten to implicate others in the game he played so expertly. As a cultural symbol, the tramp desperately attempting to demonstrate "good character" was but the flip side of the "respectable gentleman" secretly harboring bad intentions and unsavory motives. By dire necessity, tramps became masters of a confidence game that endangered not only middle-class Americans' property, but also their propriety. As The Tramp's tale of one man's restoration to respectable society demonstrates, the redeemed tramp could turn on his fellow property holders in an instant. Instead of gladly assimilating into genteel society, the novel's confidence man-hero unmasks "the hoggish insolence of the prosperous" hiding beneath the appearance of gentility.

Winning confidence and challenging the smug self-assurances of the prosperous were not merely roles assigned to down-and-out characters in working-class narratives. They were also part of the script followed by many flesh-and-blood tramps themselves. Insofar as the tramp army recruited its members from the general population of industrial workers, tramps possessed the same beliefs, values, and attitudes—in a word, consciousness—as the American working class as a whole. Unemployed workers arrived on the road educated in their class's expectations, ideologies, and figures of speech. Those few Gilded Age tramps who managed to gain access to written expression drew from a common stock of literary strategies and conventions already featured in the more formal working-class literatures of tramping. The crucible of the road, however, often gave new shape to such well-worn concepts as free labor and new meanings to what had become the stock figure of the tramp. As the Gilded Age entered its last, and most devastating, great depression in the 1890s, some tramps found ways to tell their own stories of descent and raise their own challenges to property and propriety.

## "FROM THE FRATERNITY OF HAUT BEAUS"

While exploring New York's Mulberry Street slum in 1887, the renowned journalist and housing crusader Jacob Riis came across "a particularly ragged and disreputable tramp" smoking a pipe in "evident philosophic contentment." Armed with a camera and magnesium flash, Riis offered the tramp ten cents to pose for a portrait. The tramp nodded in acceptance and then pocketed his pipe, declaring, according to Riis, "that it was not included in his contract and that it was worth a quarter to have it go in the picture." Riis readily gave in to the demand, which only confirmed to the moralistic slum reformer that he had indeed found a genuine "tramp." "The man," recalled Riis, "scarcely ten seconds employed at honest labor, even at sitting down, at which he was an undoubted expert, had gone on strike. He knew his rights and the value of 'work,' and was not to be cheated out of either" (fig. 2.1).[50]

Jacob Riis's account of how he came to shoot "The Tramp in a Mulberry Street Yard," a photograph reproduced in his landmark *How the Other Half Lives*, represents one episode in a larger Gilded Age struggle over the visible meaning of the tramp. While the competition to represent the tramp most often pitted the labor press against commercial newspapers, the contest also, by 1890 or so, increasingly involved tramps themselves as they encountered a rising generation of intrepid social investigators and reformers. While these investigators sought to deliver "realistic" representations of the "other half," their tramping subjects sometimes found ways to negotiate the terms of the encounter. Helping to define his own situation, the subject of Riis's photograph, for example, is neither an honest victim of mistaken identity, as the labor press would have it, nor a homicidal villain of middle-class fantasy. Rather, he is an agent in his own right whose deliberate gambit with the pipe betrays a shrewd recognition of the role he is being asked to play. By the same token, Riis's

Figure 2.1: Taken in 1887, fourteen years after Jacob Riis himself had retired from the road, this photograph, entitled "The Tramp in a Mulberry Street Yard," exemplifies Riis's obsessive interest in documenting what he called the "other half." As one of Riis's earliest photographs, and the first of a confirmed tramp, the picture was an important part of Riis's renowned exposé of "The Bend," a notorious slum that was eventually torn down and transformed into a recreational park and settlement house. Departing from the conventions of Victorian portraiture, "The Tramp" depicts the subject's entire body in cluttered surroundings, rather than just the upper half against a dark background. By including a squatting "lower half," Riis suggests an absence of rationality, autonomy, and spiritual unity—qualities associated with the classical bust—and emphasizes instead the tramp's subjection to his environment and his body's animal functions. Riis's own desperate experiences with homelessness in the early 1870s imbued the Danish immigrant with an evangelical fervor to expose genteel audiences to their "other half," the half that defined themselves as reputable, hardworking, and abstinent. (Used by permission of The Jacob A. Riis Collection, © Museum of the City of New York.)

own joking reference to the wage contract inadvertently acknowledges both the blurred distinctions between "honest workingmen" and "common tramps" and the cash value of picturesque "street types" to the new mass media emerging in the late Gilded Age. Riis, like all investigators, maintained the upper hand in this negotiation. But by performing as a "tramp," the Mulberry Street pipe smoker ensured that his encounter with Riis would indeed be negotiated.

Jacob Riis, who rarely distinguished between tramps and the general slum-dwelling population, was not the only investigator to record the voices of those he encountered on the streets. Two years after Riis's run-in with the Mulberry Street tramp, a nineteen-year-old Josiah Flynt Willard took off for an eight-month excursion on the road, a journey that would launch his career as the nation's premier expert on tramps. With a curious mixture of sensationalism, moralistic judgment, and sympathetic understanding, Willard authored the first ethnographic studies of tramp life, exploiting his status as a participant observer to publish in such popular outlets as *Century Magazine*, the *Contemporary Review*, and *Atlantic Monthly*. Collected in 1899 in a volume entitled *Tramping with Tramps*, a book that served as the authoritative text on tramp subculture for a generation, Willard's articles included tramps' own perspectives on the road. On the basis of this fieldwork, Willard challenged the middle class's conventional wisdom about tramps, overturning fearsome stereotypes that had been born during the crisis years of the 1870s. Tramps, Willard contended, "are not, as is . . . popularly supposed, the scum of the environment." "On the contrary," he argued, "they are above their environment, and are often gifted with talents which would enable them to do well in any class, could they be only brought to realize its responsibilities and to take advantage of its opportunities."[51]

While Willard won the sympathy of his middle-class audience by offering a collective portrait of tramps as irresponsible but talented underachievers, another tramp investigator of the 1890s, John James McCook, challenged the reigning assumptions about tramps by writing a critical biography of one self-described "knight of the road," William W. Aspinwall. Aspinwall was a tramping worker who began corresponding with the genteel McCook in May 1893. Their remarkable collection of private letters, spanning a quarter-century but concentrated most heavily in the crucial depression years of 1893–97, provides fascinating insight into the early development of an American homeless subculture. While often deploying the representational strategies of the labor press—attempting to show himself as an "honest workingman" of "good character"—Aspinwall also claimed a Whitmanesque identity as a "Gentleman of the Road." Unable to sustain this romance, Aspinwall then used his identity as a tramp to critique and threaten the propertied classes that rejected him.

Despite Aspinwall's seemingly independent voice, its ability to be heard depended entirely upon the discretion of John James McCook, an Episcopal rector and modern language professor at Trinity College in Hartford, Connecticut. Like Aspinwall, McCook was a Civil War veteran, one of fifteen "Fighting McCooks" to serve in the Union army. A devout believer in free labor and the responsibilities of active citizenship, McCook performed a number of civic duties, but none did he pursue more vigorously than the cause of abolishing outdoor relief in all its forms. Alarmed in 1890 by the generosity of Hartford's $40,000 annual budget for "outdoor alms," McCook chaired an investigating committee to uncover corruption and recommend reforms in the distribution of relief. McCook's scrupulously detailed report revealed a thoroughly politicized relief system riddled with abuses. Town Hall grocery orders, for example, steered such luxuries as coconuts, new potatoes, and eggs (out of season) to blocks of voters in poor neighborhoods. The report spawned major reforms in Hartford's poor law administration and launched McCook's career as a sociologist and policy expert.

After consulting his Connecticut neighbor Francis Wayland, McCook turned to his next topic of inquiry, the tramp problem, with a view toward establishing a rehabilitative asylum for chronic dependents. Once the professor embarked upon his study of tramps, he never quit it, even after the Connecticut state legislature rejected his proposal for a "Tramp Reformatory" in 1897. In fact, McCook was still investigating and writing about the homeless underworld until shortly before his death in 1927. This consuming interest began in 1891 when McCook sent questionnaires to over one hundred police departments across the nation to collect case studies of homeless lodgers. After carefully tabulating his findings, the professor took his inquiry to the streets, as well as to the parks, shelters, and railroad yards where tramps could be found. McCook interviewed and photographed many homeless men he met, digging for clues to their character and the causes of their dissipation. He was known to trail a single tramp all day before approaching his subject for questioning. Such foreknowledge allowed the professor to verify the tramp's descriptions of his comings and goings. His voluminous notebooks reveal a meticulous attention to detail and a habit of double-checking even the most seemingly insignificant statement. One tramp told McCook that he never wore underclothes. "I turn aside his shirt busom," recounted McCook, "and under the cotton is the bare flesh."[52]

Unlike every other tramp he questioned, McCook never met his literary foil, William Aspinwall. Born two years after McCook in 1845, Aspinwall was, in his words, "brought up well" by "good parents" in Ohio. In 1861 he joined a volunteer regiment and battled alongside the rest of Ulysses S. Grant's forces for Union control of the Mississippi River. On May 16, 1863, in the Battle of Champion's Hill, Aspinwall was hit by buckshot in the shoulder and head, leaving him with unspecified disabilities. After his discharge from the army in 1865, Aspinwall "took to roaming about having no particular home," traveling throughout the United States and much of the world. He was still on the road in the 1890s, receiving a six-dollar-per-month military pension and fixing clocks, sewing machines, and umbrellas out of a makeshift repair kit. He also occasionally worked on farms and in woolen mills, where he repaired and operated machines.[53]

While passing through New England in May 1893, Aspinwall encountered a tramp nicknamed "Connecticut Fatty" carrying six postcards with McCook's address on them. McCook had asked Fatty to send him periodic updates from the road. The indifferent Fatty, who had already received twenty-five cents from McCook, handed the cards over to Aspinwall, suggesting that he might be able to make some money as the professor's informant. Aspinwall wrote immediately, eager to sell his story. McCook, anxious to distinguish his work from "that mercenary and commercial order of literature," refused to pay, but Aspinwall continued to write anyhow, hoping eventually to gain something from his efforts.[54] The letters to McCook accumulated rapidly, amounting to several hundred pages by the end of 1893.[55] With such rich material in hand, McCook immediately drafted a manuscript on Aspinwall that he planned to publish as a book. Eight years later the *Independent* serialized Aspinwall's story as a nine-part study entitled "Leaves from the Diary of a Tramp."[56]

Aspinwall's first full letter to McCook shows an eagerness to distinguish himself from "common tramps." "I make few friends on the Road," Aspinwall explains before launching into the details of his military service and work experience. "Now I want you to distinctly understand me," he emphasizes. "I am not a Bum":

> I would rather be kicked than go up to a house and ask for something to eat. I have went hungry many a time, almost starved before I would ask. I often wished I was more of a Bum when I was good and hungry, but I am constituted of too much pride and manhood.[57]

Despite Aspinwall's professions of "producerist" pride, a skeptical McCook immediately began a background check on Aspinwall. He followed up on references and even went so far as to arrange for the postmaster of Providence, Rhode Island, to scrutinize Aspinwall thoroughly when the

tramp arrived to receive McCook's first letter.[58] Stung by McCook's suspicions, Aspinwall became defensive and began vouching for himself as a
man of experience.[59] Explaining that his life has been one "of almost constant travels at no time staying more than one year at a place," Aspinwall
declares, "I have a great deal to write about" (June 30, 1893). In an early
letter, Aspinwall briefly describes his travels in the American South, the
West Indies, Mexico, Great Britain, Australia, and India, adding that he
has "been in all the Capitals of the states of the Union and seen the White
House and Capital [sic] at Wash.," and was planning to "strike West to the
World's Fair" after his current tour of New England. "I doubt if there is
another . . . in this broad land of America," proclaims Aspinwall, "that has
been through what I have and seen what I have seen in the way I have"
(June 11, 1893). Still hoping to receive payment for his writing after six
weeks of correspondence, Aspinwall goes so far as to equate himself with
the most popular writers of the day:

> I am willing to do a great deal for charity but I must live you understand. I
> am traveling through and am comeing [sic] in contact with all kinds of hard-
> ships and giving the truth just as it is and I think my experience in this world
> is just worth as much as Gen. Grants, Mark Twains or any other celebrated
> writer. I know well that not one of them can give the same kind of experi-
> ence that I can and tell the truth. (July 4, 1893)

Aspinwall, in effect, represents himself as a Whitmanesque man of the
"Open Road," reveling in the human diversity he encounters. Despite
McCook's request that he focus his comments on the vagrant underworld, Aspinwall insists on sharing his thoughts on the broader range of
people he has met, from southern black sharecroppers and old Confeder-
ate soldiers to Pittsburgh immigrants and Oklahoma Cherokees. Recounting a convivial evening spent in a Niagara Falls saloon, Aspinwall
expresses his pleasure at being part of a veritable festival of nations:

> There was a conglomerated mass of Human beings from all nations. The
> negro was very prominent, all drunk and getting drunker. I just took a seat
> and took in the show, it beat any variety I ever saw, Polocks, Italians and Ne-
> groes kissing and Huging [sic], fighting, shooting crap. You can judge the
> sights for Sunday. (July 9, 1893)

For Aspinwall, the ability to "take in" different kinds of people and different social environments was key to his identity as a tramp and a writer.
   Inventing new terms for his brand of tramping, Aspinwall refers to
himself as a "Gentleman of the Road" and as a voice "from the fraternity
of Haut Beaus" (May 18, 1893). For Aspinwall, tramping was not so much

a stern necessity as a vocation requiring imagination and a discriminating sensibility. Emphasizing the romance of his calling, Aspinwall indulges in Whitmanesque praise of the outdoor life. Arguing that nature readily accommodates the homeless wanderer, Aspinwall says he "would rather sit in close to this beautiful stand of watter [sic] and write than to be in the most luxurious drawing room in this land" (June 30, 1893). Sleeping beneath shade trees, eating wild berries, and otherwise glorying in nature's abundance inspire reveries of a world without private property. "I often think God intended man to live as the Indians used to," he tells McCook, "—all the land common property. What happy times if we was all in woods together" (May 31, 1893). Aspinwall even claims the tramp's life as a salubrious alternative to industrial civilization. "I think this nomadic life is a healthy life," asserts Aspinwall.

> I think if some of you Proffessors [sic], students, etc., would live more of a nomadic life and feel the enjoyment of the fresh air more and take more good wholesome exercise and live more of a rough and tumble life you would enjoy better health and live longer.[60]

Such assertions of superior authenticity support Aspinwall's "literary" identity and justify his life as a tramp.

Given Aspinwall's poverty and his vulnerability to vagrancy arrest, his claims to autonomy and privilege are never secure. While Aspinwall depicts himself as a virtual tourist able to see and enjoy all he encounters, his homelessness often becomes a spectacle itself. "The gaze and stare and remarks of people as I pass along grinds me to the quick," admits Aspinwall in his early correspondence. "I often am the object of scrutiny . . . as if I was some dangerous Beast" (June 10, 1893). Sensing, perhaps, McCook's own scrutiny, Aspinwall repeatedly uses the motif of "plate-glass windows" to convey his sense of vulnerability to surveillance and his alienation from respectable society. "Well housed people look through their plate-glass windows at the poor and destitute as they pass along the street and say there goes a drunken loafer, there goes a tramp," complains Aspinwall. "A raged [sic] coat," he continues, "covers at times a more noble disposition" (December 15, 1893).

In a world governed by the iron law of appearance, a ragged coat could prompt not only jeers, but also arrest. Although Aspinwall claims never to have been arrested for vagrancy or any other crime, he rails against the tramp acts that inhibit his wanderings. A "more Republican form of Government," he argues, would allow him to travel without fear of incarceration. As it stands, "the Tramp Laws of the New England states shows [sic] that a poor unfortunate man has no chance" (June 10, 1893).

Because appearance could mean the difference between employment and unemployment, incarceration and freedom, Aspinwall devotes much of his letters to discussing how he shaves, grooms, washes clothes, and otherwise prepares himself to meet strangers. Eager to show McCook his "good front," Aspinwall sends a photograph of himself in a new suit and straw hat. "I look like a gentleman now," he tells the professor, comparing the new photograph to a previous portrait he had taken in his road clothes. Knowing that such a respectable appearance never lasts long for men of his class, Aspinwall also reminds McCook that "it is not the business or the clothes that makes [sic] the man. I am just as good in old ragged clothes as I am in a fine tailor made suit." But by wearing a tailor-made suit, he explains:

> I am going to show the public that there is one man that is a first-class tinker
> and mechanic that can go through their cities [sic] towns and country that
> is honest and decent and can keep sober and does. And treat people with
> politeness and be respected by the public as a gentleman. (July 2, 1893)

Did Aspinwall warrant such respect? John James McCook takes up precisely this question in his nine-part essay, "Leaves from the Diary of a Tramp." Here, McCook effectively rises to the challenge of Aspinwall's claims to respectability, endeavoring to test his representations as an "honest workingman" and "Gentleman of the Road." The first installment recounts McCook's background investigation of Aspinwall, which verifies his "stories of travel" as "entirely credible."[61] Subsequent sections move from the facts of Aspinwall's identity to the content of his character. Displaying his skill as an expert evaluator of character, McCook describes his request for a photograph in which he stipulated that "there must be no fixing up, no shaving or polishing, but that everything must be taken as if on the road" (3:3010). While admitting that photographs "are exceedingly unsatisfactory in matters of this kind," McCook nonetheless accepts Aspinwall's first portrait as evidence that " 'Roving Bill' is no vulgar shovel or city bum" (3:3011) (fig. 2.2). The second portrait, however, taken at Aspinwall's own expense without any prior instructions from McCook, draws the professor's suspicion. The tailored suit and straw hat seem "needlessly conspicuous," and Aspinwall himself "takes almost too much pains to vindicate the dignity of his . . . calling." McCook then reports Aspinwall's "naive confession" that he occasionally gambles and "drink[s] too much Beer." Aspinwall's purported "sturdy feeling of self-respect" no longer appears justified (6:332–34).

Exposing Aspinwall's feeble confidence game is but a prelude to Mc-Cook's greater challenge of deflecting the tramp's increasingly strident

Figure 2.2: This picture of William W. "Roving Bill" Aspinwall was taken at a photographer's studio in Bennington, Vermont, on June 8, 1893. John James McCook commissioned the portrait, stipulating that "there must be no fixing up, no shaving or polishing, but that everything must be taken as if on the road." While McCook delighted in the result, Aspinwall himself preferred a more "polished" look and paid for a second portrait featuring a new tailored suit and straw hat. This second photograph, which raised McCook's suspicions of Aspinwall's character, has unfortunately deteriorated. (Used by permission of Butler-McCook House & Garden, Antiquarian & Landmarks Society.)

criticisms of the professor and his social class. While Aspinwall had always wanted to write letters on a wide range of topics, the short messages he received from McCook contained only narrow questions regarding the habits and morals of tramping men. As the wave of corporate and bank failures during the spring of 1893 plunged the nation into its most severe depression in history, Aspinwall began to chastise McCook for his limited understanding of working-class life. When McCook sends Aspinwall his plans for a proposed tramp reformatory, Aspinwall shoots back that "there is a good deal of reforming that should be done outside of tramps and vagrants" (August 6, 1893). The "tramp nuisance," Aspinwall quips in a later note, " . . . is a great nuisance to a great number of tramps themselves" (August 14, 1893).

Aspinwall uses his identity as a tramp to claim a superior understanding of social reality. "Theory will do but Practice makes perfect," writes Aspinwall. "I have had the Practical Knowledge [of poverty] but I know you have had nothing but a theoretical knowledge" (December 10, 1893). In order to give McCook a taste of such "practical knowledge," Aspinwall abandons his high-minded tone as a "Gentleman of the Road" and becomes a social reporter and critic who documents the distress he sees all around him.

Writing from Pittsburgh on September 8, Aspinwall describes the city's "men all loafing around the streets," victims of economic depression. The rail lines "on both sides of the river," he explains, are "lined with men going both ways" in search of work, "the picture of despair on their countenances and asking how the times was where I had been" (September 8, 1893). The following spring, after closing his small repair shop in Pittsburgh, Aspinwall joined that migratory stream. From Aspinwall's side of the road, McCook's notion that tramping was an individual pathology appeared ridiculous. The "present shutting down of business will make thousands of tramps," Aspinwall tells McCook, "because everyone is a tramp when once on the road." Warning that "some one third of the male population of this country will be living a nomadic life," the tramp argues that "the general government should enact some laws to furnish all idle men work of some kind." If nothing is done, he concludes, "America will go back to the uncivilized state worse than the savage Indians before Columbus discovered this country" (April 29, 1894).

In response to Aspinwall's increasingly militant attitude, the final installment of McCook's essay focuses exclusively on what the professor calls the ultimate "pathos of the road." Aspinwall's grim tone, McCook explains, is evidence of the "melancholy" that plagues all tramps, even those with "bourgeois symptoms." "I am getting tiard [sic] of Roaming around," McCook quotes Aspinwall as writing in 1894, "and I would be Happy indeed if I only had a permanent Home." "When I get out of work and financially Busted," Aspinwall explains further, "I think there is no other alternative only to take to the Road." McCook then describes "a long period of commonplace industry" and residential stability in

Aspinwall's life when McCook greeted the tramp's "brief and dull" letters "with a half sigh for what had disappeared from his life—and mine!" (9:1540–43).

Soon enough, however, McCook again receives a letter headed "On the Road Walking." But instead of the usual romantic musings, the letter contains a tone of "political gloom" and a "high standard of pessimism" that, McCook explains, frequently appears among disillusioned vagabonds. "And you folks wonder why there is [*sic*] Tramps," snarls Aspinwall after several frustrating weeks on the road. "You are not educated up to the causes of all these social plagues. You will be in time." McCook then quotes Aspinwall on the coming class war "between the centres of wealth and the Common People" in which the tramp will figure prominently:

> Labor and all the common people are now so strong as to be almost uncontrolable [*sic*] and threatens [*sic*] to burst forth and engulf the world in Chaos. . . . There is a half million Nomadic helthy [*sic*] tough Ho-Bos in America. If I had them organized equiped [*sic*] and disciplined, they would make the grandest army that ever shouldered a gun and would be invincible. I would have no trouble in getting them transportation. They would beat their way and subsist at the back doors of towns they passed through.

McCook concludes "Leaves from the Diary of a Tramp" with Aspinwall's ominous prediction of class warfare. Responding to this threat, McCook blithely explains that he has written Aspinwall back to ask "whether it has occurred to him what would happen to his Army of Tramps if a train of wagons laden with free beer were to be sent to meet them." "I shall hear from him promptly," McCook explains as he closes his essay, " . . . and confidently expect to find him once more in his earlier and more cheerful mood" (9:1543–44).

Aspinwall's prediction of a half-million man march attested to the enduring power of the tramp army as a symbol of working-class rage. McCook's derisive retort, on the other hand, represented a middle-class need to come to terms with a tramp army that, after over two decades, was still stubbornly refusing to demobilize. By defanging Aspinwall's tramp army, McCook slayed the very dragon that had inspired his own efforts to humanize the tramp. McCook portrayed the world of William W. Aspinwall in intimate, even loving, detail in order to counter what he called the "panicky look" and "blood-curdling ferocity" that characterized earlier writings about tramps.[62] Granting Aspinwall an audience advanced McCook's larger project of quelling popular fears about the "tramp menace." Aspinwall's quaint meditations on the road and transparent confidence games played right into the professor's hands, for McCook largely saw tramps as rather harmless victims of personal pathologies. Having exposed Aspinwall's frailties, inconsistencies, and irresponsibility, McCook was equipped with a ready response to the tramp's stock provocation. After all the frenzied vigilante, legislative, and military activities of the 1870s, it turned out that beer wagons were all the nation needed to thwart the rising tramp army.

Such satirical humor masked enduring anxieties about the great army of tramps even as it provided those anxieties a rich outlet of expression. McCook's joke paralleled the comic tramp's antics on the vaudeville stage, a vogue that coincided with the vast upsurge in homelessness in the 1890s. By then America's tramp army had not only grown to unprecedented proportions; it was also undergoing a qualitative change. The great tramp army was now developing into a veritable floating subculture with its own vernacular, social networks, institutions, and urban neighborhoods. A permanent feature of American life, tramps took up key positions in the nation's expanding economy, especially in the West, where new agricultural and extractive sectors demanded a cheap and flexible labor force. For hundreds of thousands of young men, the old republican ideals of independent proprietorship receded to the horizon as new habits of casual labor and lodging grew up on the "wageworker's frontier." When this burgeoning subculture staged its real-life Industrial Army marches of 1894, labor tribunes struggled to define the protest in terms of republicanism, while the mainstream press mobilized new comic caricatures to deride what it termed "Coxey's Army." But the Industrial Army movement was neither the chaotic rising of a desperate lumpenproletariat described by William Aspinwall, nor the beer-laden carnival imagined by John James McCook. Rather, the Industrials' "petition in boots" represented the first collective expression of "hobohemia," an emergent subculture of western hobo labor whose presence would both beguile and bedevil the nation for decades to come.

# 3.

# "HALLELUJAH, I'M A BUM!"

In early 1894 the teenager who would become the nation's first proletarian writer and first literary millionaire quit his job shoveling coal and hopped a freight train out of California. Enduring insufferable heat, freezing cold, hostile train crews, and showers of coal sparks that caught his overcoat on fire, Jack London chased "General" Charles T. Kelley's 1,500-member Industrial Army as it made its way to Washington, D.C., to petition Congress for unemployment relief. Despite his youth, London was a seasoned hobo, a "profesh" in road parlance, having "decked" his first train two years earlier at the age of sixteen. Now, in April, London joined hundreds of other hoboing men in pursuit of Kelley, whose March on Washington had begun ahead of schedule when a nervous Oakland police force ordered the army to leave town.

While London clung tenaciously to boxcars, Kelley's Army got sidetracked at Council Bluffs, Iowa, where it entertained crowds, collected donations, and awaited a special train to carry it further east. "The Army made quite an imposing array," London noted in his diary the day he reached Council Bluffs, "with flags & banners & Gen. Kelly [*sic*] at their head astride of a fine black horse presented by an enthusiastic Council Bluffs citizen." Marching in the "first Regiment of the Reno Industrial Army," London gloried in the camp camaraderie, even after the railroads refused the exhausted, hungry, and rain-soaked marchers further transportation. Not deterred, Kelley's men fashioned 150 flat-bottom boats to sail down the Des Moines River to the Mississippi. Like Huck Finn, who would serve as his early literary model, Jack London reveled in his river adventure, but the sparsely populated territories of the Midwest could not provide enough food for Kelley's "navy." As he neared Mark Twain's hometown of Hannibal, Missouri, London listened to his stomach. "Am going to pull out in the morning," he scrawled in his diary on May 24; "I can't stand starvation." Two days later London caught a "cannon ball" for Chicago, where he slept in a fifteen-cent lodging house and toured the celebrated grounds of the World's Columbian Exposition.[1]

Jack London was just one of many unemployed workers to be swept up, however briefly, in the colorful protests of the Industrial Army movement during the spring of 1894. Originally the brainchild of Jacob Coxey, an eccentric monetary reformer, and Carl Browne, a flamboyant veteran of western labor crusades, the call for a nationwide March on Washington reverberated throughout depression-wracked America. From Boston to San Francisco, unemployed men responded to the rallying cry "*On to Washington!*" and left behind whatever homes they had to tramp, sail, and ride their way toward the nation's capital to deliver what Coxey christened the "petition in boots." The original assemblage of 122 marchers, which formed outside of Coxey's home in Massillon, Ohio, called itself the Commonweal of Christ. But the subsequent movement that arose in the West took on more militant overtones. Western contingents, organized explicitly as Industrial Armies rather than Commonweals, were far larger, more numerous, more popular with local residents, and more aggressive in demanding transportation, shelter, and sustenance from public and private authorities. Indeed, only three notable contingents formed in the Northeast. Even Coxey was originally to lead his march out of Chicago until concerns that the Commonweal would attract too many recruits prompted a shift to Massillon.[2]

While Coxey's Commonwealers earnestly tramped their way to Washington, western Industrials stole train rides and, on at least fifty occasions, commandeered entire freight trains. In the West, remarked one observer, "the petition in boots really came to mean petitions on wheels."[3] Despite their determination, fewer than half of those who began marching ever reached Washington. The obstacles posed by hunger and poverty, as well as by railroad detectives, local police, state militias, and the United States Army itself, simply proved too great for most armies to overcome.

Kelley's Army finally disintegrated in June after being waylaid on the Ohio River. Some stragglers eventually did meet up with Coxey's Commonweal and together confronted a United States Congress that was utterly indifferent to their plight. As for Jack London, he took off to see Niagara Falls but ended up being arrested on the "charge of Tramp" as he pulled into Buffalo. While police were dispersing the remnants of Coxey's Army camped near Washington, London was serving thirty days in the Erie County Penitentiary. Upon his release, young Jack took to the rails once more, filling his notebooks with the road stories that would launch his career on the new mass literary market.[4]

The drifting but ambitious Jack London defied contemporary descriptions of Industrial Army members. Predictably, middle-class pundits like Francis Wayland characterized the protesters as a "soap-shunning and vermin-haunted rabble."[5] In the marchers' defense, labor tribunes trotted out familiar references to "producers," "honest workingmen," family breadwinners, and, of course, Civil War veterans. Sallying forth under the banner of republicanism and seeking to transform, in General Kelley's words, "homeless wanderers into sturdy farmers and property owners," movement leaders had little use for freewheeling teenagers like Jack London.[6] Such job-shirking adventurers only fed the suspicions of those who, like economist Thorstein Veblen, saw the men as "idlers" seeking "a temporary means of subsistence and entertainment."[7]

But while much of the rhetoric and symbolism of the movement looked backward to a lost republican world of patriarchy and producerism, the very membership and methods of the Industrial Armies heralded the birth of a radically new subculture of western hobo labor.[8] In 1894 that subculture was still in its infancy, lacking the customs, infrastructure, and collective identity that would soon come to mark hobo life. But over the next two decades, as corporate capital made the West over in its own image, young wageworkers flocked to the mines, forests, lakes, harvest fields, construction sites, and countless other places where hoboes found casual and seasonal labor. As hobo labor grew, so did urban lodging-house neighborhoods, which sheltered jobless workers and then shipped them back out to the field. It was in these "main stem" and "slave market" districts where hoboes met, mingled, and together forged a group identity that drew upon shared experiences of class, plebian notions of whiteness, and peculiar expressions of masculinity.

If the term "hobo" was a language innovation used to describe this new species of homeless man, then "hobohemia," a word popularized in the 1920s by Chicago school sociologist Nels Anderson, captured the countercultural aspects of life on the "wageworkers' frontier."[9] Hoboes were bohemian not only because they were comparatively rootless, but also because they were transitional figures, straddling the residual working-class world of the nineteenth century and the emerging one of the twentieth. They had broken from their class's settled beliefs and values but had yet to fashion new ones to take their place. Like the politically revolutionary Jack London, hobohemia strained against the assumptions of working-class republicanism. The counterculture also rejected domesticity as well as the "stifling, shut-in air" and "petty routine" of factory and office labor that so oppressed Jack London.[10]

By the turn of the twentieth century, this counterculture possessed its own defining folk song, whose lyrics, scrawled on the walls of railroad cars and jail cells throughout the industrial West, defined the hobo as anything but an "honest workingman":

> Oh, why don't I work
> Like the other men do?
> How the hell can I work
> When the skies are so blue?
> *Chorus:*
> Hallelujah, I'm a bum,
> Hallelujah, bum again,
> Hallelujah, bum a handout—
> Revive me again.[11]

"Hallelujah, I'm a Bum" proved so popular that Salvation Army missionaries could no longer sing the hymn it parodied. The Industrial Workers of the World, which sought to mobilize hobohemia for its crusade against wage labor, eventually adopted "Hallelujah, I'm a Bum" as its unofficial anthem. Even as they parodied the smug platitudes of the propertied middle class, the song's sardonic lyrics captured an emerging sense of the road as a rough haven for white wage-earning men.

As the young Jack London discovered in prison, the world of the hobo was no idyllic refuge from wage dependency. Nevertheless, for many workers, what London referred to as "the call of the road" was just as decisive in directing them to hobohemia as the lash of unemployment.[12]

## THE OPENING OF THE WAGEWORKERS' FRONTIER

A year before the March on Washington, on the very grounds toured by Jack London, Frederick Jackson Turner announced to an audience of fellow historians at the World's Columbian Exposition that the American frontier was officially closed. Since Columbus's arrival, Turner argued, America's "virgin" land had drawn settlers westward, assimilating generations of homesteaders and giving rise to distinctly American traditions of democracy, propertied independence, and rugged individualism. Now, as the census of 1890 showed, the "frontier line" that had once separated "savagery and civilization" lay in the Pacific Ocean, pushed there by an expanding population. With the "safety valve" of the West shut off, unable to drain the surplus of propertyless workers that urban industrial civilization produced, what would become of the American Republic?[13]

The thousands of unemployed wage earners streaming to the road in 1893 gave this question special urgency. The West, instead of absorbing these masses with its promise of free land, was now manufacturing its own population of homeless wanderers, many of whom joined Industrial Armies. As a product of the West, the "petition on wheels" raised the possibility that the historic frontier, rather than being the Republic's salvation, might lead to its undoing. Unleashed from the tempering influence of broad-based property ownership, the masculine "savagery" long associated with the "wild West" seemed no longer redemptive, but dangerous. "A different class of beings from Coxey's followers are these western crusaders," observed one reporter. "In the main they are stalwart young fellows, hardened by exposure and full of animal life; harder men to deal with than the meek, listless Coxey Commonwealers."[14] While journalists often ridiculed the Massillon contingent as clownish "tramps," detachments from Los Angeles, San Francisco, Portland, Seattle, Salt Lake City, Denver, Houston, St. Louis, and smaller western towns inspired alarm. Coxey's Army itself, recalled one observer, was justifiably "laughed at," "but the imitators of Coxey, who sprang up in other parts of the country, acted in a much more dangerous manner. They robbed, held up trains, intimidated individuals, and even terrified local Government officials."[15]

Such descriptions of lumpen lawlessness stood in stark contrast to Frederick Jackson Turner's mythical vision of a bygone frontier society of sturdy yeoman farmers. Turner's nostalgic "frontier thesis," in fact, called attention to how the "new" West was becoming increasingly incorporated into the business enterprise of the East. Migrants no longer reached the West by wagon train, but rather by railroads, which also transported the region's raw materials back to cities for processing. Moreover, those who traveled the westward route did so not as pioneers seeking freeholds, but as laborers pursuing temporary wage work. American workers knew the perils of western migration long before Turner pronounced his thesis. "Don't go West," the *Iron Molders' Journal* instructed its readers in 1877, citing high unemployment, poor wages, and low rates of property ownership.[16] "The man without capital," concurred *John Swinton's Paper* in 1885, "has no place any more in the West."[17] That same year, a western migrant who would later command the Los Angeles Industrial Army condensed his career as an itinerant carpenter into a biting commentary for his union's journal:

The plundered victim of greed bade adieu to friends and kindred, took a last look at boyhood's home and started on his weary march to the Occident. From Ohio to Missouri, tramping over the plains, scaling the snow-clad Rockies, a pitiless fate follows in his footsteps. Now he takes a spin into the Black Hills, now he turns to Carbonate Camp and again he is in New Mexico.

He follows the wide valleys, he is on the line of every railroad, but somehow or other, there is always a surplus crop of his tribe. . . .With his face toward the setting sun he renews his toilsome march and finally reaches the Pacific shore. . . . Here he finds a population enacting the same scene he has witnessed everywhere. . . . Alas, the promised land is a myth.[18]

This passage records a moment of mythical crystallization when the promise of the West as an outpost of small independent producers is exposed as false. The March on Washington dramatized this same disillusionment by reversing the historic direction of frontier development and sending marchers eastward in their treks of protest.

While the Industrial Armies declared the "producers' frontier" to be closed, the movement also signaled that a new "wageworkers' frontier" had opened. Coined by Carlos Schwantes, a western historian one hundred years removed from Turner, the term "wageworkers' frontier" captures the rough, unfinished quality of early corporate capitalist development in the West.[19] Virtually every economic sector there operated seasonally, gathering up and then dispersing armies of transient workers. By the turn of the century, the region was teeming with men who collectively harvested wheat on the Great Plains; picked fruit and vegetables in California's Central Valley; felled trees in the Pacific Northwest; mined iron, coal, and copper in Minnesota, Colorado, Utah, Arizona, and Montana; and constructed the railroads, towns, and cities that comprised the very infrastructure of the industrial West.

This transient labor force was always multinational and multiracial, although the composition of each sector's workforce changed over time. Japanese, Chinese, and eventually Filipino communities along the Pacific coast sent huge numbers of young men to work in mining, agriculture, and railroad building. Likewise, southern and eastern European immigrants regularly shipped out in construction and common labor gangs, even to the far West. Scandinavians concentrated in the Great Plains and upper Midwest, working the harvests and, in time, dominating Minnesota's Iron Range. Mexican workers, meanwhile, crisscrossed the Southwest as "foreigners in their native land" and also eventually traveled into the Anglo Midwest to work as harvesters, factory operatives, railroad section hands, and construction laborers of all sorts. By World War I, they were increasingly joined by gangs of black laborers, which were common in the South but which began to appear more frequently in the Midwest and West as African Americans migrated to the industrialized North.[20]

Interspersed among all these groups were vast numbers of native-born white workers who quickly distinguished themselves by their individual restlessness, irregular work habits, and alienation from settled communities. These white migrants were overwhelmingly young and single, and, unlike their foreign-born and nonwhite counterparts, traveled individually or in small groups. While their social characteristics matched those of the 1870s tramp army, these footloose homeless men became known as "hoboes," differentiating them from both other migratory groups and previous generations of wayfarers.

Precisely why and how the term "hobo" came into use remains a mystery. In the absence of any traceable etymology, contemporary observers turned to various origin myths, each more imaginative than the other. Some believed the Latin *homo bonus* ("good man") to be the root. Others privileged the familiar salutation "Ho, boy!" or the descriptive "hoe-boy." Searching further afield, a creative few, such as William Aspinwall, argued that "hobo" was an anglicized version of foreign phrases like "Haut Beau." Whatever its precise derivation, the word first emerged within the Gilded Age working class, most likely among western tramps themselves, before migrating into general middle-class vernacular in the 1890s. While western newspapers referred to "hoboes" in the late 1880s, if not earlier, Josiah Flynt Willard introduced the term to a national readership in his 1891 *Contemporary Review* article entitled "The American Tramp." Willard used "hobo" in a pejorative sense to denote the more aggressive western version of the work-shunning "professional tramp."[21] Western workers themselves, however, came to adopt the term as a "badge of honor" to distinguish themselves from other groups of homeless men, whom they derided with terms like "tramp" and "bum." By World War I, hoboes had devised a classificatory system that put themselves at the top of a homeless hierarchy: "A hobo is a migratory worker. A tramp is a migratory non-worker. A bum is a stationary non-worker. Upon the labor of the migratory worker all the basic industries depend."[22] For most other Americans, "hobo" came to signify a new kind of homelessness, one so pervasive among white workers of the West that it actually fostered a transient community of its own.

Like the "great army of tramps," the most striking feature of this hobo community was its unprecedented mobility. The very experience of migrating westward was usually but an initiation into a life of frequent travel.

The extraordinary volatility of late-nineteenth-century western labor markets, heightened by seasonality and dramatic boom-bust cycles, made unemployment a routine feature of the wageworker's frontier. The traditional sources of relief that tied the unemployed to local communities in the East were scarcer in the unsettled West. Moreover, as many work sites were geographically isolated or were located in smaller towns and cities where labor markets were homogenous, losing one's job almost always entailed migration, quite often of long distances.

To facilitate such extreme transiency, hobo laborers perfected the dangerous art of freight hopping to an extent unrealized by their eastern counterparts. "Now it is notorious," remarked Jack London in 1902, "that Eastern tramps do not know how to 'railroad.'" Indeed, those whom London dismissed as "the lesser local tramps" of the East traveled in regions where work sites were relatively concentrated and often accessible by foot.[23] Western geography, by contrast, required more aggressive methods of travel. As early as 1876, the *New York Times* noted great numbers of "migratory, poverty-stricken individuals" in the West stealing train rides with "an unlimited amount of cheek."[24]

With each passing year, hoboes added to their collective repertoire of ride-stealing techniques, devising ingenious methods for mounting and "holding down" cars without being detected by vigilant train crews ("shacks" in hobo lingo) or railroad police ("bulls"). Daring migrants like Jack London not only rode inside boxcars (nicknamed "side-door Pullmans") and outside on the "bumpers" or couplings, but also "decked" the tops of trains and clung to the "rods" or "gunnels" beneath the cars, speeding along just inches above the track. Thousands of hoboes died each year traveling in such fashion, and many more suffered severe injury. Accidents claimed the lives of nearly twenty-five thousand railroad trespassers between 1901 and 1905 alone, the years during which Jack London publicized his skillful feats of "train flipping" (fig. 3.1).[25]

While London seemed to enjoy the sport, other job seekers had little choice but to steal train rides since passenger rates were high and employers were often unwilling to pay transportation expenses. As a result, hoboes considered access to railroads to be "every American's inalienable right," a right to which the Industrial Armies' train-stealing episodes so dramatically staked a claim.[26] Railroads tacitly recognized this right when labor markets were tight or when employers wished to depress wages, such as during harvest seasons. But when labor demand was low, railroad detectives and train crews often brutally suppressed trespassing, making job searches all the more difficult and treacherous.

While freight hopping was a common response to joblessness, the will-

Figure 3.1: In 1894 John James McCook paid "Providence Bob" and "Philadelphia Shorty" fifty cents each to demonstrate their various methods for riding the rails. Later published in the *Independent* as part of McCook's "Leaves from the Diary of a Tramp" series, this picture and McCook's accompanying description of "train jumping," prompted Jack London to write a scorching rejoinder for the *Bookman* entitled "Rods and Gunnels." While McCook referred to the two tramps as "riding the rods," London, speaking as a seasoned "profesh," indignantly explained that the pieces of hardware were in fact "gunnels" that could be ridden by "anybody with arms and legs." "The average Eastern tramp and the average Eastern tramp investigator," London charged, "are utterly ignorant of what the rods are" and of "railroading" generally. Only western hoboes, he continued, possessed the "nerve, and skill, and daring" to "ride the rods" in authentic style—that is, atop the trucks of a passenger car. Taking his romance of the road to Nietzschean proportions, London concluded his critique of McCook with a description of hoboes as "primordial noble men . . . lustfully roving and conquering through sheer superiority and strength." (Used by permission of Butler-McCook House & Garden, Antiquarian & Landmarks Society.)

ingness to travel also exposed hoboes to different kinds of work and even provided them with bargaining leverage as they negotiated wages and job conditions. On the wageworkers' frontier, a contract was anything but sacred, and job shirking was a regular part of every hobo's career. As one "employment agency proverb" put it, turnover was so high on the wageworkers' frontier that each job required three crews: one going, one coming, and one on the job.[27] Unlike hoboes, immigrant migratories tended to ship out together in great labor gangs and see jobs through to their end, or walk off together in mass. Many employers of gang labor preferred to hire

southern and eastern European immigrants because, as one railroad official put it in 1908, they "[stick] right through from April to November."[28]

Hoboes, on the other hand, floated from job to job, rarely staying with
one job for more than a few weeks. In the spring of 1897, for example, a
floater from Illinois named Charles Morgan stole train rides to Kansas
City, where he worked successive stints in a carriage maker's shop, a
power plant, and two packinghouses. Finding it all "very hard work" with
little pay, Morgan turned to the Union stockyards and a house-painting
firm and then rode to Chicago. There, he continued shifting from job
to job before returning to the prairies in time for the early harvests.[29]
Hoboes like Charles Morgan demonstrated not only high rates of transiency between jobs, but also great volatility and independence while on
the job. "Hobos are easily piqued," commented sociologist and former
migratory worker Nels Anderson, "and they will 'walk off' the job on the
slightest pretext, even when they have the best jobs and living conditions
are relatively good."[30] This low threshold for difficult labor, abusive treatment, and poor wages rose considerably during economic downturns when
employment was scarce. Even so, impatience with exploitative working
conditions remained a marked feature of hobo labor on the wageworkers'
frontier.

Hoboes used railroads not only to broaden their job choices but also,
from time to time, to "lay off" of work altogether. In 1898 one western migratory characterized the hobo as a worker who, "perceiving that he could
live without constant working, took to the road and brought his trade into
use when necessity pressed."[31] With the free labor ideal and the "promised
land" of the West having fallen into disrepute, few hobo workers saw any
reason to accumulate savings or acquire property. By the early twentieth
century, this nonacquisitive ethic had taken firm root in hobo subculture,
raising the alarm of middle-class observers, who considered such profli-
gate behavior as a "maladjustment." "It seems that when a laborer has
earned a sum which road tradition has fixed as affluence, he quits," wrote
economist Carleton Parker in 1915. "This sum," Parker continued,

> is known as a "jungle stake," and once it is earned the hobo discipline calls
> upon the casual to resort to a camp under a railroad bridge or along some
> stream, a "jungle," as the vernacular terms it, and live upon this "stake" till
> it is gone. Thereupon he goes north to a new maturing crop. Weeks spent
> among the casuals by two investigators lead them to attach great impor-
> tance to this custom.[32]

Interviewing seasonal and migratory workers for the United States Industrial Relations Commission between 1913 and 1915, labor investigator

Peter Speek uncovered similar practices of nonaccumulation. Sam Gray, a thirty-five-year-old hobo who passed his winters in Milwaukee and Minneapolis, for example, "never liked to work steady. He only worked as to get enough money to be fed and clothed. He does not care to save money."[33] Of another informant, a migratory harvest and railroad construction laborer named Thomas Lee, Speek reported that "after years of struggle, hopes and disappointments, he gave up the idea of becoming a farmer. After that he did not care to save money; when he had it he 'blew it in.'"[34] In this instance, "blowing it in," or spending it, expressed resignation and fatalism before the unattainable free labor ideal of proprietorship.

But while some reluctantly resigned themselves to living on a token "stake," other migratory workers considered their conspicuous rejection of acquisitivism to be a positive component of their identity. "What should I save for?" asked one seasonal laborer in attempting to explain to a Chicago social worker why he was unwilling to join a winter ice-cutting crew. "I'm real sorry to disappoint you, Miss," he continued, "since you seem so set on the idea of me working on the ice, but to tell the truth I really wouldn't think it was *right* to do it. I'd just be taking the work away from some poor fellow who needs it, and it wouldn't be right for a man to do that when he has plenty of money in his pocket."[35]

The ethical code that gave rise to such unapologetic rejections of acquisitivism also encouraged expressions of satisfaction, even defiant pride, with the hobo life. Frederick Mills, a member of Carleton Parker's investigative team researching migratory and seasonal labor in California in 1914, was surprised to learn that 70 percent of the "casuals" questioned expressed "no desire to escape from the life of a 'floater.'" Mills linked this lack of "desire" to an absence of "initiative."[36] But these widespread patterns of wage earning and nonaccumulation were also values nurtured and enforced by hobo subculture. Indeed, these values were precisely what put the "bohemia" in "hobohemia."

If hoboing was, to a degree, an individually chosen strategy for minimizing wage dependency and insulating oneself against exploitation, then the success of this strategy hinged on informal networks that made hoboing a collective enterprise as well. Hobo life bred close, if temporary, friendships. On the road, men frequently formed partnerships for reasons of safety, frugality, and company. While riding in a boxcar in 1897 in route to the Kansas wheat harvests, a nineteen-year-old Carl Sandburg proposed such a partnership to a young fellow traveler. "He had a face and a way of talking I liked so much," recalled Sandburg, "that I asked him how it would be for the two of us to travel together and share and share alike for a few weeks."[37] Although this prospective alliance did not work out (the young farmhand was heading for Alaska), Sandburg and other hoboing men routinely pooled resources and split the tasks of scavenging, begging, and wage labor.

This ethic of reciprocity and mutualism, which informed virtually every aspect of life on the road, found its most striking expression in the legendary hobo "jungles." These "marvels of cooperation," as one observer called them, were strategically located outside the immediate purview of local officials and residents but close to running water and railroad division points.[38] It was here, in these surrogates for the settled working-class communities they had abandoned, that hoboes ate, drank, bathed, washed and mended clothes, and otherwise shared in the camaraderie of the road (fig. 3.2). "I have seen them where there was plenty of Beer and Alcohol," explained William Aspinwall to John James McCook:

> . . . and plenty to eat—cooked in old tin cans and any old tin vessel that could be picked up. The grub was bummed or begged from butchers, bakers and private families and some of it gotten by the slight [sic] of hand . . . nothing but old tin cans to cook in. It takes a cook to get up meals in such a style, and how patiently they will wait on each other.[39]

In the literature of hoboing, the jungle often appears utopian, and indeed it sometimes was, in the sense that bohemian communities experiment with forms of living that deviate from despoiled norms. But the cooperative structure of jungle camps and hobo life in general derived more from necessity than from a shared romance of the road. Put simply, hoboes lacked the support networks usually available to residentially stable workers. In a world of strangers, migrants drew upon their class experiences to improvise new forms of obligation and mutual aid.

The Industrial Army movement itself, whose camps were little more than glorified hobo jungles, was an example of such improvised responses to rootlessness. Marchers floated in and out of the camps, joining them when jobless and leaving them to search for work. Indeed, Thorstein Veblen's charge that the Industrials were "idlers" seeking "subsistence and entertainment" was to some degree correct. For many, the movement was a way of "getting by" during a depressed spring labor market. "'Coxey's Army,'" as one sympathizer wrote, "was made up of men who found nothing in work but food, clothing, and slavery. In the spectacular march to Washington there was food, clothing, fame of a certain sort, excitement, a possible dream of spoils, and, at any rate, freedom."[40] After 1894 hoboes would have less use for such spectacular marches, relying more on their own resources and support networks. Especially along the main stems of

Figure 3.2: Apart from riding the rails itself, no aspect of hobo life was more celebrated than the "jungle," the hobo's resort while on the road. Hidden from view, but not far from town, jungles hosted, in the words of one investigator, an "ever-changing, ever-moving army of migratory workers and migratory non-workers" who came to rest, eat, wash up, and trade information. Virtually all accounts of jungle life include examples of both hearty camaraderie and the various dangers that always threatened to disrupt the jungle's idyll. Because thieves, rapists, confidence men, and other hazardous characters often drifted into jungles, prompting police raids, hoboes remained vigilant while encamped, wary of each newcomer. For this reason, most jungle residents scattered when confronted by an investigator's camera, leaving behind nothing more than a bare and nondescript campground. One exception, featured here, was staged in 1895 near Hartford, Connecticut, by John James McCook and his son. The tramps received a free picnic, while McCook captured a rare shot of a legendary jungle. (Used by permission of Butler-McCook House & Garden, Antiquarian & Landmarks Society.)

western cities, hoboes were beginning to make a home for themselves on the wageworkers' frontier.

## THE MAIN STEM

In the depression year of 1907, an eighteen-year-old Nels Anderson, coming off a stint with a railroad grading crew in Montana, passed through Omaha's hobo district along Douglas Street and marveled at its size. Amidst a throng of men studying the chalked placards in employment agency windows, Anderson and his traveling companion looked down the crowded sidewalks and estimated five thousand men milling about on the streets, drinking in saloons, mooching at backdoors, or "trying to get freight trains for somewhere else."[41] In little more than a day's time, Anderson would join the freight-hopping contingent and depart Omaha for Chicago, from where, in turn, he would travel on to Kansas City, Denver, and Salt Lake City in a grueling search for work.

By the time Nels Anderson arrived on Douglas Street, the lodging house neighborhoods that had first taken shape during the tramp crisis of the 1870s had developed in urban centers across the continent, from New York and Boston to Seattle and San Francisco. In both the older commercial and manufacturing hubs of the Northeast and the newer cities of the Midwest and West, districts inhabited almost exclusively by ever-changing populations of homeless men anchored the circulation of labor within metropolitan regions. From Chicago to the Pacific coast, these districts comprised a veritable network, making possible Nels Anderson's elaborate hobo journey and tying together far-flung branches of hobohemia. Located downtown, just outside towering new central business districts and adjacent to railroad yards, docks, and major thoroughfares, hobohemian neighborhoods commanded high profiles, and newcomers like Anderson made their way toward them "as if by instinct."[42] "You didn't have to ask how to find it," recalled Stewart Holbrook of the Pacific Northwest's "skid roads," "for it had a character of its own."[43]

Such neighborhood character flourished throughout the West, even in smaller towns. But metropolises with expansive hinterlands hosted particularly robust main stems that virtually defined their city centers. Minneapolis's Gateway district, located between the city's two railroad depots in the heart of downtown, was a key hobo resort of the Midwest, accommodating 105 lodging houses and 6,000 men.[44] On the West Coast, San Francisco's South of Market was the largest hobo mecca, lodging upward of 40,000 men per night by World War I.[45] Dwarfing even these was Chicago's hobohemian district, centered on West Madison Street but encircling the Loop and extending at least one-half mile in each direction. In 1908 one researcher estimated that between 40,000 and 60,000 men took shelter in the neighborhood's 200 to 300 lodging houses and hotels. A dozen years later, Nels Anderson calculated the population as ranging from 30,000 during flush summer labor markets to 75,000 during depressions and slack winter months. Whatever the precise numbers, it was clear that by the early twentieth century, Chicago had earned the title "Hobo Capital of America."[46]

Why did such crowds flock to the main stem? The greatest single lure was that which drew Nels Anderson to Douglas Street in 1907: the labor market. "Hobohemia," Anderson later wrote in his study of Chicago, "brings the job-seeking man and the man-seeking job together."[47] Districts like Chicago's West Madison Street functioned less as a source of work for hoboes than as an infrastructure for housing, marketing, and transporting their labor to the hinterlands. As the greatest single labor exchange in the country, if not the world, Chicago possessed thirty-nine different railroads radiating out to a periphery that included half the nation's population. The tracks that carried grain, cattle, coal, iron, and other raw materials and finished commodities across the hinterlands also conveyed hundreds of thousands of workers who supplied seasonal labor to an area stretching west to Omaha, east to Pittsburgh, south to Nashville, and north to Minneapolis.[48] West Madison Street served as a clearinghouse for much of this labor, feeding workers to distant job sites and receiving a steady return flow of migrants when jobs ended. Hoboes often made several trips to the main stem between May and November, staying only a week at a time or less before heading back out to peripheral work sites.

By the turn of the century, job seeking in the hobohemian "slave markets" invariably involved a visit to an employment agency. Although employment agencies existed for every segment of the labor hierarchy, from highly paid professionals to unskilled casuals, those specializing in the marketing of hobo labor were the most numerous, shipped the farthest, and had the greatest turnover of customers. Some hobohemian agencies operated year-round, but many opened only during the frenzied hiring seasons of spring and summer, conducting business with nothing but a chalkboard and a telegraph in an empty storefront. The sidewalks outside of Minneapolis's eighteen employment agencies got so crowded during the early summer that men stood "so close together you couldn't put a newspaper between their elbows!"[49] Nels Anderson estimated that Chicago's fifty employment agencies placed a quarter-million migratory workers per year, most through shipments of over several hundred miles.[50]

A few agencies charged commissions to employers only, but most levied fees against applicants as well. These fees varied according to labor market conditions so that during periods of slack labor demand, workers might pay upward of five dollars for temporary positions worth only one or two dollars a day. Such extortionist practices inspired resentment among migratory workers, who routinely referred to employment agents as "labor sharks." Despite this rancor, inhabitants of hobohemian neighborhoods took recourse to employment agencies for numerous other services apart from job placement. Those agencies that operated year-round were especially likely to sell cheap food and liquor, offer haircuts, or even provide benches or floor space for sleeping. Indeed, a number of agencies were essentially saloons or lodging houses that also served as labor exchanges during hiring seasons.[51]

While employment agencies embodied the main stem's core economic function, lodging houses defined the district as a homeless man's resort and lent the main stem much of its unique "character." Incoming migrants frequently made it their first order of business to survey their sleeping options, which, depending upon their cash reserves, ranged from a hotel to a park bench. Despite the assortment of places that passed for shelter on the main stem, most hoboes took refuge in commercial lodging houses, a late-nineteenth-century shelter innovation designed to capture the floating wage-earner's dollar.

Cheap temporary lodgings had long existed for sailors, stevedores, and other occupational groups whose mobility or poverty precluded more settled arrangements. Commercial lodging houses for the general market of tramping workers, however, made their first appearance in depreciated sections of working-class neighborhoods, such as the lower Bowery, after the Civil War.[52] The depressions of the Gilded Age inspired many urban property owners to convert commercial spaces of all sorts, from workshops and warehouses to theaters and factories, into makeshift lodging houses. Jacob Riis, John James McCook, and numerous other late-nineteenth-century slum investigators lavished attention on the most notorious "flops" and "stale-beer dives" of homeless man districts, where tramps paid a penny or two a night for the privilege of sleeping on a cellar floor. In his famous exposé, *How the Other Half Lives,* Riis even offers a second-hand description of one saloon that charged a penny a night to customers who slept suspended by their armpits along a clothesline. "In the morning," Riis explains, "the boss woke them up by simply untying the line at one end and letting it go with its load; a labor-saving device certainly, and highly successful in attaining the desired end."[53]

Despite such sensational, and undoubtedly apocryphal, reports, most lodging choices along the main stem were not so grim. Virtually all hoboes, it is true, spent some nights without shelter, "carrying the banner" in the streets during seasons when demand for lodgings outstripped supply. Some homeless men, from time to time, also slept in saloons, whose owners often accommodated paying customers. But most hoboes on the main stem found room in commercial lodging houses that varied in price and comfort.

For ten to fifteen cents, a lodger could pass the night in a hammock, rough bunk, or cot in an open dormitory ward. For double the price, he could get a dilapidated bed in a partitioned cubicle or "cage." Cubicles were merely stalls, measuring as little as five by seven feet, constructed of wood or corrugated iron partitions. Although a three- to five-story lodging house might hold several hundred cubicles that were all open to the ceiling, these cells nonetheless provided a modicum of private space. At the same time, they remained at least half as expensive as a cheap hotel room. For lodging house owners, partitions could double or triple rent potential. Consequently, cubicles rapidly became a hobohemian standard by the turn of the century. As early as the 1880s, lodging house owners, who recognized the enduring rent potential of migratory workers, began to fashion purpose-built hotels offering cubicles and small private rooms. By 1920 these high-rise "workingmen's palaces," developed by large builders with institutional loans, had completely eclipsed their makeshift counterparts and now dominated the hobohemian landscape.[54]

In addition to supplying the bare necessities of work and shelter, the main stem also offered brighter attractions that engendered its reputation as "the Rialto of the hobo."[55] While Nels Anderson remained sober and chaste, keeping his attention firmly focused on job hunting, others romped in "hobohemia's playground," enjoying the saloons, brothels, gambling resorts, vaudeville houses, fortune-tellers, cigar stores, barbershops, secondhand stores, and other commercial establishments catering to the tastes of homeless men (fig. 3.3).[56] Despite their poverty, hoboes frequently arrived on the main stem with wages in hand, looking to spend them in convivial surroundings. The pace of commercial exchange was often fast, and businesses along these strips suffered volatile boom-bust cycles corresponding to job seasons, not to mention depressions. Noting the flurry of economic activity on West Madison Street, one charity administrator admitted that while the neighborhood was "sordid, dirty, and unpleasant," it also possessed "a curiously quickening and vibrant atmosphere."[57] This vibrancy derived not only from the commerce, but also the distinct cultural milieu in which this commerce took place, a milieu one young habitué described as "irresistible."[58]

Although hoboes defined themselves largely in terms of their labor on the wageworkers' frontier, the hub or headquarters of hobo culture was in the city. While on the job, hoboes were scattered among thousands of remote work sites. But on the main stem during periods of layoff, they met and intermingled, spent their money, and participated in organizational life to a degree unimaginable in the mines, forests, construction sites, and harvest fields where hoboes labored. Encounters in the city gave the hobo world a sense of continuity and coherence despite the almost constant migrations such a life entailed. Renewing old friendships and meeting up with acquaintances from previous jobs were common activities on the main stem. "In the slave market," recalled one hobo, "buddies on former jobs find each other again, much as American tourists meet their former fellow-passengers in Westminster Abbey, the Louvre, or at the American

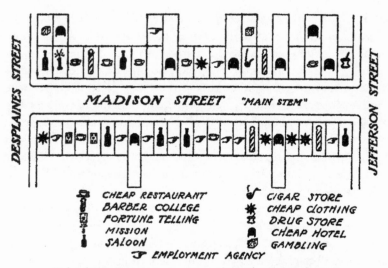

CHEAP RESTAURANT
BARBER COLLEGE
FORTUNE TELLING
MISSION
SALOON
EMPLOYMENT AGENCY

CIGAR STORE
CHEAP CLOTHING
DRUG STORE
CHEAP HOTEL
GAMBLING

Hobo institutions on one street along the "Main Stem."

Figure 3.3: Featured in Nels Anderson's classic study of hobohemia, this map of one block of Chicago's West Madison Street illustrates both the concentration and variety of services available on the "main stem." Dominated by hoboes and their fellow travelers, these districts represented the epitome of mixed-use real estate, functionally dividing the "home" into a series of commercial establishments. As the plethora of restaurants, saloons, hotels, and employment agencies—not to mention the fortune-teller, cigar store, and gambling dens—suggests, most so-called "homeless men" were not completely "down and out." Rather, as "unattached" seasonal laborers, they often thrived in a déclassé world of urban commerce. (Nels Anderson, *The Hobo: The Sociology of the Homeless Man*, 1923)

Express."[59] Through these reunions and other contacts, hoboes garnered information on job prospects, housing, and transportation. They also shared ideas and participated in activities not readily expressed or pursued while on the job.

Facilitating such self-expression was the highly segregated character of these neighborhoods. On West Madison Street in Chicago, reported one observer, "there are few people on the sidewalks who are not hobos, and the saloons and sidewalks are overflowing with them."[60] The main stem kept hoboes physically separated not only from the settled middle and working classes, but also often from other groups of migratory workers, such as African American gang laborers. While African Americans remained underrepresented in the floating army of industrial labor through the early twentieth century, those black workers who did pursue seasonal jobs on the wageworkers' frontier found themselves systematically barred from the main stem, at least in Chicago. The Great Migration during World War I sent a half-million African Americans to the industrial North, more than doubling Chicago's black population. Despite the need among single black men for cheap temporary lodgings, African Americans rarely ventured to West Madison Street. Instead, black lodgers remained on the Near South Side, where segregated lodging houses stood adjacent to railroad yards, meatpacking plants, and family residences. The paucity of such African American hotels, however, meant that urban black families routinely took in boarders and lodgers at higher rates than urban white families.[61]

Also excluded from the main stem were the huge numbers of Asian American workers who labored in virtually every sector of the wageworkers' frontier. Shut out from the cheap hotels and employment agencies of hobohemian neighborhoods, these workers formed their own "homeless" districts, the most famous of which was San Francisco's Chinatown. Like the main stem, Chinatown was largely a bachelor world of lodgings houses, brothels, theaters, gambling halls, and employment agencies. This racial ghetto became famous as a center of commercial vice and slum tourism, but the primary function of the neighborhood was to house migrant laborers, which it did in brutally efficient fashion. The relatively luxurious "cage" hotels of the main stem were unheard of in Chinatown. Instead, laborers crammed into open dormitories where they slept in shifts on double or triple bunks. Like the Filipino workers of nearby Manilatown and the Japanese migratories dispersed throughout the city's lodging house districts, San Francisco's Chinatown residents periodically shipped out to peripheral work camps, where they labored on the same jobs as their white counterparts but earned a fraction of the pay.[62]

Unlike black and Asian migratories, southern and eastern European laborers did not face legal exclusion from hobo districts. Nevertheless, these immigrants rarely turned to the hotels or employment agencies of the main stem. Studies of Chicago's hobo population consistently revealed an overwhelming majority of native-born workers, with long-settled immigrants from northern and western Europe or Canada making up the balance. Those southern and eastern European immigrants who did haunt hobohemian neighborhoods, remarked Nels Anderson, seemed "out of place."[63] Rather than take to commercial lodging houses, single wage-earning immigrants tended either to board with private families or, in the words of one neighborhood investigator, "form a non-family group of their own."[64] Researchers for the Pittsburgh Survey in 1907 and 1908 were surprised to find a "comparatively small" main stem there, a fact they accounted for by explaining that Pittsburgh's immigrant males, who made up a large portion of the city's laboring population, "are not to be found in the common lodging houses." The researchers discovered instead that the foreign born "live with their families or herd with boarding bosses in their own sections of the city. The lodging house population has its roots rather in the English-speaking population."[65]

Immigrant communities gave rise to their own distinct hiring networks, as well as lodging arrangements. Greek and Italian laborers, for example, found jobs not through the hobo slave markets, but through the *padrone* system of labor agents. Despite their ethnic ties to workers, *padroni*, like main stem agents, often levied exorbitant fees against job applicants and conspired with employers to keep wages low. Even so, the *padrone* system remained an entrenched part of immigrant labor through the 1920s.[66]

For hoboes, the main stem was a domain of the racially privileged, for regardless of their homeless condition, they enjoyed an individual mobility and access not shared by their excluded counterparts. One of these privileges was the relative freedom they enjoyed from the supervision of their social betters. With only each other to impress, white migratories did not have to show a "good front" or represent themselves as "honest workingmen," leading one hobo to say that he felt better on the main stem than "anywhere else in the world."[67] Anxiety about demonstrating respectability gave way to a certain social ease that allowed hoboes to flaunt their peculiar freedoms and countercultural identities. Several years after Nels Anderson visited Omaha, a tenderfoot hobo named Charles Ashleigh ventured into Minneapolis's Gateway district and immediately noted a distinct "swagger" and "debonair humour" among the men gathered there. "These workers," Ashleigh recalled,

> were so different from the farmers . . . [and] different, also, from the city workers, although like them they were dependent on wages. There was an atmosphere of recklessness and daring about these fellows, who strolled along the streets in their blue overalls, or khaki trousers, with grey or blue shirts, open at the throat, and their black slouch hats.[68]

The lack of a strong police presence in these low-rent neighborhoods encouraged such flamboyant poses. "The police paid very little attention to bums, hobos, sailors, or transient laborers who came into the city for a few days spree," explained one former migratory. "A hobo was not conspicuous" on Chicago's West Madison Street, recalled another main stem resident, and could therefore move about at will without drawing suspicion or prompting arrest.[69]

Hoboes protected this comparative freedom, almost paradoxically, by discouraging certain kinds of expression. In casual conversation, hoboes routinely withheld personal information and adhered to a protocol of not inquiring into the personal pasts of others. While hoboing his way from St. Paul to the West Coast in 1920, Harvard graduate Powers Hapgood traveled with a companion for several days before learning his name. "The people around here don't ask each other their names but wait . . . a long time before they find them out," Hapgood wrote in his journal. "That's the way it has been ever since leaving Minnesota."[70] Another migratory similarly recalled that "a hobo had a 'line' or several lines about himself, pat and brief, and then clammed up." Someone who pried too deeply or told too much about himself aroused suspicion. Merely asking a name was considered an invasion of privacy, "the mark of the cop, the dick, or the spy."[71]

This circumspection augmented the anonymity of the main stem, a neighborhood that, despite the reunions and conviviality, remained for the most part an ever-shifting world of strangers. As urban hobohemias grew and developed in the 1890s, they began to attract all sorts of men, besides migratories, interested in keeping their identities secret. Criminals on the run, radicals in hiding, family deserters, chronic alcoholics, thieves, murderers, rapists, and various down-and-outs embarrassed by their failures all mingled together, each contributing to the main stem's distinct subcultural milieu.

In a sense, these neighborhoods realized the nightmare scenario envisioned by the nineteenth-century middle class: a bustling world of commercial exchange ridden with confidence men and hidden intentions. While the middle class had combated these fears with a genteel cult of sincerity and, in later years, a strict adherence to social etiquette, hoboes responded with an etiquette of their own. The ritual circumspection among main stem residents offered a degree of protection to those who did not enjoy even the semblance of middle-class privacy. Passing their nights in crowded lodging houses and spending their days parading the streets, homeless men secured a measure of privacy by keeping their identities and personal pasts largely to themselves. Such anonymity actually facilitated social interaction. "You can be loose and easy when from day to day you meet strangers you will know only an hour or a day or two," explained Carl Sandburg.[72] If personal questioning marked the undercover agent and garrulousness indicated a petty confidence man, then circumspection signified trustworthiness and potential camaraderie. The protocol of caution and guardedness, therefore, allowed hoboes to identify each other and interact with a minimum of suspicion.

Despite, or rather because of, this protocol, the "code of hobo ethics" that guided behavior on the road also governed life on the main stem.[73] "When one has money he gives it to the man who needs it," explained Powers Hapgood, "and when he is broke he asks the price of a meal from the man who has it." Hapgood also reported standing on a Fargo, North Dakota, street corner with two companions when a fourth man approached them offering to sell his jackknife. One of Hapgood's companions "pulled a dollar out of his pocket and, when the man extended his knife toward him, he pushed it away and merely said: 'Remember me some time if you see me broke.'"[74] Such reciprocity allowed many hoboes to survive, or extend, their periods of unemployment in hobohemian districts. In 1913 labor investigator Peter Speek recorded one migratory's holiday in Milwaukee. "Two weeks he 'rested,' drank with other 'floaters' in the saloons . . . went to shows, and courted the girls." After his cash ran out, this hobo "started to look for work, during which time he was helped out by his temporary friends—other laborers . . . who continued to come in from work with money."[75]

In the city such mutualism often took the form of treating others to rounds of drinks, a prevailing custom in the working-class saloon culture of the late nineteenth and early twentieth centuries. Saloons were central to workingmen's lives at the turn of the century, providing a range of goods and services beyond alcohol. Offering cheap meals, baths, check cashing, reading material, employment information, and meeting spaces for unions and other neighborhood organizations, saloons functioned as veritable "workingman's clubs" for those living in crowded tenement quarters.[76] For those who laid their heads on lodging house bunks, park benches, or the bare ground, saloons took on even more importance. William Aspinwall told John James McCook, for example, that he avoided "dry" towns because his itinerant way of life depended on saloons.[77] Predictably, McCook responded to Aspinwall's earnest defense of saloons with suspicion, knowing full well that festive drinking remained a critical part of the homeless man's life.

The saloon ritual of treating, so central to the everyday affirmation of working-class masculine solidarity, took exaggerated form in a hobo world that alternated periods of intense labor at isolated work sites with those of relative leisure, albeit unemployed leisure, in densely populated urban centers. Arrival on the main stem thus often involved, as one investigator put it in 1914, "a period of more or less riotous living."[78] Hoboes landing downtown, recalled Charles Ashleigh,

spent their money royally. After working for a couple months or more in a construction camp, where they slept in wooden bunks, or in a lumber camp, they would come into town with their pockets full of money; and then there would be a prodigious celebration! Everybody was welcome to share in the "stiff's" prosperity; and everyone did![79]

This practice of accumulating wages and then spending them in convivial surroundings affirmed the "code of hobo ethics" while rejecting in dramatic fashion the more prudent goal of steady saving.[80]

By drawing together propertyless workers who had little hope of ever attaining the Lincolnian goal of an independent homestead, the main stem nurtured the kind of countercultural rebelliousness that the more isolated William Aspinwall hesitated to express. While Aspinwall's need to demonstrate "good character" always compromised his claims to the "Open Road," hoboes on the main stem were comparatively free to strut their autonomy and independence. "It's good to come to a new city with the feeling that you're the mental and physical superior to everybody in it," one hobo recalled his companion as saying on the main stem in 1917. "He meant," the hobo explained, "that, as a wanderer, as a migratory, he was entirely free from obligations to superiors. He had no social position to protect, no employer to bootlick."

In their journals, memoirs, letters, and testimonies to investigators, migratories repeatedly celebrated their freedom from employers' demands, "factory whistles," or just the "empty, dreary life" that the workaday world entailed. The freedom of the hobo, as one expressed it, meant the ability to "escape any disagreeable situation by donning overalls, cutting down your standard of living, and battering your meals if you want to."[81] Preserving this freedom meant avoiding the obligations not only of steady work, but also of home. Enjoying the conviviality of what was, in Nels Anderson's words, "quite definitely a man's street," hoboes flaunted their homelessness as a positive freedom from the constraints of "woman's sphere."[82]

## "(WHITE) MAN'S COUNTRY"

The privileges of mobility that hobohemia drew upon and fostered accrued almost exclusively to white men. Indeed, in the parlance of the road, the term "white man" was synonymous with "hobo." Both were used to distinguish migratories of northern and western European extraction not only from black, Mexican, and Asian migrants, but also from the "Mediterranean races" and eastern European immigrants found all over the wageworkers' frontier. As one observer of hobohemia put it in 1914, "a 'white man' is a laborer of any nationality who speaks English, eats American food and travels alone."[83]

As this idiosyncratic definition suggests, "whiteness" served as a mercurial and contradictory, if monumentally important, marker of social difference in early-twentieth-century America. On the road, as elsewhere, racial consciousness and practice located "whiteness" not merely in opposition to "blackness," but also in ever-changing relation to numerous other racialized statuses, ranging from "Anglo-Saxon" and "Teuton" to "Oriental" and "Negro." As persons who might once have been labeled "Celts," and therefore of only provisional whiteness, hoboes negotiated their racial identity within a shifting hierarchy of racialized migrants that included Greeks, Italians, Mexicans, Chinese, and other groups.[84]

Precisely what it meant to be "white" on the road depended, in part, on the laws and customs governing access to work, food, transportation, and shelter. Along the main stem, saloon owners, employment agents, lodging house managers, and merchants served, in a sense, as racial gatekeepers, routinely excluding African Americans, foreigners, and non-English speakers in favor of their privileged hobo clientele. In the field, employers often ran segregated job sites, setting up either a "white man's camp" or a "foreigner's camp," depending on the available labor supply.[85] Some railroad construction contractors, for example, never hired workers of different nationalities or racial groups for the same job, while others made sure to set up segregated bunkhouses and commissaries. The rules of mixing and separating varied widely over time and across the wageworker's frontier, but virtually all those who hired and managed migratory laborers kept a vigilant eye on the racial profile of their payroll. "We can mix the Mexicans and the hoboes," one camp commissary official explained, "or the Mexicans and the Negroes, but not the hoboes and the Negroes."[86] Whether hobo and black laborers could not be mixed because of racial animosity or interracial solidarity was left, in this instance, unexplained.

The degree to which hoboes themselves demanded such segregation as a means to preserve and defend their whiteness remains an open question. On the one hand, hoboes seem to have tolerated the presence of some "nonwhites" on the rails and in the jungles. Anecdotes exist of whites and blacks, for example, sharing boxcars and jungle meals, and even partnering up for a time.[87] Noting in 1923 the presence of Mexicans and African Americans in some jungle resorts, Nels Anderson even went so far as to call the hobo jungle "the melting pot of tramping" where "absolute democracy reigns."[88] The settled conventions from which men broke while on the road apparently included that of racial segregation.

On the other hand, nonwhites were not integrated on the road as equals. In their encounters with African Americans, for example, hoboes frequently struck a tone of racial superiority, referring to black migrants with epithets that reaffirmed their own "whiteness." One hobo interviewed by John James McCook referred to his black traveling companion as his "shine," proprietary language that emphasized his own racial dominance.[89] Hoboes also routinely refused to join labor gangs that contained black members, and African Americans rarely quit jobs at isolated work sites for fear of encountering hostile hoboes on the road. Contradicting his earlier characterization of the hobo jungle as a sphere of "absolute democracy," Nels Anderson recalls in his memoirs the threat of racial violence that prevented black construction workers from striking out on their own in the West. Of the men Anderson himself worked with on railroad construction crews, there were none, as he remembers, "who did not have some degree of racial bias."[90] Race thus served to segment and stratify the migratory labor market on the wageworkers' frontier in complex ways. Various racialized systems of migratory labor paralleled and, at times, overlapped with one another, contributing to the racial distinctiveness of hobohemia. Hobo subculture, in turn, reinforced the racialized sense of entitlement, privilege, and access connoted by the term "white man."

A preserve of working-class whiteness, hobohemia was also an important domain of masculinity. The severe sanctions that prevented women from joining the great army of tramps in the 1870s continued to hold sway in the early twentieth century, despite the occasional young woman who traveled in disguise.[91] Built by a mobile army of labor, the wageworkers' frontier was what one observer called "a man's country," with small proportions of women even in the cities.[92] Of course, unattached single women did flock to cities like Chicago to work as clerks, domestics, salespersons, and factory operatives. Most of these "women adrift" joined other households, either as live-in servants or as lodgers with private families. Some took advantage of the commercial rooming houses that sprang up at the turn of the century in what came to be called "furnished room districts." Those who could not afford such arrangements often turned to charitable boardinghouses such as the YWCA or other philanthropic shelters catering to "placeless women." Although these young urban laborers enjoyed a degree of individual freedom previously unknown to women their age, they were effectively barred from experiencing the freewheeling pleasures and perils of life on the road.[93]

While dominant gender rules restricted eligibility for hobohemian membership to men, hoboes themselves nurtured a group identity that was highly gendered. Like Francis Wayland and others who first defined tramping as a social problem, hoboes delimited their world through gender, identifying hobohemia with the absence of feminine manners, morals, and domesticity. One hobo, describing a group of fellow workers in 1919, emphasized the subculture's distinctly masculine and "uncivilized" characteristics:

Youths, rough and rude, but all the more manly for that, other men blasted and seared in countenance—all conversing in a language which, in another sphere, would be accounted blasphemy—but in their estimation only emphatic—with their own moral code (it may not be yours), but in their case the one most suitable to their mode of life.[94]

Hoboes frequently explained their migratory way of life as a strategy for avoiding the "other sphere" of women. One migratory told Nels Anderson that he took to traveling "mainly to keep away from women—that is, women who wanted to marry." While hoboing was for most a life-cycle stage that ended with marriage, young hoboes in the thrall of hobohemia saw domesticity as a threat to their "manly" independence. The hoboes of West Madison Street, recalled Elizabeth Gurley Flynn from her first visit there, "regarded the city workers as stay-at-home softies—'scissorbills.' They referred to a wife as 'the ball and chain.'"[95]

On the other hand, hoboes often idealized their relationships with those women who served them either as sources of charity or sex. Believing women to be more charitable than men, hoboes on the road routinely sought handouts from women, most often at backdoors while the man of the house was away. Women also helped to underwrite hobo life on the main stem by working as missionaries, social workers, waitresses, boardinghouse keepers, and other service-oriented roles. In Chicago "Mother" Greenstein's restaurant on South State Street was famous among hoboes for its free bread-and-coffee lines, as well as for "Mother's" refusal to allow any man to go away hungry.[96] As the maternal nickname suggests, hoboes often rationalized such dependence upon women by construing their relationships in terms of surrogate motherhood.

The hobohemian gender imagination complemented such nurturing Madonnas as "Mother" Greenstein with "whores" who fulfilled the desire for sex without requiring submission to matrimony or the rituals of courtship. Describing himself as "not the kind of fellow to be tied down to a woman," one divorced hobo considered his periodic trips to the brothels of the main stem as the perfect way of enjoying female company without giving up his freedom. "If I want anything now, I go to a good whore and pay for it. Then I can go about my business."[97] When John James McCook asked another migratory if he ever frequented prostitutes, his informant responded matter-of-factly, "a man can't get along without that—it's God's arrangement."[98] The commercial sex markets that flourished in American cities in the late nineteenth and early twentieth centuries frequently found their headquarters in hobo districts. Although "a man's street," the main stem employed armies of young women to solicit sex, not only in established brothels, but also in saloons, gambling dens, and lodging houses. One slum investigator in Boston determined that there were two types of housing for homeless men: brothels disguised as lodging houses and lodging houses that permitted prostitution.[99] On the wageworkers' frontier, prostitution was thoroughly integrated into the commercial life of the hobo's "Rialto." The migratory who had never paid for sex while laying off on the main stem was the exception, rather than the rule.

## HOBOSEXUALITY

Just as prostitution facilitated and reinforced hobohemia's all-male gender ideals, so, too, did homosexual activity within the subculture further shield hoboes from feminine influences. While most men on the road preferred the temporary company of a woman, some hoboes did have sex with each other. Just how many did so is unclear. Outside commentators often exaggerated hoboes' homosexuality in order to cast further disrepute on the subculture. Homeless men also sometimes overstated the frequency of same-sex liaisons among their cohorts in order to legitimate their own behavior. But while investigators of hobohemia and their informants disagreed as to the extent of homosexuality on the main stem, virtually all concurred with Nel Anderson's conclusion "that homosexual practices among homeless men are widespread."[100]

As just one prominent part of a larger multiethnic, multiracial, and cross-class bachelor world flourishing in late-nineteenth- and early-twentieth-century American cities, hobohemia overlapped with that subculture of urban bachelors whose preferences for male company included sex.[101] Like hobohemia, this gay world drew upon the cultural and neighborhood associations of the working class, operating through networks of cafeterias, poolrooms, saloons, theaters, social clubs, parks, baths, and rooming and lodging houses. Gay subculture thrived in homeless man districts like the Bowery and West Madison Street, which served as crossroads for large groups of transient men and provided venues for highly visible modes of erotic interaction. Main stem districts throughout the country gained reputations for harboring erotic activity of all sorts. By the early twentieth century, nonmigratory men frequently made their way to hobo neighborhoods, seeking male or female prostitutes or the erotically charged entertainment often found in hobohemian theaters and saloons.[102]

On or off the main stem, hoboes shared in the largest and most important single-sex environment that brought young working-class men to-

gether from vast geographic areas. For many, a stint on the road represented their first time away from home. Freed from family, neighborhood,
and small-town supervision, young hoboes often experienced their entry
into hobohemia as a sexual coming-of-age. A visit to a female prostitute or
a brief affair with a young woman in a new town was the most common
form of sexual initiation. Some, however, awoke to their sexuality in the
arms of other men. One eighteen-year-old hobo told Nels Anderson of his
first sexual experience, which occurred during the Kansas wheat harvests
when he was seduced by another migratory. "Disgusted with himself," the
teenager returned home to his family, got a steady job, and wondered how
he could ever have fallen into such "relations" on the road. As spring approached, the boy "began to get uneasy" and once again hit the road, this
time seeking out sexual partners and getting "a certain pleasure out of
the practice."[103] By the time Anderson met him, the boy was thoroughly
integrated into West Madison Street's gay life. Recalling a similar teenage
experience, one former hobo captured the confusion of feelings that frequently accompanied these sexual awakenings on the road:

> By this time I was beginning to marvel at the queer way in which this young
> man spoke. His train of speech was getting more and more affectionate . . .
> and when he kept endearing me with his words, and caresses, I began to get
> a queer sensation which I could not for all the world of me account for. It
> was a sort of a soothing thrilling feeling which seemed to urge itself on as
> soon as he touched me. It seemed as if I didn't want him to take his hand off
> my thigh and when at last he did take it off I had a feeling of utter loneliness.
> I had never experienced anything like this before and the fact that I was with
> a man made it all the more difficult to explain.[104]

While this teenage hobo was at a loss to explain his erotic feelings, sociologists who observed the prevalence of homosexual behavior within
hobohemia pointed to the road's absence of women and cramped housing
conditions as the root causes of "perversion" among hoboes. Hobohemia
certainly brought men into close physical contact, especially in lodging
houses and boxcars. Jack London's description of a boxcar journey toward Kelley's Army in 1894 effectively captures this sense of closeness:
"The light was dim, and all I could make out was arms and legs and bodies inextricably confused. Never was there such a tangle of humanity.
They were all lying in the straw, and over, and under, and around one
another."[105] While London never indicated an erotic dimension to this
"tangle of humanity," another hobo remembered sleeping "body to body"
in a boxcar with someone who had "stealthy fingers." "Once I awoke after
a crawly nightmare," he recalled, "to find my fly-buttons undone and my

private parts exposed to public view."[106] Focusing on working conditions, labor investigator Carleton Parker cited the lack of sufficient housing and clothing as contributing to "sex inversion." "Often the men sent off from the employment agencies are without blankets or even sufficient clothing," explained Parker, "and they are forced to sleep packed together for the sake of warmth. Investigations are beginning to show that there are social dangers which a group of demoralized, womenless men may engender under such conditions."[107]

But the mere opportunity for sexual relations does not explain desire or performance. Indeed, while close quarters and shared beds may have facilitated sex between hoboes, they also generated taboos against homosexual behavior. Like military men, hoboes living in close contact with one another often raised strict prohibitions against eroticizing their relationships. The protocol of circumspection and reciprocal guardedness that alerted hoboes to thieves and detectives was also designed to ward off amorous advances. A suspicious Carl Sandburg kept his distance from a hobo he met on the road who "had a slick tongue and a fast way of talking." Unlike other hoboes, this one "liked hearing himself talk about himself." After sharing a jungle retreat for an hour with this hobo, Sandburg finally learned his motives when "he happened to lay a hand upon me in a way I didn't like. . . . I could see he wanted to take care of me in a way I didn't care for."[108]

Hoboes could reject, sometimes violently, road partners revealed to be "fairies."[109] But while rejected mates attested to the limited appeal of homosexual behavior within hobohemia, those who did accept sexual advances bore witness to the prominent role that sexuality could play in the bonds between hoboes. In his study of gay life in Chicago's hobohemia, Nels Anderson notes several "attachments between men and between men and boys 'that surpass the love of woman.'" "Many of these are not more than a few days' duration," continues Anderson, "but while they last they are very intense and sentimental."[110]

More common than the reciprocal and mutually constituted homosexual associations between hoboes were the predatory relationships between older hoboes, or "jockers," and young initiates, or "punks." These relationships, widely discussed and lampooned among hoboes and nonhoboes alike, signified not only hobohemia's homosexual undercurrent, but also the subculture's larger gender ideology that encouraged masculine domination. Coercing, cajoling, or enticing punks into sex, jockers offered in exchange protection, money, or general instruction in the skills of begging, freight hopping, and securing food and shelter. Jockers commonly approached punks on the road, in the jungles, in parks, or even on the streets of urban hobohemias. In 1921 one probation officer of Chicago's Juvenile Court working on South State Street alone charged eighty adults with contributing to juvenile delinquency through "perversion." "One need not be in the [hobo] class long before he learns of the existence of the practice," testifies Nels Anderson, "and any boy who has been on the road long without having been approached many times is an exception."[111]

The jocker-punk relationship pervaded the various literatures of hobohemia, informing social welfare reports, autobiographical accounts of initiation, and even popular hobo folklore. Indeed, before popular singers and folklorists in the 1920s bowdlerized "The Big Rock Candy Mountain," this most famous of hobo folk songs originally recounted in sardonic fashion the luring of a boy into a jocker's lair through promises of "cigarette trees," "lemonade springs," and "soda water fountains." In the final verse, the boy spurns his jocker in terms so graphic that folklorist John Greenway felt compelled to expurgate them:

> The punk rolled up his big blue eyes
> And said to the jocker, "Sandy,
> I've hiked and hiked and wandered, too,
> But I ain't seen any candy.
> I've hiked and hiked till my feet are sore
> I'll be damned if I hike any more
> To be ★ ★ ★ ★ ★ ★ ★ ★ ★ ★ ★ ★ ★ ★ ★
> In the Big Rock Candy Mountains.[112]

The sexual bonds between older and younger hoboes conformed to the erotic interests and expectations not only of hobo laborers, but also of seamen, sailors, prisoners, and other male working-class groups disengaged from family and neighborhood.[113] Jockers generally abided by the conventions of predatory masculinity, refusing to be penetrated, not taking feminine nicknames, and otherwise, in the words of Nels Anderson, "substitut[ing] the boy for the woman."[114] Many inside the subculture regarded involvement with a jocker as a sign of weakness or "femininity" rather than of homosexual interest or "queerness." "The boys who become slaves to 'jockers' are of the weaker and more degenerate type," explained one former hobo. "The tramp always ruled the 'punk' by fear. He practised the same crude and brutal psychology that the pimp practised over the weak women of the underworld."[115]

Consequently, many young hoboes considered the evasion of predatory jockers as crucial to preserving their manhood. Mac McClintock, author of "The Big Rock Candy Mountain," rated his boyhood battles with jockers as the most strenuous aspect of his initiation into the hobo world at the turn of the century. "There were times when I fought like a wildcat or ran like a deer," recalled McClintock, "to preserve my independence and my virginity."[116] Recounting his first hobo trip made at age thirteen, the flamboyant radical activist Ben Reitman described being kidnapped by a jocker named "Ohio Skip" who ordered Reitman to "do as I say. I'm your jocker and I'll take good care of you." Reitman escaped only after rival jockers, interested in stealing Reitman and another punk, began a fight with Ohio Skip that left all parties wounded.[117]

Not all jockers employed coercion. Nor did all punks resist advances. For some, taking up with jockers over long or short terms was simply "an easy way to get by." With few skills or contacts and limited knowledge of migratory labor markets, teenage hoboes relied more heavily on stealing, begging, and selling sex than did others. Punks could also negotiate more equitable relationships with jockers, with each partner "going fifty-fifty" and taking turns at sexual positions. Punks might even interpret the "bottom" position in terms of dominance, rather than weakness or submission. The jocker "on top," after all, was servicing, as well as being serviced by, the punk "on bottom." Even those hoboes who reviled punks heaped still greater contempt upon road kids who turned to missions or welfare agencies for support. "The mission beggar or 'mission stiff' is a very unpopular person in hoboland," states Nels Anderson in explaining the willingness of young hoboes to work as punks, "and the boy does not care to do anything that will bring him into disrepute."[118]

Hobo sexual practices, especially the jocker-punk relationship, must be understood in terms of the general assumptions about sex and gender that pervaded working-class culture in the late nineteenth and early twentieth centuries. For workers, masculinity or "manliness" derived not so much from sex, or the sex of sexual partners, but rather from gender status: that is, the bundles of attributes, values, and behaviors believed to be desirable or normal in men. Whereas middle-class men increasingly defined their manliness through heterosexual relationships with women, working-class culture, as George Chauncey argues, "regarded manhood as a hard-won accomplishment, not a given," and as something "confirmed by other men and in relation to other men, not by women."[119]

The saloon rituals of treating, for example, not only affirmed hoboes' countercultural solidarity as "workers" who scoffed at middle-class values, but also as "men" who rejected feminine manners and morals. Hoboes similarly demonstrated their manliness on the job by challenging bosses who demanded submission or insulted their independence and autonomy. Rituals of competition, such as boxing, wrestling, and gambling, also provided arenas within the subculture for hoboes to establish, challenge, and reaffirm their manhood.[120] Included in these rituals was the phallic domination of women and other "nonmen" such as "fairies" and "punks." By hobo standards at least, jockers were not necessarily "gay," "queer," or even "homosexual." Rather, they were like other hoboes, except that they dominated punks, instead of women, in order to affirm their own manhood. As Nels Anderson and others observed, debased punks often sought to reclaim a measure of their masculinity by exploiting others in similar fashion.[121]

The fragility of the hobo's gender status, in the face of predatory jockers and other ritual challenges to manhood, explains both the vigilance with which many hoboes defended their masculinity and the lengths to which some might go in demonstrating manliness. Having fallen prey to the sexual will of a jocker in his adolescence, Ben Reitman, for example, expressed extreme gender anxiety in much of his private writings, referring time and again to his physical cowardice and limited sexual potency.[122] After being stripped, prodded, burned with cigarettes, and tarred by a band of vigilantes during the San Diego free speech fight of 1912, Reitman's "whole being was centered on San Diego," obsessed as he was on recovering the manhood he believed to have been debased.[123] His goal was to face persecution once again in order to demonstrate his physical courage and strength. So profound was this struggle with his own diminished manliness that the otherwise thoroughly public Reitman failed to give direct voice to his early experiences of rape and submission. Reitman only referred to his victimization through a feminine alter ego, the apocryphal "Boxcar" Bertha Thompson, whose alleged autobiography derived largely from Reitman's own experiences.[124]

If hobohemia's strong emphasis on manliness as a "performance" illuminates the place of the jocker in hobohemia's gender ideals, then the subculture's extreme emphasis on single-sex camaraderie also sheds light on the more equitable homosexual relationships between hoboes.[125] These relationships in many ways merely extended into the sexual realm the bonds that all hoboes shared with each other as men. Describing an evening at a saloon frequented by migratory workers, for example, one former hobo named William Edge captured both the erotic extremes to which some men took their camaraderie and the limits that others, like Edge, placed on theirs. "Two workers whom I knew by sight," commented a disapproving but unsurprised Edge, "were dancing in a disgustingly homosexual manner." At the same time, Edge expressed frustration at his own inability to converse or connect in any way with the available women at the bar: "How I wish these girls were men. I could talk to the men. . . . But these girls!"[126]

Memoirs, novels, and other accounts of hobohemian life commonly contain similar examples of uneasiness with female companionship and a reluctance to settle down. "He loved her," writes Charles Ashleigh in his autobiographical novel *Rambling Kid*. "But not so much as he loved the stiffs."[127] Ashleigh, like most hoboes, was heterosexual, and the "love" he expressed for his fellow "stiffs" was brotherly, not erotic. But other hoboes took the common sense of the road, which taught that men should avoid entanglements with women, to its logical extreme. "In the homosexual relations there is the absence of the eternal complications in which one becomes involved with women," writes Nels Anderson, summarizing his interviews with gay men of the road. "They want to avoid intimacies that complicate the free life to which they are by temperament and habit committed."[128]

By refusing to domesticate their sexuality, hoboes justified middle-class fears about homeless men's lack of sexual restraint, fears that had emerged with the tramp crisis of the 1870s. But for hoboes, this lack of feminine influence was essential to their distinct identity as swaggering wayfarers unbound by the conventions of work and home. By the early twentieth century, hobohemia's main stem flourished as an urban counterculture, hosting an ever-changing male population that thrived on ritual performances of manhood and the anonymous commercial life of the streets. On its own, this counterculture represented a serious challenge to a nation guided by reigning middle-class beliefs in private nuclear families, moderate domestic consumption, and steady work. But hobohemia would not remain merely a world apart, a disquieting alternative to the norms of mainstream society. Shortly after the turn of the century, hobohemia developed a radical politics of its own that departed dramatically from the nineteenth-century republicanism of the Industrial Army movement. Under the direction of powerful hobohemian organizations such as the Industrial Workers of the World, hoboes began to mobilize their subculture for revolution.

# PART II

## HOBOHEMIA AND HOMELESSNESS IN THE EARLY TWENTIETH CENTURY

# THE POLITICS OF
# HOBOHEMIA

O n September 1, 1908, a barnstorming band of nineteen hoboes departed Portland, Oregon, on a 2,500-mile journey across the wageworkers' frontier. Led by J. H. Walsh, one of hobohemia's premier labor activists and sidewalk impresarios, the gang jumped aboard a cattle car and rode to Seattle, where they spent a night in jail for trespassing. A few days later, they headed east and continued hopping freights across the Great Plains, preaching the gospel of revolutionary industrial unionism in every main stem, hobo jungle, and boxcar they encountered along the way. Unlike the Industrial Armies of 1894, the self-described "Overalls Brigade" had their sights set not on the nation's capital of Washington, D.C., but rather on the hobo capital of Chicago, where the fourth annual convention of the Industrial Workers of the World (IWW) was about to open.

Flamboyant propagandists and fund-raisers, members of the Overalls Brigade were also active delegates seeking to wrest control of the conflict-ridden IWW from what they derisively termed the "homeguard," a faction that favored the ballot box as a path to socialism. As migratories without home or vote, the hobo delegation rejected ward and parliamentary politics, as well as the binding contracts painstakingly negotiated by traditional trades unions. Instead, they advocated direct action, embracing strikes, sabotage, and other forms of on-the-job protest as the only political weapons capable of destroying capitalism. The hoboes' detractors called them the "bummery," warning that a floating population of seasonal workers could hardly be relied upon as a revolutionary vanguard. But the hour belonged to the bummery. Proclaiming a millennial vision of "One Big Union," the hobo insurgents won the day, ousting the homeguard and dedicating the IWW to direct economic action exclusively.[1]

The Overalls Brigade's triumphant return to the West heralded the dawn of a new era in hobohemia. No longer mere symbols or foot soldiers in the struggle against the wage system, hoboes now possessed an independent political movement of their own, one that promised the emancipation of all labor. Grave concerns remained, however, about the effectiveness of a revolution headquartered in the hobo's "Rialto." After all, job shirking, binge drinking, sexual promiscuity, and family desertion were not exactly qualities that recommended themselves to leading an international movement aimed at fundamental social change. But instead of burnishing their reputations as "honest workingmen," J. H. Walsh and his floating fraternity celebrated their identities as "sons of rest" who preferred the "simple life in the jungles" to the workaday world of the homeguard.[2] In so doing, the bummery propagated a folklore of the hobo that would outlive both the IWW and the subculture from which it emerged.

The Overalls Brigade itself gave birth to this folklore on its hobohemian tour of the West. Shortly before the trip, Walsh had organized his men into a red-uniformed Industrial Union Band that parodied popular gospel hymns and sentimental ballads for street-corner crowds. In route to Chicago, the floating delegation peddled ten-cent song sheets that contained four of their most popular numbers, including "Hallelujah, I'm a Bum," a decade-old hobo song that the activists transformed into a revolutionary anthem:

> Whenever I get
> All the money I earn,
> The boss will go broke,
> And to work he must turn.
> *Chorus:*
> Hallelujah, I'm a bum,
> Hallelujah, bum again,
> Hallelujah, give us a handout—
> To revive us again.[3]

Having "sold like hotcakes" on the road, the song sheets inspired Walsh to issue an entire book of such parodies upon his return from the 1908 convention.[4] Given the provocative title, *Songs of the Workers, on the Road, in the Jungles, and in the Shops—Songs to Fan the Flames of Discontent,* the *Little Red Songbook,* as the volume came to be known, went through dozens of editions and remains hobohemia's most important cultural artifact.[5] Along with the stories and commentaries of the road published in the IWW's numerous newspapers and pamphlets, the *Little Red Songbook* provided hobohemia with a powerful set of myths to enhance its group definition, vindicate its countercultural status, and mobilize its members for political action. The impact of this propaganda was swift and far-reaching. "Where a group of hoboes sit around a fire under a railroad bridge," noted Carleton Parker in 1914, "many of them can sing I.W.W. songs without a book."[6]

In addition to fostering communal ties, this new folklore also advanced the contentious proposition that hoboes, by virtue of their footloose detachment from the bonds of settled community, were by nature the "real proletarians" and more revolutionary than other groups of stationary workers.[7] Assigning hobohemia the world-historical task of "labor's emancipation," IWW propagandists submerged the racial and gender components of the hobo's identity under the more potent category of class. While this strategy accorded with the IWW's official policy of color-blindness and gender inclusion, it also subtly reinforced the exclusionary biases upon which the subculture was based. By promoting hobohemia as the most authentic bearer of proletarian consciousness, Wobblies, as IWW members were nicknamed, relegated not only the homeguard, but also women, African Americans, Mexican Americans, and a whole host of immigrant groups from Europe and Asia to supporting roles in the hobo revolution. The IWW's decade-long reign over the main stem delivered a floating subculture to the very center of American labor activism. One of the most enduring legacies of this reign, however, was a Wobbly frontier myth that venerated the hobo as a manly white pioneer of the industrial West.

## ORGANIZING THE MAIN STEM

For all their talk about direct action, western Wobblies did little on-the-job organizing in the years immediately following the bummery's coup. Instead, their first order of business was to stake a claim to the main stem as the headquarters of their revolution. The same anonymity and freedom from supervision that attracted hoboes to slave market districts also drew the Wobblies, for only in the city could activists deliver their radical message to large numbers of migratories without worrying about employer interference.

The most effective such activist was J. H. Walsh, who arrived in Spokane after the 1908 convention to breathe new life into the city's IWW local. Within the space of a few months, Walsh's innovative soapboxing campaign not only recruited over a thousand new members, but also established an organizing model for other locals to follow. The songs, jokes, street theater, and fiery sermons used in Spokane soon became part of the

Wobblies' stock-in-trade on main stems throughout the West. One memorable routine began with a speaker shouting, "I've been robbed! I've been robbed!" As a crowd gathered, the orator then delivered his punch line: "I've been robbed by the capitalist system!"[8]

The IWW's claims to the main stem did not go uncontested. Indeed, Walsh's high-profile organizing efforts in Spokane sparked a fierce struggle over urban public space, a struggle that would take place in dozens of hobohemian districts over the next decade. To counter the growing power of Walsh's local, which Walsh effectively wielded to boycott Spokane's employment agencies, city officials pulled the Wobblies' soapbox out from under them by banning street-corner orations. In response, hundreds of Wobbly hoboes hitched freights to the city to defy the ban and serve their time in prison.

By the time Spokane capitulated to the protesters in March 1910, similar free speech fights were breaking out all over the wageworkers' frontier. With the notable exceptions of San Diego, where the dynamiting of the *Los Angles Times* building sparked the official suppression of street speaking, and Everett, Washington, where the conflict started over the IWW's support of striking sawmill workers, these pioneering free speech campaigns were launched not to protect American civil liberties or the First Amendment. Rather, Wobbly activists fought to preserve hobohemia's collective autonomy and to challenge the stranglehold that employers and their recruiting agents had on the hobo job market. As peace descended on Spokane, another fight erupted in Fresno when an agent complained to police that sidewalk agitators were damaging his efforts to recruit workers for a dam construction project. When the city revoked the IWW's speaking permit, the *Industrial Worker* responded with the call of "All Aboard to Fresno," and hundreds of Wobblies arrived from as far as St. Louis to join the protests.[9]

In addition to marking their territories through free speech fights, Wobblies also set about the quieter task of delivering basic services to their hobo clientele. Strategically located in the heart of the main stem, IWW halls offered kitchens, beds, reading rooms, employment information, and large meeting halls, where hoboes congregated on a nightly basis. Wobbly halls, observed Carleton Parker, "are not so much places for executive direction of the union as much as gregarious centers where the lodging house inhabitant or the hobo with his blanket can find a light, a stove, and companionship. In the prohibition states of the West, the I.W.W. hall has been the only social substitute for the saloon to these people."[10]

Chicago organizer Ralph Chaplin kept the distinct needs of hoboes in mind as he planned to open IWW offices on West Madison Street. "The outlook of the stiffs on life was different from that of homeguard mass-production workers," explained Chaplin. "The true migratory had no home. He needed a place to park his 'bindle' and to brew an occasional pot of 'java' in addition to flopping on the floor." It was the need to provide lodging, as well as a social center, that especially prompted Chaplin to organize a West Madison Street hall. Although Chicago was the site of the IWW's founding convention, its general headquarters, and both the Russian propaganda and Jewish recruiting centers, the city had no place expressly for English-speaking migratory workers until 1914. Russian and Jewish members, stated Chaplin, were contemptuous of migratories who showed up with their packs and expected to flop at their halls overnight. So Chaplin and others raised funds for a hobohemian hall on West Madison that quickly became a mecca for hoboes throughout the wageworkers' frontier.[11]

In establishing their presence, Wobblies challenged not only city officials, the chamber of commerce, and employment agencies, but also the main stem's notoriously popular commercial life. Through their cultural programs and institutions, the IWW sought to rival the saloons, theaters, gambling dens, and prostitution resorts for control over the hearts, minds, and dollars of wintering migratories. Indeed, Wobblies castigated municipal officials for not enforcing anti-vice codes on the main stem. Sounding more like Anthony Comstock or Carry Nation than Joe Hill, the *Industrial Worker* complained that "little is said by the respectable citizens about the permanent dens of vice which smell to heaven, and which line the streets of the tenderloin quarter, and which need a thorough fumigation like that dealt out to Sodom and Gomorrah."[12] Less strident was a migratory who testified that he joined the IWW for the cultural alternative it offered to the "Rialto":

Have you ever thought of how we, the workers in the woods, mines, construction camps or agricultural fields, are really approached and "entertained" when we visit our present centers of "civilization" and "culture"? What is the first thing we meet? The cheap lodging house, the dark and dirty restaurant, the saloon or the blind pig, the prostitutes operating in all the hotels, the moving picture and cheap vaudeville shows with their still cheaper, sensational programs, the freaks of all descriptions who operate on the street corners, from the ones selling "corn removers" and shoestrings to various religious fanatics and freaks. Did you ever see a sign in the working class district pointing the way to the public library? I have not. Did you ever meet a sign in any one of the rooming houses where we are forced to live, advertising a concert or a real play of any of our great writers, such as Ibsen, Shaw, Suderman, Gorky, Tolstoy, Shakespeare or others? Never.[13]

Responding to this perceived need for cultural uplift, the IWW nurtured a remarkably far-reaching intellectual life on the main stem. In prominent hobohemian cities like Chicago and San Francisco, hobo districts gained reputations as centers of cultural activity, drawing intellectuals and bohemians from bordering neighborhoods. In addition to the Wobbly halls themselves—which ran regular programs of films, concerts, plays, lectures, debates, and discussion groups—radical bookstores also played an important role in organizing hobohemia's intellectual life. "In every large city there are hobo book stores which make a specialty of radical periodicals," explained one migratory, "for even if the hobo does not generally belong to a socialistic society, he has been taught to think about class struggle. He may read the Hobo News, or he may read Jack London, or the Masses, or the Industrial Standard."[14] Nels Anderson concurred that the hobo was "an extensive reader" who disapproved of the "Capitalist press," adored Jack London, and passed along reading material as soon as he finished it. Anderson also attributed the popularity of radical bookstores on the main stem to the hobo's hesitation to use the public library, "dressed as he usually is."[15]

Possessing the flexibility typical of hobohemian institutions, bookstores not only served as a substitute for the library, but also for the saloon, restaurant, and even lodging house. Bookstores on Chicago's main stem, for example, collected mail, held items for safekeeping, and sometimes hosted lodgers. Virtually all served as meeting places for radicals. The Radical Book Shop on Chicago's North Clark Street, for example, was a favorite haunt of IWW organizers and officers, and also "a hangout for radicals of all shades of red and black, as well as for the Near North Side intelligentsia."[16] The Clarion Book Shop, on the other hand, had only loose ties to Wobblies, although the store's owner was active in hobohemian politics.[17] Perhaps the most prominent bookstore on Chicago's main stem was the Hobo Bookstore, also called the Proletariat, located on West Madison Street one block away from the IWW general headquarters. Daniel Horsley, the store's proprietor, gave frequent lectures "along Marxian lines" and entertained activists of all political affiliations.[18]

In the hobo capital of Chicago, hobohemia's cultural attractions also included the Dill Pickle Club, an institution Sherwood Anderson praised in 1919 as one of "the bright spots in the rather somber aspects of our town."[19] Founded by Jack Jones, a Wobbly organizer and former husband of Elizabeth Gurley Flynn, and managed for a time by the anarchist Ben Reitman, the Dill Pickle evolved from a center for labor organizing and radical agitation to a bohemian resort that attracted many kinds of intellectuals, artists, poets, and performers. Carl Sandburg, Edgar Lee Mas-

ters, Sherwood Anderson, Vachel Lindsay, Clarence Darrow, Ring Lard-
ner, Emma Goldman, Eugene Debs, Theodore Dreiser, and Big Bill Haywood were among those who lectured, performed, and congregated at
this original "little theatre" off of Washington Square on Chicago's Near
North Side. In its early years, the Dill Pickle provided a place where
hoboes, intellectuals, artists, and radicals of all stripes could meet and exchange ideas. "It opened its doors wide to everybody who had a message,
a grievance, a hope, or a criticism, constructive or destructive," recalled
one regular, "who wished to raise his voice against oppression, prejudice
and injustice in all their multiforms."[20]

By far, the largest and most popular venues for raising voices were the
public parks scattered throughout most hobohemian districts. Pershing
Square in Los Angeles, Pioneer Square in Seattle, and Washington Square
in Chicago were all important hobo resorts, especially during temperate spring and summer months. Listening to soapboxers in "Bughouse
Square," as Washington Square was nicknamed, was the single most popular daytime recreation among hoboes laying over on Chicago's main
stem.[21] Located adjacent to the Dill Pickle Club, the Newberry Library,
and the countless cafés of the Near North Side, Bughouse Square was a
"ragamuffin bohemia," "a pocket edition of Greenwich Village," which
brought speakers and performers of all sorts together with common
hoboes.[22] "Bohemia and Hobohemia," quipped Nels Anderson, "meet at
'Bughouse Square.'" On Saturdays and Sundays, three or four orators
performed in different corners of the park at one time, entertaining ever-
changing audiences of hoboes and local residents from morning to midnight.[23]

Most speakers preached from radical gospels, although many prosely-
tized from the Good Book itself, exhorting hobohemia's wayward souls to
answer the Lord's call. J. H. Walsh first organized his Industrial Union
Band to drown out Christian evangelists, and Wobblies constantly battled
the Salvation Army for control of the main stem's parks and street corners. But despite hoboes' well-known disdain for the missions, they generally abided a full spectrum of opinion in public arenas like Bughouse
Square. As the ferocity of the free speech campaigns demonstrated, main
stem residents jealously guarded the soapbox as a forum of free expression. "If you don't believe it," remarked Nels Anderson, "just go into a
town where the soap-boxer is suppressed and see how bitter the 'bos'
are."[24]

Written as well as spoken words helped to spread the IWW gospel on
the main stem. Wobblies were famous for their many newspapers and
pamphlets, but the *Industrial Worker* published by J. H. Walsh's Spokane

local was undoubtedly the most important for hoboes. The newspaper's advertisements alone betrayed its readership, for the names of Spokane's many lodging houses, coffee shops, and secondhand clothing stores littered its pages. The *Industrial Worker* also reached beyond Spokane to main stems throughout the West. In March 1909 the newspaper began a series of articles detailing the most prominent roads, jungles, and work sites of the wageworkers' frontier.[25] This field guide to hobohemia offered tips on various local judges, residents, train crews, and police forces around the West. "Try and make them believe you are German," one article suggested to hoboes looking for a handout in Ritzville, Washington.[26] Virtually every issue also featured "slave market news" that reported not only on the amount of hiring being done on a given main stem, but also on the hours, wages, job conditions, and fees that migratories could expect to find there. These reports channeled labor market information to workers who had previously relied upon word-of-mouth or "employment sharks," as private employment agents were nicknamed (fig. 4.1). For Wobblies, gaining some measure of control over the supply of labor to work camps was a first step toward seizing command of the camps themselves. By organizing the main stem, the IWW laid the groundwork for direct action in the field.

Workplace activism finally arrived on the wageworkers' frontier in 1913, long after the IWW had established itself in the hobohemian districts of the West. The fieldwork began in California when "camp delegates" departed the main stems of Redding, Sacramento, Fresno, Bakersfield, Los Angeles, and San Francisco to recruit seasonal laborers on the job. Delegates swept through the orchards, harvest fields, and forests of the Central Valley and Sierra Nevada spreading propaganda and attempting to organize the floating army of "wage slaves."

Bolstering these efforts was the notorious Wheatland hop pickers strike at E. B. Durst's ranch near Marysville, California, in August 1913. This strike, led by several Wobbly hoboes who spoke for the multinational workforce of twenty-eight hundred, ended in a shoot-out that left four men dead, including a district attorney, a deputy sheriff, and two workers. In the wake of Wheatland, and the sentencing to life imprisonment of two Wobblies charged with murder, forty new IWW locals opened and one hundred soapboxers marched up and down the state signing up thousands of new members.[27] Wobblies were notorious for disrupting normal labor camp routines, finding any excuse to agitate fellow workers on the job. "They stand on a nail keg and organize a strike," remarked one employer, "and inside of a day one of them hits camp, hell's a-poppin'."[28]

While the California campaign succeeded in "fanning the flames of

**BLANKET STIFF AND EMPLOYMENT SHARK--WHICH SIDE IS YOUR HUMP ON?**

Figure 4.1: This cartoon from a 1909 edition of the *Industrial Worker* targets not employers but employment agents, whom western hoboes blamed for high labor turnover, low wages, poor working conditions, and extortionist fees. In the five years following the 1908 convention, the IWW sponsored countless boycotts and soapbox campaigns against main stem labor "sharks" rather than attempting to organize migratories in the field. These efforts spawned numerous free speech fights that brought the Wobblies wide renown on the wage-workers' frontier. (*Industrial Worker*, June 10, 1909)

discontent," it failed to achieve better wages, improved living and working conditions, or increased job control for the state's seasonal workforce. Delivering real on-the-job power to hoboes became the central concern of the IWW's organizing drive in the Midwest. In April 1915 IWW delegates at special conference of harvest district locals voted to form the Agricultural Workers' Organization (AWO), which soon became headquartered in an old cheap hotel building in Minneapolis's Gateway district.

As in the California effort, the AWO used mobile job delegates to travel from town to town organizing groups of harvesters. Unlike the California movement, the AWO focused on concrete issues of wages, hours, and working conditions. By September job delegates were signing up one hundred new members per week, a rate that the campaigns of 1916 and 1917 subsequently eclipsed. So stunning was their success that the AWO effectively transformed the whole experience of harvest migration, not only securing gains on the job but also ridding jungles and boxcars of gamblers, stick-up artists, and extortionist railroad police. Claiming seventy thousand members in 1917, the AWO expanded operations into the lumber and mining districts of Montana, Idaho, and the Pacific Northwest.[29]

These organizing drives brought Wobblies to new prominence in hobohemia, a prominence far beyond the union's actual membership. The AWO channeled enough dues to the IWW that in 1917 the parent organization opened a large new general headquarters on West Madison Street equipped with an up-to-date print shop, meeting hall, scores of offices, and a twenty-foot sign atop the building. "Our new general headquarters dominated the 'skid road,'" recalled Ralph Chaplin.

> Every migratory worker on the "skid road" wore a Wobbly button, and there were IWW stickerettes on every lamppost. Open-air meetings were blocking traffic. Halls weren't large enough to accommodate crowds that turned out for Wobbly meetings and entertainments. The revolution was on![30]

Less partisan observers from all over the wageworkers' frontier confirmed a dramatic rise in Wobbly power by 1915. Carleton Parker estimated that 73 percent of the "floating laborers" he talked to in California held radical views consistent with the IWW.[31] Parker's undercover investigator Frederick Mills found IWW symbols, slogans, and messages posted on makeshift "hobo bulletin boards" wherever migratories congregated. "The extent and activity of this organization's workings are almost beyond belief," Mills wrote in his journal.

> One sees notices everywhere. You hear "Wobblies" spoken of favorably in "jungle" conversations. There is widespread knowledge of and interest in its doings that is of far more than passing importance in any consideration of the problems connected with this organization.[32]

As this "widespread knowledge" and interest attest, the IWW had infused hobo subculture with political zeal. "To-day if you will get into a box car and meet a crowd of hoboes," Ben Reitman wrote sometime after 1915, "you will almost imagine that you are in the Socialist or I.W.W. meeting." Because of the IWW, he added, "the hobo has evolved from a despised shiftless creature to a powerful useful man."[33]

The dramatic rise of the IWW provoked an equally dramatic response on the part of employers and law enforcement officials. The assault came

in 1917 as the United States entered a global war that the Wobblies denounced. The IWW's opposition to World War I gave employers the cover
they needed to launch a massive counteroffensive against the union, ac-
cusing Wobblies of being traitors and even spies for Kaiser Wilhelm.

Taking leadership in strikes that curtailed wartime lumber and copper
production, Wobblies also suffered attack from countless vigilante groups
allied with local police departments and business interests. These attacks
laid the foundation for the devastating "Big Pinch" of September 5, 1917,
when United States Justice Department agents simultaneously raided
IWW headquarters, halls, and private homes around the country. These
agents gathered up virtually all of the union's records and property and
arrested one hundred members under federal espionage laws. Subsequent prosecutions under newly passed state and federal sedition and
criminal syndicate statutes sent leading Wobblies to jail or underground.
The infamous Palmer Raids of 1919 and the virulent Red Scare that followed further inhibited Wobbly activities. By 1920 this once premier hobo
organization stood on the verge of collapse.[34]

But just as the hobo-martyr Joe Hill did not die in the hearts of all those
fighting oppression (as sentimental Wobblies were wont to say), so, too,
did the IWW's radical vision survive the war, albeit in altered form. In
hobohemia, political leadership passed to less prominent organizations
that had once competed with the IWW for members, but that now swelled
with former Wobblies seeking new affiliations. Despite their pervasive influence on the main stem, Wobblies had never possessed an absolute mo-
nopoly on hobohemia's political activity. Less radical organizations had
arisen right alongside the IWW, offering hoboes an alternative to the agi-
tational style and uncompromising politics of their more militant counterpart. In 1914, for example, an organization calling itself the Itinerant
Workers' Union, or Hoboes' Union of America, opened an office and cooperative lodging house on Seattle's skid road. This union banned both
Wobblies and evangelists, established its own hiring hall, and bargained
collectively for casual labor jobs, refusing to furnish strikebreakers.[35] Numerous similar organizations appeared on main stems throughout the
wageworkers' frontier in the early twentieth century.[36] But the only one to
rival Wobblies for dominance over hobohemia was the International
Brotherhood Welfare Association (IBWA), a mutual aid society founded,
like the IWW, in 1905.

The IBWA developed originally as the brainchild of James Eads How,
the son of a railroad executive and grandson of the noted civil engineer
who built the Eads Bridge, the first steel span across the Mississippi River.
As a young man, How studied theology at Harvard, Oxford, and the

Meadville Theological Seminary in western Pennsylvania, where he acquired an asceticism that would come to mark the "Millionaire Hobo." Giving away most of his possessions and wearing only threadbare suits, How worked his way through Fabianism, monasticism, and vegetarianism before using his family's estate and the tolls from the Eads Bridge to launch the IBWA on behalf of the migratory worker. How fashioned his organization around a millennialist vision of hoboes that derived from the social gospel and Christian socialism. "If he is penniless we sustain him," How declared. "He always repays the kindness when he finds work.We try to show him that he will play an important part in the coming change and that he must take an interest in the study of industry and social and economic conditions."[37] Like the Wobblies and previous labor commentators on the tramp, How considered homeless men to be "a chosen people" who would lead the nation toward a classless society.[38]

Unlike the Wobblies, however, How believed the best path toward such a society was not direct action, but rather education, cooperation, and uplift.The IBWA's emphasis on mutual association and even spiritual development distinguished it from labor unions, although members saw their work as laying "the foundation for the effectual unionization of the migratory workers."[39] In its mission statement of 1919, the IBWA declared itself to be "a clearinghouse for labor," which sought to "organize the unemployed and assist them in obtaining work"; "furnish medical, legal, and other aid to its members"; "utilize land and machinery in order to provide work for the unemployed"; and "educate the public mind to the right of collective ownership in production and distribution."[40]The IBWA's organizational and propaganda efforts centered around the *"Hobo" News*, a monthly paper distributed by the IBWA through street sales. Sold for five cents in hobohemian neighborhoods, the *"Hobo" News* reached as many as twenty thousand homeless men each month and helped to shape hobohemian identity and politics.[41]

The IBWA also established multifaceted locals in some twenty main stems around the country, including a few in eastern cities like Baltimore, Buffalo, and Philadelphia and far western centers like San Francisco.The heart of the organization, however, was in the Midwest, especially St. Louis, Kansas City, and Chicago. IBWA halls in these cities enjoyed a popularity almost on par with the IWW. Referred to as "Hobo Colleges," an idiosyncratic term that reflected How's educational focus, these halls provided "a forum for discussion of hobo plans . . . and a club-room for hobos, other than saloons."[42] Offering hot meals, dormitory lodgings, a reading room, and job information, IBWA halls required only maintenance, and perhaps a nominal fee, for admission.[43]The largest, most active, and most famous of the Hobo Colleges first opened in 1908 just off of Chicago's West Madison Street under the direction of the ubiquitous Ben Reitman. Although the hall's precise location changed almost yearly—most IBWA halls were open only between November and May, when urban hobohemias were flush with unemployed migratories—it always remained on or close to West Madison and always secured a hall large enough to accommodate one hundred persons. When Reitman departed Chicago to manage Emma Goldman's speaking career, others took over operations of the IBWA branch. Although the hall never lived up to Reitman's grandiose plans, the Hobo College maintained a remarkably consistent and prominent profile in Chicago through the 1920s.[44]

Virtually from its inception, the IBWA recognized a common interest with the IWW, but struggled to remain a distinct and separate entity. "There is nothing in common between the two organizations," announced the *"Hobo"News* just before the "Big Pinch" of September 1917. At the same time, the paper also stated "that a lot of injustice is done and lies fostered by the Capitalist press about the I.W.W. movement."[45] This delicate balancing act of offering arm's length support for the IWW was made all the more difficult by those Wobblies who plotted to bring the IBWA into their orbit. Seeing James Eads How as a hopelessly bourgeois dreamer who impeded their own organizing efforts, Wobblies constantly harassed IBWA soapboxers and attempted to pack their meetings. The problem was especially acute in Chicago, where the Hobo College was large, active, and therefore offered a particularly tempting target. Despite these efforts, the IBWA resisted being taken over and remained an independent voice on the main stem until World War I.[46]

What the Wobblies could not accomplish while at the height of the IWW's power they finally achieved during the union's period of decline. The crushing blow dealt to the IWW in 1917 thrust the IBWA to greater prominence, increasing its membership exponentially. With the diminished activity of the IWW, former Wobblies and migratory workers of all stripes turned in ever-larger numbers to Hobo Colleges and the pages of the *"Hobo"News*, leaving their radical imprints on both. As a result, the IBWA came under increasing surveillance by Justice Department agents, who confirmed the growing links between the two organizations. On October 10, 1917, for example, Seattle police arrested one Eric Anderson for public speaking and selling the *"Hobo"News* without a permit. Anderson told the federal investigators called to the scene that the IBWA was not affiliated with the IWW, but admitted that many IBWA members were also Wobblies. The items found on Anderson at the time of his arrest indicated dual sympathies, if not membership: red-covered constitutions of both the IBWA and IWW and letters from John X. Kelly, secretary of the IBWA, instructing him to "beat it" to Seattle to soapbox for the organization.[47] Others arrested in IBWA and IWW raids expressed various attitudes toward the two groups. Some swore off any connection between the two organizations, while others declared allegiance to both. One hobo arrested in Kansas City claimed that IBWA members there routinely raised funds to aid in the legal defense of persecuted Wobblies.[48] Another intelligence report from Dayton, Ohio, in 1921 stated that "men who are in the field selling the 'Hobo News' are also spreading I.W.W. propaganda" and that "radicals of all organizations apparently have a common meeting place at [the IBWA's] headquarters at 320 W. Second Street."[49] In some places at least, IBWA and IWW operations were closely intertwined, if not identical.

After 1918 federal intelligence officials considered the IBWA to be a front group "used to camouflage meetings of radicals."[50] In 1919 one military intelligence investigator reported breathlessly that "this organization supposed to have been founded by a 'harmless hobo' whose motives were to help and assist unfortunates is now being manipulated by unscrupulous agitators and being used for propaganda purposes to stir up unrest and dissatisfaction and foster the principles of the Soviet form of government."[51] On the basis of this and other reports, intelligence agencies secured the cancellation of the *"Hobo" News'* second-class mailing privileges and increased surveillance of the paper's street sellers and distributers.[52]

In addition to intelligence reports, evidence from post–World War I copies of the *"Hobo" News* itself indicates a clear ideological shift in the IBWA. Changes in the tone and very structure of the newspaper reflected the growing influence of IWW-inspired militancy. In the July 1919 issue, for example, an untitled and unsigned article declared a long list of IBWA goals that included: to "make us masters of the machinery of production instead of its slaves"; "give every worker the full value of the product of his labor"; "abolish the landlord, the lendlord, and the capitalist"; and "abolish classes." Such departures from the previous emphasis on education, uplift, and welfare work were commonplace in 1919. Its special May Day issue of 1919 even took the risky step of affirming the IWW's notorious antiwar principle that "workers shall never take up fire-arms or the tools of production against their fellowmen."[53] After 1918 the IBWA also began issuing its own hobo song sheets and songbooks, whose contents, including "Hallelujah, I'm a Bum" and "Solidarity Forever," were almost entirely lifted from previous editions of the *Little Red Songbook*.[54] In Chicago the Hobo College and the array of surrounding bookstores had taken a notably radical turn (fig. 4.2).[55]

The "Blanket Stiff"

He built the ROAD—
With others of his CLASS, he built the road,
Now o'er it, many a weary mile, he packs his load,
Chasing a JOB. spurred on by HUNGERS goad
He walks and walks, and wonders why
In H—L, he built the road.

Figure 4.2: By 1920 "The 'Blanket Stiff'" had become a familiar figure in hobohemian political iconography. The illustration first appeared in the *Workingman's Paper* and was subsequently adopted by the *Industrial Worker* in 1910. In 1919 the *"Hobo" News* began featuring it on the newspaper's masthead. An IBWA pamphlet of the early 1920s entitled *Legal Robbery of the Workers* also carried this graphic on its cover, and by 1923 an oil painting of "The 'Blanket Stiff'" had become a permanent fixture in Chicago's Hobo College. Its use by the IBWA after the Justice Department's crackdown on the IWW during World War I is evidence of the growing links between the two organizations. (*Industrial Worker,* April 23, 1910)

Radical members of the IBWA also sought to fill the void left in the field of direct job action by establishing the Migratory Workers Union (MWU) in 1918. The MWU was financed largely by James Eads How, though, like most aspects of the postwar IBWA, it was not controlled by him. Union officers saw the MWU as "organizing industrially" for the purposes of getting "these men, the 'Hobo Workers,' together for the good of all of them. Better wages, shorter hours and decent living conditions will be demanded."[56] With a view to winning the financial support of How, organizers of the MWU drew up a moderate constitution that called for the repeal of vagrancy laws; the federal inspection of work camps; the abolition of prison contract labor and chain gangs; free transportation for migratory workers; the abolition of private employment agencies; and a shorter work day. By the time Nels Anderson investigated the union's activities in 1922 and 1923, the union was virtually defunct, although Anderson did state that it had once wielded considerable influence in Indiana and Ohio.[57]

The increased visibility of radicals in the IBWA after 1918 engendered conflict within the organization, conflict that usually centered on the figure of James Eads How. Radicals considered How an obstacle to increased militancy, while moderate officers like John X. Kelly blamed How's cavalier and democratic managerial style for leaving the IBWA vulnerable to Wobbly influence.[58] Despite How's attempts to foster solidarity, a rupture occurred during the IBWA's 1922 convention when the presiding chair with close IWW ties refused to recognize the more moderate delegation associated with How.[59] One result of this rift was the creation of a more radical monthly newspaper, the *Hobo World*, to rival the *"Hobo" News*. Although publication of the *Hobo World* appears to have been irregular, the paper billed itself through the mid-1920s as the "Official Bulletin Published Monthly of, for, and by the Migratory Workers."[60]

As this newspaper's masthead suggested, the struggles between main stem moderates and radicals were to a large degree conflicts over the right to speak for the hobo. Both the IWW and the IBWA sought to represent hobohemia, and both wrestled with the conflicting imperatives that such representation entailed. On the one hand, these organizations placed a premium on their own authenticity as instruments of subcultural expression—"of the hoboes, by the hoboes, and for the hoboes," as the *"Hobo" News* put it. Moderates and radicals therefore both had to demonstrate their subcultural credentials and faithfully depict, even endorse, the peculiar countercultural traits of their hobo rank and file. On the other hand, Wobblies and IBWA members also considered hobohemia as on the vanguard of larger social changes and as representing broader constituencies apart from merely those on the main stem. To both groups, hoboes were "a chosen people" burdened by the world-historical mission of ushering in the glorious socialist future. "Nowhere else can a section of the working class be found so admirably fitted to serve as the scouts and advance guards of the labor army," wrote one contributor to the IWW newspaper *Solidarity* in 1914. "Rather, [hoboes] may become the guerillas of the revolution—the franc-tireurs of the class struggle."[61]

Integral to the IWW's and IBWA's task of organizing the main stem, then, was the effort to shape the very identity of the hobo. On what basis did hoboes stand as distinct from other groups of stationary and migratory workers? How much ideological freight could the hobo be made to bear? These questions of identity politics found abundant expression in the imaginative body of hobo folklore propagated by the IWW and IBWA. In its attempt to represent both an authentic "song of the jungles" and a universal cry for liberation, this folklore articulated the contradictions inherent in mobilizing hobohemia for the purposes of revolution.

## "THE SONG OF THE JUNGLES"

Despite their political differences, both the IWW and the IBWA sought to give voice to hobo subculture. In the pages of the *"Hobo" News*, the *Industrial Worker*, and other main stem papers, migratories saw common concerns and interests expressed in an idiom that was distinctly their own. While their primary task was to spread revolutionary propaganda, these papers also generated a sense of community through the stories, poems, illustrations, reports, and other commentaries they collected from migratories in the field. Hobo newspapers often specifically solicited contributions from ordinary readers, especially snappy poems or short stories that brought together key elements of the hobo identity. These contributions ranged from serious articles reviewing conditions at munitions factories to the more numerous examples of doggerel.[62] Nels Anderson observed more than one hobo carrying his own press clippings in his pocket. Without these contributors, wrote Anderson, "radical sheets like the I.W.W. publications and the Hobo News would not appeal to the homeless man. The radical press in turn serves as a pattern by which hobo writers fashion and color their literary productions."[63] The sheer number of contributors to the *"Hobo" News* suggests the importance of the paper as an arena for self-representation among migratory workers. Between 1919 and 1921, over eighty different names appeared in the paper's bylines, with little more than a handful belonging to members of the paper's staff or the IBWA's executive board.[64]

Despite this general accessibility, these radical newspapers exercised strict editorial control in order to shape the cultural meanings of the hobo. The pages of the *"Hobo" News*, in particular, exhibited conflict over its editorial policies, especially after the paper's ideological shift in the postwar period. "We need a hobo magazine that will express life and labor and fight our battles," complained one reader disenchanted with the paper's "scientific socialism" and "technical" economic theories, which, this reader maintained, did not interest the "average working stiff." The *"Hobo" News'* editors responded to this criticism by asking, "Do you think we can get people to use their thinking boxes if we get out a paper full of Weary Willie copy?" "We invite stories from the road," they continued, "but we welcome the philosophy of the down and out who has the foresight to see better things and how to get them."[65]

This brief debate highlighted the tensions at work in the IWW's and IBWA's strategies for representing hobo subculture. Neither radicals nor moderates celebrated hobohemia for its own sake, but rather sought to use the hobo's raw counterculture as a lever to advance their larger labor and socialist agendas. Many hoboes, on the other hand, defined themselves as much against other groups of workers as they did against capitalists. What the *Industrial Worker* referred to as "the meek and tractable home-guard" was a favorite target of hoboes who voiced their preference for "the carefree life of the American Indian" over the settled existence of most industrial workers.[66] Such sentiments raised questions about just what a post-revolutionary world would look like in the hands of Wobbly hoboes. Was hobohemia truly a viable alternative to the norms of home and family that prevailed virtually the world over?

IWW and IBWA commentary tried to avoid such outrageous conclusions by drawing upon older themes of alienation and patriarchal loss in their depictions of the hobo's homelessness. In one IBWA pamphlet written by M. Kuhn, for example, the author characterized the hobo's plight in terms of his "detach[ment] from the soil and the fireside." "By the nature of his work and not by his own will," Kuhn argued, "[the hobo] is precluded from establishing a home and rearing a family."[67] Wobblies also frequently invoked the lack of home life as evidence of oppression. Frederick Mills recorded the words of one speaker at an IWW hall in Sacramento in 1914: "You people think you live, don't you? You think you are happy. Well, answer just one question, and answer it truthfully. Will every married man in this crowd raise his hand?" Out of the two hundred men present, recounted Mills, none raised his hand. "Well, do you call that living?" the speaker asked. "Even the black chattel slave had a chance to propagate his race. You men don't know what it is to have a home, a wife, a child, and yet you think you live."[68]

Others, like the popular IWW short story writer Ralph Winstead, used sentimental images of domestic life to highlight the "perversions" of hobohemia. "I never went into a brothel by preference," announces a Winstead hobo character in the pages of the *Industrial Pioneer*. "I have trembled at the thought of a sweet woman's arms clasped about me in love. I have stood with my throat choked with a string of burning lumps— outside of some bourgeois's home, and watched a while the antics of the clean children playin' on the lawn."[69] Alluding similarly to the prevalence of prostitution and perhaps homosexuality among geographically and socially isolated workers, another Wobbly contributor claimed that all hoboes

> want to see and partake in all the manifestations of civilized society, we want amusements, comfort, leisure. We also want a clean and healthy environment composed of both sexes, we want a home, family, children. We want to see ourselves and our ideals in life perpetuated in our own offspring. And may I say that I hold this to be a blessing for humanity. Whoever does not strive and fight for the good things of life is, in my opinion, dangerous to society. But due to our perverse social system we are prevented from satisfying our desires and the majority of our class accepts whatever is offered as substitute.[70]

While such commentaries undoubtedly reflected many hoboes' longings for stable homes, they also represented an imaginative effort to link the class struggle to thwarted desires for monogamous sex and feminine civilization. Indeed, by conflating sexual "perversion" and deviancy with a "perverse social system" that denied men the blessings of "civilized society," Wobbly writers launched a powerful critique of exploitative labor conditions that many nonradical reformers found compelling. By World War I, a chorus of Progressive opinion condemned unregulated capitalism on the wageworkers' frontier for denying men "decent homes" and "the society of decent women."[71] Carleton Parker was especially eloquent and influential in his analysis of migratory workers as "tragic symptoms of a sick social order." In Parker's view, hoboes were merely "finished products of their environment," an environment that was fundamentally "perverted":

> There can be no greater perversion of a desirable existence than this insecure, undernourished, wandering life, with its sordid sex expression and reckless and rare pleasures. Such a life leads to one of two consequences: either a sinking of the class to a low and hopeless level, where they become through irresponsible conduct and economic inefficiency a charge upon society; or the result will be revolt and guerilla labor warfare.[72]

Sensing accommodation with Progressives like Parker, many Wobbly hoboes rejected such negative valuations of hobohemia and espoused the "guerilla labor warfare" so feared by reformers. Instead of depicting the single-sex environment of migratory labor as a "perverse" consequence of wage relations, supporters of the bummery hailed hobohemia as the last manly holdout against capitalist civilization's degrading feminine embrace. In the *Little Red Songbook*, for example, the migratory's loss of home and family is the proletariat's gain. As the very title of "Hallelujah, I'm a Bum" suggests, the hobo's exploitation and detachment from the bonds of "civilized society" provided a freedom to discover an authentic proletarian identity. "The Mysteries of a Hobo's Life," for example, written by Matt Valentine Huhta (alias T-Bone Slim) for the songbook's 1916 edition, depicts initiation into hobo subculture as simultaneously an exile from "civilized society" and an induction into manhood and class-consciousness:

> I took a job on an extra gang
> Way up in the mountain.
> I paid my fee and the shark shipped me
> And the ties I soon was counting.
>
> The boss put me driving spikes
> And the sweat was enough to blind me
> He didn't seem to like my pace,
> So I left the job behind me.
>
> I grabbed a hold of an old freight train
> And around the country traveled
> The mysteries of a hobo's life
> To me were soon unraveled.
>
> I traveled east and I traveled west
> And the "shacks" could never find me.
> Next morning I was miles away
> From the job I left behind me.
>
> I ran across a bunch of "stiffs"
> Who were known as Industrial Workers.
> They taught me how to be a man—
> And how to fight the shirkers.
>
> I kicked right in and joined the bunch
> And now in the ranks you'll find me,
> Hurrah for the cause—To hell with the boss!
> And the job I left behind me.[73]

Invoking hobohemia's gendered rituals of solidarity and anti-acquisitiveness, "The Mysteries of a Hobo's Life" depicts migratory labor as a community of authentic masculinity that also signified the larger body of productive labor.

Not surprisingly, jungle life provided a particularly popular theme in Wobbly folklores of the hobo, for it was in the absence of domesticity, civilization, and workplace subordination where the IWW's imagined community of masculinity flourished. Echoing William Aspinwall's romantic musings on the outdoor life, the *Industrial Worker* carried lyrical passages in praise of jungle life as "an idyl of springtime."[74] Meanwhile, contributors to the *Little Red Songbook* frequently made reference to jungles as masculine refuges from work and home. In "The Suckers Sadly Gather," written by railroad construction worker Richard Brazier, migratories who earnestly seek work are "suckers," while those who repair to the jungles to dine on stolen chicken "are happy as can be."[75] Brazier, who joined J. H. Walsh's Spokane local in 1908, amplified these sentiments in "Meet Me in the Jungles, Louie," a song composed to the tune of "Meet Me in St. Louis, Louie." Here, a worker "out of a job" and "dead on the hog" comes home to find that his wife has evicted him for failing to pay the bills. The emasculated breadwinner then hits the road to join a host of jungle-dwelling hoboes:

> Louie went out of his shack,
> He swore he would never come back;
> He said, "I will wait, and take the first freight,
> My friends in the jungles to see;
> For me there is waiting out there,
> Of a mulligan stew a big share.
> So away I will go and be a hobo,
> For the song in the jungles I hear."[76]

Contrasting "the song in the jungles" heard by Louie was the siren song of domestic life, which carried "scissorbills," "sissies," and other "homeguard" workers to the embrace of feminine civilization. In a cartoon drawn by Joe Hill and published in a 1913 issue of the *Industrial Worker,* for example, a migratory worker chases a female apparition whose diaphanous dress and wispy hair encodes the settled existence of civilized society as distinctly feminine (fig. 4.3).[77] With a crown atop her head reading "job," the female form speeds along on a unicycle tied to one foot. In her one hand is a magic wand, a phallic possession held out of the man's grasp. Closer to his reach is a pork chop, which the woman holds out with her other hand. Also beckoning the migratory is a homeguard perched in a rocking chair on the front porch of a grocery store. The homeguard, who may be "A. Kockrotch," the grocery store proprietor, calls upon the hobo to "stay in one place and vote the Socialist ticket." In chasing the woman, Joe Hill's migratory pursues the illusory promises of capitalist civilization. But just as deceptive is the homeguard's call to settle down. The search for steady work and domesticity, this cartoon sug-

**CONSTITUTIONAL GUARANTEE:—LIFE? LIBERTY? AND THE PURSUIT OF—A JOB!**

Figure 4.3: Joe Hill's cartoon offers a distinctly hobohemian perspective on work and home. Here, a job appears as a young maiden holding out a pork chop to a pursuing migratory. Instead of chasing this temptress, who will always stay out of reach, Wobblies like Joe Hill urged hoboes to resist the wiles of feminine civilization and make their home in the masculine community of the IWW. (*Industrial Worker,* April 24, 1913)

gests, removes the migratory from his true home in the masculine community of hobohemia.

In its conflation of class-consciousness with virile masculinity and the rejection of feminine civilization, Wobbly folklores exploited the associations with "savagery" that homelessness had carried since the tramp crisis of the 1870s. When Francis Wayland first defined the tramp as a "savage" refugee from the feminine sphere of home, little did he know that not only Wobblies, but also other sociologists like John James McCook and popular writers like Jack London would win renown by romanticizing the tramp's primitivism and lack of civilized restraint. London's narratives of "*blond-beast* adventure" on the road fascinated not only hobo readers, but also white middle-class audiences, who, by the turn of the century, had come to fear their own "overcivilization."[78]

As London's "blond-beast" reference to Nordic whiteness suggested, these fears expressed racial as well as gender anxieties that white men were growing soft and weak amidst the civilized refinements of home.

New groups of exotic immigrants pouring into urban centers and building powerful new political machines fed into the sense of crisis. So, too, did women, who increasingly crossed the threshold of the home into the public sphere seeking work, leisure, and even political power. Finally, changes in the very structure of middle-class work itself, which was becoming more sedentary and bureaucratized, gave rise to insecurities about the loss of bodily vigor and manly independence. As an antidote to the racial disease of "overcivilization," middle-class white men welcomed appeals to "experience," outdoor activity, and "the strenuous life," and sought what one commentator called "a saving touch of honest, old-fashioned barbarism."[79] Such therapeutic barbarism could be found, among other places, in lively accounts of the road, where wayfaring white men rediscovered primitive strengths and virtues and, in so doing, played out middle-class fantasies of escape and regression.

IWW propaganda drew enormous symbolic power from this discourse of "overcivilization." Wobblies exploited bourgeois concerns about white masculine virility to craft an authoritative myth about the hobo that linked themes of racial regeneration and authentic manhood with those of class warfare.

Nowhere did hobo radicals find a richer or more fecund source for their folklore than in the myth of the frontier. Our oldest story of national origins, the frontier myth, which Frederick Jackson Turner's address at the World's Columbian Exposition had revived in compelling fashion, explains American historical development in terms of the recurrent regressions to primitivism experienced by several generations of white pioneer settlers. According to the myth, each wave of settlement penetrated deeper into the howling wilderness, bringing white "civilization" into violent contact with Indian "savagery." Through warfare, white settlers did not displace savagery, but rather incorporated it into their very identity as a frontier people and used it to redeem the effete, corrupt, and degenerate commercial centers of the East. A closed frontier, then, removed a crucial pillar of American identity. For, according to the myth, it was only the constant exposure of white masculinity to the "saving touch" of savagery on the frontier that kept the race vigorous and the nation free from European-style corruptions.

As psychological compensation for this imagined loss, the frontier West enjoyed more cultural currency in the early twentieth century than it did when the frontier was supposedly "open." The writings of Owen Wister, the paintings of Frederic Remington, and the very public persona of Theodore Roosevelt all attested to the symbolic importance of the West to an American middle class thinking obsessively about the fate of white masculinity in an urban industrial age.[80]

The IWW and IBWA did not, of course, seek a middle-class audience. But hobo and middle-class readers alike responded to a common stock of symbols, icons, keywords, and rhetorical clichés that came with the shared national culture, however conflicted that culture may have been. As a particularly resonant and complex symbol, the frontier West figured prominently in radical hobo folklore as the mythic space of hobohemia. At times, as in one IBWA pamphlet, hobo activists described the East-West distinction as an ideological spectrum: "The Conservative East and the Progressive West."[81] But more often, hobo folklore constructed the West as a crucible of vigorously masculine and revolutionary activity in contrast to the East's settled domesticity and docility. Even the homeless of the East were submissive and dull, hoboes argued, while floaters on the wageworkers' frontier were manly and dynamic. "In Chicago," wrote IWW sympathizer William Edge, "the hobo is self-conscious."

> In New York, Pittsburgh, Cleveland, Baltimore, the hobo was an adventitious migratory. He went dumbly from job to job, impelled by the relentless forces of modern capitalism. He was simply a man beaten by an economic system. In Chicago, the hobo seemed to be a hobo by choice. The men were large, strong, conscious of their disinheritance. They seemed not to be victims of circumstances; they came to Chicago of their own free will, to "get by" during the winter. They knew what they were about. They had definite standards. They did not allow themselves to be kicked about from job to job. They had worked on the wheat all summer, or on war jobs. Now that winter was coming, they had left for Chicago. The hegira was not accidental; it was as conscious as the migrations to Palm Beach or the Riviera.[82]

After the 1908 convention, IWW propaganda repeatedly contrasted eastern laborers, who were "church-going," "weak-kneed," and "servile tools" of capital, with western workers, who were "strong-limbed, resolute, self-reliant . . . the finest specimens of American manhood." The hobo, proclaimed the *Industrial Union Bulletin* in 1908, "is the leaven of the revolutionary industrial union movement in the West, and his absence . . . from the East, accounts in large measure for the slowness of the Eastern workers to awaken from their lethargy."[83] While the bourgeois West offered individual escape and regeneration from an East plagued by immigration, feminism, and corporate domination, the West of hobo folklore provided a uniquely masculine environment for the collective expression of revolutionary class power. Just as anti-labor writers frequently drew from the frontier myth to characterize strikers as "savages," so, too, did Wobblies symbolically substitute capitalists for Indians, depicting themselves as hardened members of a superior race going to war against a "savage" social system to save an enfeebled working class.

Wobblies combined Frederick Jackson Turner's frontier thesis with the natural selection principles of social Darwinism in order to explain the development of a revolutionary race of white men in the industrial West. Fred Thompson, former hobo and editor of the *Industrial Worker*, described the "process of selection" through which he believed western hoboes evolved: "Those who least tolerated the ways of the east, went west. There most of them did not become settled or tied in a specific location—there weren't enough females to tie them. They were footloose."[84] In the absence of women, Thompson suggested, men naturally took to the road, forming veritable tribes of nomadic wanderers. Another hobo, contributing to the *Industrial Worker*, emphasized the frontier hobo's emancipation from a governing moral order that was at once capitalist and feminine. "When a large strike of long duration occurs in the east," he wrote, "the more rebellious of the unmarried men go west." "These workers," the writer continued, "are the real proletarians. . . . They are irreligious. Their words and ethics are not those of the ruling class. The one, last tie that binds other workers to society is lacking; there are no family ties. . . . This is the class that the masters fear . . . and nothing will sooner cause a fight than to apply to them the epithet 'homeguard.'"[85]

According to Wobbly myth, the wageworker's frontier cut men loose from enslaving domestic regimes, creating "natural" revolutionaries whose primitive habits of movement and collective association furthered the cause of industrial unionism. Like Theodore Roosevelt, Wobblies sought to use the West's "saving touch" of barbarism to regenerate "morally flabby" white men of the East. But unlike Roosevelt, who tried to invigorate an effete upper class to seize hold of corporate, national, and imperial leadership, Wobblies targeted an eastern working class that had fallen under the spell of "the conventions of bourgeois society." "The nomadic worker of the West," wrote one contributor to *Solidarity* in 1914, is

> infinitely less servile than his fellow worker in the East. Unlike the factory slave of the Atlantic seaboard and the Central States, he is most emphatically not "afraid of his job." . . . No wife or family encumber him. The workman of the East, oppressed by the fear of want for wife and babies, dares not venture much. He has perforce the tameness of the domesticated animals.[86]

Here, the call to break free of domestic bondage is not merely an appeal to the "strenuous life," but a summons to war against the dominant social order. By linking the hobo's revolutionary freedom with the "savage" characteristics of the frontier, however, this passage employs notions of gender and race that Theodore Roosevelt himself would have found familiar. According to the writer, prolonged exposure to mixed-sex communities and domesticity weakened white men, causing them to lose their natural instinct for adventure and, one may assume, violence. Their servility is inscribed upon their very bodies through the metaphor of tamed domestic animals. In contrast, western workers who ventured into the untamed West awakened the vestigial beasts within and lost fear of their masters. The hobo, in effect, was a latter-day "Leatherstocking," a socialist "noble savage," who assimilated the savage ways of the wageworkers' frontier in order to destroy the savage social order that created it.

The most extended exposition of the hobo frontier myth was Charles Ashleigh's essay "The Floater," published in the *International Socialist Review* in 1914. In this essay, Ashleigh detailed the hobo's masculine strength, virility, and fearlessness while depicting the eastern working class as feminized and anemic. Recapitulating hobo folklore's Darwinian environmentalism, Ashleigh described the East's "permanence of industry" as producing a stable working-class family life: "a debased and deteriorated family life, it is true, lacking in all the pleasant and restful features usually associated with that term, but, nonetheless, marriage, the procreation of children and some amount of stability are assured by the conditions of industry." In addition, monotonous and imprisoning factory labor engendered a "loss of nervous and physical vitality and the creation of bodily weaklings" among the eastern working class.[87]

In the West, however, where manufacturing had not yet dominated, extractive sectors like lumbering, mining, and agriculture employed seasonal male labor exclusively, making home and family life impossible. In this all-male outdoor environment, according to Ashleigh, labor grew up strong and sturdy, uncompromised by the refinements of eastern civilization. Western workers were "sun-tanned, brawny men, most of them in early manhood or in the prime of life, dressed in blue overalls or khaki pants and blue cotton shirts." Animated by a "growing spirit of passionate rebellion," the very bodies of these workers exhibited class power:

> The arduous physical toil in the open air does not have the same deteriorating effect as does the mechanical, confined work of the eastern slave. The constant matching of wits and daring needed for the long trips across country have developed a species of rough self-reliance in the wandering proletarian of the West. In health and in physical courage he is undoubtedly the superior of his eastern brother.[88]

Ashleigh's references to "rough self-reliance," "health," and "physical courage" highlight hobo folklore's preoccupation with the hobo's body, a preoccupation derived in large part from the strong corporeal component of hobohemian masculinity. The very physicality of their labor provided hoboes with a ready basis for imagining their manhood in terms of brawny strength. The IWW's cult of physical daring, which led more than one Wobbly activist to an early grave, infused hobohemia's emphasis on bodily vigor with new political meanings. Facing vigilante attack with courage was so highly valued that "hobo agitators" such as Frank Little, who was tortured and lynched by vigilantes during a copper mine strike in 1917, routinely waded into unfriendly districts knowing full well the dangers that awaited them.[89]

While such demonstrated courage denoted a masculine readiness to receive and possibly inflict violence, IWW iconography depicted powerful male bodies to symbolize working-class power. An illustration submitted by "Bingo" to *Solidarity* in 1916, for example, celebrates the AWO's victories in the harvest fields with an idealized image of a tall, striding migratory. Entitled "Now for the Eastern Invasion!" this drawing depicts the "Harvest Spirit" as a brawny hobo with a black cat and wooden sabots, heading off to organize "eastern industries" (fig. 4.4).[90] Two other *Solidarity* illustrations similarly represent the IWW's class power in terms of virile masculinity. In "Somebody Has Got to Get Out of the Way!"—also by "Bingo"—solidarity among striking miners of the Mesabi Iron Range is represented by a club-wielding giant. Towering above the landscape, this figure is on the verge of clobbering the "Steel Trust," symbolized by a fleshy aristocrat and his minions (fig. 4.5).[91] Another untitled illustration from a 1917 edition of *Solidarity* similarly features a muscular and gigantic worker who bears the inscription "I.W.W." This figure appears only in a loincloth as he dismantles a fortress built with stones symbolizing "low wages," "long hours," "militarism," "rotten conditions," and "speedup system" (fig. 4.6).[92] Only manly force could break up such a sturdy edifice.

Such images represented a dramatic break from nineteenth-century labor iconography. Older labor banners tended to carry, on the one hand, images of skilled tradesmen and, on the other, allegorical depictions of female virtues such as Truth, Justice, Faith, Liberty, the Republic, and the People. The IWW led an early-twentieth-century shift toward masculine proletarian iconography, a shift that occurred in European labor movements as well.[93] Designed to represent the power of mass industrial unionism, these new images reflected the waning strength of craft unions, which fought incessant corporate campaigns to reduce skilled workers' control over the production process.

In addition to exploiting the weaknesses of skilled labor, the IWW's

Now For the Eastern Invasion!

Solidarity, October 14, 1916.

Figure 4.4: This illustration looks hopefully to the future after the successful organizing effort on the Great Plains in 1916. Here, the brawny "Harvest Spirit" heads for nearby timber and oil districts, while the factories of the East wait on the horizon. Wobbly folklore propagated the notion that the wageworkers' frontier, where women and family life were largely absent, produced the kind of strong virile men needed to emancipate the weak and effeminate workers of the East from "wage slavery." (*Solidarity*, October 14, 1916)

proletarian iconography also drew symbolic power from a larger "cult of muscularity" gripping the early-twentieth-century middle class.[94] Brawny working-class men found depiction not only in Wobbly propaganda, but also in highbrow paintings, sculptures, and statuary and lowbrow newspapers, magazines, and advertisements. Public statues of hammer-wielding laborers and classical poses of working-class bodybuilders always implicitly carried threatening messages to middle-class viewers, who worried about their own bodily strength. To manage these disruptive class associations, displayers of such virile art purified working-class bodies through an aesthetics of nudity or a health-related emphasis on physical fitness.[95]

IWW propaganda sought to bring these latent associations to the surface, allowing the working-class body to realize its disruptive and destructive potential. Representing labor's power not as a narrow trade or a universal ideal but rather as the raw muscular "savagery" of unskilled proletarians, Wobblies devised a folklore that exploited middle-class racial

## Somebody Has Got to Get Out of The Way!

Solidarity, August 19, 1916.

Figure 4.5: IWW illustrations such as this one transformed traditional labor iconography by depicting proletarian workers in terms of masculine virility. This impassive and otherwise featureless figure symbolizes the solidarity of striking miners on the Mebasi Iron Range. Unlike Wobbly propagandists, the miners themselves defined their solidarity not around virile manhood, but rather in terms of home, family, ethnicity, and community life. (*Solidarity,* August 19, 1916)

and gender anxieties and figuratively encompassed the general body of industrial labor.

Despite its inclusive intentions, however, Wobbly folklore propagated a fiction of working-class unity that discounted, and indeed erased, the gender, ethnic, and racial differences that divided the body of labor. Making the hobo stand for the whole of the working class denied expression to the experiences of other laboring groups, both migratory and sedentary, whose on-the-job militancy was equal to, if not greater than, that of hoboes. Indeed, the IWW's most memorable strikes involved whole families of workers, including wage-earning children, who stood picket in the industrial centers of Massachusetts, New Jersey, Ohio, western Pennsylvania, and elsewhere to defend the very "homeguard" communities denigrated by Wobbly hoboes. The Wobblies' masculinist iconography to the contrary, radical Finnish miners on the Mesabi Iron Range, for example,

*Solidarity,* April 28, 1917.

Figure 4.6: This piece of Wobbly propaganda draws upon not only the classical male form but also the early-twentieth-century "cult of muscularity" that flooded American culture with depictions of powerful male bodies. The IWW often exploited this larger cultural fascination by making explicit the subversive class messages inherent in much of this virile art. In this case, raw muscularity dismantles the edifice of industrial capitalism. (*Solidarity,* April 28, 1917)

defined solidarity in terms of settled community life and built support for the IWW only with the help of women and children. To these homeguard workers, the cause of industrial unionism was inseparable from the bonds that tied laboring communities together, including those of family, neighborhood, ethnicity, and religion, as well as shared experiences of work and manhood.[96]

Western Wobblies who traveled to the ethnic enclaves of the East to advise and lead strikes often neglected the importance and even sanctity of these community ties, sometimes raising the ire of their homeguard hosts. When the first hoboes arrived in McKees Rocks, Pennsylvania, in 1909 to assist striking steelworkers, for example, the migratories threw their bedrolls on an eastern European church alter, raising the ire of their striking fellow workers.[97]

This tension within the movement also had more serious and long-lasting consequences. While immigrant strikers infused the IWW with new community-based meanings, the union's failure to establish a more permanent presence in manufacturing districts was partially the result of a western hobo leadership that saw home as a prison. Building mass industrial unionism in the East, and indeed most of the West, involved patient and intense local activism over a long period. Nurturing the fragile bonds between ethnic groups and combating the violent opposition of employers, local officials, and native-born skilled workers required immense organizational skills. Such work was beyond the ken of many western hoboes, who preferred to fly to and fro industrial flashpoints, "fanning the flames of discontent."[98]

Wobbly folklores of the hobo also perpetuated the myth, widely accepted to this day, that hobo labor alone built the industrial West. Hoboes, however, formed only one of the migratory streams that crisscrossed the wageworkers' frontier. Everywhere hoboes labored, they did so alongside other seasonal workers who never stepped foot on the main stem. Chinese, Japanese, Filipino, Greek, Italian, Mexican, Serb, Croat, Hungarian, Polish, and Finnish were just some of the nationalities represented in the extractive and agricultural sectors of the West. Unlike hoboes, these workers maintained tight connections to their home communities. Many had even set out from home under specific authorization and orders from their families. While hoboes worked only long enough to save up a "stake," which they subsequently "blew in" on the main stem, their foreign-born counterparts tended to stick to the job, carefully husbanding their earnings, which they often sent back home.[99] For this reason, hoboes frequently expressed scorn for immigrant "scissorbills" who seemed to be "owned by their jobs."

But sojourning immigrants could be every bit as feisty as hoboes. Indeed, individualistic hoboes who simply drifted off the job when the spirit moved them often lacked the solidarity that characterized immigrant protests. Japanese farmworkers in California, for example, confronted their employers over wages and job conditions on numerous occasions, winning their demands so often that they inspired envy among native-born white migratories. Japanese migrants, testified one Wobbly official, "act more solid together than do the natives." Writing for the *Industrial Worker* in 1911, another organizer agreed that the Japanese are "masters in the art of bringing John Farmer to his knees." "My advice," he told his hobo readership, "is learn the tactics used by the Japanese. Go thou and do likewise."[100]

Wobbly folklores of the hobo could not speak to such experiences as those of Japanese farmworkers. Like the Industrial Army movement of 1894, which differed dramatically from the IWW in terms of political ideology, the western Wobblies responded to the increasing diversity of the

American working class with a folklore and iconography of white American manhood intended to represent class unity.

At its worst, this folklore reflected the explicit racism of those hoboes who prized their membership in hobohemia as a racial privilege. Many IBWA locals, which tended to define themselves exclusively as hobohemian organizations, refused admission to African Americans as well as to "the traditionally lazy races of the Mediterranean coast." One secretary of Chicago's Hobo College even belonged to the Ku Klux Klan.[101]

The IWW stridently and incessantly denounced such racism, both in its hobo propaganda and elsewhere. Yet in celebrating hoboes as the "real proletarians," Wobblies tacitly reproduced in culture the very structure of exclusion that denied women, nonwhites, and recent immigrant groups access to the main stem. Wobbly myth construed hobohemia as mediated only by class, when, in fact, the subculture was explicitly defined by racial and gender segregation. Through this conceptual sleight of hand, IWW propaganda made a veritable fetish out of the hobo. Within a decade of the Justice Department's assault on the IWW, the larger culture would embrace the fetish and recode Wobbly folklore as an authentic example of white frontier Americana, making little reference to the social and economic conditions of migratory labor.

Even while it served in the capacity of revolutionary propaganda, radical hobo folklore entailed a masculine romance of the road that, stripped of its strident class rhetoric, appealed to many white middle-class men. By World War I, watered-down versions of the hobo myth had become a staple of the new mass media and urban popular culture. In some versions, hoboes appeared as curious and compelling anomalies to the settled norms of white America. In others, they became satirical mouthpieces for urban bachelors who scorned the ways of marriage and family.

As the hobo myth spread throughout the culture, it provoked strong reaction from Progressive reformers and investigators concerned about the growing influence of hobohemia over urban life. To these reformers, the main stem population was indeed a vanguard, not of a multiracial and multinational working class, but of an encroaching modernity and economic rationalization that increasingly drew native-born white Americans away from the traditional relationships of home. Through their struggle with a population they deemed homeless, these activists redefined the very meanings of home for modern industrial society.

# "A CIVILIZATION
WITHOUT HOMES"

**I** n June 1921 Nels Anderson retired from the hobo life with one final freight-hopping excursion across the wageworkers' frontier. Like thousands of other men riding the rails that summer, Anderson headed toward Chicago's West Madison Street. But, unlike the others, he did not search out the slave markets there. Having "resolved to leave the 'bummery'" in favor of a more sedentary white-collar career, Anderson sold his tool chest, bought a five-dollar suit, and asked for directions to the University of Chicago. Arriving on campus fresh from the road, Anderson drew stares and wondered if he would have to "give up the university idea." That night he ducked into an alley and bedded down next to a smokestack. In the morning he put on his suit, searched for work, and plotted his strategy for gaining admission to the university's graduate school. If everything fell into place, he would enter full-time study with Robert Park, Ernest Burgess, Albion Small, and the other pioneers of "Chicago sociology."[1]

To these scholars, sociology was more than a mere academic enterprise. It was a mode of urban exploration and encounter, a way of seeing that transformed the city itself into a "social laboratory" for the study of human behavior in a modern urban environment. Robert Park called himself "an intellectual vagabond exploring and writing about the life of the city."[2] To Nels Anderson, academic labor was merely a better way of "getting by."[3] His new career offered not only a way off the road, but also a means of exploiting his migratory past. Indeed, it was largely on the basis of Anderson's hobo experiences that the department admitted the otherwise poorly credentialed candidate. Park and his colleagues championed "participant observation," the willingness, as Anderson put it, to "descend into the pit, assume a role there, and later ascend to brush off the dust."[4] Anderson was not merely a participant observer, but an actual participant who, as evidenced by the stack of data cards he collected in route to Chicago, could use his status as a subcultural "insider" to chart life on the margins of urban industrial civilization.

The fit between Anderson's new career and his old one was not always neat. The former hobo quickly tired of the "weary willie humor" that followed him down the academic hallways.[5] Indeed, he eventually left Chicago to complete his doctorate at New York University, hoping to shed the hobo stigma.[6] Despite these problems, Anderson's tenure at Chicago proved fruitful for all involved. Robert Park and Ernest Burgess quickly tutored their new recruit in sociological methods, arranged funding from local welfare organizations for fieldwork, and directed him to write a report on Chicago's homeless population. When Anderson delivered his report one year later, Park, without even consulting the author, dropped everything and hastily prepared it for publication. With the appearance of *The Hobo: The Sociology of the Homeless Man* in 1923, Nels Anderson became the nation's leading authority on homelessness and one of the most recognized sociologists in the country. He had not even yet earned his master's degree.[7]

*The Hobo* rewarded Robert Park as well. By reaching a broad audience, Anderson's book introduced the methods and insights of Chicago sociology to the general public and, not incidentally, attracted funding to the department for further research projects. The volume also launched a new series of books by the University of Chicago Press on urban sociology. This series, in which nearly two dozen studies by Chicago sociologists appeared in less than two decades, brought Robert Park and his department international acclaim and left a profound impact on American culture at large.[8] Through their vivid descriptions of urban life, Chicago sociologists defined not only new research methods, but also new ways of comprehending the chaotic dynamics of the modern city.

Befitting its inaugural role, *The Hobo* raised fundamental questions about life in the new twentieth-century metropolis, questions that Anderson himself felt ill equipped to address. The task of drawing broader meaning from Anderson's study fell to Robert Park. "What is the matter with the hobo's mind?" Park asked in 1925. Certain that hobohemia expressed something essential about the tremendous pace of contemporary urbanization, Park defined the hobo as "a belated frontiersman, a frontiersman at a time and in a place when the frontier is passing or no longer exists." The hobo, then, was a man out of time, a relic from a world that had once rewarded freewheeling masculinity.

Accordingly, Park considered the folklore propagated by the IWW and

IBWA to be the hobo's only important contribution to American culture. These jungle songs, Park explained, belonged to a bygone age of restless individualism and enterprise when the hobo's "romantic temperament" had fueled frontier development. In the age of corporate consolidation and urban concentration, however, the hobo's "wanderlust" amounted to "locomotion for its own sake."[9] "The man whose restless disposition made him a pioneer on the frontier," writes Park in the preface to Anderson's book, "tends to become a 'homeless man'—a hobo and a vagrant—in the modern city." Those who had once subdued a continent were now society's cast-offs, rendered obsolete by the urban industrial order. Bereft of their historic mission, hoboes (and, by extension, all Americans) had to accommodate themselves to the modern age and learn to make their homes not on the hardscrabble frontier, but among the interdependent social networks of the new metropolis.

But while Park saw the hobo as an artifact from the past, he also recognized something new and distinctly modern about the homeless man. For one thing, the hobo had, in fact, made his home in the modern city. Wobbly lore glorified "the simple life of the jungles." But homeless men spent most of their time in the central cores of the nation's largest cities. Here, the hobo's world centered around a complex of hotels, restaurants, and the latest popular entertainments. His methods and frequency of travel were also distinctly modern, and his personal relationships seemed transient and superficial, far from the primary attachments that had once characterized the face-to-face communities of small-town America. Like the armies of clerks and other young white-collar workers assembling in downtown districts, homeless men on the main stem led ever-shifting lives marked by alienated labor, public sociability, and casual lodging that mocked traditional notions of home. The hobo, from this perspective, did not so much recall a frontier past as foreshadow a homeless future.[10]

In deliberating over the homeless man's significance to the new industrial metropolis, Robert Park and Nels Anderson drew upon not only their own observations, but also the previous efforts of welfare officials and reform journalists to map America's lodging house districts. Since the turn of the century, urban investigators had scoured main stem neighborhoods and studied the subcultures taking root there. As the research mounted, references to "vagrants," "tramps," and even "hoboes" began to disappear in favor of a new language of "homelessness" and "casual labor." Although the new terms were as ideologically loaded as the old ones, they appeared to be more exact, scientific, and better suited to new urban conditions. The "homeless," as the head of Chicago's Bureau of Charities put it in 1911, included "any man who has left one family group and not yet identified himself with another . . . unattached single men." The term especially applied to "those men of the homeless class who live in cheap lodging houses in the congested part of any city."[11]

By focusing attention on the main stem, the language of homelessness articulated a new perspective, one that framed the problem in terms not so much of human nature—that is, of men's eternal masculinity—as of the new urban environment itself. "Human nature," writes Robert Park in his preface to *The Hobo*, ". . . is very largely the product of the environment."[12] As part of a larger industrial civilization that tended to reduce the relations of home and work to a series of short-term contracts, the main stem manufactured homelessness like Ford produced Model T's.

The new work on urban homelessness that culminated in the publication of *The Hobo* represented a dramatic departure from the underlying assumptions and concepts that had governed responses to the "great army of tramps" in the late nineteenth century. Regardless of their politics or even their social positions, commentators from Henry George and Francis Wayland to Jack London and John James McCook interpreted tramps as failures in the human struggle to evolve up the scale of civilization. Tramps were "savages" who had somehow slipped through the cracks of the nation's civilizing institutions. The solution, then, was to fill those cracks, to prevent men from escaping "the restraints of orderly life," as McCook put it.[13] Whether the remedy prescribed was universal property ownership, the Single Tax, or tramp reformatories, the common goal was to restore tramps to the high road of civilization.

From the point of view of the twentieth-century main stem, however, the problem did not appear so simple. Indeed, to many commentators on urban homelessness, it was modern civilization itself, defined as the administered world of market exchange and wage labor, that created the pathology of the lodging house. In his magisterial history of the American family published in 1919, Arthur Calhoun worried that the highly mobile and thoroughly commercialized life of the big city was transforming the United States into a nation of hotels. "It would seem," Calhoun remarks, "that our current capitalism is willing to try the experiment of a civilization without homes."[14] For Calhoun and others, the solution lay not in a reversion to "savagery," or even a "saving touch of barbarism." Rather, most of the new commentators put their trust in civilization differently defined. The problem then became one of how to administer a bureaucratic solution without replicating the very conditions of urban alienation that had given rise to homelessness in the first place.

As "homeless" gradually replaced "tramp" in the discourses of social welfare and social science, the latter figure took on a new life in the realm of urban popular culture. The accumulated stereotypes and layers of meaning that, over the years, had rendered "tramps" and "hoboes" no longer useful as social scientific concepts (except, as in the case of Nels Anderson's book, in attracting lay readers) made them ideal for vaudeville, comic strips, and early film comedies.

Still laden with associations of unbridled masculinity, the tramp figure nonetheless changed dramatically as it moved to the center stage of urban popular entertainment. The tramp's aggression was no longer equated with unredeemed "savagery." Nor was it necessarily even put into service on behalf of a dispossessed working class. Rather, through his rough-and-tumble antics, rapid-fire humor, and cunning deceptions, the comic tramp represented the spirit of the city itself speaking in the voice of a streetwise urban bachelor. Like their homeless counterparts on the main stem and the participant observers of Chicago sociology, comic tramps highlighted the very issue of performance and role-playing in urban life. If the modern city increasingly reduced what Robert Park called "the art of life" to "skating on thin surfaces," then solving the problem of homelessness entailed far more than arranging new forms of shelter.[15] It involved no less than restoring authentic community and a coherent, integrated sense of self.

REFORMING THE MAIN STEM

Nothing so characterized early-twentieth-century proposals for addressing the problem of homelessness as the "comprehensive solution." Five-, ten-, and twenty-point plans for reforming homeless men abounded, virtually all calling for coordinated action at the local, state, and national levels. Plans differed in their specifics, but in the years before World War I, most focused on railroad trespassing and the need for labor colonies to "restore" habitual vagrants "to normal social conditions." By the time of Nels Anderson's *The Hobo,* increased calls for free employment bureaus, subsidized transportation, and a state system of workingmen's hotels signaled a new recognition that most "tramps" were indeed active workers in seasonal, migratory, and casual labor markets.[16] Reformers once bent on eradicating hobohemia now sought to manage it.

Despite the abundance of proposals, no local, state, or national authority ever attempted a comprehensive solution to homelessness in these years. Instead, action proceeded in piecemeal fashion at the municipal level, often orchestrated by private charity and welfare organizations. Like the more ambitious programs outlined in reform journals, these local efforts also sought to bring lodging house districts and their inhabitants under some kind of ameliorative authority and administrative control. Progressive Era housing and social welfare activists especially poured their energies into three major reform initiatives that, unglamorous and limited as they were, nonetheless reshaped life on the main stem: municipal lodging houses, building and sanitary codes, and philanthropic workingmen's hotels. All three reform efforts delivered new comforts and improvements to the lives of casual lodgers in the early twentieth century. But these reforms all deserve special notice as failures, for none of them removed the designation of "homeless" from the men they targeted. Indeed, by succeeding as much as they did, these initiatives further incorporated homelessness into the very fabric of urban life.

The municipal lodging house represented the most dramatic and important response to the problem of homelessness since the infamous "tramp acts" of the Gilded Age. Intended to shift the burden of overnight lodgings from the police to social welfare authorities, the municipal lodging house entailed a rehabilitative component that approximated the loftiest goals of the tramp reformatory or labor colony. "It is our hope," wrote officials of New York's Department of Public Charities in 1914, "to make the Municipal Lodging House something more than a mere sleeping quarters for tired, hungry men out of work. We aim to make it a great human repair shop, manned and equipped to rebuild the broken lives of those who enter its doors for help."[17]

By 1914 the idea of municipal lodging was over three decades old, having survived numerous depressions and waves of unemployment. Early boosters of the idea trumpeted their scheme: police stations would halt overnight lodgings and instead direct vagrants to the municipal lodging house, which would open its doors in early evening; inmates would register, strip, shower, have their clothes fumigated, and be led to rows of cots; in the early morning, inmates would arise, dress, work in the wood yard, stone pile, or on road repair before being served a breakfast of bread and coffee and released to the streets. To prevent freeloading, the lodging house would allow inmates to return for one or two additional nights only.[18]

The uniformity of this rehabilitative ideal stood in stark contrast to the diversity and unevenness of municipal lodging practices in the late nineteenth and early twentieth century. Some cities retained police stations as lodging sites but merely instituted a work test, which was often later dropped. In many cases, such as Boston in 1879 and Baltimore in 1893, such lodgings were not municipal at all, but private ventures spearheaded by charity organizations and relief committees that had secured cooperation from police.[19] Other cities, like Denver, Philadelphia, and Detroit, contracted with private agencies to operate their lodges.[20] New York City opened and ran its own municipal lodging house in 1896 after Jacob Riis had appealed to Police Commissioner Theodore Roosevelt to close police stations to homeless men. City authorities responded by providing cots on a barge floating in the East River.[21] Finally, many cities, large and small, never adopted municipal lodging at all. Despite the best efforts of various charity organizations and social reformers, for example, the cities of Pittsburgh and Philadelphia continued to lodge homeless men in police stations into the 1930s.[22]

The history of Chicago's municipal lodging house illustrates the bureaucratic confusion such experiments entailed and the ultimate futility of addressing the broader problem of homelessness through such temporary expedients. Since the 1880s, "a pavement of human bodies" regularly lined the basements, corridors, and stairwells of Chicago's police stations and other public buildings during cold winter nights.[23] In December 1901 the City Homes Association, a philanthropic organization dedicated to slum clearance and model housing, convinced city authorities to replace these facilities with its own rehabilitative lodging house located outside the Loop. The immediate result was a dramatic reduction in demand, the total number of lodgings dropping from just under ninety-three thousand in 1901 to just over eleven thousand in 1902.[24]

Declaring success, the City Homes Association transferred operations in 1903 to the police department, which subsequently relaxed interview, fumigation, and work test requirements. The following year, one investigator reported conditions at the facility to be worse than the old police stations, with dirty undrinkable water, unwashed bedding, poor food, and standing orders forbidding any talk among inmates.[25] During the depression year of 1908, lodging house operations transferred to the health department, which reimposed the four-day maximum stay and the mandatory interview, fumigation, and two hours of wood chopping per day. After the crisis passed, authorities dropped these requirements once more, only to reimpose them again during the depression of 1914–15. With the revival of flush labor markets during World War I, Chicago's municipal lodging house closed entirely for five years, subsequently reopening with the publication of *The Hobo* in 1923. Following Anderson's recommendations, the city placed the lodging house under the control of the Department of Public Welfare and emphasized its role as a social services and information bureau rather than a rehabilitation center.[26]

The history of Chicago's municipal lodging house highlights the persistent problems that faced reformers everywhere: the difficulty of separating worthy from unworthy, the inadequacy of casework solutions in the

face of mass unemployment, and the temporary nature of the rehabilitative component. Another enduring problem also vexed the lodging house.
Except during times of recession, the vast majority of homeless men did
not need to resort to municipal facilities and, in fact, possessed ample resources to support themselves in commercial lodgings. "Most [homeless
men]," explained the superintendent of New York City's municipal lodging house, "are independent in attitude and fairly self-satisfied regarding
their economic and social status."[27]

Recognizing as much, many advocates of municipal lodging also called
for bringing cheap hotels under municipal or even state control. "Private
commercial lodging houses should be under inspection of some sort," argued one charity administrator in 1904, "otherwise they may prove dangerous competitors to the [municipal] lodge."[28] With the closing of police
station lodgings, commented another official in 1907, "indecency . . . fled
to the [commercial] lodging house, and it is necessary to pursue it
there."[29]

Pursuing indecency meant not only enforcing new restrictions against
drinking, gambling, and prostitution, but also improving the very physical
surroundings of lodging house life.[30] Activists such as Lawrence Veiller,
author of the first modern building codes and founder of the National
Housing Association, believed that imposing higher standards of sanitation, construction, and design on commercial lodgings would elevate not
only the comforts of the lodgers, but also their morality. Like his contemporary Jacob Riis, Veiller believed that the immediate housing environment "leaves its ineffaceable records on the souls, minds, and bodies of
men, there to be read by all able to understand."[31] Accordingly, when
Veiller became a full-time housing official in New York City in 1898, he
brought the city's lodging houses under a new system of licensing and inspection. Lodging house owners were now required to equip their buildings with spring mattresses, clean bedding, and bathing facilities. They
also had to abide by occupancy restrictions and provide adequate lighting
and ventilation.[32]

Housing activists scored similar victories in other cities. After founding
Chicago's municipal lodging house, the City Homes Association spearheaded the passage of the city's first residential building code, which
regulated, among other things, the dozens of cheap hotels lining West
Madison Street.[33] Similar code changes occurred in San Francisco after
the earthquake of 1906. Suddenly, housing inspectors there possessed the
power to close any lodging house on sight. In 1909, the same year that
California approved a statewide housing code, authorities in San Francisco turned down three-quarters of all proposals for new lodging house

construction.[34] Minneapolis adopted even more stringent regulations in 1910. This city's code was so detailed that it specified the placement of lodging house spittoons.[35]

These new codes sought to ensure the health, safety, and very basic comforts of lodging house customers. But the regulations were also intended to drive up the cost of cheap shelter for the poorest lodgers. In 1907, when New York City strengthened its earlier code, one approving official announced that the revisions would "in all probability force every ten-cent lodging house in the city out of business."[36] At the very least, another added, the new regulations "will decrease the number of beds allowed, a fact which, together with alterations on a rather extensive scale, will undoubtedly raise the price of beds in the cheapest houses."[37] Some would have preferred to close lodging houses by edict. But, as one commentator lamented, the general public believed "that the poor man is entitled to any sort of shelter that he can pay for." The only practical solution, therefore, was to "raise the prices of the 'tramp joints.'"[38] By intervening in the lodging house market, reformers hoped to steer previously self-supporting lodgers into the arms of social welfare authorities.

Another tactic was to compete with commercial lodging houses by building inexpensive workingmen's hotels, which themselves would protect the physical and moral hygiene of lodgers. New York City real estate developer Darius O. Mills led these efforts in 1897 by opening the first philanthropic hotel for single men on Bleecker Street (fig. 5.1). "If the Mills Hotel had accomplished no other good than diminishing the number of [commercial lodging] houses by its cheap lodging rates," commented T. Alexander Hyde in 1898, "it would be enough to earn for its founder the title of 'benefactor of his kind.'" Assessing the impact of the Mills Hotel on the city's lodging house industry, Hyde determined that many of the lowest-priced establishments had been forced to close, a result that boded well for future philanthropic endeavors. "An effort should now be made to banish even the last of these dens by cooperative enterprise," wrote Hyde.[39] Such enterprise meant finding investors who were willing to settle for 5 percent returns in order to keep lodging prices low and food supplied to customers at cost. The lodger received, in the words of Darius Mills, "the fullest possible equivalent for his money." At the same time, philanthropically minded investors saw profits, even if they fell short of the returns ordinarily expected from urban real estate.[40]

Scores of hotels modeled on the Mills plan appeared on numerous main stems in the years before World War I. Chicago in particular attracted prodigious philanthropic efforts. On New Year's Day 1914, Charles G. Dawes, noted financier and future vice president under Calvin Coolidge,

Figure 5.1: With its impressive facade and enormous scale, the Mills Hotel, located on Bleecker Street in New York City, articulated the grand philanthropic design of its founder, real estate developer Darius O. Mills. When Mills opened the doors of his 1,500-room "workingmen's palace" in 1897, he promised to provide single men with clean and morally hygienic lodging at a low subsidized price. But the Mills plan had its critics. Some argued that by turning a cheap lodging house into such a respectable and visually imposing landmark, Mills's experiment actually promoted and legitimated the casual lodging practices associated with hoboes. By World War I, a growing cohort of social workers and housing activists came to view the philanthropic hotel movement as part of the larger urban problem of "homelessness." Meanwhile, lodgers themselves sometimes took a jaundiced view of the Mills experiment, as evidenced in this piece of doggerel recorded by Philip Wylie:

> The elevator boys are rude
> The porters scream and yell.
> The swill is better than the food.
> God damn the Mills hotel!

(*Municipal Affairs*, March 1899)

opened the Rufus F. Dawes Hotel on South Peoria Street in Chicago's hobohemia. Named after the founder's dead son, the Dawes Hotel cost $100,000 to build and lost money in its early years. Even so, the Dawes maintained its low prices of five cents for a ward bed, ten cents for a small room, and eight cents for meal.[41] Two years later the Young Men's Christian Association christened a nineteen-story, 1,800-room hotel located five blocks off of Chicago's Loop. With its highly centralized administration, the YMCA hotel operated twenty-eight different departments, including an employment agency, and required that every registrant "pass muster for cleanliness and decency."[42] Eclipsing even the YMCA's efforts was the Salvation Army, which ran three hotels on Chicago's main stem: the Workingman's Palace, the Reliance, and the New Century. By World War I, these large subsidized hotels, along with numerous smaller enterprises, had become a major presence in hobohemia, having forced out the "barrelhouse" lodgings entirely.[43]

Despite the energy and capital poured into such semi-charitable enterprises, the philanthropic hotel movement was laden with contradictions that severely limited its success in combating homelessness. Most obvious was the contradiction between competing for the low-priced lodging market and maintaining high levels of respectability. Marble staircases, potted plants, and impressive facades might lend an air of upscale decorum, but domesticating impoverished transients was a different matter entirely. The YMCA's emphasis on "cleanliness and decency," for example, could and did exclude those most often defined as homeless: hobo laborers who frequented the cheapest lodging houses. Fearing that model lodging houses would become "congenial places for the 'tramp and 'bum,'" some reformers urged that they "be confined to the worthy class of men who need a home—sober, industrious men of the most limited means."[44] In describing the patrons of the Mills Hotel as predominantly "drummers, clerks, professional men, artists, and laborers," philanthropic boosters often stressed the white-collar respectability of their clientele.[45]

But others called this respectability into question. After touring the Mills Hotel in 1905, one inspector declared it to be "in no respect superior" to New York's other big lodging houses.[46] Indeed, despite attempts to screen and supervise patrons, the Mills Hotel, the YMCA, and other such philanthropic establishments gained widespread reputations as hubs of homosexual activity.[47]

Philanthropic hotels also carried the more profound risk of promoting the very casual lodging practices they ostensibly sought to suppress. Although the goal of philanthropic lodging was "to make a real home for men, keeping them out of saloons and other evil resorts," the effect was often to formalize and legitimate a temporary lodging system that separated men from family life.[48] "The family is the bulwark of morals, nay, of the very life of the nation," stated T. Alexander Hyde, who considered philanthropic hotels "a necessary evil." "If hotels must exist," Hyde declared, "let them be on the plan of the Mills Hotel."[49] A writer for *Municipal Affairs* in 1899 noted numerous objections to the Mills plan, quoting extensively from a letter penned by "one of the best known of New York's philanthropic people":

> Certainly you must feel that such a life is very bad for the men who lead it, and for the community of which they form a part, and the more comforts and conveniences which are added to it, the more attractive it becomes. These men are, many of them, sons who are neglecting their parents, husbands who have deserted their wives and children, and at any rate they are men who ought to have duties and who ought to want to have homes, they are voters who ought to have a stake in the welfare of the community. What sort of creatures can they be, living in barracks, without a tie, a duty, or any happiness of any decent human sort?[50]

As this critic feared, philanthropic hotels merely raised the physical standards and increased the scale of casual lodging. Building and sanitary codes achieved the same effect. By encouraging safe, sizable, purpose-built hotels, these reforms forced less well capitalized competitors out of business and attracted the investments of those who could assemble large parcels of land and construct modern lodging houses to code. These changes furthered the ongoing differentiation of urban space by rationalizing main stem real estate markets. As land use became more uniform, architecture more specialized, and building scales larger, homeless districts became safer places in which to invest, as well as to sleep.[51] The effort to make lodging houses more respectable only served to entrench hobohemian institutions and the qualities of homelessness they supported.

In adopting the new language of homelessness, urban reformers signaled their awareness of this larger problematic. The term "homeless," as one charities official put it in 1911, did "not necessarily imply a forlorn or penniless condition."[52] Neither did it denote a lack of shelter. Rather, "homelessness" referred to a practice of casual lodging that challenged reigning middle-class conceptions of home. Simply put, while the middle class in the nineteenth century defined home in cultural terms as a locus of personal obligation and nurture, lodging house subculture laid bare the labor and market relations that undergirded all housework. By purchasing on a casual basis the services of home—shelter, food, bathing water, laundry, entertainment, and even sex—homeless men reduced a highly sentimentalized and almost sacred aspect of middle-class life to the cash nexus. Just as the descriptive terms of cheap lodging came down to price—the ten- and twenty-five-cent lodging house—so did lodging proprietors themselves renounce the cultural attributes of home in favor of bare market relations. "We are in the hotel business to make a living," explained one hotel developer to Nels Anderson.

> We give the men the best service they can pay for. We give nothing away and we ask for nothing. . . . We hold that the men have a right to criticize us and come to us if they are not satisfied with the service we give. That is business. The man who pays seventy-five cents for a bed has a right to seventy-five cents' worth of service. If a man can only pay twenty-five cents for a bed he is entitled to all that he pays for and is entitled to kick if he doesn't get it.[53]

This focus upon the commercial transactions through which homeless men bargained for domestic services lent early-twentieth-century homelessness investigations their distinctive air of "realism" and sense of exposure. Just as prostitutes commodified sex, homeless men stripped housing of the familial attributes of home in their nightly exchange of wages for rent. Commentators routinely referred to main stem districts as "false" and "artificial" environments bereft of authentic social relations. Housing activist, social welfare administrator, and University of Chicago professor Edith Abbott argued that "Madison Street is an important business street . . . [but] not a community by itself, for it is not a community at all."[54] Albert Wolfe, who published a pioneering study of Boston's lodging houses in 1906, issued an even stronger judgment. "At every possible vantage-point," Wolfe declared, "the artificiality and deceptive sham of lodging-house life—the false freedom of lodging-house irresponsibility must be attacked. . . . [T]he lodger must be given more of the *personal* element in life."[55]

In identifying lodging house life as artificial and impersonal, Wolfe and others redefined homelessness as a product of modernity. For previous students of tramp life, like John James McCook, homelessness was simply a product of nature. The "artificial man," as McCook put it, was "the average man [who] grows up to live a regular life and to work as part of it." On the road, men departed from their "artificial" routines of work and home and rediscovered a rich primal identity in which they grew "vigorous and strong" and learned to "commune with nature, [and] live and die the lord of creation again." When a husband, son, or father becomes a tramp, argued McCook, "it is all over with the artificial man. The original savage resumes its sway. Nature is triumphant."[56]

For lodging house investigators, home still operated as the binary opposite of homelessness. But the lodging house problem itself raised the question of what "home" really meant in the dawn of the twentieth century. Next to the rationalized, bureaucratized, and commodified world of the main stem, home appeared as a bastion of presocial human ties that the advances of modern urban civilization threatened to render anachronistic.

While the nineteenth-century tramp had rediscovered his primal self at the expense of civilization, the twentieth-century homeless man had gained a civilization by sacrificing home. The lodging-house problem, then, was not so much one of vermin, disease, or even vice. After all, the new moral, sanitation, and building codes, along with the appearance of cut-rate "workingmen's palaces," had served to curtail these blights upon the city. Rather, the problem of the lodging house was precisely that of the modern city itself. "The lodging-house question," wrote Albert Wolfe, "is . . . an important phase of the general problem of the home,—of the maintenance of the home ideal against certain social and economic forces which in the present era are tending strongly to disrupt it." These forces, Wolfe continued, "all conspire to produce the peculiar restlessness, the gregariousness, the nomadism, characteristic of the modern American populace. It is a population which moves rapidly with no impediments save a valise and trunk."[57] The city had become a virtual lodging house writ large, a "hotel civilization" of transients without a sense of place or permanent attachment.

In such a context, was it even possible to restore "the *personal* element in life" without sacrificing the gains of civilization? This question burned in Progressive Era critiques of the urban scene, stimulating imaginative responses from across the political spectrum.

## "THE HOTEL SPIRIT"

Henry James may not have known tramps, but he did know hotels. While visiting New York City on a blustery evening in January 1905, James ducked into the famous Waldorf-Astoria to escape the "sleet and slosh" of the streets (fig. 5.2). Within an instant an "amazing hotel-world" closed around him. Behind the swarming air and brilliant pandemonium of eating and drinking, laughing and dancing, buying and selling, the novelist detected an "admirably ordered" and "administered" set of laws governing what was, in essence, "a complete scheme of life." James himself was something of a stranger to this "hotel-civilization," for he had just returned to the United States after a twenty-year absence. With the eye of a detached "restless analyst," James surveyed a land that had become one of

Figure 5.2: When New York City's Waldorf Hotel merged with the adjoining Astoria Hotel in 1893, the newly created Waldorf-Astoria became the largest hotel in the world and set the standard for palatial elegance and luxury accommodations (ca. 1910). Entering the hotel's "endless labyrinth" in January 1905, Henry James was overwhelmed and unnerved by the "material splendour" of the place, as well as by the "extraordinary complexity and brilliancy" of the laws governing its operation. While James used the "hotel spirit" as a metaphor for commercial civilization's subtle but increasing powers of social control, others, like housing activist Lawrence Veiller, saw only decadence, lack of domesticity, and poor citizenship on display at such palace hotels as the Waldorf-Astoria. (Used by permission of The Byron Collection, © Museum of the City of New York.)

constant motion and chatter, of "immense promiscuity" and superficial associations. In America "organic social relations," especially families, fragmented and dispersed amidst the public bustle of unbridled commerce. The hotel, James decided, had become "a synonym for civilization" because more than any other form, it expressed that most "ubiquitous American force": "the genius for organization." In prompting their hotel guests into a "supremely gregarious state," the "master-spirits of management" created and fulfilled their customers' desires, manipulating them like "an army of puppets." Even more amazingly, these masters pulled their guests' strings in such a way as "to make them think of themselves as delightfully free and easy." As the repatriated author continued his travels north, south, and west over the next six months, he became even more convinced that "the hotel-spirit" was indeed "the American spirit most seeking and most finding itself."[58]

The "truth" that had seized Henry James on that winter's day in 1905—"that the present is more and more the day of the hotel"—also dawned upon other urban investigators who harbored less literary, but greater reform ambitions.[59] While James worried about the homogenizing and controlling effects of the "hotel spirit," observers like Robert Park invoked the hotel metaphor to describe the new metropolis's lack of intimacy and informal social control. "A very large part of the population of great cities," wrote Park in one of his earliest essays, "live as the people do in some great hotel, meeting but not knowing one another." "The effect," Park concluded, "is to substitute fortuitous and casual relationships for the more intimate and permanent associations of the smaller community."[60] In order to explore these new relationships and associations, Park and his students fanned out across Chicago's hotel districts, seeking to capture the spirit of urban life on its vanguard.

The sheer number and variety of hotel districts in cities across the nation enhanced the richness of Henry James's and Robert Park's metaphor. Indeed, the hotel metaphor itself derived from the simple observation that increasing numbers of Americans at every economic rung were making their homes in the most transient of accommodations. As one hotel keeper put it in 1903:

> We have fine hotels for fine people,
> good hotels for good people,
> plain hotels for plain people,
> and some bum hotels for bums.[61]

At the time of Henry James's visit, half of the "fine people" at the Waldorf-Astoria were permanent guests, wealthy persons seeking status, perfected service, and an escape from the dreary routines of housekeeping in the lavish surroundings of the world's largest hotel. "Bums," meanwhile, flocked to huge new "workingmen's palaces" not only for the price, but also for their distinct subcultural milieu. Both of these extremes—the upper- and lower-class "palaces"—came under critical attack as bastardized substitutes for home. In 1910 Lawrence Veiller went so far as to equate high-priced residential hotels with the most squalid of urban tenements: "The bad effect upon the community of a congregate form of living is by no means limited to the poorer people. Waldorf-Astoria at one end of town and 'big flats' at the other end are equally bad in their destruction of civic spirit and the responsibilities of citizenship."[62]

If the "congregate form of living" had been merely confined to the top and the bottom of the economic scale, then critics could have at least taken comfort in the great middle (formerly "producing") class, which had long provided a model of domestic stability and citizenship. Unfortunately, the hotel spirit had infected not only "fine people" and "bums," but also "good" and "plain people" as well. Indeed, professionals, businessmen, and young white-collar workers composed the fastest-growing segment of the new hotel-dwelling class. Theirs was a flourishing world of apartment hotels, residence clubs, rooming houses, light housekeeping rooms, and a multitude of other arrangements that fell under the rubric of "hotel."[63]

In 1903 the *Architectural Record* singled out the middle class—"the business Bohemians"—for blame as it recounted the phenomenal growth of residential hotels over the previous three years. Before the turn of the century, the journal stated, such buildings were virtually unknown. But since then, developers had filed 101 new proposals for various types of "apartment hotels" (including "three monster hotels for transients") with New York City's building department alone. This trend, the editors concluded, represented "the consummate flower of domestic irresponsibility" and "the most dangerous enemy American domesticity has yet had to encounter."[64]

The *Architectural Record* shared its alarm with a growing number of sociologists, economists, and students of urban life. The problem of homelessness had spilled over the boundaries of the main stem, reaching deep into the city's native-born middle class. "All that has been found true of the population of the better-class rooming-houses is true of the 'homeless man' in an exaggerated fashion," argued Harvey Zorbaugh in his study of Chicago's Near North Side. One of Robert Park's many students to examine hotel life, Zorbaugh observed that roomers "are typical of an increasingly large population in the modern city, who . . . in the ever increasing anonymity, mobility, and segregation of city life are coming to constitute a half-world, a world apart."[65]

Studying Philadelphia in 1910, economist Simon Patten similarly noted the hotel spirit catching hold of the city's salaried workers and small businessmen. These Americans, Patten wrote, had given up the responsibilities of home and family and, in so doing, had surrendered their traditional roles as civic leaders. Unlike the native-born middle class, which increasingly sought the individual comforts and freedoms of hotel life, America's new immigrants maintained home and family ideals even amidst their poverty:

> The great middle class, once the city's pride, are rapidly becoming a homeless class, living in boardinghouses or [becoming] patrons of cheap restaurants. Their homes are also childless or reduced to the one-child basis. In the America of today they have little influence and in that of tomorrow they will have no part. The future of Philadelphia is the future of its recent immigrants.[66]

Fears that America's future did indeed belong to its immigrants fed into a national discourse of "race suicide," a term coined in 1901 by sociologist Edward A. Ross and subsequently popularized by President Theodore Roosevelt. Arguing that American civilization required "good breeders" as well as "good fighters," Roosevelt warned that native-born whites' declining birthrate imperiled both white racial supremacy and the nation's global hegemony.[67] Census figures showed that those who reproduced the least—old-stock whites living in cities—were also rapidly shedding the responsibilities of homeownership. Meanwhile, southern and eastern European immigrants proved increasingly willing to save their often-meager earnings to purchase homes of their own.[68] Once again, the hotel spirit, which seemed only to infect native white populations, came in for blame. By diverting young white middle-class men and women from the path of marriage and family, wrote Albert Wolfe, casual lodging contributed to the problem of "race suicide." In racial terms, argued Wolfe, hotel dwellers were "appreciably above the population of the thickly inhabited tenement districts where birthrates are the highest." But these racially superior men and women were refusing their racial duty, rejecting Roosevelt's call to virility and fertility and embracing instead the decadent, barren, and supremely "overcivilized" world of the hotel. "The sooner marriage rescues them from the lodging-house world and its sophisticating, leveling, and contaminating influences," Wolfe declared, "the better it will be both for individuals and for society."[69]

Despite the views of Albert Wolfe, the lodging house controversy did not primarily focus on issues of overcivilization or racial decadence. Rather, commentators on the hotel spirit tended to interpret the racial characteristics of hotel dwellers as a function of their exposure to modernity. Most agreed that as African Americans and immigrants grew accustomed to urban industrial life, they, too, would succumb to what Henry James called the "ubiquitous American force" of the hotel. This force, as James noted, emancipated individuals from settled communities, but also imposed new structures and standards of its own.

As an emblem of modernity, the hotel resembled the metaphorical "iron cage" that Max Weber so memorably described as characterizing life in the modern industrial order. The bureaucratic organization of private enterprise and the state had delivered modern building codes, streamlined transportation networks, and any number of services, commodities, and entertainments to urban dwellers throughout industrialized society. But as persons became integrated, both as workers and consumers, into the large new hierarchies of administration, they entered the "iron cage" of instrumental rationality. Their world and their very lives no longer possessed their former religious or moral significance. Human beings, in Weber's words, had become "specialists without spirit, sensualists without heart." Alienated from their own primal natures and the essential bonds of family and community, individuals performed as mere bureaucratic functionaries, as cogs in the machine of capital and the state. "This nullity," Weber continued, "imagines that it has attained a level of civilization never before achieved."[70]

As an agent of this new instrumental rationality, the hotel spirit had disenchanted the "home," reducing it to the functions of "housing." Hotel dwellers thus stood on the vanguard of a modern corporate order that reached into the very seat of human belonging and identity. The rooming house, wrote Harvey Zorbaugh, is "a world of thwarted wishes, of unsatisfied longings, of constant restlessness . . . of atomized individuals, of spiritual nomads."[71] Roomers were homeless in the most profound sense of the term, for they had become estranged from their own authentic selves.

The changes at work in the new metropolis inspired little hope that these nomads would ever be able to find their way back home. "Under the conditions of modern city life," wrote another of Robert Park's students, Norman Haynor, "the establishment of a 'real home' is difficult, and in many cases impossible to attain." According to Haynor, the "real home" was the primary model of human obligation and fulfillment, balancing the needs of the individual with those of the group. In trading their "real homes" for "hotel homes," young urban dwellers exchanged responsibility for freedom and a rooted identity for alienation:

The American home is also coming to be more and more of a "hotel home," psychologically speaking. In addition to new creature comforts American families are acquiring new ways of behaving. Like the emancipated couples of the hotel world, a growing number of urbanized families are small, mobile, and loosely integrated. . . . In large cities the individual home, with its numerous activities and relative permanence, is obviously passing. . . . The detachment, freedom, loneliness and release from restraints that mark the hotel population are only to a lesser degree characteristic of modern life as a whole. The hotel is, in fact, a symbol of changes that are taking place not only in the manner and morals of American society, but wherever the influence of machine industry is felt.[72]

In describing the transformation from "real home" to "hotel home," Haynor drew from the earlier, pathbreaking work of Ferdinand Tönnies, a German sociologist who in 1887 had charted the modern shift from *Gemeinschaft,* or community, to *Gesellschaft,* or society. Tönnies characterized *Gemeinschaft* as a pre-industrial world based upon the organic bonds of family, village, and tribe. As *Gesellschaft* rose to dominance, new formal, legal, and contractual relations increasingly severed the traditional communal bonds of old. The state, the corporation, and a slew of other bureaucratic structures, argued Tönnies, had utterly redefined social life, divesting home and family of their former meanings and functions.[73]

Tönnies's ideas of *Gemeinschaft* and *Gesellschaft* provided the key conceptual building blocks of modern sociology, shaping the social scientific understanding of American homelessness in the early twentieth century. Historian Arthur Calhoun adhered to Tönnies's evolutionary account as he chronicled the changes in the American family since the colonial era. Reviewing the contemporary American "addiction" to hotel life in the third and final volume of his study, Calhoun concluded that the traditional American family was on the way out. Schools, churches, courts, and businesses had effectively usurped the offices of home. Despite occasional "cases of exaggerated familism," observed Calhoun, "the higher and more obligatory relation is to society rather than to the family." "The family goes back to the age of savagery," Calhoun explained, "while the state belongs to the age of civilization." In the modern world, he concluded, "home interests can no longer be supreme."[74]

As Calhoun and others meditated on the new hotel civilization, they frequently linked the rise of what Tönnies called *Gesellschaft* to the passing of the old-fashioned boardinghouse. Along with the informal boarding arrangements that absorbed young footloose men into family households, the boardinghouse had provided the most important substitute for home in the nineteenth century. There, nonfamily men could receive lodgings and common meals served in familylike surroundings.[75] When it was thriving, the boardinghouse evoked middle-class fears of family breakdown. But in the twentieth century, reformers esteemed boarding as a lost bulwark against the hotel spirit. "A generation ago many of the men who are now our commercial leaders made their homes as young men in old-fashioned boarding-houses," one activist wistfully recalled. "They were surrounded during the most precarious period in their lives by many of the safeguards of a good home."[76] Albert Wolfe likewise argued that with their common meals, parlor discussions, and the ever-watchful eyes of matronly keepers, boardinghouses provided "something of the home element" to anchor potentially prodigal tenants.[77]

The dramatic expansion of the migratory and white-collar workforce in the late nineteenth century overwhelmed the small-scale boardinghouse system. Armies of hoboes, clerks, salesmen, and secretaries now flocked to commercial hotel districts, where they forged new identities based upon independent living and the public commercial attractions of the street. The shift away from boarding to the impersonal and formal arrangements of the hotel was rapid and almost total. By World War I, boardinghouses had virtually disappeared from the urban scene, replaced by new enterprises that could deliver domestic services at scale.[78]

Representing the triumph of specialization, labor subdivision, and economies of scale, the new system not only accommodated more people, but also functionally divided the single boardinghouse into a specialized network of hotels and their support institutions, such as cheap cafés, restaurants, and laundries. Impersonal and contractual relations had replaced those of the integrated, face-to-face boardinghouse world. The hotel tenant, wrote Albert Wolfe, had become "simply and solely . . . a rent-paying organism." Lodging house keepers interviewed by Wolfe declared time and again that "it is best not to know too much about your lodgers."[79] Harvey Zorbaugh reported a similar perspective among Chicago's hotel managers. "The keeper of the rooming-house has no personal contact with, or interest in, his roomers," claimed Zorbaugh. "He is satisfied to collect his rents and to make a living. It is an entirely commercial consideration with him."[80] The hotel-restaurant axis had achieved a "marvelous accuracy of calculation," remarked Albert Wolfe. But managerial experts lacked the "personal element" that boardinghouse "matrons" had once used to fashion a meaningful substitute for home.[81]

As the "matron" references suggest, deeply ingrained notions of gender informed the early-twentieth-century elegy to the boardinghouse, and indeed to *Gemeinschaft* in general. Critics of hotel life imagined both the boardinghouse and *Gemeinschaft* as matriarchies. In the boardinghouse, as in the pre-industrial village, the primary relationship between mother and child provided the basis for the broader bonds of home and community. Just as *Gesellschaft*, in the words of historian Ann Taylor Allen, appeared to bring "the repression of female by male values," so, too, did the hotel seem to represent the triumph of masculine civilization over feminine culture.[82]

To some, those women who chose hotel life appeared as monstrous perversions of their sex, for they had turned against their very nature to embrace the masculine-identified hotel spirit. Rather than accept her natural role as a bearer of group identity and culture, the emancipated woman entered the hotel world, giving up "the chief source of her effectiveness and power," as the *Architectural Record* put it. "She resigns in favor of the manager," the journal explained. "Her personal preferences and standards are completely swallowed up in the general public standards of the institution." The managerial, institutional qualities of the hotel squelched personal difference and authenticity and imposed an impersonal standard on all who entered. Forfeiting "their effective influence over their husband [*sic*] and children," hotel women cast themselves and their homeless men adrift upon the iron waves of modernity.[83]

In singling out women for blame, the *Architectural Record* put its finger on one of the driving forces behind the new hotel arrangements. Turn-of-the-century women increasingly forsook their household chores in favor of a vibrant public life only found in the city. From the suffrage movement and reform organizations to women's clubs and department stores, the new urban culture afforded women unprecedented opportunities for public interaction and enterprise. For many women, the rise of the hotel engendered not alienation or anxiety, but a new optimism about the possibilities for genuine self-expression and fulfillment.[84]

Feminists like Charlotte Perkins Gilman especially viewed the demise of *Gemeinschaft* as a salutary development that would liberate women from the heavy chains of home. A former boardinghouse keeper, Gilman interpreted the new hotel spirit as the guiding force of civilization's progressive evolution toward sexual equality. She designed and publicized her own plans for a feminist hotel, where the tasks of cooking, cleaning, and child care would fall to trained professionals. For Gilman, the technologies and organization of hotel life—the very fruit of *Gesellschaft*—offered a civilized alternative to an anachronistic family structure that had exploited and oppressed women for centuries. Women, she argued, would only reclaim their labor and establish independent identities of their own in a fully developed "hotel civilization."[85]

Gilman's feminist designs inspired numerous experiments with commercial and cooperative housekeeping in the early twentieth century. In 1906 novelist and socialist proselytizer Upton Sinclair launched with great fanfare Helicon Hall, a cooperative colony modeled on the scale and organization of the modern hotel. Located in Englewood, New Jersey, the colony employed staff members (including a young janitor named Sinclair Lewis) to cook, clean, and look after the children. After four months and much publicity, fire destroyed the building, putting an end to the hotel experiment. Despite Helicon Hall's demise, Sinclair never lost his conviction that what Lawrence Veiller condemned as the "congregate form of living" was, in fact, the future of socialist housing.[86]

Indeed, the hotel provided Sinclair not only a model for Helicon Hall, but also a literary figure with which to resolve the plot of his most famous novel, *The Jungle*. The book's protagonist, Lithuanian immigrant Jurgis Rudkus, suffers virtually all the injuries that corporate capitalist society can inflict. Jurgis toils in a Chicago packinghouse, working amidst nauseating conditions for less than subsistence wages. His wife dies during the birth of their child, who subsequently drowns in the muddy streets of his slum neighborhood. Jurgis loses his job, done time in jail, and hoboes on the wageworkers' frontier before returning to Chicago as an unattached homeless man.

This portion of Jurgis's story unfolded quickly for Sinclair. But the question of how to resolve the hero's homelessness stymied the author and initiated a prolonged bout of writer's block. As a former dime novelist, Sinclair knew that he had to lead Jurgis back home. But what, in such a thoroughly despoiled social system, was home? A Wobbly novel would have ended with Jurgis joining the revolutionary fraternity of the wageworkers' frontier. A more romantic or nostalgic book might have reassigned him back to the *Gemeinschaft* world of his peasant homeland. But in 1905 Sinclair was a newly converted socialist, convinced that the progressive logic of urban industrial civilization would inexorably lead to the collective and cooperative organization of society. Thus, when Sinclair returned to his writing, he delivered his homeless protagonist to a hotel. Jurgis becomes an employee and resident of not just any hotel, but one owned by "the best boss in Chicago" who is also a state organizer for the Socialist Party. Here, Jurgis at last finds rest and, for the first time, looks with confidence upon the future, which he knows will be socialist. "Such was the new home in which Jurgis lived and worked," concludes *The Jungle*'s storyline, "and in which his education was completed."[87]

Unlike Upton Sinclair or Charlotte Perkins Gilman, most commentators, socialist or not, took little comfort in the triumph of *Gesellschaft* and denounced the hotel spirit in all its forms. In response to feminist designs for cooperative housekeeping, Sinclair's socialist friend John Spargo declared that "a glorified Waldorf Astoria is inferior to a simple cottage with a garden."[88] Robert Hunter, who converted to socialism at the same time as Sinclair, agreed, condemning hotel life at any level as "irresponsible and unnatural," "devoid as it must be of the wholesome restraints of home."[89] Socialists such as Spargo and Hunter lavished attention on the lodging house problem not in the hopes of redeeming it for cooperative living, but to condemn it as a baneful product of capitalism. After reviewing the "studied homelessness" of contemporary American city life, Arthur Calhoun concluded that "the real menace to family and home is . . . the relentless workings of the profit system." Convinced that socialism was the logical "next stage in social evolution," Calhoun predicted that the demise of capitalism would bring about the regeneration of both family life and the privately owned home.[90] Odd as it seems, most socialists heralded the return to John Spargo's "simple cottage," advocating broad-based home-ownership, rather than the cooperative utopias of Gilman or Sinclair. In 1911 the *Appeal to Reason*—the very Socialist Party newspaper that had first published *The Jungle* in serial form—vigorously declared that "Socialism will enable EVERY FAMILY IN ALL THE WORLD TO OWN A HOME."[91]

Reducing urban densities and rolling back the congregate form of living appealed not only to socialists but also to a loosely organized coalition of housing activists, urban planners, home economists, architects, developers, and others who came together under the banner of "the new suburban ideal."[92] Unlike the socialists, these reformers did not declare war against the profit system, but rather endeavored to make mass homeownership part of that system. The professionals and managers who promoted suburban living thrived in Max Weber's "iron cage" and embodied the very essence of *Gesellschaft*. They did not, therefore, seek a return to the pre-industrial village. Neither did they share Henry James's modernist faith in the potential of the city's diversity and dynamism to emancipate the human spirit. James, after all, opposed modernity's "master-spirits of management" precisely because their excessive social control always threatened to extinguish individual difference and freedom.

Suburban boosters, on the other hand, sought to harness what James called the American "genius for organization" to the task of private home building. The same technological, managerial, and financial innovations that had created the magnificent hotel world of the Waldorf-Astoria could also be used to assemble new suburban enclaves that functioned as part of the metropolitan order. Grosvenor Atterbury, general architect of the Russell Sage Foundation's Forest Hills Gardens plan in New York and foremost advocate of suburbanization, argued as early as 1906 that reducing the cost of the single-family home was the only true solution to the modern housing problem. Atterbury contended that achieving such economies in home construction meant applying the techniques of mass production to the building industry. "Carried to its logical conclusion," the architect explained in a charities journal, "this principle would result in a system of standard dwelling manufacture . . . like that which has already given the worker his cheap shoes, and his ready-made suit of clothes."[93] With its inexpensive undeveloped land, the urban periphery offered a new frontier upon which the "master-spirits of management" could reengineer the American home.

Reformers acknowledged, however, that proprietorship on the suburban frontier held far different meanings than it did in the days of the homesteading pioneers. Relying on institutional financing, suburban homeownership was a form of consumption that delivered the trappings of *Gemeinschaft* with all the efficiency and coordinated effort of *Gesellschaft*. No longer did ownership of land and house endow citizens with economic independence or a productive shelter against unemployment. Rather, single-family homes, as numerous suburban enthusiasts stressed, instilled in their owners a sense of familial belonging, rootedness, and place. The eventual return to mass homeownership, Arthur Calhoun remarked, would signal "the evolution of a spiritualized family based not on economic necessity but on aesthetic, idealistic, spiritual values and loyalties."[94] Garden City advocate Annie Diggs argued in a similar vein in 1902 when she declared that the suburban home would provide an almost spiritual antidote to "the essential sin of divorcing the children of men from their Mother Earth."[95] Alienated from Mother Earth as productive property, suburban homeowners would return to the land as consumers of an exchangeable commodity.

Just as proprietorship would heal the alienation arising from the hotel spirit, physical separation from the diversity and publicity of urban life would restore authentic social ties. While lodgers and roomers sought basic domestic services on the streets or in neighboring cafés, shops, saloons, and laundries, suburban residents would maintain these services within the context of the family. Although it relied on organizational and technological innovation, the suburban ideal was also a regressive endeavor to remove the home from public commercial life, to privatize domestic consumption, and to reestablish the familial intimacy that had once characterized the sentimental home. Isolated from urban commerce, industry, and recreation, the suburban home represented a retreat from the anonymous and gregarious excitement of hotel civilization.

As philanthropic organizations increasingly brought their ambitious design programs to life in the form of model working-class suburbs, social scientists like Robert Park and Ernest Burgess began to imagine urban growth as an ever-expanding series of concentric circles radiating outward from the city center.[96] Residences would naturally flow to the new rings, while businesses and industries would fill the backwash left in the old ones. Indeed, by the 1920s lodging house districts, with their mixed uses and floating populations, appeared to Burgess as "disorganized" zones awaiting "reorganization" into single-use commercial, administrative, or manufacturing hubs.[97]

With powerful, well-financed, and highly articulate advocates working in its favor, the suburban ideal eclipsed the hotel spirit after World War I, becoming the norm against which the deficiencies of the hotel world were measured. Apart from material feminists like Charlotte Perkins Gilman and idiosyncratic socialists like Upton Sinclair, lodging house advocates lacked a coherent voice and organized movement. Instead, individual hotel dwellers continued to vote with their feet, choosing the congregate form of living for reasons of economy or lifestyle.

Of course, one sustained and compelling critique of the suburban ideal did attract much attention during the early twentieth century. But the source of this critique—the vaudeville stage—hardly inspired reverence. Indeed, the popular entertainments that daily trumpeted the superiority of city life over the suburbs served only to undermine the credibility of urban advocacy and focus anti-urban ire. It did not help matters that vaudeville's assault on home and family came largely in the guise of a slovenly homeless man. With his grotesque features and aggressive demeanor, the early-twentieth-century comic tramp appeared to fulfill Francis Wayland's Gilded Age stereotypes about "savage" men of the road. But the antics of tramp comedy, vulgar and id-driven as they were, played out a cultural logic and spirit belonging to the twentieth century, not the nineteenth. Born in the working-class concert saloon as a figure of betrayed republicanism, the comic tramp moved to the center stage of urban popular culture at the turn of the century, becoming one of the era's most remarkable emblems of modernity.

## THE COMIC TRAMP

In its indictment of the hotel spirit, the *Architectural Record* noted that virtually all of New York's apartment hotels were located in theater districts, indicating just how thoroughly the new hotel world was enmeshed in the commercial amusements of the city.[98] It is fitting, therefore, that the homeless man would find his most memorable depiction not in the pages of reform journals, but in the commercial entertainments that formed such a vital part of hotel civilization. While *Charities* and the *Survey* offered sober-minded glimpses into the lodging house world, comic strips, cheap novels, advertisements, films, and especially vaudeville saturated the city with humorous representations of homeless men, making the comic tramp, in Charles Musser's words, the "single most popular figure in turn-of-the-century culture."[99] "In the first decade of the 1900s," recalls Douglas Gilbert, "tramp comics swarmed through vaudeville almost as a national symbol; legit musical stages were heavy with them; and joke magazines and newspaper strips . . . detailed their haphazard lives with jesting abandon."[100] Frederick Opper's "Happy Hooligan," Zim's "Weary Willie," W. C. Fields's "tramp juggler," and, of course, Charlie Chaplin's legendary "Little Tramp" led the parade of early-twentieth-century comic figures that drew their inspiration from the main stem.[101]

The tramp vogue grew to such proportions that charity and law enforcement officials accused vaudeville and the comic press of hampering their efforts to curtail homelessness. "Instead of instituting measures against the tramp," lamented one frustrated anti-vagrancy activist in 1908, the American people have "raised him to the heights of a national joke." While acknowledging that "the stage tramp is the most irresistibly funny of comic characters," this critic charged tramp comedy with encouraging a "tolerant and indulgent" attitude toward the homeless, thus dampening public enthusiasm for reform.[102]

Critics had reason to worry. The comic tramp—like the numerous Irish, Jewish, blackface, and other caricatures with whom he shared the stage—reveled in the promiscuous freedoms of urban life. If vaudeville represented, in literal translation, "the voice of the city," then the comic tramp was the voice of vaudeville. Just as the vaudeville show itself mimicked city life with its rapid succession of diverse acts, so, too, did the vaudeville tramp embody the physical excitements, oversize appetites, and jarring dislocations of urban culture. Like homeless men on the main stem, comic tramps recklessly abandoned any semblance of home, authenticity, or even a private self in favor of the exterior pleasures and duplicitous play of the streets. In 1914 one modernist theater critic summarized this new comic type:

He is a happy, tattered, slovenly, red-nosed rogue; glorying in his detestation of work and water and gaily oblivious of the rights of property. He lies for the pure joy of lying and his hunger and thirst are absolutely unappeasable. His costume has become traditional. A battered hat, through which his hair sticks out; the remnants of a once black coat; ragged pants, too large for him, supported by a string round the waist, from which is suspended his trusty tomato can; a gaping pair of shoes cover sockless feet—the whole effect being surmounted by a grin of inordinate proportions which seems to stretch nearly round his head. He is full of chuckling mirth and has a vocabulary large enough to start a new language. He has a super-ingenuous manner, which he especially assumes when he most intends to deceive, while the excuses that he can give for avoiding anything which looks in the least like work may be contradictory but are without end.[103]

As this passage suggests, tramp comedy, for all its reference to modern urban life, operated within a tradition and an aesthetic that stretched back to the carnival celebrations of early modern Europe. Like tramp humor, the transgressive play and insubordinate comedy of carnival carried an implicit critique of the dominant social order. Under certain conditions, carnival's festive outbursts could actually spark popular resistance to established authority. Under other conditions, the festival's implied critique defused oppositional politics, allowing people to "blow off steam" in an officially sanctioned and circumscribed ritual. Regardless of its ultimate political meaning, carnival drew its symbolic power by figuratively overturning the rules, hierarchies, and presumptions that ordinarily governed the world.[104]

Like tramp comedy, the focus of carnival's humor was the human body, which it twisted and distorted into grotesque configurations. As Mikhail Bakhtin explains in his seminal study of the "carnivalesque" in the novels of François Rabelais, the classical body represents official culture by appearing smooth, polished, closed, and finished. In the classical pose, the body remains separate and distinct from its surroundings and is animated only by a pair of thoughtful eyes signifying individual rationality and autonomy. The grotesque body, on the other hand, repudiates these limits, expanding to outlandish proportions. Take, for example, the publicity photograph of Nat M. Wills, the most popular tramp comedian at the turn of the century (fig. 5.3). Here, "the Happy Tramp," as Wills was known, brings together the key elements of the grotesque body. Rather than smooth finished lines, Wills's portrait is "all protuberances and orifices, shoots and branches," his hair flying out from his head, his coat frayed and jutted, his eyes bulging and vacant, and, most important for the purposes of the grotesque, his mouth open, the space between his teeth almost gaping.[105] "The grotesque face," remarks Bakhtin, "is actually reduced to the gaping mouth; the other features are only a frame encasing this wide-open bodily abyss."[106]

Figure 5.3: Taken in 1907 at the height of his popularity, this publicity photograph of Nat M. Wills, "the Happy Tramp," captures the look of vaudeville's premier tramp impersonator. Born in 1873, Wills was among the first generation of variety theater comics to make the shift from "blackface" to "grayface," thereby inventing a new stage character. As Wills's frayed and wide-eyed appearance suggests, tramp comedy incorporated elements of the grotesque into its aesthetic, indulging in the inversive and insubordinate play that marks the carnivalesque. As products of nineteenth-century working-class culture, performers like Wills initially targeted corporate capital in their comic parodies. But as working-class variety gave way to vaudeville, which adhered to urban middle-class tastes and standards, Wills and others increasingly aimed their barbs at the sentimental home and the Victorian restraints of "character." Although Wills credited the free, unrestrained, and spontaneous humor of real tramps with inspiring his own stage routine, the actor depended heavily on professional joke writers for his material. (Used by permission of The Billy Rose Theatre Collection, the New York Public Library for the Performing Arts, Astor, Lenox, and Tilden Foundations.)

If the comic tramp harked back to the fools and clowns of medieval Europe, he also gave evidence of a more immediate ancestry. In many ways, turn-of-the-century tramp comedy merely updated that most popular of nineteenth-century carnivalesque forms, the minstrel show. Most tramp actors had, in fact, originally performed in blackface, adjusting their burnt-cork makeup to fashion a new urban type. According to Douglas Gilbert, the blackface acts of vaudeville, which themselves had been adapted from older minstrel performances, "were brother comics of the tramps . . . the grease color and occasional accent [being] about the only changes found."[107]

While differing in important ways, both tramp and blackface routines ridiculed and brutally caricatured members of oppressed groups, denying representation of their basic humanity. In so doing, these routines sanctioned and perpetuated the subordination of those they portrayed. But comic tramps followed in the nimble footsteps of their minstrel predecessors by also encouraging audience identification. To the degree that spectators could see themselves in the characters portrayed onstage, they became implicated in the countercultural and anti-authoritarian antics performed there. When a tramp or blackface monologuist took aim at the high and mighty, deflating their pretensions through cunning, guile, feigned naïveté, or grotesque parody, audience members roared with approval, while also maintaining a sense of their own superiority.[108]

Whereas blackface minstrelsy arose in the antebellum era to explore and confirm the racial differences upon which slavery was predicated, tramp comedy emerged in the Gilded Age as an articulation of the new class divisions created by universal wage labor. The tramp characters that first took stage in Gilded Age concert saloons thus served as figures of a despoiled republican legacy, a legacy that the labor press and popular dime novels also struggled to keep alive. Like the tramps that appeared so often in working-class print culture, tramps of the stage lamented the loss of patriarchal identity and republican independence and trumpeted their own worthiness as honest "producers."[109] By 1890 the tramping worker, down on his luck but still "honest," had largely disappeared from the stage in favor of the tramp as tramp—that is, as a confirmed member of a despised and rejected subculture.

In his comic guise, the tramp took on lighter shades of black. As tramp performers blackened up, they played out the cultural logic of the nineteenth-century labor movement. "Wage slavery," this logic held, threatened to reduce white workers to the status of subordinate African Americans. By donning burnt cork to portray countercultural lower-class whiteness, the stage tramp perpetuated this imaginative link between class subordination and racial degradation. In his subordinated and degraded state, the tramp performer was now free to ridicule and lampoon the very pieties about home and work that earlier portrayals of "honest workingmen" had upheld.

The success of such a performance, however, depended upon an audience capable of identifying with the outcasts portrayed onstage. In the plebian rowdiness of the nineteenth-century concert saloon, such audience identification posed little problem. But as enterprising businessmen began to refashion variety theater in the 1880s and 1890s to attract a broader urban audience, one that included middle-class women and families, much of the concert saloon's lowbrow repertoire suddenly seemed inappropriate.

Ambitious show business entrepreneurs like B. F. Keith and Edward F. Albee endorsed only entertainment that would "appeal to all classes of people equally" and not give offense to middle-class theatergoers especially.[110] These entrepreneurs invented vaudeville by consolidating independent variety houses into integrated networks of purpose-built theaters, contracted performers, booking agents, and managers. Such economies of scale required a mass audience, which, in turn, meant carefully selecting from among the bawdy and insubordinate routines that made up the working-class variety show. Theater managers tended to shun acts that were too racy or subversive for fear of driving away middle-class customers. On the other hand, shows entirely devoid of what vaudeville historian Kathryn J. Oberdeck calls "popular realism"—that is, visceral representations of lower-class urban types—failed to attract middle-class spectators, who enjoyed the spirited diversity of urban life.[111] In this middle ground between refinement and vulgarity, high culture and low, the turn-of-the-century vaudeville act was born.

As an irreclaimably vulgar and indeed "savage" type, the comic tramp almost failed to make the transition to vaudeville. Comic actor Lew Bloom, who claimed to be "the first stage tramp in the business," recalled an early performance in 1885 that had "gone big" with the crowd but infuriated the theater's manager. "I guess it must have been so lifelike that the manager thought it was too shocking," Bloom explained. The argument ended in a fistfight and Bloom's arrest—"a fine martyrdom for the sake of art," as the *New York Telegraph* put it.[112]

Tramp actors like Bloom took for granted their popularity with the cheap seats, but also understood that they had to finesse the charge of vulgarity and insubordination. The claim to "lifelike" realism, such as that made by Bloom, was an especially common strategy for justifying tramp humor. Comic tramps routinely characterized their acts as authentic and even edifying depictions of the homeless life. Many even told elaborate tales about how they had conducted their own in-depth investigations of tramp subculture in order to limn true-to-life stage personas. Walter Jones claimed to have patterned his popular "Charley Tatters" character on a particular tramp he spied from a train window. He "was such a good type of his class," recounted Jones, "that I got out my pencil and sketched him on the spot."[113] Charlie Chaplin told different stories about the genesis of his Little Tramp character. But one early tale involved meeting a hobo in San Francisco's South of Market district. Over dinner and drinks (which Chaplin paid for), the hobo expanded on the irresponsible joys of the road. Chaplin delighted in the conversation, taking in the man's gestures, expressions, and mannerisms. "He was rather surprised when we parted, because I thanked him so much," recalled Chaplin. "But he had given me a good deal more than I had given him, though he didn't know it."[114]

What this story gave Chaplin's Little Tramp was a justifying authenticity that all tramp comedy required. "Mine for realism" was the motto of Nat Wills, whom critics considered "the best impersonator of tramp characters on the American stage."[115] Attributing his stage success to his extensive study of tramp life, Wills regaled reporters with stories about marching in Coxey's Army, traveling in boxcars, and sleeping in flophouses, all for the sake of his art. Wills professed to be "scientifically" accurate in his portrayal of the Happy Tramp, maintaining that he developed the character through several years of participant observation. The actor even favorably compared his own ethnographic eye to that of Josiah Flynt Willard, the nation's premier sociological authority on tramp subculture at the turn of the century.[116] Claiming to have worked, like Willard, for the police as an "expert advisor" on tramps, Wills time and again expressed great sympathy for the homeless and urged his audiences to see the bright side of the road:

> I have gone among them to get material for my impersonations, and I want you to believe me when I say some of the most charming gentlemen it has been my good fortune to meet were tramps; men who had no visible means of support, no homes, no families, no friends, no professions, and no place in the social scheme. These men have been keen-witted humorists, deep-thinking philosophers and profound students both of nature and the abstract problems of the universe. . . . The funniest tramps I have ever seen were off the stage.[117]

Such glowing descriptions of the "real" tramp helped to legitimate the stage tramp's eccentric view of the world, encouraging audiences to identify with his insubordinate play. By characterizing their objects of parody as possessing special insight, actors such as Wills betrayed not their "scientific" knowledge, but their own working-class backgrounds that predisposed them to take kindly to tramps. Few tramp comics, or vaudevillians generally, came from middle-class homes. The vast majority grew up with a firsthand understanding of tramp life, an understanding born not of study, but of personal experience with the vagaries of wage labor. Indeed, with their peripatetic lifestyles, seasonal unemployment, and penchant for cheap lodging houses, vaudeville actors closely resembled the migratory workers and homeless men they lampooned onstage.[118]

Such resemblance proved an asset before plebian audiences, which thrived upon the comic tramp's bottom-up critiques of corporate capital. Such class-specific humor defined working-class variety comedy, and some of it survived the bowdlerization of vaudeville, filtering into performances intended to "appeal to all classes of people equally." "I think the men who run our big railroads are only a little different from cannibals," joked Nat Wills as the Happy Tramp. "You see, cannibals cut men up to eat and the owners of railroads cut men down so they can't eat."[119]

Despite the occasional jibe aimed at Andrew Carnegie, J. P. Morgan, or John D. Rockefeller, tramp comedy generally did not emphasize the battle between capital and labor. Indeed, the comic tramp managed to survive the shift from working-class variety to vaudeville only by pointing the spotlight away from class distinctions and toward those differences that increasingly separated urban folk from the rest of America.

The primary object of tramp parody was not work, but home, not the boss or the owner, but the wife and the mother-in-law. While poking fun at the foibles of city life and satirizing the array of urban types, vaudeville never accepted country or suburban living as a viable alternative. Like early motion pictures, which were first exhibited in variety theaters, vaudeville heaped contempt both upon country rubes who dared to venture into the city and city couples who foolishly traded their hotel apartments for suburban homes.[120] Comic tramps routinely outwitted day-tripping shoppers and newcomers to the city who easily fell prey to sidewalk confidence games. While tramps often concluded their routines on the receiving end of an Irish cop's billy club, they also frequently triumphed in their capers. At any rate, they always succeeded in disturbing the peace, especially in quiet country cottages or suburban homes. These lords of misrule disdained the conventions of marriage, child rearing, and domesticity almost as much as they detested work. In tramp comedy, home was an intolerable prison that separated men from the carefree pleasures of the city. As one common gag put it:

Dusty Roads: All married folks are not unhappy.

Weary Will: Only the men.[121]

Such humor went over well in the cheap seats. Indeed, Nat Wills won favor not only among critics, but also in the "peanut gallery," which "whooped it up" whenever the comic appeared on stage.[122] Despite the efforts of show business managers to create a broad-based entertainment industry that adhered to middle-class values, tastes, and interests, vaudeville remained dependent upon the patronage of working-class men, who still made up the majority of theatergoers. According to one survey conducted in 1911, 4 percent of New York's vaudeville audience even categorized itself as "vagrant," "gamin," or "leisured."[123] Such sporting types no doubt cheered Nat Wills as a champion of irresponsible bachelorhood. But the comic tramp also appealed to that larger group of male workers who defined their masculinity in relation to other men, rather than to home and family.

It is no wonder, then, that IWW songsters and soapboxers like J. H. Walsh, Mac McClintock, and Richard Brazier raided vaudeville for the song parodies and comic routines that they made part of Wobbly lore. Ruthlessly ridiculing the sentimental home and celebrating unfettered masculinity, the *Little Red Songbook* shares a common heritage with the *New Tramp Joke Book*. Both trace their roots to working-class variety theater.[124] While vaudeville censored tramp comedy's stinging critiques of capital, Wobbly propagandists liberated the suppressed material and refashioned it into a masculine romance of the road that was also a call to revolution. Far from appealing "to all classes of people equally," Wobbly humor took hold only among those hardened male workers who equated the rejection of women's sphere with labor's emancipation.

Instead of preaching revolution, vaudeville fanned the flames of the hotel spirit, inviting middle-class spectators to join its playful rebellion against sentimental domesticity. Those middle-class men and women who most enjoyed vaudeville were also those who increasingly made their homes in rooming houses, apartment hotels, and light housekeeping rooms. These hotel dwellers saw an important piece of their own identity played out on the vaudeville stage, especially by comic tramps. As Nat Wills and others ran roughshod over home and family life, white-collar patrons did not recoil in horror, but rather cheered the inversive play that legitimated their own departure from domestic conventions. In 1903, for example, middle-class theatergoers enthusiastically supported *A Son of Rest*, a musical comedy vehicle that effectively catapulted Nat Wills from vaudeville to "legitimate" theater and film. The comedy featured Wills as a tramp who impersonates a woman's absent husband in order to defraud her elderly father of $2 million. The confidence game succeeds, enriching the Happy Tramp and, of course, destroying any semblance of domestic order or integrity.[125] Just before the curtain falls, an impeccably dressed and out-of-character Nat Wills appears onstage, inviting applause for his skillful impersonation of a tramp who himself had proven an expert impersonator.

The comedy of parody and impersonation appealed to urban audiences imbued with the hotel spirit. To many observers, especially those associated with Chicago sociology, the gregariousness and public display associated with hotel living had transformed the city into a theater writ large, where everyday social encounters involved elaborate performances and self-representations. Living "as people do in some great hotel," remarked Robert Park, urban dwellers lacked intimate knowledge of each other and related instead through "conventional signs—fashion and 'front.'" The symbolic interaction and role-playing theories that so characterized Chicago sociology sprang from what Park called the urban "art of life," the theatrical and performative aspects of city living.[126]

Before the rise of hotel civilization, sentimental ideologies of home had nurtured the concept of "character," a model of selfhood that emphasized qualities of interiority, autonomy, stability, and integrity. Desperate to show "good character," Gilded Age tramps like William Aspinwall instead raised the specter of the confidence man who masked his ill intentions beneath a glib facade. As the hotel spirit took hold, the concept of "character" gave way to a new model of "personality" that stressed fluidity, malleability, and performance. Presuming a certain degree of theatricality to everyday life, city dwellers made their peace with the confidence man, accepting him as a roguish aspect of their own urban identities.[127] Promoting what critics called a "tolerant and indulgent" attitude toward tramps, actors such as Nat Wills encouraged audiences to see themselves in the outrageous confidence games played out onstage. For those who delighted in the role-playing parodies of A Son of Rest, winning confidence through the skillful manipulation of a "front" was simply part of the urban "art of life."[128]

The homeless man proved an ideal figure with which to explore this new performative model of selfhood, for no other urban type depended so heavily on the art of self-representation. The tramp, observed Hutchins Hapgood in 1910, "is thoroughly a public man[,] . . . as public as the street. All the world is admitted to his inner life."[129]

Whether socially transparent or merely guarding a polished front, homeless men shrewdly recognized the stakes of their performances. As

Jack London explained in 1907, every hobo, at one time or another, re-
sorted to theatrics in order to "get by":

Upon his ability to tell a good story depends the success of the beggar. First
of all, and on the instant, the beggar must "size up" his victim. After that, he
must tell a story that will appeal to the particular personality and temperament of that particular victim. . . . As in a lightning flash he must divine the
nature of the victim and conceive a tale that will hit home. The successful
hobo must be an artist. He must create spontaneously and instantane-
ously—and not upon a theme selected from the plenitude of his own imagination, but upon the theme he reads in the face of the person who opens
the door.[130]

London's readers were well familiar with the beggar's art, for virtually
every major study of homeless life, from the Elizabethan literature of
"roguery" to the modern ethnographies of Josiah Flynt Willard and Nels
Anderson, cataloged the various ploys and ruses associated with mendi-
cancy.[131] But latter-day writers such as London, Willard, and Anderson
added a new conceit to this discourse of impersonation and improvisation.
These ethnographers not only observed homeless subculture; they became
part of it, dressing, talking, and behaving in character as they conducted
their investigations. As former hoboes, London and Anderson were "at
home" among the down-and-out and, in fact, often felt themselves to be
participant observers in middle-class culture.[132] Even they, however, remarked on the performative qualities of their investigations.[133] Indeed, the
genre of tramp ethnography became popular in the early twentieth century
precisely because it attended to the subjective experiences of role-playing
as much as it did to the objective conditions of homelessness.[134]

The first and most famous tramp ethnographer was Josiah Flynt
Willard, who originally donned the disguise of the tramp in protest
against what he called the "feminine atmosphere" of his genteel home.[135]
Raised in a matriarchal household headed by his strong-willed aunt
Frances Willard, cofounder of the Women's Christian Temperance Union,
the rebellious nephew escaped to the road, first as a rambling teenager,
then as a professional journalist. Emancipated from home, Willard became "a finished actor" who delighted in dressing up, changing his demeanor and tone of voice, and learning the various languages of the
underworld.[136] Along with Jack London, who dedicated his book *The
Road* to him, Willard popularized the genre of cross-class undercover investigation at precisely the time when tramp comedy was sweeping vaudeville.[137] Like tramp comics, masquerading journalists such as Willard
lavished attention on the art of impersonation, discussing their performa-

tive techniques right along with their observations of the homeless life. When Nat Wills compared himself with Willard, he did so to stress his own astonishing expertise as a tramp impersonator, a skill that Willard's ethnographic studies also dramatized.

Although Willard celebrated himself as a refugee from the Victorian restraints of "character," his battle with alcoholism, followed by his death in 1907 at the age of thirty-eight, raised speculation that the pioneer of "realistic sociology" might have taken his game too far.[138] In the eulogizing commentary that accompanied his posthumously published autobiography, Willard's literary associates explored the tramp investigator's disturbingly intense devotion to disguise and role-playing. While most obituaries suggested that Willard had "gone native," his closer friends saw him as trapped in a never-ending cycle of impersonation and performance. Willard never returned home from the road, remarked poet Arthur Symons, because home really did not exist for him. Utterly lacking an inner life or a coherent, stable sense of self, Willard lived in "complete abandonment to his surroudings."[139] The famous tramp ethnographer only really felt at ease, another friend explained, when "given the *Mask of No Identity.*"[140] Just as the hotel spirit had estranged urban dwellers from the font of human belonging and attachment, so had the theater of the streets alienated Willard from his own authentic self. The play of personality, intimated Willard's eulogizers, exacted a toll in the loss of coherent identity.

If investigative disguise threatened individual autonomy and difference, so did the commercial entertainments of the city, albeit on a far different order. Henry James might have noted as much if he had gone to a variety show instead of the Yiddish theater during his 1905 tour of America. Behind the scenes at vaudeville, James would have found the "masterspirits of management" working feverishly to manipulate their customers' expectations and desires, just as they had with the "army of puppets" at the Waldorf-Astoria. A critical element of hotel civilization, vaudeville was the first modern show business, applying what James called the American "genius for organization" to popular amusement. Booking agencies, theater chains, talent pools, and standardized performance requirements transformed the informal and unpredictable variety stage into a "performance machine," with each fifteen-minute act serving as an interchangeable part.[141] "With its emphasis on bureaucratic organization and enormous scale," explains Robert W. Snyder, the corporate empire of vaudeville was "part of America's second industrial revolution."[142]

While vaudeville celebrated the liberation of "personality" from the constraints of "character," the gregariousness and hilarity of variety shows were the administered outcomes of a show business bureaucracy. Whereas earlier theater customs encouraged a lively give-and-take between audiences and performers and even between audience members themselves, vaudeville darkened the house, elevated the players, and insisted on strict audience decorum, discouraging the kind of enthusiastic applause often heard from the "peanut gallery."[143] To keep audiences in rapt attention, writes vaudeville historian Albert F. McClean Jr., stage comedians honed "their fifteen-minute performances as precisely and as skillfully as diemakers, knowing that in their specialty there was no middle ground between success and failure." "Success" in this instance meant contagious mirth as a uniform audience response, with no silences, repartees, ambiguities, or pauses for reflection permitted.[144]

Although Nat Wills attributed the popularity of his impersonation to the tramp's native "spontaneity," Wills, in fact, left nothing to chance. Instead, the comic subscribed to *Madison's Budget,* a trade journal of gags and song parodies, and retained a stable of professional joke writers to keep his material fresh and to scout ahead on the vaudeville circuit for pertinent local matter.[145] As performers like Wills standardized their routines, audiences struggled to retain the autonomy and initiative they had previously enjoyed in working-class variety. While patrons remained active agents in their own amusement, they did so against the design of vaudeville, which restricted the parameters of participation and encouraged the passive consumption of staged entertainment.

Eventually, the administered laughter of show business dulled the rough edges of tramp comedy. After World War I, vaudeville gave way to new mass entertainments, especially the motion picture and then radio, that sought to broaden their appeal beyond urban audiences. As the "voice of the city" fell silent, so did the comic tramp's raucous and eccentric celebrations of the hotel spirit.

Tramp comedy remained as popular as ever through the 1920s, and second-generation tramp comics such as Charlie Chaplin and Emmett Kelly enjoyed a celebrity far exceeding that of their predecessors such as Nat Wills and Lew Bloom. But these new tramp characters succeeded only by accommodating themselves to the suburban ideal. Chaplin's early films, especially those he made at Keystone, feature a vulgar, brutish, and libidinous tramp whose bawdy slapstick owed much to Nat Wills. Public criticisms and private warnings from the National Board of Censorship, however, inspired Chaplin to refine his film persona after 1916, when middle-class suburbanites began attending movies in large numbers. The new Charlie, one affectionately referred to as the Little Tramp, mixed comedy with pathos, slapstick with romance, and redefined the tramp's struggle as a thwarted search for domestic happiness (fig. 5.4).[146]

Figure 5.4: Merely one of many characters played by Charlie Chaplin during his early career, the Little Tramp emerged by 1915 as Chaplin's trademark film persona. While Chaplin told different stories about how he conceived the Little Tramp, the character was actually part of a larger comic tramp craze that dated back to the 1890s. The violent and bawdy antics that characterized Chaplin's early films at Keystone and Essanay eventually gave way to more refined and fully rounded performances, such as that depicted in this film still from *City Lights* (1931). Chaplin's use of homelessness as a source of pathos, as well as license, coincided with the decline of "hotel civilization" and the emergence of suburbia as a middle-class norm. Unlike other tramp characters who attempted the transition to film, such as Nat Wills's "Happy Tramp" and Frederick Burr Opper's "Happy Hooligan," Chaplin won enduring renown by transcending the urban humor and aesthetics of early tramp comedy. Such character development also allowed Chaplin to broaden the range of his social and political commentaries, as evidenced in his most famous feature, *Modern Times* (1936). (Used by permission of © Roy Export Company Establishment.)

Figure 5.5: Like Charlie Chaplin's Little Tramp, Frederick Burr Opper's "Happy Hooligan" changed dramatically as the "hotel spirit" associated with hobohemia increasingly gave way to the suburban ideal of nuclear family life. As a cartoonist for *Puck* in the 1880s and 1890s, Opper had won acclaim by lampooning the domestic concerns of the "Suburban Resident" (sometimes named "Howson Lot"), including his fear of tramps. In 1899 Opper created the "Happy Hooligan" for the Hearst papers, prompting vehement criticisms from turn-of-the-century moralists who objected to the strip's vulgarity and sadism. As the character's simian features and Gaelic dialect suggest, Opper's tramp drew upon the racialized stereotypes of Irish "savagery" that had originally informed the "tramp menace" of the 1870s. During the 1920s, however, the "Happy Hooligan" received a makeover, losing his tattered rags (though not his tomato can hat) and gaining a natty bow tie, clown-checked jacket, and smooth black pants without the patches. By the early 1930s, this once grotesque tramp had acquired a home, a dog, and a white picket fence to go along with his heart of gold. (Frederick Burr Opper, "Happy Hooligan," 1904)

Similarly, when Emmett Kelly developed his circus clown routine in the late 1920s, he strove to depict his "Weary Willie" "as a forlorn and melancholy little hobo who always got the short end of the stick and never had any luck at all, but who never lost hope and just kept on trying."[147] By the 1920s even such outrageous tatterdemalions as Frederick Burr Opper's "Happy Hooligan" had cleaned up their acts, trading in their dirty rags and slapstick humor in favor of ill-fitting suits and heartwarming story-lines (fig. 5.5).[148] The comic tramp so completely shed his earlier carni-valesque associations that he even began gracing the cover of the *Saturday Evening Post*. In the hands of Norman Rockwell, the sadness and loneli-ness of the down-and-out became a source of gentle, rather than vulgar, humor.[149] Such middlebrow humor required the comic tramp to recover his interiority and depth of feeling. Instead of celebrating the hotel spirit, these new characters emphasized the pathos of homelessness and the uni-versal need for belonging and attachment.

The sentimentalized comic tramp joined a pantheon of new literary and folkloric depictions that, once again, redefined the very meaning of homelessness for American culture. As the suburban ideal subdued the hotel spirit after World War I, changes on the wageworkers' frontier, and in the political economy of industrial employment generally, dramatically reduced the pool of migratory hobo labor. By the time Nels Anderson published *The Hobo*, the rowdy subculture that had presided over the main stem since the late nineteenth century appeared to be on its way out, a casualty of the same "ubiquitous American force" that had created and then diffused the hotel spirit.

As urban industrial civilization tamed the wageworkers' frontier and shifted the locus of residential life from the downtown hotel to the subur-ban home, observers like Robert Park increasingly began to look upon hoboes as "belated frontiersmen" whose domestication warranted a sense of nostalgic regret rather than triumph. No longer fearing that the home would become an anachronism amidst a rising hotel civilization, investi-gators now rushed to capture the folkways of those rough undomesticated men who had yet to take their places on the "crabgrass frontier."

# PART III

## RESETTLING THE HOBO ARMY, 1920–1980

# THE DECLINE AND FALL
## OF HOBOHEMIA

W hile traveling in Mexico in 1926, novelist John Dos Passos met Gladwin Bland, a former Wobbly hobo who, over a decade earlier, had gone south to fight in the Mexican Revolution. Now retired from the revolutionary struggle and running a small business, the expatriate regaled Dos Passos with stories of the old wageworkers' frontier. Looking back with "a certain satirical detachment," Bland recalled "the days when he believed the I.W.W. were really building a new society within the shell of the old." The hobo's radical faith now appeared tragically naive, for postwar developments had strengthened, rather than hollowed out, the corporate capitalist state. Indeed, it was hobohemia that had become the empty shell, eviscerated both by long-term economic changes and by well-organized efforts to curtail hobo labor and radicalism. Listening to Gladwin Bland spin his yarns, Dos Passos decided that the story of hobohemia's decline and fall was the epic of the age, a narrative that bridged the lost republican world of Walt Whitman and the assembly-line civilization of Henry Ford.[1]

Upon his return to the United States, Dos Passos began work on *The 42nd Parallel,* the first volume of his extraordinary *U.S.A.* trilogy, which charts the fate of America's democratic promise through the first three decades of the twentieth century. Without quite knowing how it would end, Dos Passos launched his "narrative panorama" with the story of Mac, a character modeled on Gladwin Bland.[2] Mac first hits the road as a teenager, after his parents' death and the financial ruin of his socialist uncle Tim. Before the boy leaves home, his dissipated uncle offers a piece of parting advice: "Don't ever sell out to the sonsofbitches, son; it's women'll make you sell out every time."

As Mac rides west along the forty-second parallel, the hoboes he meets reinforce Uncle Tim's admonition and encourage him to "whore round" rather than settle down. At an Upton Sinclair lecture in San Francisco, Mac meets a Wobbly organizer who signs the young hobo up for the revolution, warning him that "a wobbly oughtn't to have any wife or children." But a woman named Maisie turns Mac's head, offering companionship and comfort in exchange for the lonely asceticism of the wageworkers' frontier.

"I guess I've sold out to the sonsobitches all right," laments Mac after he has married Maisie, fathered two children, and begun payments on a bungalow. Maisie "always wanted new things for the house" and demanded that Mac earn more money. Moreover, she burned his copies of the *Appeal to Reason* and the *Industrial Worker*, berating him for his "ungodly socialistic talk." Slamming the door on Maisie for the last time, Mac resolves to leave his family and recapture the masculine freedom and camaraderie of the road. "I'm free to see the country now," Mac says to himself, "to work for the movement, to go on the bum again."[3]

Like Gladwin Bland, John Dos Passos cast a jaundiced eye on the IWW's revolutionary romance. After beating his way to Mexico, Mac again suffers a failure of nerve, moves in with a woman, and rides out the Mexican Revolution in petty bourgeois comfort. There, Mac drops out of sight, not only from the class struggle but also from *U.S.A.* Indeed, he is the only major character from *The 42nd Parallel* not to reappear in *1919* or *The Big Money*, though other migratory workers do surface from time to time as Mac's ghostly traces. Dos Passos originally intended to continue Mac's story and had planned on making Ike Hall, who first initiates Mac into hobohemia, the central character of *The Big Money*. But Mac's romance of the road was a narrative dead end, unable to represent the realities of New Era capitalism.[4]

Most obviously, this romance denied voice to huge sections of the industrial working class, not only women, who accounted for one-quarter of the nation's wageworkers in the 1920s, but also African Americans and new immigrants.[5] Dos Passos suggests the political consequences of this failure in *1919*, when whiskey-drinking Wobblies tell a race-baiting wayfarer named Joe Williams to "carry a red card and be a classconscious worker." Joe responds by saying that such politics "was only for foreigners, but if somebody started a white man's party to fight the profiteers and the goddam bankers he'd be with 'em."

Soon afterward, Joe has his skull crushed in a bar fight, after punching a black Senegalese soldier for dancing with a white woman.[6] The color line that had always bounded hobohemia—a line that excluded southern and eastern European immigrants as well as Asians, Mexicans, and

African Americans—eventually strangled the subculture, diffusing its oppositional politics.

White supremacy and nativism were not the only factors that made the hobo an inadequate vehicle for Dos Passos's epic. The story of hobohemia also failed to capture the new forms of social and economic organization that emerged after World War I, especially the quickening trends toward consumerism, the service trades, assembly-line production, and suburban living.

The reigning symbol of these changes was the automobile, which had replaced the locomotive as the emblem of industrial progress. In the decade after World War I, the auto industry had transformed the nation, spearheading the economy and inspiring new modes of production, novel forms of personnel management, and modern systems of corporate organization. The automobile also redefined the very meaning of "the road." Hoboes had once prized their footloose mobility as the supreme privilege of their subculture. Now, the whole nation was on the move, bypassing the railroads entirely for newly paved ribbons of highway. The age of speedup and mass communications had marginalized hobohemia, leaving it behind like a deserted right-of-way or a sidetracked boxcar. The subculture still harbored its refugees from the wage system but had become too inflexible and indeed immobile to pose a serious threat to the corporate capitalist order.

Punctuating the hobo's isolation, Dos Passos concludes *U.S.A.* with one final ghastly allusion to Mac. At the edge of a concrete highway, a grotesquely damaged "Vag" stands with his thumb out, utterly defeated, dispirited, and on the brink of starvation. Overhead, well-heeled "transcontinental passengers" fly in a glistening airplane, bearing witness to the progressive annihilation of space through time. The road itself has become obsolete:

The transcontinental passenger thinks contracts, profits, vacation-trips, mighty continent between Atlantic and Pacific, power, wires humming dollars, cities jammed, hills empty, the indiantrail leading into the wagonroad, the macadamed pike, the concrete skyway; trains, planes; history the billion-dollar speedup. . . .

The young man waits on the side of the road; the plane has gone; thumb moves in a small arc when a car tears hissing past. Eyes seek the driver's eyes. A hundred miles down the road. Head swims, belly tightens, wants crawl over his skin like ants:

went to school, books said opportunity, ads promised speed, own your own home, shine bigger than your neighbor, the radiocrooner whispered girls, ghosts of platinum girls coaxed from the screen, millions in winnings were chalked up on the boards in the offices, paychecks were for hands willing to work, the cleared desk of an executive with three telephones on it;

    waits with swimming head, needs knot the belly, idle hands numb, beside the speeding traffic.

A hundred miles down the road.[7]

As *U.S.A.*'s concluding vignette, Vag stands as a grim epitaph to bohemia and a gruesome measure of the IWW's romantic delusions. While the Wobbly romance of the road suffered a stern critique in *U.S.A.*, it endured a more ignoble fate in the realm of popular culture, which domesticated, rather than demythologized, hobohemia. By the time Dos Passos started work on his trilogy, popular writers of all sorts had already begun to record the songs, stories, vernacular, and folkways from "the classic days of hobodom that are now passing."[8] These preservation efforts recast hoboes as "romantic relics out of the historic past, nostalgic memories of a way of life that was no longer possible."[9] But the folklore and picaresque narratives that emerged in the 1920s popularized this romance only by bowdlerizing Wobbly lore and stripping hobohemia of its erotic associations and radical political meanings. The new canon of hobo lore also largely ignored the social and economic conditions of migratory labor and the commercial attractions of the main stem.

To those who would erase the class struggle from hobohemia's memory, John Dos Passos's *U.S.A.* trilogy offered a powerful corrective. But the romantic quest to preserve the hobo's rugged and freewheeling spirit as a source of nostalgic inspiration for machine age America continued to attract widespread attention. Much as sympathetic nineteenth-century commentators looked past the concerns of living American Indians to indulge their own romance of a vanishing race, twentieth-century folklorists saw the closing of the wageworkers' frontier as a regrettable but inevitable cost of civilization. In 1940 the *New York Times Magazine* made this analogy explicit when it declared that "the typical hobo is fast replacing the Indian as the 'vanishing American.'"[10]

Such romances obscured both the causes and the larger significance of hobohemia's demise. Change on the wageworkers' frontier was inevitable, but the decline of hobo labor was not simply a by-product of industrial civilization's irresistible march into the future. Indeed, modern capitalism had first commissioned hoboes as agents of expansion, only to encounter the unforeseen problems raised by such a standing army of hobo labor. Far from a mere obstacle to modernization, hobohemia was a powerful modernizing force in its own right that, through its peculiar oppositions and countercultural expressions, gave shape to the postwar world depicted in *U.S.A.*

As would become clear in the Great Depression, when John Dos Passos struggled to conclude his epic, the fall of hobohemia did not signal the end of homelessness. Neither did it entail the complete elimination of a rail-riding subculture. Rather, the social and economic transformations that attended the closing of the wageworkers' frontier altered the context of the main stem, giving it a new political economy, social composition, and cultural meaning. Even in its twilight, hobohemia continued to abet, resist, and at all levels articulate the broader changes at work in the young American century.

## THE CLOSING OF THE WAGEWORKERS' FRONTIER

> The "blanket stiff" now packs his bed
> Along the trails of yesteryear— . . .
> Now dismal cities rise instead
> And freedom is not there nor here—
> What path is left for you to tread? . . .
> Do you not know the West is dead?
> —Ralph Chaplin, "The West Is Dead,"
> *Industrial Pioneer* (October 1923)

As Ralph Chaplin penned his nostalgic tribute to hobohemia, an aging Jacob Coxey strolled down West Madison Street with Nels Anderson, remarking to the sociologist that "the old timers will not be here much longer." Looking back, Anderson realized that Coxey had been right. The hobo, Anderson wrote, was clearly "on his way out" even as he conducted his landmark study in 1921 and 1922. This study, claimed Anderson, "was out of date as soon as it was written," for the subculture it surveyed was already vanishing.[11]

The turning point, as Anderson noted, was World War I. The war had not only prompted a devastating crackdown on hobo political organizations, most notably the IWW and the IBWA, but had also accelerated long-term social and economic trends that diminished the need for hobo labor. Much of this labor had always been temporary, existing only as long as it took to build the infrastructure needed to produce, process, and distribute the natural resources and finished commodities of the industrial West.

With railroad track mileage peaking and actually beginning to decline in 1916, for example, smaller maintenance crews replaced the construction gangs that had once employed the likes of Nels Anderson. As large-scale building projects drew to a close, the demand for lumber fell off, reducing the numbers of blanket stiffs in the timber fields.[12] Mechanization also claimed hundreds of thousands of jobs in construction, agriculture, and mining. Trucks, tractors, chain saws, and steam shovels all came into general use after the war, as did the undercutting, tamping, tie-shaping, spike-driving, and other kinds of machines that transformed the nature of work in several major sectors.[13] By 1933 the harvest combine alone had displaced over 150,000 hands on the Great Plains.[14]

Those who continued to come out for harvest and other seasonal jobs in the West tended increasingly to be "homeguard" workers: men, women, and families who traveled short distances by automobile to earn extra money. Indeed, the West itself, where single men had once made up 60 percent or more of local populations, had taken on the more settled characteristics of the East, with larger numbers of women and families and smaller proportions of freewheeling bachelors. By the 1920s the civilizing forces of the machine, the home, and the settled community had tamed the wageworkers' frontier.[15]

As main stem populations grew older and more sedentary, they bore witness to changes prompted in part by hobohemia itself. Economic imperatives, new technologies, and demographic trends drove modernization on the wageworkers' frontier, and in the nation at large in the early twentieth century. But this modernization always involved human agencies, especially employers and government officials, who harnessed and directed the broad forces of change. Modernization, in fact, resulted from policies and practices implemented in part to address the crisis precipitated by America's floating army of single white male workers.

The disappearance of boxcar-riding harvest stiffs from the Great Plains, for example, was as much a response to the IWW's successful organizing drives as it was a result of technological innovation. Indeed, combine technology had existed since the mid-nineteenth century, but farmers had not been moved to adopt it until the war. The rise of the Agricultural Workers' Organization, coupled with high wheat prices, inspired employers to displace what the governor of Kansas called "as wild and undependable and overpaid a labor supply as had ever bedeviled an industry."[16] Moreover, the technology that halted hobo migrations on the Great Plains also precipitated the exodus of small farm families who could no longer compete with the large mechanized fields.[17] Modernization, then, did not necessarily entail the settling of populations. Rather, the forces of "civilization" stabilized some while setting others in motion.

The example of the Great Plains also demonstrates the prominent role played by law enforcement in dispersing hobo labor. After the war, farmers and state employment officials launched a vigorous campaign to recruit harvesters from the ranks of commuting "automobile tourists." Automobiles, the reasoning held, shortened the harvests by moving workers quickly in more direct routes. Cars also delivered harvesters in smaller units of three to five men, which employers found easier to manage and the IWW more difficult to organize. "The most serious situation which confronted and still confronts the organization," editorialized *Industrial Solidarity* in the 1920s, " . . . is the worker traveling by auto. . . . All attempts to organize the men prove futile." Expert observers of the harvest labor problem concurred with the IWW's assessment. "The man making the harvests in a car," remarked one investigator, "is spared many of the contaminating influences" of the boxcar.[18]

To protect harvesters from such influences, public and private authorities vigorously policed railroad yards and jungle sanctuaries, preventing hoboes from stealing rides and congregating in or near town during harvest season. Although Nels Anderson made it from Utah to Chicago in 1921 without getting arrested, he found the railroads crawling with police, often "thick-necked sergeants" recently discharged from the army, who did their best to challenge "the hobo's honorable art of getting over the road."[19] That same year, an official commissioned by the United States Department of Labor to investigate harvest conditions watched as armed railroad police in Colby, Kansas, marched a thousand hoboes to the town's employment offices, ordering them to take jobs or immediately leave town.[20] Across the state in Kansas City, Len DeCaux and "scores of other harvest-bound stiffs" actually drew fire from police all day and night as they tried to board freight trains.[21] In Kansas, at least, the shift from hobo to resident labor was not merely the natural result of population growth, but a planned outcome backed by the coercive power of the state.

While these measures chased many hoboes off the road, they did not eradicate migratory labor. Indeed, migrants displaced local labor forces in numerous sectors, such as Michigan's berry orchards and the Southwest's fruit and vegetable fields, during the ten years after World War I. "The hobo has merely changed his vehicle," observed one charity official in 1925. "It used to be the blind baggage or the bumpers. Today it is the flivver. And he takes his wife and kids along, too."[22]

Migratory families did indeed increase in number as hobo labor declined, in part because many employers preferred them over single drifters. Farmers in Washington State vigorously encouraged the migration of family groups, even going so far as to provide housing, auto camps, and portable schools for harvesters who arrived with families in tow.[23] In

1921 a correspondent for the *"Hobo" News* reported that hiring agents in the Pacific Northwest specifically warned single male "floaters" not to apply for seasonal work.[24] Some experts even advocated the permanent settlement of harvest families as a "fortunate and practical" response to the problem of hobo labor.[25] By replacing individual migrants with family migrants, employers hoped to quell the civil unrest and labor conflicts associated with the hobo army. As Carey McWilliams puts it:

> Migrant families do not gather about soup kitchens, nor do they travel in boxcars or form improvised armies for protest demonstrations. They have, in fact, an extraordinary capacity for making themselves inconspicuous; . . . They drift into the community, not as a procession, but in single families, car by car, at different hours and by different routes.[26]

Judging migrant families to be isolated and "inconspicuous," therefore easily controlled, employers and state officials shared the prejudices of Wobbly folklore, which derided family obligations as impediments to revolution. In the early 1930s, after family groups had reached a majority among migratory farmworkers in the West, renewed militancy in the harvest fields exposed the falsehood of such folklore. Family migrants, it turned out, could be even more combative and assertive on the job than boxcar-riding hoboes.

If union and strike activity among the new migrants defied hobo folklore's disparaging attitude toward wage-earning families, then it also challenged hobohemia's collective racial imagination, which often equated "whiteness" with manly independence and "nonwhiteness" with being "owned by the job." The massive strike wave that swept through California's agricultural valleys in 1933 and 1934, for example, was largely the work of Mexican, Filipino, Chinese, and Japanese farm laborers, none of whom had been part of the main stem's "white" counterculture.[27]

Many of these non-Anglo members of the communist-led Cannery and Agricultural Workers Industrial Union had originally come to California in response to aggressive employer recruiting drives aimed at ridding the state of single white "bindle stiffs." By World War I, white labor had not only grown expensive and troublesome; it had also blatantly affronted California's arcadian version of white supremacy. The specter of impoverished white men drifting about without home or vote imperiled the state's cherished racial ideals of white proprietary citizenship. The hundreds of thousands of Mexican immigrants, traveling by truck or car in family groups, who poured into the harvest fields of the Southwest after World War I had been invited to solve a crisis that was not only one of labor, but also of race.[28]

Deprived of the privileges of whiteness, this new labor source soon descended into working conditions as exploitative and abusive as any in the nation. One chamber of commerce official from Los Angeles hailed the Mexican worker as "the most tractable individual that ever came to serve us."[29] With the strikes of the early 1930s and the deportations and vigilante violence that followed, such estimates of Mexican tractability appeared farcical. Indeed, almost immediately after the strikes, growers and state officials began searching once again for a more docile labor force. This time they turned to impoverished "Okie" migrants who entered the fields to reclaim scarce wage labor for white folks (fig. 6.1).[30]

Before the anti-immigrant backlash of the 1930s, employers in the Midwest followed the lead of California's growers in recruiting Mexicans to replace less dependable hoboes. "The Mexicans are now our best available labor supply," one Illinois railroad official told economist Paul Taylor in 1928. "They work hard and get the work out. You do not have to keep after them all the time. You can depend on them to be at work day in and day out. The hoboes do the work better but they are always moving around. They are not reliable."[31] While Taylor found many supervisors and hiring agents who voiced exasperation with "white workers" who drifted from job to job, he also noted a growing disenchantment with Mexican laborers, many of whom were adopting the wayfaring habits of their predecessors. "The Mexicans were steady," explained one Chicago employment agent in 1928, "but this year they seem to be more shifting. They are becoming 'short stake' men like the hoboes. They used to want all-year jobs. . . . . Now they are satisfied with short seasonal jobs if the rate seems all right."[32]

Such examples of "white" behavior among immigrant laborers became even more pronounced as hoboes disappeared from seasonal jobs. The army of Filipino migratories, which grew dramatically through the 1920s and early 1930s until Congress virtually eliminated immigration from the Philippines in 1934, closely resembled the hobo army that had come before it. Made up almost entirely of young men unencumbered by families, Filipino migrants often traveled thousands of miles per year, moving seasonally from Alaska fish canneries to Pacific Northwest fruit orchards to Montana railroad construction sites to the Imperial Valley. Like hoboes, these immigrant workers possessed an urban "playground" and base of operations, not on the main stem but in Seattle's Chinatown. By the late 1920s, they could also be seen hopping freights individually or in small groups, taking advantage of freedoms that had once been the preserve of white men. Just as some Mexican migrants took on the characteristics of hobo labor, so, too, did Filipino floaters shift about, lay off work, form unions, and strike for higher wages.[33]

Figure 6.1: In the years following World War I, employers all over the wageworkers' frontier began to replace hobo labor with what they perceived to be more vulnerable, and therefore docile, groups of workers. In an effort to counter IWW militancy and stem the crisis of white male homelessness, California's growers, for example, recruited families of Mexican immigrants, such as the one photographed by Dorothea Lange in 1936, to work their fields. Within a decade, however, such families proved to be even more contentious than their hobo predecessors, eventually launching the largest strike wave in the history of American agriculture in 1933. The success of these strikes, which began with the spring pea harvests, prompted growers once again to seek new sources of labor, including Okie migrants from the Southwest, to replace Mexican harvesters. Waylaid by a flat tire as they searched for work in the pea fields, the family depicted here faced a powerful coalition of anti-union and anti-immigrant forces determined to restore a tractable labor force to the fields. (Courtesy of the U.S. Farm Security Administration Collection, Library of Congress.)

In a sense, the peculiar traits associated with hobohemia did not disappear. They merely changed form. New groups of migrants flooded "white man's country," transforming it into a multinational and multiracial domain.

The shift in the road's racial complexion resulted from the efforts of not only employers and their hiring agents, but also a new generation of industrial relations experts who approached the problem of hobo labor as a crisis of nationhood, as well as industry. In 1914 labor economist Carleton Parker described hoboes as "a class inferior, unequal, and with fewer rights than normal American tradition seems to promise to its citizens." The gross inequality that marked the lives of Asian, Mexican, African American, and immigrant workers of all sorts rarely drew the concern of investigators like Parker. Indeed, racial subordination was part of "normal American tradition," hardly deserving comment. Deprived and subordinated white workers, on the other hand, were "tragic symptoms of a sick social order," a sign of disease on the body politic.

Since at least the days of the Industrial Army movement, hoboes had invoked their "whiteness" in staking claims both to citizenship and to the fruits of industrial civilization. As agents of the state, Progressive labor investigators took these claims to heart and began searching for ways to resettle the hobo army and reintegrate white floaters back into the polity.[34]

Like those who explored main stem "homelessness" in the early twentieth century, Progressives who set out on the wageworkers' frontier jettisoned the old language of "tramps" and "hoboes" and talked instead of "migratory," "seasonal," and especially "casual labor." These new terms placed the hobo squarely in the labor market and, in so doing, emphasized the role of modern wage relations in the making of hobohemia's peculiar counterculture. The discourse of "casual labor," like that of "homelessness," also entailed a broader critique of industrial civilization as a noxious environment that spawned unnatural offspring. "The casual migratory laborers," argued Carleton Parker, "are the finished product of an economic environment which seems cruelly efficient in turning out human beings modeled after all the standards which society abhors." By helping to ameliorate that environment through public policy recommendations, Parker hoped to redeem the hobo and restore "normal American tradition."[35]

Parker had first come to the hobo labor problem in 1914 while heading the California Commission on Immigration and Housing's investigation of the Wheatland hop pickers' strike. Parker's final report included a strong condemnation of the living and working conditions of California's migrant laborers. Roundly criticized by growers, state officials, and his own employers at the University of California, Parker's report also offered something of an apology for the IWW, an organization that, the report noted, gave white hoboes psychological compensation for their marginal lifestyles.

Pressured to resign from both his state commission and university jobs, Parker continued to investigate white migratory labor, serving on the United States Commission on Industrial Relations and as a federal strike mediator for the War Department. Through his reading in Freudian psychology, Parker came to see the Wobbly hobo as a "psychological by-product of the neglected childhood of industrial America," a rebel who responded to his unnatural subordination through aimless wandering and occasional outbursts against conventional society. By bringing industrial America up to full-fledged "adulthood," argued Parker, business leaders and government officials could cure these extreme cases of "industrial psychosis" and quell the simmering discontent that had spread throughout the nation's working class. "The stability of our Republic," declared Parker, "depends on the degree of courage and science with which we move to the task."[36]

Moving to the task meant embracing a new vision of political economy, one that measured wage levels and working conditions against both the expectations of individual workers and the needs of the polity. Parker's ideas about the interlocking relationship between economics, psychology, and politics—work, self-esteem, and citizenship—derived in part from long-standing working-class debates about the "living wage."

As Lawrence B. Glickman explains it, the living-wage ideal first emerged in the late nineteenth century as workers gradually abandoned the republican dream of a "producers' commonwealth." With wage employment an economic fact of life, the mainstream labor movement embraced the concept of a living wage that would bestow upon breadwinners an "American Standard of Living." Never fixed, nor tied to the "natural law" of the market, the American Standard was to provide white male wage earners with the means and leisure necessary to support a family, participate in civic affairs, and enjoy the fruits of consumer society. As working-class identity shifted from "producerism" to "consumerism," argues Glickman, "class consciousness moved from the shopfloor to the storefront," infusing such hallowed terms as "proprietorship," "citizenship," and "nationhood" with new meanings.[37]

During the Progressive Era, a growing company of middle-class reformers adopted similar visions of the political and economic order. Industrial relations experts especially came to view wage levels as socially constructed, rather than natural, and the economic conditions of wage earners as integral to the health of the nation's political institutions.[38] The living wage and the American Standard provided commentators with a rich ideology both for judging the fitness of "nonwhites" for membership in the polity and for measuring the extent of the hobo labor problem. As white men unable or unwilling to support a family, exercise citizenship, or even consume rationally, hoboes embodied the crisis of nationhood that lay at the heart of living-wage debates.

To most scholarly observers of the postwar era, hobohemia was merely the tip of an iceberg, a peculiarly flamboyant expression of the estrangement and rootlessness endemic to industrial workers generally. Even homeguard workers, most commentators agreed, drifted about from job to job, routinely sloughing off the responsibilities of family, neighborhood, and nation. One of the reasons for such widespread alienation, argued Robert Park in his 1925 essay on the hobo, is that modern industry "tends inevitably to the casualization of labor." This truism had taken hold over a decade earlier with the "historic discovery of labor turnover." Management experts had spread alarm among industrialists about the astonishingly high percentages of workers who changed jobs once or more times per year. In manufacturing, annual turnover rates of 100 to 250 percent were common, while in the extractive and service sectors, employees left work in such high numbers that companies turned over their entire payrolls every month or two.[39]

Such shifting about, of course, had characterized the industrial economy from the very beginning. Only in the early twentieth century did turnover become defined as "*the* problem of industrial society," prompting countless studies, commissions, and commentaries on the "casual state of mind." The mechanization of industry, it turned out, had dramatically increased the costs of training employees, making the turnover of machine operatives far more expensive than that of traditional common laborers. While employers fixated on cost, others took a broader view of the problem, seeing workers' alienation from the job as part of a larger crisis in the nation's civic health. By the end of World War I, the effort to eradicate casual labor had swelled into a virtual crusade. "The idea of decasualizing irregular workers," stated one expert in 1919, "represents in the field of employment the same concept that 'saving the sinner' does in religion and moral effort." "It is the men and women who work steadily, have continuing responsibilities, and who are permanent members of some community," he continued, "who are the foundation upon which American democracy rests."[40]

The struggle to move the hobo off the road was but one phase of the larger endeavor to transform the political and moral economy of employment, thereby firming up the foundation of American democracy. World War I represented a watershed in this crusade, for the labor shortages, federal regulatory measures, and working-class militancy prompted by the war inspired employers throughout the economy to seize upon the recommendations of industrial relations experts like Carleton Parker.

Seeking to steady their payrolls and reduce "antisocial" activity on the job, industrialists invented the new field of personnel management, designed to implement the carrot of "welfare capitalism" as a counterpart to the stick of anti-radicalism and the open shop. In replacing the "drive system" and the "foreman's empire" with formal hiring, training, and disciplinary procedures, employers offered their workers a new bargain, one that rewarded loyalty, productivity, and workplace quietism with job security, fair treatment, steady promotions, and an array of others benefits linked to seniority. The decade after the war witnessed the vast expansion of company pension plans, annual vacations, insurance policies, mortgage loans, stock ownership, sports teams, and employee representation schemes.

Moreover, many companies now used long-range planning to keep their payrolls steady throughout the year, minimizing seasonal fluctuations in production and employment. By expanding and rationalizing markets though advertising and diversifying product lines, firms hoped to maintain a continuity of demand and production.[41]

Such measures had a powerful impact on some industries, such as lumbering, that employed hobo labor. Plagued by Wobbly-sponsored work stoppages during the war, western lumber operators succumbed to pressure from federal labor officials, Carleton Parker among them, and raised wages, improved living and working conditions, and installed the eighthour day as an industry standard. After the war, company owners established the West Coast Lumbermen's Association, which offered workers the "square deal" of family housing and more regular employment in a deliberate attempt to undermine hobo subculture. The consequence of such policies was to reduce labor turnover substantially in the timber fields by the mid-1920s.

Welfare capitalism yielded similar results throughout the New Era economy, pushing down turnover rates and encouraging workers to tie their fortunes to a single employer. Chronically high unemployment rates across the manufacturing sector achieved the same effect, motivating employees to stay put rather than take their chances in a slack job market.[42]

While corporate welfarism helped to create a more sedentary workforce, it never solved the problems of unemployment, low wages, long hours, seasonal layoffs, or unhealthful working conditions. Most workers benefited little from the new welfare measures, which largely failed to live up to the promises trumpeted in corporate publicity campaigns.

But, as Lizabeth Cohen has argued, these campaigns did have the unexpected consequence of convincing industrial workers that their employers bore a moral responsibility for ensuring their welfare. Even as workplace activism declined in the 1920s, employers' welfare work quietly encouraged the working-class vision of a "moral capitalism," which, like the living-wage ideal, emphasized the critical role of wage relations in promoting a healthy family life and a sound democratic polity.[43]

Such a vision contrasted sharply with what the *Industrial Worker* had hailed in 1912 as the "tramp's view of work," which advocated that men maintain an "irreducible minimum of artificial desire," including the desire for "furniture, pictures, houses, theaters, expensive clothes, wives, [and] children," so as to reduce their dependence upon wages. In the mid-1920s, even the IWW, though never endorsing moral capitalism, joined the general appeal to domestic order, arguing that "the welfare of ourselves and our families is the fundamental principle underlying all human life." Having ousted the last remnants of the "bummery," Wobbly leaders devoted what was left of their movement to organizing the homeguard. "It is . . . the man who has home and family ties," announced the *Industrial Unionist* in 1925, "who is going to put up the hard battle against capitalism."[44]

That battle, as well as the struggle to fulfill the promise of moral capitalism, resumed in earnest in the 1930s when a tide of homelessness dwarfing all that had come before it inundated the land. By then, hobohemia had undergone a transformation in the larger culture commensurate with the changes that had swept across the wageworkers' frontier. The battleground over the hobo shifted from the job site and the main stem to the realm of print culture, where writers narrated competing versions of hobohemia's decline and fall.

The contests that took place in the 1920s over the hobo's memory signified broader debates over the meaning and trajectory of the new political-economic order that the fall of hobohemia had heralded. In representing the hobo's past, postwar writers and folklorists prefigured, and in some cases shaped, future debates about homelessness, especially when unprecedented numbers hit the road during the Great Depression.

## CONTESTING HOBOHEMIA

In 1925, the same year that the *Industrial Unionist* pledged allegiance to the homeguard, Floyd Dell offered readers of the *Century Magazine* a narrative commemoration of the hobo. Anticipating John Dos Passos's epic novel, Dell's short story, entitled "Hallelujah, I'm a Bum," telescopes the story of hobohemia's rise and fall into the life of Jasper Weed, a middle-American son of a browbeaten father and overbearing mother. As a teenager, Jasper labors in a factory to help save the family home until one day his urbane aunt Miriam, a vaudeville actress and therefore disreputable in the eyes of Jasper's parents, arrives from the big city. Pulling Jasper aside, she implores her nephew not to throw his life away paying off "a dirty mortgage." "That house has ruined enough lives, Jasper," she tells him. "*Don't let it get you, too!*"

That night Jasper makes for the railroad tracks. He takes quickly to the hobo life but almost gets trapped into settling down to suburban comfort. Hitting the road once more, he vows to exchange "domestic slavery and misery" for the bonds of manly friendship, which he forges through work, travel, and, after a time, organizing fellow hoboes into the Industrial Workers of the World. Working tirelessly "to create a new society within the shell of the old," Jasper fans the flames of discontent until murderous vigilantism and police violence dampen his enthusiasm for revolution. With war raging in Europe and jingoistic hysteria gripping the United States, Jasper quietly quits the class struggle and beats his way to New York, where he meets "a kind of a tramp he had never seen before—the artist kind."

To Jasper, the painters and poets of Greenwich Village were "old friends in a new guise," for, like hoboes, they eschewed the conventions of work and home and embraced what they called "vagabondia." At studio parties Jasper learns about free love and modeling clay. In return, he teaches his new friends how to sing Wobbly anthems.

Jasper's star rises quickly among the Village crowd when a federal grand jury indicts the former Wobbly on espionage and sedition charges. On the eve of his conviction, Jasper's eyes are opened to the cultural gulf that separates him from his bohemian friends. To them, the courtroom struggle was nothing more than "an idle curiosity," a grand and exciting "spectacle" that illustrated "the folly of heroism, the uselessness of endeavor." Jasper's lover, Inez, denounces revolutionary politics as "a kind of madness" and tells Jasper that he became a Wobbly "because it gave you a good excuse for keeping on being a tramp." While Inez implores him to remain, like her, "an idler and a vagabond" with "no responsibilities" toward the world, Jasper declares that he does not "want to be a bum all my life" and pressures Inez into marrying him. Like a footloose hobo, Inez runs away, spending only one last passionate night with Jasper before he is scheduled to begin his twenty-year prison sentence.

Disillusioned with his early romance of the road, chastened by his exposure to bohemian life, and alienated from a postwar world that offers him no place, Jasper jumps bail and disappears into Russia. There, he hopes to help build "a whole new civilization" but suspects, along with his lover, that his heroism will only get him "hanged or shot."[45]

Floyd Dell's bitter tale of persecution and exile was one of many to find in the vanishing hobo an emblem for the predicament of American culture in the New Era. Upton Sinclair, Hart Crane, Edward Dahlberg, John Dos Passos, and several lesser-known writers also treated hobohemia's dissolution as a symbol of political and cultural impasse, a roadblock that boded ill for the prospects of democratic culture. Taken together, these writers crafted a master narrative of hobohemia's decline and fall, one that served, to borrow from Michael Denning's assessment of *U.S.A.*, as a charter for the new radicalism that would emerge in the early 1930s, "its starting point, its founding mythology."[46]

The key to this founding mythology was not only a strident rejection of postwar definitions of "normalcy"—especially the "revolt against the village"—but also a critique of bohemian decadence. The trenchant self-criticism that marks "Hallelujah, I'm a Bum," where Dell confesses in an aside that "I was one of those artistic tramps living in Greenwich Village," eventually culminated in Malcolm Cowley's memoir *Exile's Return*, which chronicles the nihilistic degradation of Greenwich Village and the "Lost Generation" of American modernists. Jasper's exile left the Village in the hands of idlers and vagabonds like Inez, bereft of any countervailing political commitments that might, in the words of Cowley, prove "dangerous to Ford Motors or General Electric." Despite their misgivings about the IWW's revolutionary romance, radicals like Dell hoped to revitalize modernist counterculture, invoking the fading world of the hobo as a departure point for what Dell called "intellectual vagabondia."[47]

Dell was hardly the first writer to look to the road for inspiration. The vast shadow cast over American letters by Walt Whitman virtually guaranteed that poets would seek the "open road" in the subculture of tramps and hoboes. As early as 1873, the year the word "tramp" first emerged as an epithet, Whitman's close friend and biographer John Burroughs expounded on "the exhilarations of the road," praising "the commonest tramp" as "a wild bird amid cage."[48] Various volumes of "hobo ballads," "tramp poems," and "songs from vagabondia" soon followed, all based on the picaresque adventures of those who followed the hobo trail in the name of art.[49]

Vagabond poetry reached its most creative stage during World War I when Harry Kemp and Vachel Lindsay published their well-received books of verse. By this time, however, the realism of tramp ethnography and the revolutionary rhetoric of Wobbly folklore had so compromised pastoral visions of the road that both Kemp and Lindsay disavowed their relationship to hobo subculture. Kemp's near-death experience while hopping a freight and the "filthy talk" he encountered in a jungle camp outside of Kansas City prompted the vagabond poet to shed his "old idealisation of the life of the tramp" and abandon the road for good.[50] Lindsay, meanwhile, included among his "rules of the road" injunctions against laying up in cities, traveling by railroad, pairing up with others, and being lewd and uncivil. For Lindsay, "preaching the gospel of beauty" meant avoiding the commercialized and corrupted world of the main stem.[51]

Numerous other hoboes pulled away from the road right along with

Kemp and Lindsay as new social, political, and economic conditions conspired to reduce the main stem's vitality. Whereas before the war, a venturesome few had entered hobohemia with literary ambitions, afterward the direction of migration reversed itself, sending former Wobblies into the bohemian haunts that had spawned the likes of the vagabond poets. Searching for a safe countercultural haven, some hoboes, like the fictional Jasper Weed, found their way to Greenwich Village, which had once treated the "one-eyed giant" Big Bill Haywood as a celebrity.

The cross-fertilization of hobo labor and bohemia bore most fruit in the hobo's capital of Chicago, where Jack Jones, a former railroad construction worker and IWW organizer, opened the Dill Pickle Club in 1917. Originally intended as an informal flop and meeting hall for hobo activists, the Dill Pickle received its memorable name and bohemian reputation during the war when the official crackdown on radical activities prompted Jones to close shop and open a new club on the Near North Side. Located just off of Washington Square, the club soon became the headquarters of the "Chicago Renaissance," attracting all manner of modernist poets, artists, dancers, actors, singers, and intellectuals, as well as hobo radicals. With the exodus of literary talent to New York in the 1920s, the club soon descended into a speakeasy, what one former devotee called a "sex-sideshow for gin-soaked collegiates and other perennial adolescents out for an intellectual jag." Police harassment finally finished off the Dill Pickle in 1931. By then, the club had become a symbol of Roaring Twenties decadence.[52]

If the Dill Pickle was a symptom of the main stem's decline as a center of radical counterculture, then the career of Dr. Ben Reitman, a leading figure at Jack Jones's club, illustrates how these changes, almost paradoxically, raised the profile of hobohemia in American culture. Although he eventually became a physician, Reitman had come of age on Chicago's main stem, having grown up among the brothels, saloons, and hotels that lined West Madison Street. As an adult, Reitman had led unemployed marches, founded the Chicago chapter of the IBWA, and almost martyred himself to the cause of industrial unionism when vigilantes tortured him during a 1912 free speech fight. After several years of managing Emma Goldman's speaking career, Reitman returned to Chicago in 1919 when Goldman was deported. The hobo world he found there had changed, as had Reitman. No longer possessing a taste for radical politics, the "King of the Hoboes" refashioned himself as a "Main Stem Dandy," cutting a Byronesque figure with his Windsor tie, ruffled shirt, flowing cape, and oversize walking stick (fig. 6.2).

When he was not taunting former Wobblies at the Dill Pickle, Reitman

Figure 6.2: With his curious mixture of bohemianism, radical activism, and cultural entrepreneurialism, the flamboyant Dr. Ben Reitman embodied the shifting fortunes of Chicago's main stem (ca. 1919). Abandoned at a young age by his father, a Russian Jewish immigrant peddler, Reitman grew up in the heart of Chicago's First Ward just as it was developing into the "Hobo Capital of America." A self-described victim of "Wanderlust," Ben first hit the road at age twelve and continued to ride the rails even after a wealthy benefactor offered to pay his way through medical school. Although he eventually graduated and sporadically served as Chicago's "clap doctor" and "whorehouse physician," Reitman spent most of his early adulthood in the world of hobohemian politics, founding the Chicago branch of the International Brotherhood Welfare Association in 1907. After meeting the famed anarchist Emma Goldman the following year, Reitman left town with her, spending the next decade as her manager and lover. With the main stem already in decline by the time of his return to Chicago in 1919, Reitman once again refashioned himself, this time as the "Main Stem Dandy." He offered lectures and tours to social workers, sociologists, writers, artists, and sightseers of all sorts, exerting immense influence in particular on the Chicago school of sociology. With his help, scholars and other commentators came to view hobohemia as primarily a world of "intellectual vagabondia," rather than of migratory labor. (Used by permission of Ben L. Reitman Papers [BLR neg. 14], Special Collections, University Library, University of Illinois at Chicago.)

cultivated his relationships among Chicago's many social service agencies and also among the sociologists at the University of Chicago. Indeed, Reitman became the most important liaison between Chicago sociology and the city's underworld in the 1920s, shepherding many of Robert Park's graduate students through their urban explorations and inspiring several of the department's better-known studies. Nels Anderson's *The Hobo* came about largely through meetings with Reitman, who suggested the plan of investigation, helped to secure funding through the United Charities, and served on the special committee arranged to oversee the project. In return, Anderson and other Chicago sociologists raised Reitman's status as an independent social worker and semi-official defender of the down-and-out. They also spoke regularly at Reitman's "Hobo College," which the good doctor had transformed into a lyceum dedicated to bringing hoboes "in contact with philosophy and psychology, with art and letters and music." Park and Herbert Blumer even assisted Reitman in writing a sociological study of his own, an investigation of pimping entitled *The Second Oldest Profession*.[53]

Ben Reitman proved to be a key figure, not only in helping the Chicago school to exploit its "social laboratory" of the city, but also in shaping Chicago sociology's urban vision. When Nels Anderson first heard Reitman lecture on the subject of homelessness, he was struck by how closely the Main Stem Dandy linked hoboes with the bohemian world of the city. "Reitman's knowledge of hoboes," Anderson recalled, "was restricted to their nonwork lives" on the main stem and "did not include their contribution to society as workers."

A former migratory laborer who felt quite out of place in the rarefied surroundings of the University of Chicago, Anderson was particularly sensitive to popular images of the hobo as a happy-go-lucky ne'er-do-well. Indeed, Anderson consciously modeled his book against Josiah Flynt's investigations, which ignored seasonal labor and unemployment and emphasized instead the role of alcoholism and "Wanderlust" in the making of tramps. Burdened by the need to justify his own background and the importance of his research, Anderson presented the hobo as "one of the heroic figures of the frontier" and defined the main stem primarily as "the labor exchange for the migratory worker," rather than as the hobo's "playground."[54]

In contrast to the former migratory worker Nels Anderson, Robert Park, who called himself "an intellectual vagabond exploring and writing about the life of the city," shared Reitman's essentially cultural interpretation of the hobo, seeing him as a product of the emancipated urban environment that had given rise to intellectual vagabondia.[55] In his own essay on "The Mind of the Hobo," Park slighted the main thrust of Anderson's argument and characterized the homeless man instead as "a bohemian in the ranks of common labor," a reluctant worker who possessed a fundamentally "artistic temperament."[56]

Indeed, it was Park who developed the very concept of "hobohemia" and originally wanted to use the word as the title of Anderson's book. As it happened, the publisher rejected the plan because Sinclair Lewis had already produced both a short story "Hobohemia" and a play *Hobohemia*, which, like Dell's "Hallelujah, I'm a Bum," satirized the pretensions of Greenwich Village (one reviewer noted that the title was the most successful feature of Lewis's play). Anderson, in any case, made little of the connections between the "Latin Quarter" of the Near North Side and the "slave market" of West Madison Street. "The Main Stem" would have been a more appropriate title for Anderson's study, for the geography it mapped ran from the lodging houses and employment agencies of the city to the jungles and job sites of the hinterlands.[57]

Park, who considered Walt Whitman the purest embodiment of the hobo spirit, must have been a little disappointed in *The Hobo*. While the book provides fascinating insight into the key customs, institutions, and personalities of Chicago's homeless district, it balks at making a broader statement about the city as a quasi-bohemian "state of mind." Park's student Harvey Zorbaugh later compensated for Anderson's failure in his study of Chicago's rooming-house "bohemia" on the Near North Side, arguing that "the bohemian way of life becomes increasingly characteristic of the city at large."[58]

In this respect, *The Hobo* was something of an anomaly in the 1920s, for as hobo subculture became released from the social and economic conditions of its origins, it began to take on a life of its own, encouraging others to view the hobo world, in the words of Rolf Linder, as a "non-conformist life-*style*" rather than as a "vagrant *way* of life."[59] Emancipated from the restraints of migratory labor, the hobo was now free, in the person of Ben Reitman or even Jasper Weed in "Hallelujah, I'm a Bum," to purify and distill the countercultural elements that life on the wageworkers' frontier had fostered. Floyd Dell's bohemian idler Inez recognizes as much when she implores her lover to admit that "a tramp is a tramp" regardless of his or her social position. "You call it organizing the seasonal workers," she argues. "I call it bumming around with the kind of people you like best."[60] In Dell's story and in urban culture generally, hobohemia thus operates less as a distinct subcultural milieu anchored to a specific form of labor than as a free-floating spirit that permeated the city and invited all comers.

As the artifacts of hobo life, such as "Hallelujah, I'm a Bum," became increasingly alienated from the specific conditions of their production, they became the subject of a cultural contest that pitted radicals like Floyd Dell and John Dos Passos against more conservative and populist commentators. While Dell claimed leftist intellectuals and artists as the rightful inheritors of the hobo tradition, a new generation of pioneering folklorists sought to domesticate hobohemia as a proud example of vernacular subculture. These folklorists were part of a larger postwar effort to preserve those native American folkways that collectors believed to be imperiled by the standardizing forces of mass culture and the exotic subcultures of urban immigrants.

As native white males, hoboes exerted particularly strong appeal. "The hobos sang true American songs," asserted one student of hobo lore in 1925, "not the odious noises composed by thick-voiced aliens, but the simple, plaintive airs of long sentimental and heroic ballads which are as native to America as the prairie corn."[61] Although rarely as blatantly nativist as this writer, folklorists routinely published lists of "hobo cant" and "Wobbly talk" in journals such as *American Mercury, American Speech,* and *Dialect Notes,* while Carl Sandburg included seven "hobo songs" in his 1927 *American Songbag,* the first commercially successful anthology of its kind. Musicians such as Jimmie Rodgers, Cliff Carlisle, and the old Wobbly Mac McClintock further popularized hobo lore by recording songs of the road for the burgeoning country music market.[62]

These preservation efforts culminated in 1930 with the publication of George Milburn's *The Hobo's Hornbook,* a compendium of eighty-six folk songs and poems and a glossary of slang that firmly established the hobo's place in the canon of American folklore. "Tramps and hoboes are the last of the ballad makers," announces Milburn in the book's preface. "Not in the Tennessee hills, or among the Sea Island Negroes, or in any other such arrested community is there a more vigorous balladry than that which has been flourishing for the past fifty years in America's peripatetic underworld." A scholar at the University of Oklahoma, Milburn had traveled within this "arrested community" for one year during 1926 and 1927, roaming about the country and keeping notebooks of the songs, stories, and vernacular he heard along the way.

Making no reference to urban lodging-house neighborhoods, Milburn instead focused on the jungle as the locus of the hobo's most authentic cultural practices. "Denied the usual diversions of the modern world," the professor explains, hoboes turn "to devices that flourished centuries ago." In a classic statement of what James Clifford calls "eleventh-hour ethnography," Milburn warns that if collectors wish "to catch and embalm specimens of the American vagrant's balladry," then "it must be done before many years pass, because both tramps and hoboes are anachronisms bound for extinction." Despite his account of ethnographic heroism, Milburn culled most of his materials from previously published sources: vagabond poetry, the *"Hobo" News*, the *Industrial Worker*, and especially the *Little Red Songbook*. His primary achievement was not to collect but rather to recode this material as instances of an anachronistic premodern folk culture.[63]

Supplementing the work of professional folklorists in the postwar era were numerous picaresque hobo narratives and autobiographies, most of which, like Jim Tully's celebrated *Beggars of Life*, ignored descriptions of labor and main stem life and focused instead on freight riding, jungle talk, and colorful bohemian characters consumed by wanderlust.[64] Even Nels Anderson exploited this broad appetite for hobo lore in 1930 by publishing *The Milk and Honey Route: A Handbook for Hobos* under the pseudonym of Dean Stiff. Disguising his authorship so well that few recognized his voice, Anderson-as-Stiff argues that "the true picture of the hobo and his life in that best of possible worlds, Hobohemia, remains to be drawn." In contrast to the scholarly work of *The Hobo*, *The Milk and Honey Route* provides a vernacular guide to hobohemia, making little reference to work or even lodging houses, but offering abundant information on jargon, jungle life, and the tricks and techniques of begging and freight hopping. Like other hobo authors of the period, Dean Stiff celebrates the bohemian glory and unconscious purity of the hobo world, a world that would always remain closed to the "uninitiated." "The hobo," explains Stiff, echoing the words of Robert Park, "can and does live the life of the consummate artist without being aware of it."[65]

Even those folklorists who did maintain a focus on the hobo's work often domesticated the meanings that hobo subculture attached to that labor. Lamenting that the wageworkers' frontier was "now populated largely by laborers who support families, and who own automobiles, tailored clothes, and bank accounts," one contributor to the *Century* in 1925 recalled the songs and stories that had once animated western bunkhouses and jungles:

> Behind these plain tales could be seen the leaders of men realizing their dreams, the driving forces of industrialism, the constructive uses of finance, the whole operation of a vastly organized industrial movement, and, finally, the conquering of another empire for mankind as the grand result. The hobo laborers felt all this, if they did not express their feelings in so many words. It was a sense of being an actor in a drama, of being a human element

in a great movement that was consciously directed toward some mysterious and romantic end, which made them perform heavy toil joyously, place high importance on their simple traditions and little rules of labor.[66]

Through a crude sleight-of-hand, this author inverts the master narrative that would come together under the auspices of John Dos Passos and Floyd Dell. In the above passage, the triumph of corporate capitalist hegemony, rather than the failed revolutionary struggle of the Wobblies, becomes the hobo's "great movement." While this romance of empire, this paean to industry, is tinged with nostalgic regret for a lost world of untamed white masculinity, it nonetheless treats the new postwar political economy as the laudable achievement of hobo labor, the fruit of pioneer sacrifice.

Fascinating for what they reveal about the cultural politics of memory in the New Era, the contests over the historic meanings of the hobo—the competing narratives of hobohemia's rise and fall—take on even greater significance in the context of the Great Depression when mass homelessness infused debates about hobohemia with special urgency. The lines drawn during these early debates conditioned responses to the trauma of the 1930s, as artists, intellectuals, relief workers, government officials, and even the newly homeless themselves struggled to determine whether hobohemia was a dangerous and subversive "underworld," a domesticated folk culture, or a starting point for a new revolutionary movement.

With lodging houses, railroad yards, and jungle camps filling up once again with refugees from the wage system, demands for a "moral capitalism," or an end to capitalism entirely, reached the ears of the nation's political and business elites, prompting new social and economic policies designed to exorcise the specter of hobohemia. In developing federal relief, recovery, and welfare measures, the architects of the New Deal order answered the predicament posed by John Dos Passos's Vag with a figure of their own, one that President Franklin D. Roosevelt termed the "Forgotten Man."

As the nation would soon learn, the decline of hobohemia had radically changed the rules of the road. With the onset of the depression, boxcars and jungle camps now teemed with persons who found no shelter in hobohemia's memory, for they possessed no claim to the kind of "normal American tradition" that had promised native white men the full privileges of citizenship. Just as *U.S.A.*'s romance of the road failed to accommodate those workers excluded from the main stem, so, too, did the New Deal's rhetoric of the Forgotten Man recall and recover only a fraction of those traversing the nation's landscape in the 1930s.

# FORGOTTEN MEN

Fifteen years ago my public duty called me to
an active part in a great national emergency,
the World War. . . . In my calm judgement, the
Nation faces today a more grave emergency than
in 1917. . . . These unhappy times call for the
building of plans that rest upon the forgotten,
the unorganized but the indispensable units of
economic power, for plans like those of 1917 that
build from the bottom up and not from the top
down, that put their faith once more in the
forgotten man at the bottom of the economic
pyramid. . . . It is high time to admit with
courage that we are in the midst of an emergency
at least equal to that of war. Let us mobilize to
meet it.
—Gov. Franklin Delano Roosevelt, "The 'Forgotten
Man' Speech," Albany, New York, April 7, 1932[1]

One month after presidential candidate Franklin Roosevelt
announced his intention to mobilize the "Forgotten Man,"
three hundred unemployed men from Portland, Oregon, clambered
aboard a Union Pacific freight train for the first leg of a 3,000-mile journey to Washington, D.C. Like the Industrial Armies of 1894 and the Overalls Brigade of 1908, this new contingent fashioned itself as an "army" of
activism, stealing rides, commandeering entire freight trains, and living
off donations it collected along the way. Unlike their freight-hopping forebearers, however, these latter-day hoboes were all genuine war veterans
with a special claim on the nation's conscience. Calling themselves the
Bonus Expeditionary Force (BEF), a play on the American Expeditionary
Force that had been dispatched to France in 1917, the marchers sought
the immediate cash payment of their "bonus," insurance certificates that

Congress had authorized in 1924 as "adjusted compensation" for service in World War I. The bonus was due to be distributed in 1945, but with the onset of the Great Depression, veterans clamored for early payment, desperate for the roughly $1,000 each claim would bring.

The idea for a Bonus March did not originate in Portland. Indeed, by May 1932 demonstrations for the bonus had become commonplace in the nation's capital, attracting large and small groups of veterans from across the country. The American Legion, the Veterans of Foreign Wars, and the Communist Party had each sent representatives to Washington in support of the bonus and had sponsored countless other petitions and local marches. Of all the various demonstrations, however, none captured the country's imagination like the journey of the Portland BEF. These crusaders generated more headlines and inspired more veterans to join the campaign than any other group. Their success was due largely to the opposition they encountered, as private and public authorities tried in vain to disperse the marchers.

The BEF first attracted national press coverage in Council Bluffs, Iowa, when railroad officials sidetracked the "petition on wheels," much as they had done to Jack London and Kelley's Army thirty-eight years earlier. As the police watched passively, the marchers uncoupled cars, disconnected air brakes, and occupied trains until the railroad allowed the men to continue on their way. Subsequent skirmishes and standoffs between the BEF and its adversaries drew even more attention to the marchers. Public support for the bedraggled veterans swelled to such a degree that the governors of Illinois, Indiana, Ohio, Pennsylvania, and Maryland consented to provide National Guard escorts all the way to Washington. By the time they pulled into the District of Columbia on May 29, Portland's Bonus Marchers had become depression celebrities, flesh-and-blood Forgotten Men staking their claim on the nation's capital. Over the next two weeks, twenty-five thousand veterans poured into Washington, creating the largest body of demonstrators the city had ever seen and sparking the most dramatic crisis of the Great Depression.[2]

As veterans continued to arrive, even after the Senate overwhelmingly rejected the bonus bill on June 17, the charismatic and somewhat unstable commander of the Portland BEF, Walter W. Waters, assumed leadership of the growing Bonus Army encamped in Washington. A former army sergeant with a shadowy past, the thirty-four-year-old Waters had been plagued by unemployment and mental illness, possibly stemming from the war, ever since his discharge in 1919. "My inability to take root in fertile soil," explained Waters, "may have been due to the unsettling effects of the War on me." Breaking all family ties and even changing his name upon his return to civilian life, Waters drifted about the West, working the harvests and various other casual labor jobs until settling down in Portland in the late 1920s. At the time of the Bonus March, he had been unemployed for eighteen months, a casualty in the great battle for common labor that the Great Depression had unleashed.[3]

Waters's first order of business as "Commander-in-Chief" of the Bonus Army was to impose strict military discipline on the thousands of hungry veterans massed in Anacostia Flats and other camps around the city. Under the watchful eye of Washington's shrewd chief of police, Pelham Glassford, Waters mustered his men into companies and regiments, created a chain of command, set up commissaries, called roll, and conducted regular inspections of the shacks and tents that the marchers called home. In re-creating regular army life as faithfully as possible, Waters hoped to combat the impression that the campers were disreputable "bums," "tramp and hoboes" looking to feed from the public trough. But to observers like Gladwin Bland, who traveled to Washington to join the Bonus Army, the camps suggested less an army bivouac than "an immense hobo jungle."[4] For the former Wobbly hobo, memories of hobohemian counterculture provided the best measure of the Bonus Army's political meaning and potential.

Waters and other leaders, however, rejected the comparison to hobohemia and successfully encouraged their men to adhere to the military model. As an "army," the movement not only kept its demands narrowly focused on veterans benefits, but also offered itself as a spectacle of nationhood, one that exchanged the New Era values of individualism, domesticity, and striving for those of fraternity, camaraderie, and sacrifice. Indeed, this unemployment demonstration took the form of a Bonus March precisely because the military presented such a powerful model of masculine citizenship at a time of "great national emergency," as FDR put it. In combining the masculine romance of the road with the soldierly ideals of war, the Bonus Army sought to strengthen the attenuated bonds of nationhood and reconsecrate the obligations and privileges of citizenship.

To the real United States Army, under the command of Chief of Staff Douglas MacArthur, the demonstrators' military pretense was an affront to legitimate government and a threat to established order. MacArthur saw the camps as "animated by the essence of revolution." A few intelligence officers even believed that MGM Studios in Hollywood, which they referred to as a "100 per cent Jewish" organization, had financed the Bonus March with funds from the Soviet Union. President Herbert Hoover himself eventually became convinced that the Bonus Army had fallen under the influence of the Communist Party and was planning a coup d'état in the manner of the Bolsheviks. In July the president and his advisers began to plot a strategy for reoccupying the public grounds held by the Bonus Army.[5]

Despite the administration's fears, the veterans' movement conspicuously lacked a revolutionary consciousness, a fact noted by many leftist observers such as John Dos Passos and Gladwin Bland. "I attempted to enlighten a few of my fellow veterans as to the cause for their plight," Bland wrote Dos Passos after his visit to Washington, "but they kind of backed away declaring: 'Oh the hell with the Red propaganda.' . . . poor misguided devils."[6] Dos Passos himself, who traveled to Anacostia Flats on assignment for the *New Republic*, thrilled at the sight of the campground but also perceived divisions in the Bonus Army similar to those that had haunted hobohemia. While communists hoped that the veterans would prove a vanguard of the working class, right-wing populists saw the Bonus Army as a sphere of white male privilege opposed to big business and radicals alike. The BEF's analogue of war, commented Dos Passos two years after the march, had given "the powers that be the scare of their lives," but it had also brought out "disgruntled medicine salesmen and con men with fancy colored shirts." Might these demagogues, Dos Passos asked, eventually enlist the Bonus Army's "Forgotten Man . . . into fascist organizations where he will be used as the praetorian guard of the imperial monopolies?"[7]

As Dos Passos's concerns suggest, the cultural politics that had shaped the contest over hobohemia's memory in the 1920s played out in flesh-and-blood on the grounds of Anacostia Flats as left-wing and right-wing factions battled for control of the movement. While communists and their allies made regular pilgrimages to the camps, right-wing populists, such as Detroit's popular radio priest Charles E. Coughlin, also appeared, giving speeches, distributing literature, and offering donations. Coughlin's $5,000 gift to the Bonus Army came with the stipulation that the marchers "keep clear of all communistic leaders and all communistic suggestions."[8] Such admonitions came not only from well-wishers like Coughlin, but also from BEF officers themselves, who posted anti-radical warnings everywhere in camp, repeating them weekly in copies of the *BEF News*. Indeed, Police Chief Pelham Glassford had arranged Walter W. Waters's rise to command of the BEF in return for the "elimination of radicals" in the Bonus Army.[9] Waters and his MPs proved so ruthless in their treatment of suspected "reds" that Glassford, fearing a riot, eventually had to restrain the BEF vigilantes.

Dissension in the ranks precipitated a leadership crisis as rival factions created their own newspapers and chains of command. Waters himself resigned twice, only to regain his position through the aid of Glassford. He also eventually called for the dissolution of the BEF altogether. On the eve of the "Battle of Washington," when the U.S. Army evicted the marchers from their camps, Commander Waters announced the formation of the Khaki Shirts. Supporters described the group as a permanent political organization of veterans modeled on "the Fascisti of Italy and the Nazis of Germany."[10] The legacy of the Bonus March appeared to belong to the men with the "fancy colored shirts."

But by 1934, when Dos Passos wrote a foreword for a communist account of the Bonus Army, the writer had come to see the Forgotten Man as susceptible not only to the populism of the Right, but also to the official populism, "the rosy democratic smokescreen," of Franklin Roosevelt.[11] A clear beneficiary of the Bonus Army crisis, the canny FDR maintained a strategic silence on the matter throughout the summer of 1932, observing events from the governor's mansion in Albany, New York, as the crisis unfolded to the White House's disadvantage. In a muted show of support for the president, Governor Roosevelt quietly dispatched Nels Anderson, an official in his Temporary Emergency Relief Administration, as an emissary to New York's Bonus Army. Anderson extended the governor's offer of jobs and free transportation to all marchers who returned home.[12] Failing in his mission, as all knew he would, Anderson predicted that dispersing the "army of occupation" would create more havoc than had its arrival.[13] He proved correct on July 28 when General Douglas MacArthur, assisted by Majors George S. Patton and Dwight D. Eisenhower, exceeded orders and drove the Bonus Army out of Washington, using tear gas, bayoneted rifles, and even several tanks (fig. 7.1).

As Anacostia Flats smoldered the next morning, Roosevelt sat in bed with the *New York Times* and pondered the photographs, which appeared to him like "scenes from a nightmare." The rout, the candidate understood, had sealed his election.[14] But FDR also realized that his would be the next administration to encounter such armies of protest. In keeping with the analogue of war, Roosevelt sketched plans to recruit an unemployed army of his own, one that would mobilize America's Forgotten Men for public works and save them from the "fancy colored shirts" on the Right and the "reds" on the Left. But, as many argued at the time, while such an army might recover those white men "at the bottom of the economic pyramid," it might also serve as a potent rival to home and family. The masculine camaraderie of camp life was a poor substitute for domesticity and the suburban ideal. Mobilizing to meet the crisis of homelessness and exorcize the specter of hobohemia would ultimately in-

Figure 7.1: As a prelude to the larger assault led by General Douglas MacArthur later that day, Washington police moved on the morning of July 28, 1932, to evict Bonus Marchers from their condemned quarters on Pennsylvania Avenue. During the melees that ensued, such as the one depicted here, police shot and killed two marchers, while brick-hurling veterans seriously injured one officer. As the struggle over the flag suggests, the marchers viewed their movement as an emblem of nationhood, evoking a vision of citizenship defined in terms of fraternity, sacrifice, and masculine privilege. By demanding their "bonus," the protesters cast their relief as an entitlement of manhood, rather than as charity. Inspired by the Bonus Army's plight, lyricist Yip Harburg composed a song in the fall of 1932 that idealized the fraternal bondings of American men at war, at work, and on the road. Whereas hoboes had sought handouts primarily from women, the refrain of Harburg's plaintive composition emphasized the fraternal obligations of citizenship: "*Brother,* Can You Spare a Dime?" (Courtesy of the National Archives and Records Administration.)

volve restoring men to home. Only when equipped with newly won purchasing power would the Forgotten Man resume his authority as both breadwinner and citizen.

## A NEW DEAL FOR THE AMERICAN HOMELESS

Three weeks after a buoyant Franklin Roosevelt rode to his inauguration with a dour-looking Herbert Hoover seated beside him, Nels Anderson supervised a one-day census of the nation's homeless population. Extrapolating from the figures sent in by hundreds of volunteers across the country, Anderson conservatively estimated that 1.5 million Americans had spent the night in public shelters or out-of-doors. Commercial lodging houses, which remained filled to capacity throughout the Great Depression, harbored additional uncounted masses, probably numbering into the millions. Signaling the severity of the crisis, social scientists like Anderson now excluded residents of cheap hotels from the rubric of "homeless," reserving the term for those unable to pay for shelter of any sort.[15]

As in earlier depressions, private charities responded first to the problem, soliciting donations, acquiring buildings, and banding together in special committees for "Homeless and Transient Men."[16] City and state governments soon joined these efforts, establishing public shelters for "unattached non-family men," while granting impoverished families the courtesy of outdoor relief.[17] In cities across the country, homeless men crowded into main stem districts, where relief officials had refashioned old buildings into open dormitory wards. By 1932 Chicago was housing over twenty thousand men a day, more than the city served *annually* during the 1920s.[18] On West Madison Street and elsewhere, the public shelter had eclipsed the employment agency as the defining institution of the old "slave market."

In most every state, archaic settlement laws required those seeking relief to demonstrate residence, which was often defined as a period of five years.[19] Catching those who fell between the cracks of local and state relief systems became the mission of the federal Transient Program, one of the most imaginative and ambitious measures of the early New Deal. Created in May 1933 under the Federal Emergency Relief Administration (FERA), the Transient Program was largely the brainchild of those charity officials and social scientists who had long studied and addressed the problem of homelessness.

In 1932 officers of the YMCA, YWCA, Salvation Army, and other groups had come together to form the National Committee on the Care of the Transient and Homeless (NCCTH). NCCTH members had sponsored well-publicized investigations, such as Nels Anderson's census of the homeless, and had lobbied strenuously for federal action, eventually designing and administering the Transient Program itself. By 1935, when the federal government liquidated the division in favor of the massive new Works Progress Administration (WPA), the Transient Program had operated almost six hundred camps and centers around the country and provided relief to roughly 1 million individuals. For transient families, indoor relief remained "taboo," as FERA director Harry Hopkins put it. The transient camps themselves, therefore, largely housed unattached persons with no legal settlement.[20]

The intense relief efforts surrounding transients, as opposed to the "resident homeless," stemmed not only from their anomalous legal status, but also from the extent to which they recalled hobohemia. The resident homeless, who collected in local downtown shelters, were much older, less exclusively male, and much more ethnically and racially diverse than the hoboes of old.[21] By contrast, transients, who had hit the road in response to their poverty, bore a striking resemblance to their footloose predecessors. Like hoboes, these "pioneers without a frontier," as social workers referred to them, were overwhelmingly young, single white men migrating into and out of urban areas.[22] While most observers found the resident homeless to be in "a dull, bewildered mood, inactive and unprotesting," relief officials sensed a restlessness among the transients, one that needed to be directed into useful pursuits, lest it get channeled into criminal or otherwise antisocial behavior.[23]

Despite the relative familiarity of the transient population, the publicity campaign orchestrated by the NCCTH, a campaign that included congressional hearings and numerous journalistic exposés, gave rise to sensationalized accounts of "lady hoboes" and "wild boys" wandering the nation. As symbols of gender disorder, family breakdown, and community disintegration, women and children of the road spoke powerfully to fears of social collapse. But in terms of policy and administration, these two groups posed few special problems for relief officials.

Homeless women had indeed become more visible than ever, as female wage earners faced unemployment rates even higher than those of men. But single women rarely ventured on the road, where, in the words of one Transient Program official, they were "likely to encounter both suspicion and prejudice from citizen and police alike," not to mention violence at the hands of other transients.[24] As a consequence, unattached women comprised only 1 to 3 percent of the general transient population. Even so, "ladies of the road" were rife in journal, magazine, and newspaper stories through the early 1930s. Most accounts offered grotesque images of undomesticated womanhood that recalled Progressive Era condemnations of "hotel women." "Show me a 'lady hobo,'" wrote one commentator for *Scribner's*, "and I'll show you an angular-bodied, flint-eyed, masculine-minded travesty upon her sex."[25]

In 1934 Walter C. Reckless, who had studied under Robert Park with Nels Anderson in the 1920s, offered a particularly compelling analysis of the lady hobo crisis in an *American Mercury* article entitled "Why Women Become Hoboes." Having conducted extensive investigations of homeless women and recorded in lurid detail the experiences of one "woman of the road" in particular, Reckless predicted that "one of the many social pathologies which will result from the present depression is the growth of a chronic female hobo class." This prospect, argued Reckless, signaled a drastic restructuring of gender norms. Hobohemia had traditionally been "a man's world," with "accepted practices and activities" that made the homeless life "bearable, if not attractive, to men." Women, on the other hand, historically lacked any "hobo lore and tradition" and tended to accept charity only "as members of families." Having to invent customs of their own, lady hoboes were now becoming aggressive in their manners, using their bodies as working capital, and taking on multiple sex partners as they traveled. By making these and other "adjustments" to gender and sexual norms, concluded Reckless, women will "invade hobohemia and the jungles just as women generally have encroached upon all the other original provinces of men."[26]

While the lady hobo symbolized the depression's assault on the "original provinces of men," homeless children, the notorious "wild boys of the road," provided an even grimmer index to the future of patriarchal authority. As one NCCTH member put it in 1933, transient boys "have become the answer to the photographer's prayer and scarcely a magazine appears today without pictures of young fellows jumping freight trains, huddled in box-cars, cooking Mulligan stew in the jungle, thumbing passing automobiles and hitch-hiking across the country."[27]

As with the lady hobo, the panic over wild boys far exceeded the scope of the problem. Nels Anderson and others estimated that about 10 percent of the nation's transient population was under twenty-one years of age. As some pointed out, only a small fraction of those labeled as transient "children" were under sixteen, and the vast majority were between the ages of eighteen and twenty-one.[28]

In fact, the age distribution of depression-era transients virtually mirrored that of earlier homeless populations that had congregated in urban "slave markets" around the country. "We built up the West with boy transients," testified Nels Anderson before Congress in 1933, "and never worried about them until the last two or three years."[29] "A compound of sentiment and propaganda," concurred another Transient Program authority, had elevated "road kids" into an object of popular fascination and horror.[30] The media brimmed with portraits of wandering youth, such as William Wellman's hit movie of 1933, *Wild Boys of the Road*. Such accounts proved so powerful that they even received blame for inciting boy transiency.[31] The most important effect of the wild boy panic, however, was to generate a groundswell of support for the Transient Program under FERA.

The folklore of lady hoboes and wild boys emphasized the innocence and vulnerability of the homeless and the need to save them from the corruptions of the hobo underworld. Just as Gilded Age labor newspapers never tired of distinguishing their "honest workingmen" from "common tramps," so, too, did depression-era journals and magazines heap commendation upon the "new homeless" through favorable comparisons with old-guard "hobohemians." While the late-nineteenth-century working class used the language of "producerism" to legitimate the tramping unemployed, 1930s relief officials referred to their clientele as "white collar" and "middle class," terms that signified respectability in the early twentieth century. In San Francisco a "Who's Who in the Breadline," put out by the city's main charity bureau, contended that "the old-time 'hobo,' 'stiff,' and 'bum'" was "almost lost in the crowd" of engineers, dentists, draftsmen, and other professionals. Social workers contrasted the industry and domesticity of the new homeless with the antisocial and anti-family attitudes of the hobo. "The 'jungle'—the retreat of the old-time hobo and tramp—receives but slight attention from the homeless men of today," asserted one student of the "new poor" in 1933. "They are generally wanderers in search of a job and 'a new opportunity' [and] . . . carry over to a large extent the attitudes and sentiments which governed them at home."[32]

Firsthand narratives of homelessness also replicated old formulas, depicting the descent into homelessness as a progressive loss of identity and a reversion to "savagery." Writing for the *Forum* in 1933 after two unemployed years on the road, for example, Frank Bunce narrated his expulsion from white-collar work and middle-class respectability into the world of flophouses, boxcars, and jungle camps. "I have lost loyalties to my country, to God, to mankind," declared Bunce at the end of his tale. "Having lived like an animal," he explained, "I am taking on the ethics of an animal; . . . I have become, in short, a public menace."[33]

Two years later Tom Kromer produced an even bleaker portrait of homelessness, stringing together episodes of aimless drifting through bread lines, jail cells, boxcars, and even the bed of a gay man who offered food and shelter in exchange for sex. Providing no place-names nor any specific temporal frame, Kromer's *Waiting for Nothing* represents homelessness as a state of utter alienation:

> People I have known, I remember no more. They are gone. They are out of my life. I cannot remember them at all. Even my family, my mother, is dimmed by the strings of drags with their strings of cars that are always with me in my mind through the long, cold nights. Whatever is gone before is gone. I lie here and I think, and I know that whatever is before is the same as that which is gone. My life is spent before it is started.[34]

To relief officials, the dangers of homelessness lay not only in the profound disaffiliation described by Kromer but also in the possible reaffiliation of formerly respectable men with hobo subculture. In the nomenclature of depression-era relief, the terms "hobo" and "hobohemian" were reserved for those who had launched their homeless careers before 1930, "when bumming," as one seasoned vagabond reportedly put it, "was still a profession."[35] Social workers viewed these men as recruiting agents for the road, masters who taught their apprentices how to adjust to the homeless life. In 1934 Ellen Potter, chair of the NCCTH and director of the Transient Program, estimated that the "chronic hobo" type composed 10 percent of the total transient population, the rest being "average normal individuals." But, she warned, "if we do not handle this situation wisely and constructively, we run the risk of developing a nomadic tribe, irresponsible in its habits of life, subsisting ultimately as parasites upon society and potentially a dangerous group, contaminated, as it is bound to be, by the 'chronics.'"[36]

Chicago school sociologists Edwin H. Sutherland and Harvey J. Locke likewise divided the homeless population into two "distinct cultural groups," which they labeled the "Hobohemians" and the "non-Hobohemians." Hobohemians, the sociologists explained, reject "conventional standards" and institutions and feel at home in the flophouses of the main stem. Non-Hobohemians, on the other hand, "hold more traditional or conventional views of religion, home, and country. . . . Their economic philosophy is essentially that of the business man." Over time, Sutherland and Locke contended, the distinctions between these two groups diminished until the non-Hobohemians collapsed fully into Hobohemia, augmenting the power of a dangerous subculture.[37]

Wild boys magnified this threat even further, for they seemed even more impressionable than adults. "The least tangible but perhaps the most devastating hazard that roving boys encounter," contended Chicago sociologist A. Wayne McMillen in 1932, "is the infectious attitude of the seasoned hobo." "'Getting by' becomes a game. The danger is that it may become a habit."[38] Other commentators on "wandering youth" defined hobohemia as both politically and sexually deviant:

The tramping boys frequent the jungles and there witness and frequently participate in the abnormal life that goes on in almost all of these jungle camps. The adult migrant is homeless, jobless, and womanless. Being homeless he has no stake or interest in normal life. He frequently scoffs at those ideals that society values. Being jobless he lives the best he may. He derides honesty, hard steady work, and sobriety. He advocates the most extreme "isms." He laughs at law and order. The boy in the jungle is subjected to this. Being womanless the adult migrant resorts to illicit relations and perversions.[39]

To shield boys from such perversions and loosen the grip of hobohemia on the new homeless, New Dealers curtailed transiency by establishing relief camps that substituted military-style camaraderie for the illicit fraternity of the road. Harnessing the entropic energy of hobo life to the great national purposes of forest conservation and public works, both the Transient Program and the more celebrated and longer-lived Civilian Conservation Corps (CCC) established a network of rural camps across the country that attracted millions of marginal men. As President Roosevelt's earliest and favorite relief program, the CCC recruited over a half-million young men between the ages of sixteen and twenty-five in its first two years alone, offering a powerful symbol of recovery and hope to the nation. While the War Department actually oversaw the CCC, it also supplied surplus land, buildings, and materials to the Transient Program. Transient camps never achieved the same level of regimentation and paramilitary discipline as "Roosevelt's Tree Army," but the analogue of war animated the program nonetheless, as transients adhered to a regular schedule of work, meals, and lights-out in rough communal barracks.[40]

As official alternatives to the road, transient and CCC camps not only shielded floaters from hobohemia, but also contained the resurgent Bonus Armies that formed each spring. In May 1933 President Roosevelt signed an executive order allowing twenty-five thousand veterans, regardless of age, to enroll in the CCC, giving preference to those three thousand or so massed in Washington for a reprise of the Bonus March. Although he repeatedly vetoed bonus legislation for reasons of government economy, the president guaranteed all arriving veterans placement in rural relief camps. Communist organizers warned the marchers to "keep away from the CCC camps," seeing them as "the forerunner of fascism." But most demonstrators eagerly accepted the offer, enrolling either in the Transient Program or the CCC. By 1936 roughly fourteen thousand Bonus Marchers and tens of thousands of other veterans had joined the New Deal's army of relief.[41]

Much as the IWW had created a folklore of white masculinity to bind its revolutionary community of hoboes, so, too, did the transient and CCC camps promote their programs of nationalist recovery through a rhetoric and an iconography of virile white manhood (fig. 7.2). As Holly Allen remarks, race and gender myths were central to the ideological mis-

Figure 7.2: Drawing upon frontier myth, both the Transient Program and the Civilian Conservation Corps depicted their rural camps as zones of regeneration for defeated white men. Like the West of Wobbly folklore, relief camps promised to toughen and "bronze" their workers like Indians, allowing them to recover their virility through the rough camaraderie of outdoor labor. Promotional materials such as this photograph, taken ca. 1935 by Wilifred J. Mead, emphasized bulging muscles and suntans as salubrious by-products of the camps' restorative regimens. "The slogan of the Civilian Conservation Corps is 'We can take it!'" read Mead's accompanying text. "Building strong bodies is a major CCC objective." While such an emphasis on restoring the white male body provided hope for national recovery, it also discriminated against women and nonwhites (despite the official ban on racial discrimination in the CCC's charter). Furthermore, these programs proved a little too attractive to some men of the road who preferred the camaraderie of the camps to the settled bonds of home and family. (Courtesy of the National Archives and Records Administration.)

sion of the CCC. Like the Transient Program, the "Tree Army" was meant not only to provide relief but also "to model a particular vision of citizenship and national community."[42] This vision suggested that America could recover from its "great national emergency" only by restoring white men to their traditional positions of authority.

This strategy succeeded not only in calming the sense of crisis and deflecting the challenge of the Bonus Army, but also in reducing the actual numbers of men on the road. By relying so heavily on camp camaraderie as a metaphor for national recovery and regeneration, however, the Transient Program, like the Bonus Army before it, could not avoid comparisons with hobohemia. Indeed, a few boosters of the program, ignorant of the new vocabulary of relief that defined the "hobo" negatively, actually promoted the analogue of hobohemia, viewing the subculture positively in the vernacular terms of popular folklore. The director of Camp Greenhaven in New York, for example, boasted to a reporter for the *Survey Graphic* that his men had built "a jungle right on the camp property . . . complete with tin cans and gunny sacks, in the best tradition of the road." "The men hang out in it as a sort of a 'club-house,'" the director explained. "Some of them wash their clothes there. I'm told too that it has its uses for sobering up purposes." The article's accompanying photographs of men bathing by a stream attested to the jungle's popularity and emphasized transients' resemblance to hoboes.[43]

Sanctioning, it would seem, the institution of the jungle, the Transient Program encountered contradictions similar to those that had hampered the philanthropic hotel movement a generation earlier. Like the Mills Hotel, Camp Greenhaven threatened to promote the very subcultural practices it was meant to suppress. One former transient writing for the *Saturday Evening Post* called his camp "a glorified jungle where a great many men accustomed to travel at no expense to themselves were invited to settle down for a spell at the expense of the Government." Others worried that "the abnormal regimented life" of the camps would make readjustment to "normal living" impossible. Several experts also feared that the camps were harboring sexual "perversions" similar to those that ruled in the hobo jungles.[44]

As the concern about sexual deviancy suggests, the very success of the Transient Program had refocused attention on the broader problems of gender and domesticity historically denoted by the term "homelessness." Looking back on the early years of the depression from the vantage of 1936, Edwin H. Sutherland and Harvey J. Locke saw clearly that the plight of the new homeless involved far more than shelter. "Without family life and satisfying female companionship," they explained, "single men had no incentive to labor, to save, to live a normal life; instead they be-came nomadic and self-sufficient."[45]

While providing shelter and sustenance, transient camps also appeared to perpetuate and legitimate lodging practices that separated homeless men from family and community life. With the benefit of hindsight, one Transient Program official described in 1937 why the division had to be liquidated in favor of the WPA. Camp life, she explained, encouraged a "false" sense of community among the men and "tended to make a cult out of transiency." It "removed the transient from all possible contact with private employment, from normal society, and from contact with women and normal family relationships and sent him into the segregated, adoles-cent barrack life of an isolated camp."[46] As the program came to a sudden close in 1935, Harry Hopkins suggested that the transient camps had proven too successful in pulling men from the road. "It was the men who became so well adjusted to the secure, if limited, life of the transient camp," Hopkins explained, "who hoped, like certain soldiers, that the war would never end."[47]

Ending the analogue of war meant shifting the business of relief from FERA and the Transient Program to the WPA. By offering work relief to heads of households, the WPA elevated family breadwinning over military-style collectivism as a model of masculine citizenship. The WPA answered the depression's crisis of nationhood and gender—the plight of the For-gotten Man—not by massing him into an army, but by reaffirming his patriarchal authority and individual purchasing power. Like the CCC, which remained in place as a source of military socialization for the young, the WPA discriminated against women, African Americans, and eventually "aliens," both in its relief policies and its celebrated iconogra-phy. The WPA's "family provider" stood as a countervailing force to the CCC's "youth citizen-soldier." Thoroughly imbued with white racial and masculine gender ideals, both figures served as key symbols of national re-covery during the Great Depression.[48]

While the military organization of the CCC unexpectedly prepared America, especially the army, for the fighting war that was to come, the family breadwinning model of the WPA framed FDR's entire second New Deal. The housing, labor, pension, family welfare, and unemployment compensation provisions that emerged after 1934 signaled the birth of a whole new political economy, one that eventually was to settle, once and for all, America's homeless army. Until then, while the nation remained in the depression's grip, the road continued to receive new groups of mi-grants who challenged the old folklores of homelessness and narratives of hobohemia.

## FOLKLORES OF HOMELESSNESS

The easing of the homelessness crisis and the dissolution of the Transient Program paved the way for a popular revival of hobo folklore at mid-decade. During the early 1930s, when Bonus Marchers, lady hoboes, and wild boys claimed the road, the hobo remained largely absent from popular culture, except as a menacing figure who lured unsuspecting transients into his lair. One prominent attempt to celebrate the open road, Lewis Milestone's 1933 musical *Hallelujah, I'm a Bum*, failed at the box office, as audiences were not yet ready to cheer Al Jolson's depiction of a happy-go-lucky hobo named Bumper.[49] By 1935, however, the road was once again clear, capable of accommodating the various romances that Americans had attached to it since the 1890s.

Writers and poets again extolled the exhilarations of hobo life, exchanging the pretenses of civilization for the authenticity of the road.[50] Old main stem activists offered walking tours of lodging house districts and reissued the *"Hobo" News* as a tabloid of jokes, lore, and verse.[51] The small town of Britt, Iowa, which in 1900 had celebrated the comic tramp with a much-publicized and controversial "hobo convention," revived the event as an annual folk festival featuring campfire songs and a re-created hobo jungle.[52] Other organizations, such as the Rambling Hobo Fellowship of America and the Hoboes of America, Incorporated, held rival conventions that coupled "entertaining hobo high jinks" with the serious business of electing a "Hobo King." "There are more pretenders to this uneasy throne than in a Balkan state," remarked entertainment columnist Walter Winchell.[53] The sight of old friends coming out of retirement to vie for the crown embarrassed even Ben Reitman, though he knew a successful claim could bring endorsement offers, book contracts, and even parts in Hollywood movies.[54] More serious folk collectors also reemerged to gather the familiar artifacts of hobo subculture. In 1938 the WPA's Federal Writers' Project sponsored a field study of "hobo lore" that recorded jungle songs as "documents of human experience."[55]

The hobo vogue reached such heights that it even proved worthy of satire. In 1941 filmmaker Preston Sturges went against the grain of the popular folk idiom with *Sullivan's Travels*, a movie that lampooned the revival of tramp ethnography. In the film John Sullivan, a well-meaning but naive Hollywood movie director who specializes in light comedies, takes to the road in a quest to become a serious filmmaker. Instead of discovering a "folk" there, he finds masses of chillingly silent and disaffiliated men, homeless persons, not hoboes. Indeed, the only joy he encounters is in an African American church, where he gathers with other chain-gang prisoners not to worship and sing, but to laugh at a Mickey Mouse cartoon. The poor and the marginal, Sullivan learns, are bereft of any life-sustaining folk culture or redeeming authenticity. Rather, it is only mass-produced entertainment, the very kind in which Sullivan himself specializes, that soothes the pain of poverty and allows the down-and-out to realize their full humanity.[56]

In valorizing the therapeutic power of mass culture, *Sullivan's Travels* critiqued not only popular romances of the road, but also the larger folk revival of the late 1930s. With the individualistic and consumerist values of the New Era discredited by economic collapse, many Americans turned to "populist outsiders" as sources of inspiration, elevating previously disreputable figures such as outlaws, prisoners, and sharecroppers into folk heroes.[57] Offering a view of America from the bottom up, the resurgent hobo fit the profile of the populist outsider perfectly. In depression folklore, the hobo lacked the ideological sophistication of his Wobbly forebearers. But, unlike the homeless in *Sullivan's Travels,* this folk hero retained a natural integrity, independence, resourcefulness, and generosity that allowed him to endure his poverty with strength and good humor. The blurb of one popular hobo memoir published in 1937 stressed the author's unschooled authenticity and irrepressible optimism. "His narrative is simple and direct," the notice explained; "there are no barriers between him and his reader. And although he deals with some unsavory experiences, his outlook remains fundamentally healthy and reveals his native integrity."[58] Less subtle was "Hobo King" Jeff Davis's declaration in his *Hobo News Review:* "Let's 'Grab dat Rattler'—OLD MAN DEPRESSION—And 'Deck 'em till he's 'Ditched'—'Boil up a Mulligan' of PEP, COURAGE, and HOPE!"[59]

Sounding like a severely déclassé version of the president himself, this Hobo King, who, in fact, lived with his wife and children in Ohio, indulged in the "official" populist rhetoric of the New Deal. This rhetoric assured Americans that the only thing to fear was fear, that "with confidence and faith, adversity could be conquered."[60]

But the plain-speaking hobo did not always parrot mainstream prescriptions for recovery. In some cases, depression-era folklore revived the romance of the road as an alternative to FDR's family breadwinning ideal. A few even invoked old Wobbly myths in denouncing domesticity as a curse upon freewheeling men.

In Frank Capra's *Meet John Doe,* a film that both exploits and critiques the populist rhetoric of the Forgotten Man, a hard-bitten hobo known as the Colonel, played by Walter Brennan, presents a vision of the world reminiscent of Joe Hill. The Colonel's unemployed traveling companion,

Long John Willoughby (Gary Cooper), plays the part of the Forgotten Man when an unscrupulous newspaper columnist (Barbara Stanwyck) offers him money to pose as "John Doe," a "disgruntled American citizen," for a publicity stunt. Rather than suggest the immorality of the fraud, the Colonel rails against Long John's "living wage" bargain, warning his fellow traveler of the consumerist peonage that awaits him:

> I've seen guys like you go under before. Guys that never had a worry. Then they got a hold of some dough and went goofy. . . . The first thing that happens to a guy like that is he starts wanting to go into restaurants and sit down at a table and eat salads and cupcakes and tea. Boy, what that kind of food does to your system! The next thing the dope wants is a room. Yes sir, a room with steam heat and curtains and rugs and before you know it, he's all softened up and he can't sleep unless he has a bed. . . . I've seen plenty of fellas start out with fifty bucks and wind up with a bank account! . . . And let me tell you, Long John, when you become a guy with a bank account, they got you. Yes, they got you.[61]

Early New Deal relief officials would have viewed the Colonel as a dangerous example of hobohemia's influence upon the new homeless. But in *Meet John Doe*, it is Long John's resistance to the Colonel's message that sparks the mischief. Indeed, the Colonel's rejection of domestic conventions and his deep suspicion of salesmen, politicians, business leaders, relief workers, and public relations specialists appear well placed. The sinister force at work in the film is not hobohemia, but a fascist media baron named Norton who hitches his own dictatorial ambitions to the rising star of John Doe. The newspaper magnate sponsors a network of "John Doe Clubs," a seemingly innocuous association of middle-American men and women who affirm the common values of the Forgotten Man. But the John Doe Clubs are a front group for fascism, launching a populist third-party movement with which Norton hopes to capture the White House and rule America with "an iron hand."

Critiquing both the right-wing populism of the "mob" and the liberal populism of the New Deal, *Meet John Doe*, in its final version, also refuses to sanction the Colonel's bleak countercultural vision. Shortly before the movie's release, director Frank Capra removed an original ending that returned the Colonel to the film to cradle a dying Long John after his suicidal leap from city hall. In place of this ending, Capra inserted a happier one in which Long John and his chastened followers walk away from the John Doe charade, daring Norton to "try and lick" "the people." Despite its dark warnings about the fascist tendencies of the Forgotten Man and the hegemonic power of mass culture, *Meet John Doe* ultimately keeps the

Colonel at bay, allowing Long John to get the girl (Stanwyck, of course) and the people to be redeemed.[62]

While Hollywood could not bring itself to endorse the Colonel's romance of masculine freedom, neither could the political Left. In the 1930s the Left achieved enormous cultural influence, largely through the work of the writers, intellectuals, and artists associated with the Popular Front. A broad-based social movement that united communists with a larger group of independent labor, civil rights, and anti-fascist activists, the Popular Front drew inspiration from a variety of depression-era folk figures in an attempt to reimagine America as a racially and ethnically diverse cooperative commonwealth, "a nation of nations."

Popular Front activists joined the rhetorical struggle over "the people," contesting right-wing and New Deal depictions of the Forgotten Man with a gallery of populist outsiders ranging from single wage-earning women and urban immigrants to black sharecroppers and Mexican migrants. Perhaps not surprisingly, the hobo failed to take a prominent place in this gallery of the "cultural front," either as an icon of "the people" or as a starting point for social activism.[63]

Even the communist-sponsored Unemployed Councils, which represented the party's earliest attempt to reach out to non-communist activists, made little use of hobohemia, the main stem, or Wobbly folklore in their demonstrations. The Unemployed Councils took root almost exclusively in stable working-class neighborhoods, building their community networks through fraternal lodges, churches, and other ethnic-, racial-, and language-based organizations. Indeed, many members were housewives who mobilized to stop evictions, an issue that concerned few committed hobohemians.[64]

Similarly, the old-stock native whites who had formed the rank and file of hobohemia found themselves vastly outnumbered in the militant unions of the Congress of Industrial Organizations (CIO). The masses of workers swept up by the CIO in the late 1930s and early 1940s were overwhelmingly urban ethnics and African Americans who a generation or two earlier would have found themselves in the agricultural peripheries of Europe and the American South. Even the much-publicized efforts to organize migratory workers in California primarily involved Asian and Mexican workers, rather than the "bindle stiffs" who had once roamed the Golden State.[65]

Given the multiracial, multiethnic, and even gender-inclusive nature of the movement, it is perhaps not surprising that the hobo, shrouded as he was in myths of native white manhood, enjoyed so little currency as a representative of "the people" in Popular Front culture. The folklore of the hobo jungle, like those of the Bonus Army and CCC camps, rested on racial and gender exclusions that seemed to tilt ominously toward fascism. Nevertheless, just as the Wobbly romance of male virility and violent struggle persisted in the rhetoric and iconography of the CIO, so, too, did the hobo endure as a powerful symbol of both dispossession and political awakening.[66] As such, he could not simply be expunged from the gallery of labor icons. Instead, he had to be modified, cleansed of his latent racist and nativist associations, in order to remain vital in the age of the Popular Front.

The most celebrated and successful effort to adapt hobo folklore to the "pan-ethnic Americanism" of the Popular Front came in the work of Woody Guthrie, a radical writer, singer, and activist who became a radio celebrity in the late 1930s.[67] Like the Wobbly ballads of old, Guthrie's songs and stories recounted both the deprivations and the glories of the road, ultimately embracing the boxcar, the jungle, and the flophouse as the gathering fields of revolution. In *Bound for Glory*, his anthemic autobiography of 1943, Guthrie recalls earlier working-class narratives of tramping that depicted the experience of homelessness as an epiphany. "There is a stage of hard luck that turns into fun," Guthrie explains while describing a rainy night in a California freight yard, "and a stage of poverty that turns into pride, and a place in laughing that turns into fight." To Guthrie, the road was a school in "fight," in socialism and labor activism, offering an authentic community and fellowship that was inaccessible to those "hemmed up" in suburban homes and "walled in" inside downtown office buildings.[68]

But while *Bound for Glory* posits the rough and unstable camaraderie of the boxcar as a microcosm of the American working class, it emphatically insists on a racially inclusive vision of "the people." Indeed, the book's opening sentence redefines the road as a multiracial domain: "I could see men of all colors bouncing along in the boxcar." His description of the men "piled around on each other" amounts to a catalog of occupations, ethnicities, nationalities, and races, each in tension with one another but subjected to the same conditions. With "race pushing against race" on the crowded train, Guthrie emphasizes the common battle "against the wind and the rain," metaphors for the depression and fascism, that ultimately must draw the men together.

The coupling of Guthrie and his black traveling companion provides a model for such interracial solidarity. Another racially utopian moment occurs along the main stem of Los Angeles when Guthrie and a gang of other down-and-out men fight off a jingoistic mob of "native-borned American citizens" threatening "to beat the hell out of all the Japs" in town.[69] Unlike John Dos Passos's *U.S.A.*, which extinguishes its revolutionary romance in a self-defeating white supremacy, Guthrie's book maintains a faith in the road's ability to accommodate ethnic and racial difference and to lead America toward a glorious victory against international fascism.

While Guthrie opens and closes his autobiography with vignettes of a freight train that is "bound for glory," his narrative actually centers around the disintegration of his drifting family and the stream of migrants he meets when he strikes out on his own for California. The social context of Guthrie's account is not so much the movement of single male transients, but rather the mass migrations of the late 1930s that moved hundreds of thousands of agricultural families to the West Coast. In the migrant family's struggle to stay together, forge new communal bonds, and discover the larger meaning of their "hard traveling," Guthrie finds a symbol of revolutionary collectivism as powerful as that of the boxcar. On the road near Redding, California, Guthrie encounters a vast "jungle camp" filled not with hoboes, but with thousands of men, women, and children living "as close to nature, and as far from everything natural, as human beings can." The song of this jungle is a far cry from the rollicking celebration of the freight train. Indeed, this song emanates from two young sisters who sing and play the guitar with such "clear and honest" beauty that the entire camp sits quietly enraptured. For these migrants, redemption comes not from a "Hollywood put-on" or a rugged romance of struggle, but from the folk wisdom of an uprooted people.[70]

In placing his own narrative in the context of the drifting southwestern families of the late 1930s, Guthrie contributed to a new folklore of homelessness that, like that of the hobo, had its conservative as well as radical uses. While Guthrie frequently noted the presence of African American, Mexican, Chinese, and Japanese migrants on the road, John Steinbeck and many other narrators of the emerging "grapes of wrath" story focused exclusively on the "American exodus" of "Okies," white Protestants from southern plains states. Displaced by drought, mechanization, farm foreclosure, and declining agricultural prices (causes often subsumed under the legend of the Dust Bowl), Okies seemed to domesticate the very experience of homelessness both in their "plain-folk Americanism" and their common gender arrangements.[71]

Unlike lady hoboes and wild boys, migrant families posed serious problems of relief but elicited none of the panic that had accompanied the transient crisis. Indeed, most officials did not even consider migrant families to be homeless at all. Because generations of charity workers had defined homelessness almost exclusively in terms of unbound masculinity (or travestied femininity), FERA administrators did not at first even consider procedures for transient family groups. When displaced families poured into registration centers in the West and elsewhere, program officials quickly evaluated these transients as "normal in purpose and attitude," supplied them with outdoor relief, and arranged for their transportation back home, not bothering to administer any of the program's prophylactic or rehabilitative measures.[72]

Eventually, government officials even refused to label these homeless families "transients," a term tainted by its association with relief camps. Instead, these families became "migrants," a word that signaled the almost relaxed acceptance with which New Dealers met the continental shifting of populations toward the end of the decade.[73] "Migrants," asserted one former Transient Program administrator in a revisionist article of 1937, demonstrate that "mobility in itself is a desirable and necessary phenomenon if our present day economy is to function smoothly and efficiently"[74] Drifting families eased concerns about rampant mobility because they seemed to retain the habits and values of home life even if their only shelter was a canvas tent or the steel frame of a Ford. They did not indulge in romances of the road, and therefore failed to raise the specter of hobohemia. Indeed, they appeared to reaffirm traditional family structure, as well as the resolute nobility of whiteness, in the face of enormous adversity.

As a populist symbol of beset nationhood, the Okie exodus came to rival, or rather complement, the plight of the Forgotten Man. Indeed, no single image from the Great Depression is more recognizable or enduring than Dorothea Lange's "Migrant Mother," a photograph of a desperately poor woman and her children stranded in California in 1936 (fig. 7.3). As one of the period's many "icons of motherhood," Lange's portrait offers a certain reassurance to the viewer, despite the pitiful condition it records. Unlike the dynamic images of Wobbly romance, which depict the hobo as a vanguard figure leading society toward a new dawn, the "Migrant Mother" refuses such narratives, appearing timeless in her maternity. Amidst the crisis of dispossession and displacement, such "madonnas of the fields" provided symbols of stability and tradition, promising, as does Ma Joad at the end of Darryl Zanuck's movie *Grapes of Wrath*, that "the people" "will go on forever."[75]

The iconography of migrant motherhood proved so compelling that it eclipsed earlier depictions of aggressive lady hoboes who encroached upon the "original provinces of men." Even Ben Reitman's scandalous "autobiography" of "Boxcar Bertha," an apocryphal account of female homelessness that exploited the lady hobo panic of the early depression,

Figure 7.3: Taken shortly after she encountered the Mexican family with tire trouble (see fig. 6.1), Dorothea Lange's "Migrant Mother" has transcended the particular circumstances of its creation to become the most famous documentary image from the Great Depression. On a rainy afternoon in March 1936, Lange paid a ten-minute visit to a fetid pea-pickers' camp in San Luis Obispo, California, looking to capture the plight of unemployed agricultural workers. "I saw and approached the hungry and desperate mother, as if drawn by a magnet," recalled Lange. That mother, a thirty-two-year-old widow named Florence Thompson, posed for six photographs in her makeshift lean-to, the last of which became the "Migrant Mother." Even as it recorded a fatherless family on the brink of collapse, the "Migrant Mother" provided a reassuring image of endurance in the face of adversity. The photograph joined numerous other "icons of motherhood" that collectively quelled fears of female homelessness in the late 1930s. In contrast to popular images of swaggering "hobohemians," emancipated "lady hoboes," and roving "wild boys," the "Migrant Mother" resisted the connotations of homelessness, appearing static and almost timeless in her maternity. (Courtesy of the U.S. Farm Security Administration Collection, Library of Congress.)

fell under the domesticating influence of the Migrant Mother. Published in 1937, Reitman's narrative of a former Wobbly "rebel girl" reads at first like a feminist account of political awakening and liberation. Then, toward the end of the book, Bertha suddenly and inexplicably departs her career as "a hobo, a radical, a prostitute, a thief, a reformer, a social worker, and a revolutionist." Bertha instead embraces motherhood, her maternal instincts prevailing over both her wanderlust and her politics:

> I had been trying to escape my own natural need to be responsible for someone, to live for someone else, some special individual person who belonged peculiarly to myself. For years I had told myself that I didn't want to be tied down, that I wanted to keep myself free to help others, to uplift the vast mass of struggling humanity. And I knew now that I had been rationalizing my need to be a mother, dissipating it over the face of the earth when its primary satisfaction lay within reach of my own arms.[76]

While such pro-natalist myths helped to quell the cultural crisis of homelessness in the late 1930s, the Migrant Mother did not simply signal a return to old-fashioned family values. By placing mothers at its center, the new folklore of homelessness celebrated women's strength and resolve, not as "rebel girls" or wage earners, but as family protectors. Of course, the absence of breadwinning fatherhood from this folklore was precisely what endowed migrant motherhood with such symbolic power. The very image of the Migrant Mother demanded the return of the family provider or, in his absence, the granting of "welfare" to his dependents. But while certainly "pitied" as dependents, and therefore shackled to their domestic roles, women nonetheless completed the figurative family circle by providing strong companionship to their "entitled" men.[77]

The "comradely ideal" that informed public representations of men and women during the depression also structured the coupling of Forgotten Men and Migrant Mothers as symbols of recovery and recipients of New Deal largesse.[78] Domesticating these two uprooted figures did not mean replanting them in the eroded soil of rural America or massing them in congregate camps. Rather, it entailed restoring the suburban ideal to the center of American family life and revitalizing the nation through broad-based homeownership.

While the plights of the Forgotten Man and the Migrant Mother provided myths of family and national restoration, more formal sociological accounts of family collapse and recovery also emerged to sanction the suburban ideal. Several studies of family life in the 1930s stressed the importance of both flexibility and tradition in maintaining the home amidst economic crisis. In 1936 Robert Cooley Angell found that highly modern urban families who made their homes in apartments were too "loosely knit" and "individualistic" and thus quickly succumbed to the entropic forces of the depression. While urban families fell victim to the "hotel spirit," rural farm families adhered too rigidly to tradition, maintaining patriarchal authority at the expense of women's contributions. "The husband who will not let his capable wife share in family control because he feels it is his role to be the sole leader," writes Angell, spells the doom of the home. The nation's best hope, Angell concludes, are the "highly integrated, highly adaptable" families "found among the thoroughly Americanized elements of the middle class, particularly in smaller cities."[79] By nurturing companionate marriages and a modern nuclear family life, Americans could stem the disintegrating forces of the depression.

As in earlier periods, a broadly defined crisis of homelessness inspired numerous blueprints for reengineering the American home. Urban planners and housing activists like Lewis Mumford and Catherine Bauer campaigned for a wide range of residential forms, from independent cooperative apartment buildings to federally supported noncommercial housing units of all sorts. But just as the hotel experiments of Charlotte Perkins Gilman and Upton Sinclair provided little check against the rising suburban ideal, so did alternative urban plans fail to divert the New Deal from its core focus in housing, which was to subsidize the mass suburbanization of America.[80]

From the Resettlement Administration's Greenbelt program to the Home Owners Loan Corporation (HOLC) and the Federal Housing Administration (FHA), New Deal housing initiatives expressed an unwavering commitment to suburbia as the nation's dominant residential form. As vehicles of economic recovery, the HOLC and the FHA saved nearly a million mortgages from foreclosure and resuscitated a moribund building industry by insuring long-term low-interest loans for suburban homes. The same federal planning, building, and lending guidelines that underwrote suburban growth also defined old main stem neighborhoods as "blighted" districts in need of wholesale redevelopment. By the end of World War II, when demobilization and a tight housing market raised once again the specter of hobohemia, an entirely new financial apparatus was now in place to make the suburban ideal a reality for the majority of American families.[81]

The Great Depression, which began by sending millions to lodging houses, jungle camps, and public shelters, ended by confirming hobohemia's demise and recommitting the nation to the suburban domestic ideal. But the road from relief camp to suburban subdivision was long and twisted. Indeed, the Great Depression ended not with the analogue of war, but with war itself, as America mobilized to fight in Europe and the Far East. Forgotten Men suddenly found themselves back in the rough life of the barracks, while Migrant Mothers took their places on production lines and in office pools. Public shelters emptied, but the "congregate form of living" became the norm for millions of American men and women who, like Woody Guthrie's boxcar companions, made their way to defense-related jobs. Lodging houses brimmed with young workers, and hotel districts once again became centers of a vibrant commercial life.

Unlike with the Bonus Army, the demobilization of soldiers and sailors after World War II would entail far more than awarding veterans a post-dated check for services rendered in war. Rather, it would mean legislatively vouchsafing to returning GIs to the kind of homes promised by the family breadwinning model of the second New Deal. After the war, the New Deal constituency would leave behind the urban "congregate form of living" and head for the suburbs. Meanwhile, memories of the road would survive only in the imaginations of men still at war with their own domesticity.

# COMING HOME

ike most soldiers and sailors coming home after World War II, Bill Mauldin "fretted and felt good" as he awaited his discharge from the army. He felt good that his war was over, but he fretted for what the future would hold. On the face of it, Mauldin had little reason to worry. The war had made him a celebrity, a Pulitzer Prize–winning cartoonist for *Stars and Stripes* whose sardonic depictions of two "dogface" infantrymen, Willie and Joe, had been a favorite among enlisted men on the front. While returning Willies and Joes hopped freight trains, slept on park benches, and crowded into urban lodging houses in the summer of 1945, Mauldin enjoyed VIP treatment on his journey back home. Arriving in New York City, he found himself showered with movie offers, book contracts, and syndication deals. At the tender age of twenty-four, Mauldin possessed a cultural authority that few popular commentators could rival. During the war he had spoken for millions of men massed in infantry units abroad. Now he would have a chance to speak for those returning to the home front and, perhaps, help to shape their future.[1]

Still, the prospect of reconversion filled him with anxiety. Mauldin had won his fame by charting the fates of two proletarian characters who, a decade or so earlier, might have found themselves in Anacostia Flats rather than Anzio or shouldering bindles instead of rifles (fig. 8.1). Like many actual veterans who had been "road kids" or CCC recruits before the war, Willie and Joe had little experience with domestic life. Now these two Forgotten Men would have to come home. For Mauldin, this meant leaving behind the only subject matter he had ever known: the camaraderie of the bivouac, the loneliness of the foxhole, and the deluded arrogance of army brass. A strange new world of wives, babies, and jobs awaited.

*"Remember that warm, soft mud last summer?"*

Figure 8.1: Along with Ernie Pyle, Bill Mauldin provided Americans with the most compelling images of life on the front during World War II, including this cartoon from 1944. Positioned "on the left side of American politics," Mauldin brought a distinctly proletarian aesthetic to his cartoons of Willie and Joe, two infantry "dogfaces" whose grim humor took aim at the class inequities of army life. Bewhiskered and bedraggled, sleeping outdoors but retaining a fierce sense of manly independence and fellowship, Willie and Joe recalled a long line of tramp and hobo characters, from the hobohemians of Wobbly folklore and the "Weary Willies" of the vaudeville stage to the protesting veterans of the Bonus Army. These two undomesticated "dogfaces" also dramatized the distance between the rough camaraderie of the bivouac and familial comforts of the home front. Although Mauldin opposed "special privileges" for returning soldiers and sailors, his cartoons expressed the very concerns about reintegrating veterans into civilian life that inspired the Servicemen's Readjustment Act of 1944, otherwise known as the GI Bill. (Copyright 1944 by Bill Mauldin. Reprinted with permission of Bill Mauldin.)

Also awaiting were new controversies over how best to reintegrate former GIs back into civilian life. As an independent leftist with Popular Front credentials, Mauldin spoke out vigorously against the American Legion, which, he complained, regarded "the veteran as a separate and privileged part of society." Fearing the Legion's fascist tendencies, Mauldin opposed its efforts to win government largesse on behalf of veterans. Leveling a particularly damning accusation that played upon emerging prejudices, Mauldin contended that veterans who clamored "for free benefits from the Treasury" were probably bachelors, for men "who have families to support are too busy earning a living to think of a march on Washington."[2] Instead of special benefits for veterans, Mauldin favored a general "Economic Bill of Rights" for all Americans, which President Roosevelt and the Congress of Industrial Organizations' Political Action Committee (CIO-PAC) had called for during the war.[3] A year before Mauldin's return home, however, the American Legion had secured a "Bill of Rights" of its own, an omnibus piece of veterans legislation that was destined to change America. In 1945 the full impact of this legislation was lost on Mauldin, as it was on FDR himself.

The Servicemen's Readjustment Act of 1944, or the "GI Bill" as its Legion backers dubbed it, was one of 640 bills introduced in Congress to address the problem of returning 12 million veterans to civilian life.[4] When the president signed the GI Bill into law on June 22, 1944, few paid any attention. Most of those who did considered its extraordinary package of benefits—unemployment compensation, subsidized mortgages, and money for higher education and vocational training—as a fit and necessary measure to shield the country against the impact of demobilization. The end of war, most assumed, would bring a return of depression and mass unemployment, leaving the country vulnerable to roving armies of jobless veterans.[5] In addition, there were also fears that "the army had created a generation of bums," as Bill Mauldin put it.[6] Just as Gilded Age commentators linked the rise of America's "great army of tramps" to the Civil War bivouac, so, too, did post–World War II observers express concern that returning veterans would be unwilling or unable to assume positions as family breadwinners.

To counter the threat of a reinvigorated hobohemia, the GI Bill extended the suburban ideal to masses of demobilized men, seeking to transform them from bivouacking dogfaces to breadwinning husbands and fathers. Among the few who publicly opposed the bill were those who charged that the legislation would spread, rather than staunch, the spirit of the bivouac. In an article for *Collier's*, for example, the president of the University of Chicago warned that the GI Bill, far from domesticating veterans, would instead turn colleges "into educational hobo jungles."[7]

While veterans did, in fact, swarm to college campuses, doubling en-rollments by 1947, the GI Bill's extraordinary housing provisions trans-formed the nation's very landscape.[8] In so doing, this single piece of legislation achieved in a few years what a decade of New Deal relief pro-grams had failed to accomplish. Namely, it resettled the nation, bringing to a swift halt the residential shifting that had characterized American life throughout its industrial history. By 1950 the suburban ideal had become a reality for a solid majority of American families who rushed to claim the material and social benefits of homeownership.[9]

Within these new homes, nuclear family life flourished as never before. Marriage and birth rates soared, reaching twentieth-century highs after the war, while the median age of first marriage—22.6 for men and 20.4 for women—dropped to their lowest recorded levels.[10] In the span of five years, Willie and Joe had moved from foxhole to park bench to ranch house. Where they had once struggled against the restrictions of army life, they now found themselves chafing against their own domestication and the burdens of breadwinning (fig. 8.2).

As a substitute for the general "Economic Bill of Rights" envisioned by liberal New Dealers and Popular Front activists alike, the GI Bill repre-sented an opening gambit in a larger series of negotiations between the federal government, large corporations, and organized labor in the wake of World War II. The bargaining arose in response not only to the specter of the unemployed veteran, but also to an awakened militancy among in-dustrial workers, a militancy expressed in wildcat strikes during the war and a massive strike wave launched by the CIO shortly after V-J Day. By late 1946 over a quarter of the CIO's membership stood on picket lines, and general strikes had erupted in a half-dozen American cities. Through these strikes, workers articulated their demands for an "industrial democ-racy," a redistribution not only of wealth but of decision-making power over the nation's economic life.[11] In responding to these demands, busi-ness leaders gave shape to a new political economy and social order that magnified the entitlements enshrined in the GI Bill.

Many conservative business leaders rejected the idea of a new order, responding to the CIO's insurgency instead with intense anti-union cam-paigns. But while conservatives exploited the growing power of the anti-communist movement to purge the CIO of its radical leaders and secure an "open shop," others embraced a philosophy of "corporate liberalism" that encouraged making concessions to labor in order to achieve long-term economic stability. Like their welfare capitalist forebearers, postwar corporate liberals sought to give workers a stake in the system by offering benefits, promotions, and wage increases linked to seniority. But unlike

*"How's it feel to be a free man, Willie?"*

Figure 8.2: After his discharge from the army in 1945, Bill Mauldin started work on *Back Home*, a sequel to his popular account of GI life, *Up Front*. With brilliant irony, the book explores the many perils that awaited returning soldiers. In the above cartoon, for example, Mauldin expresses emerging fears that veterans were becoming trapped in breadwinning routines that deprived them of their manly freedoms. As the Cold War–fueled domestic revival took hold in the 1950s, such fears multiplied, inspiring numerous "gray flannel" rebellions against the feminized home and bureaucratized workplace. The problem of "conformity," often equated with "emasculation," soon became a topic of national concern, with commentators prescribing any number of remedies for the loss of male autonomy, initiative, and authority. One can easily imagine Mauldin's "dogface" Willie moving to the suburbs, shedding his proletarian identity, and then turning to the pages of *Playboy* magazine for dreamy images of unfettered bachelorhood. (Copyright 1947 by Bill Mauldin. Reprinted with permission of Bill Mauldin.)

the corporate welfarism of the 1920s, corporate liberalism of the 1940s and 1950s recognized the state as a key component of this new political economy. Liberal business and financial leaders, as well as academics and old New Dealers, saw the state as playing a critical role in mediating the conflicts between the nation's major interest groups, especially those of capital and labor. Corporate liberals also assigned government the task of creating and maintaining a favorable business climate, whether it be through promoting investment, regulating domestic demand conditions, or gaining access to international markets and raw materials.[12]

Most important, in light of the 1946 strike wave, was the role of government in promoting consumer spending and subsidizing the living standards of workers. The GI Bill, in this light, was more than a piece of veterans legislation. It was, in no small measure, part of a larger class bargain struck with the returning New Deal constituency—FDR's Forgotten Men—in order to forestall the kind of militant protests that had plagued the nation since the Bonus March of 1932. Negotiated through the 1940s and prolonged by the Cold War political economy of the 1950s and 1960s, this "fair deal" tied working-class aspirations for a better life to the suburban ideal of masculine breadwinning and the steady consumption of durable goods. Long-standing dreams of a "living wage" for labor reemerged in the postwar era as a "family wage" that would allow men to keep their dependent wives and children out of the workforce. As the conservative stick of anti-communism and the open shop broke the CIO's insurgency, the carrot of corporate liberalism and the family-wage pact began to appear like an offer that few workers could refuse.

With the nation entering an era of domesticity, bureaucratic unionism, and unbridled consumption, observers noticed that a stubborn residuum was refusing to accept this postwar settlement, this great class bargain. Instead of signing the family-wage agreement and moving to the suburbs, some men lingered in aging main stem districts, clinging to their old bachlor ways and casual labor habits. These districts, which urban sociologists now uniformly referred to as "skid rows," fascinated those Americans embroiled in the problems of "conformity" and masculine domesticity. Skid row attracted not only sociologists seeking to uncover the pathologies of nonfamily men, but also a new generation of bohemian artists and writers—the so-called Beats—who found in homeless man districts both a measure of their own alienation from postwar norms and a starting point for their own counterculture.

Equally important to the Beats, but far less visible to white suburanites, were those African American urban dwellers, many of them newly arrived from the South, who were systematically excluded from the postwar settlement. Suburban expansion had added a new geographic dimension to America's color line, dividing whites and blacks within the metropolitan order itself. Federal housing policy effectively barred African Americans from most new suburban developments and discouraged investment in urban multifamily units. With suburban homeownership increasingly becoming the mark of full citizenship, such "red-lining" practices augmented the subordination that a racially stratified labor market already imposed upon black Americans.[13] Bill Mauldin may have been right when he said that most veterans were too busy earning livings and raising families to march on Washington for special benefits. But for African Americans, the March on Washington movement, first launched in 1941 by A. Philip Randolph's mobile army of sleeping car porters, opened a new campaign to secure the homes, jobs, and status legislatively vouchsafed to white veterans after World War II.

As part of a larger postwar settlement, the GI Bill had effectively solved the modern problem of homelessness and reclaimed the Forgotten Man for the middle class. But in so doing, it had also encouraged the creation of a new "underclass," one defined largely in terms of race. By pushing the "crabgrass frontier" ever farther into the urban hinterlands, the GI Bill helped to lay the foundation for a postmodern homelessness crisis that began to emerge once the last remnants of skid row had all but disappeared.

## THE DECLINE AND FALL OF SKID ROW

During the postwar economic boom, when the family-wage system enjoyed greater authority than it ever had before or ever would again, skid row seemed to represent a strange exception to the general rule of mobility. With Americans moving upward into the middle class and outward to the suburbs, the men of skid row appeared to be stagnating.

The widespread use of the term "skid row" suggested as much. The label originally derived from the skidways that loggers in the Pacific Northwest had used to transport lumber to sawmills. In Seattle lumberjacks had fashioned one of the liveliest main stems in America along the "skid road" that led to Henry Yesler's waterfront sawmill. When the migratory labor market declined after World War I, the generic term "skid row" came into use, rivaling the more positively construed "main stem" and "hobohemia." Whereas the latter terms had signified a certain swaggering élan associated with the hobo world, "skid row" emphasized downward mobility (hitting the "skids") and a constrained physical environment (a "row" instead of a "stem").[14] In the wake of World War II, the older terms disappeared entirely. "Hoboes," who had once epitomized freewheeling American working-class manhood, had become "bums," confined to a few city blocks and shut out of the abundance and fulfillment that the postwar world had to offer.

Given the seemingly exceptional nature of skid row poverty and alienation, most Americans took comfort in the observable fact that homeless man neighborhoods across the country were rapidly disappearing. Having boomed during the war and demobilization, cheap hotel districts began to shrink in both population and physical size in the late 1940s. Each year suburban expansion and urban renewal claimed increasing shares of its inhabitants and buildings. One study of Chicago's West Madison district in 1958 counted a mere thirteen thousand individuals residing there, less than one-fifth the number of those estimated by Nels Anderson in 1922.[15] Another analysis of census data from forty-one skid row districts across the country found an aggregate population loss of almost 58 percent between 1950 and 1970.[16] As those remaining on skid row aged, the neighborhood took on the look of a rest home for single working-class men.[17]

As skid row slid into oblivion, journalists and sociologists kept the problem of homelessness before the public eye as never before. Indeed, even as the numbers of lodging houses and homeless men dwindled, the aberrant world of skid row attained a mythic status in the American imagination. With suburban domesticity on the rise in 1949, the *Chicago Daily News* "set Chicago buzzing," and reportedly gained twenty thousand new readers, with its twelve-part exposé of West Madison Street.[18] Numerous other newspapers followed suit, as did social scientists. Howard M. Bahr and Theodore Caplow, the two most prominent skid row sociologists, remarked in 1974 that postwar scholars had used "nearly every research method known to modern sociology" to study homeless men, adding that there was "no other type of problem area in the United States about which we are as well informed as skid row."[19]

Researchers lavished such attention on skid row precisely because of its anomalous status. Like the waterfronts, juvenile gangs, and communist cells that showed up so often in the popular movies and fiction of the 1950s, skid row represented an illegitimate subculture with bonds and allegiances separate from and resistant to those of the middle-class nuclear family. During the housing shortage of the late 1940s, this subculture appeared particularly threatening. With 6 million families doubling up, a half-million more living in makeshift shelters, and masses of undomesticated men still returning from military service, family disintegration posed a real problem.[20] In addition, the war itself had breathed new life into crowded hotel districts, drawing millions of diverse people, including African Americans and women, into the urban labor force.[21] Only in 1949 and 1950, with reconversion accomplished and the housing crisis quelled, did the immediate menace of homelessness subside. As in the 1920s, skid row became less a threat and more of a fascinating and disturbing anachronism, a throwback to another age before mass consumerism, suburban subdivisions, and high-wage jobs had liberated the American family from the "congregate form of living."

But while domesticated Americans of the 1950s viewed skid row as a perverse holdout against the modernizing forces of the age, the domestic revival itself expressed underlying anxieties and uncertainties about the new world coming into being. While the threat of a renewed depression had passed, the prospect of another war, this time against a nuclear-armed Soviet Union, lay on the horizon. Preparing for this conflict meant coordinating state, industrial, military, labor, and even cultural activities on a national scale. While bringing a measure of security to the nation, this vast bureaucratic expansion of both public and private enterprise entailed dangers of its own, including the "unwarranted influence" of the "military-industrial complex" denounced by President Dwight D. Eisenhower in 1961.[22] But the reach of state and corporate bureaucracies stretched far beyond Cold War defense industries. Together, government and business leaders engineered a new mass consumer market that propelled the country to an unparalleled state of economic prosperity. Even as it increasingly defined the parameters of the "good life," however, the new consumerism also fed anxieties about decadence, rampant commercialism, and the fraying community fabric.[23]

Like the early-twentieth-century suburban ideal, the postwar domestic revival attempted to counter the entropic effects of mass consumerism by binding the forces of modernization to a traditional vision of American family life. Postwar suburbia harnessed what Henry James had called the American "genius for organization" to engineer a therapeutic remedy for the ills created by the ongoing march of modernity. New suburban subdivisions both exploited and advanced technological, managerial, and mass production innovations in order to heal the alienation and sense of anonymity to which these innovations gave rise. Builders such as William Levitt perfected the assembly-line construction techniques envisioned by the founders of the suburban ideal a half-century earlier, putting houses on the market at the rate of thirty-five a day and selling them for about $7,500.[24] Powerful ideologies of nuclear family life "contained" the anxieties that arose in response to such impersonal economies of scale. In this way, postwar domesticity held out the promises of both freedom and security, mobility and community.[25] Against these promises stood the grim realities of skid row, which only seemed to confirm the barrenness, immobility, and insecurity of life away from the nuclear family.

Skid row men elicited pity during the Cold War era, but they also evoked disgust and not a little fear. Skid row homelessness represented a blatant affront to the nuclear family ideal, an ideal that held such extreme sway in postwar culture that few who deviated from it escaped without sanction. Dependent as they were on male breadwinning, most women, for example, could only avoid poverty and the stigma of "failure" by getting married. While single men did not necessarily face indigence, they did draw suspicion. Men who held out from marriage much beyond their mid-twenties were invariably seen as "immature" or "irresponsible," labels that impaired career success as well as social acceptance. More serious was the charge of "perversion," an omnibus term that included homosexuality within its rubric. For any man who wished to enjoy the full benefits of postwar culture, marriage was, quite simply, a prerequisite.[26]

Skid row, made up entirely of unmarried men, thus appeared deviant, even dangerously so. If Americans fought the Cold War, as Elaine Tyler May argues, through the analogue of home, then homelessness potentially threatened not only gender and family norms, but national security itself.[27] The skid row man "is not part of the team," stated Howard M. Bahr succinctly, and therefore "cannot be trusted."[28]

Like previous investigators, Bahr and others defined skid row homelessness not in terms of shelter or even poverty, but rather in terms of attachment and allegiance to a settled social system. "The essence of the concept goes beyond residential arrangements," argued Bahr and Theodore Caplow. "The man who occupies the same lodging on skid row for forty uninterrupted years is properly considered homeless." Drawing upon Robert Merton's anomie theories, Bahr and Caplow characterized homelessness as a state of "disaffiliation" caused by a variety of factors but constantly reinforced by the alienating commercial environment of the city.[29]

By defining homelessness as "disaffiliation," Bahr, Caplow, and others could have potentially launched a sweeping critique of postwar American culture, uncovering the sense of alienation and isolation lurking beneath the celebration of family unity and consumer abundance. Indeed, one psychologist argued in 1963 that far from being isolated on skid row, homelessness represented an "invisible mountain" growing at the very center of American life. This scholar contended that men from "every strata of society" were increasingly withdrawing from the bonds of family, community, and workplace. "The homeless man is a symbol of what's wrong with our society," he concluded, " . . . the beacon light warning us of the reefs up ahead."[30] Such uses of the homelessness concept, removed from the specific conditions of skid row life, became increasingly common into the 1960s. By 1973 Peter Berger and the other authors of *The Homeless Mind* could characterize modern consciousness itself as homeless without stretching or abstracting the term much beyond earlier definitions of skid row "disaffiliation."[31]

But skid row sociologists and social service professionals rarely launched such broad critiques. Instead, they characterized skid row as a world apart, an isolated enclave of damaged white men who had failed to take up their proper roles as family breadwinners. Moreover, they insisted that the very existence of skid row threatened American society by virtue of its detachment from the "affiliative bonds that link settled persons to a network of interconnected social structures." The skid row resident, argued Bahr and Caplow, was "a man out of control" and "ultimately beyond the reach of organized society." Without property, family, or job, he lived outside of the nation's "reward system" and therefore was subject to no sanction other than corporal punishment. The skid row dweller "may go along with the rules," Bahr and Caplow warned, "but there is no guarantee he will do so, and because he is not part of the system, he has no important stake in its continuity."[32]

Along with the popular press, most scholarly studies vastly exaggerated skid row's isolation and deviance. Contrary to prevailing stereotypes, for example, most homeless men worked for a living and relatively few were alcoholics. Moreover, as Bahr and Caplow's own research revealed, the men of skid row experienced levels of disaffiliation remarkably similar to those of settled workers. That is, married working-class men were only slightly more likely to vote, join organizations, go to church, and have steady friends than skid row men. Skid row, then, was less an exception to a general rule of abundance and mobility than a variation on a larger theme of poverty and alienation.[33]

Far from being an isolated ghetto, skid row hosted men of various racial, ethnic, and age groups and saw a great deal of interaction with surrounding black, Latino, and other working-class neighborhoods. African Americans, Mexicans, Puerto Ricans, and American Indians could all be found on America's skid rows, though they were rarely counted among the homeless. Sociologists tended to see these minority groups as suffering from racial and ethnic discrimination, rather than disaffiliation, and as possessing strong ties to settled minority communities.[34]

Issues of racial identity, then, continued to shape both popular and scholarly definitions of homelessness. As in the early twentieth century, homelessness in the postwar era represented a crisis of white manhood separate and distinct from the deprivations and subordinations of poor women and nonwhites. Without warrant, it seemed, the denizens of skid row were voluntarily rejecting the entitlements that "normal American tradition," in Carleton Parker's phrase, had bestowed upon white men. Instead, they were embracing the marginality that the nation had traditionally imposed upon other racial groups. Skid row bums were failing to take their rightful places as citizen-homeowners, stubbornly resisting the efforts of those who, over the previous three decades, had struggled to reintegrate white floaters back into the polity. For skid row social service professionals, the mission now was to complete this task, to solve the modern problem of homelessness once and for all.

The first step toward such a solution was the demolition of cheap lodgings, a step that corresponded neatly with the goals of urban renewalists. Indeed, most professional observers of skid row worked for redevelopment agencies and made recommendations concerning the relocation and rehabilitation of displaced skid row residents. By scattering skid row populations, these analysts argued, redevelopment would expose homeless men to the salutary affiliations of settled society. Off of skid row, commented one sociologist, men "will not only appear sicker, but will also believe themselves to be sicker" and thus "will be more likely to look for help." Echoing the reasoning of early-twentieth-century lodging house reformers, this scholar added that with the demolition of cheap hotels, bars, and shops, "it will be increasingly harder for them to 'make it' or to 'get by' as homeless men."[35]

Such expert recommendations did not, in themselves, lead to the redevelopment of skid row. They merely ratified and legitimated the larger transformations in urban geography that were already eroding the value of downtown districts throughout the nation. The postwar boom in road construction, especially after the Interstate Highway Act of 1956, advanced the suburbanization not only of residences, but also of retail, manufacturing, and administrative activities formerly housed in urban cores.[36] Federal housing policies also encouraged investors to abandon downtowns for the suburbs. The appraisal system used by the Federal Housing Administration (FHA) and Veterans Administration (VA) drastically undervalued urban real estate. VA loan guarantees, therefore, subsidized white middle-class suburban development by directing lenders away from neighborhoods judged to be aging, congested, nonwhite, or suffering from unsalutary mixtures of ethnic groups or land uses.[37]

As a zone characterized by "inharmonious" residents and activities, skid row suffered directly from the FHA's and VA's appraisal hierarchy.

Title I of the Federal Housing Act of 1934 initially allowed for building and improvement loans for all dwellings, including residential hotels. But subsequent property standards created by the FHA specifically excluded lodging and rooming houses from the definition of a dwelling and redlined these neighborhoods for their "undesirable community conditions" and "decreased mortgage security."[38] As a result, skid row districts were ruled ineligible for FHA mortgage insurance. While new building in the suburbs eventually boomed, lodging house construction never rebounded from the depression. In 1947 one sociologist puzzled over why no one was building housing for the "unattached," not even "for those unattached who earn fairly good wages and salaries." Possessing three times the available resources of the average family person, single women and men represented a strong demand for housing. But federal policies under the FHA and other agencies had created such disincentives for investing in single-room occupancy hotels (SROs), as the old lodging houses became known, that this demand remained unmet in the marketplace, as well as in the domain of public housing.[39]

With their aging buildings and economic obsolescence, postwar skid rows generated less in tax revenue than they consumed in city services and thus became known as "blighted" districts. The solution was to buy and clear blighted skid row properties so that they could be sold and developed for higher uses. With the end of war, as one financial periodical noted, business people talked "of 'rebuilding' our cities just as if they had been bombed."[40] The "Marshall Plan" for cities came in the form of urban renewal, federally funded demolition and rebuilding projects launched on a massive scale in the 1950s and 1960s. The Housing Act of 1949 allowed the federal government to finance two-thirds the cost of buying and bulldozing blighted urban properties for the purposes of selling them to developers as cleared land. A more comprehensive Housing Act that passed five years later broadened the federal role by authorizing funds for building as well as land clearance, "renewal" as well as "redevelopment." This legislation also weakened the social welfare and public housing provisions of earlier housing acts, clearing the way for the wholesale conversion of downtown districts.[41]

Skid row neighborhoods were, as one sociologist put it, "almost perfect targets for urban renewal, given their lack of economic function, their negative reputations, and the powerlessness of their residents."[42] Skid row property owners in Omaha, Denver, Minneapolis, Los Angeles, San Francisco, and a dozen other cities across the country sold their buildings to municipal authorities and watched as thousands of hotels, bars, secondhand stores, and movie theaters met the wrecking ball. In their places arose downtown malls, hotels, office buildings, civic centers, sports coliseums, college campuses, expressways, and parking lots. In Stockton, California, lodging houses that had once sheltered "bindle stiff" harvesters gave way to a cross-town freeway, a 200-room hotel complex, and an extension of the central business district. In Kansas City a luxury hotel, a thirteen-story office building, and commuter parking reclaimed several blocks of its old main stem. Meanwhile, in St. Louis, renewalists demolished half of an old hobohemian district to build the famous 630-foot stainless steel arch, a monument to the city's historic relationship to its western hinterlands.[43]

In Chicago, once the "Hobo Capital of America," years of private investment, municipal bond-raising efforts, and state appropriations for skid row redevelopment culminated in the federally sponsored Madison-Canal project drawn up in 1966. The Madison-Canal Redevelopment Company demolished almost thirty thousand cheap hotel rooms along West Madison, and office towers slowly followed in their wake. By 1980 almost 90 percent of the single-person units on this once-premier main stem were gone. Gone also was the international headquarters of the IWW, which was demolished as part of urban renewal in the late 1960s. Meanwhile, the few remaining rooming and lodging houses on the Near North Side eventually yielded to gentrified shops, condominiums, and apartments in the 1970s and 1980s, long after the postwar domestic revival had waned and the "hotel spirit" had crept back into the upwardly mobile urban middle class.[44]

Like the closing of the wageworkers' frontier in the 1920s, the decline and fall of skid row in the Cold War era was a planned event, a project launched by those who directed the forces of change in order to eliminate a noisome social problem. For most Americans, the cheap hotel was, at best, an unnecessary hangover from the bad old days of the Great Depression. At worst, it represented a dangerous departure from prevailing gender and family ideals. These ideals had attained unprecedented cultural power precisely because they provided a measure of security and belonging that seemed otherwise unavailable in Cold War America.

But even if skid row met almost universal condemnation in the postwar period, the domestic revival that shaped perceptions of homelessness inspired discontents of its own. For women, the family-wage pact entailed economic dependence upon husbands and discouraged the forging of an independent identity beyond that of wife and mother. For men, the burdens of breadwinning engendered new resentments against feminine domesticity, as well as against the workplace bureaucracies that seemed to be robbing men of their autonomy and initiative. If the suburban ideal gave rise to what Betty Friedan described as "the problem that has no name," then it also provoked the problem of "conformity," a masculine condition that found abundant expression in postwar culture.[45] Novels like *The Man in the Gray Flannel Suit*, sociological texts like *The Organization Man* and *The Lonely Crowd*, and even popular magazines like *Playboy* all offered critiques of domesticated manhood and encouraged men to fight against their own emasculation.[46]

Despite the array of remedies offered by these and other works, hardly anyone held out skid row or the memory of hobohemia as a model for rebellion. Several commentators did see skid row as a symptom of over-domestication. "The doting mother and the nagging wife must take the blame for thousands who seek escape on Skid Row," remarked one writer for *Collier's*. But even if some did recognize "the delights of an all-male Skid Row flop" in comparison to domestic containment, few entertained more elaborate romances of the road.[47] Indeed, the hobo vision of perfect freedom might have died out completely had it not been for a small band of bohemian writers known as the Beats. Alone among the period's cultural critics, the Beats embraced skid row as the starting point of their journey back to Whitman's "Open Road" of masculine independence. In reclaiming the road as the patrimony of American men, the Beats offered a final memorial to skid row and served as an important precursor to a much larger countercultural rebellion that would emerge in the 1960s.

## DHARMA BUMS AND EASY RIDERS

The decline of skid row in the 1950s inspired none of the nostalgia and ideological contests that attended the closing of the wageworkers' frontier after World War I. Few offered up elegies to these vanished Americans or sought to preserve the nearly extinguished flame of hobohemia. Until the 1960s and 1970s, when dissenting anthropologists and sociologists like James Spradley and Douglas Harper began to challenge disaffiliation theories and see skid row as a community in its own right, the world of the boxcar, the jungle camp, and the lodging house remained buried in a disreputable past.[48] The "Hobo Kings," who had won celebrity in the 1930s and 1940s with their celebrations of the road, once again slipped back into oblivion, taking their folklore with them. When they died, few took notice. By 1960 the very memory of hobohemia, like skid row itself, was on the verge of extinction.

Then came the Beats. Toiling in obscurity in the late 1940s and early 1950s, the Beats would eventually emerge as the most important counterculture in postwar America until the upheavals of the late 1960s. In launching their rebellion, Beat poets, novelists, artists, and filmmakers not only drew inspiration from a vanished hobohemia, but also headquartered their underground in the decaying cheap hotel districts of New York and San Francisco. In the late 1950s, when this previously invisible subculture achieved national notoriety and literary celebrity, the Beats brought memories of hobohemia to the surface of American culture, though these memories were as abstracted and distilled as those of their Jazz Age predecessors.

Like the bohemians of Floyd Dell's era, the Beats largely eschewed political involvement. They saw organized labor as an ossified bureaucracy that reinforced clock-punching and breadwinning habits. In the face of such corruption, the Beats maintained a broad antinomianism and libertarianism until the emergence of the New Left forced them to clarify their politics.[49]

Railing against Cold War militarism, bureaucratic organization, suburban domesticity, and the family-wage pact, the Beats defended skid row as an embattled refuge from the shackles of postwar conformity. In 1960 the foremost Beat writer, Jack Kerouac, published an essay on the "vanishing hobo" that blamed the demise of the road on an "increase in police surveillance." The police, wrote Kerouac, have "nothing to do but pick on what [they] see out there on the landscape moving independently of the gasoline power army police station." Chased from the road by overzealous county sheriffs and Civil Defense patrols, Kerouac explained, the hobo gives up his "camping ambitions" and retreats to skid row to "get drunk." Kerouac concludes his essay by issuing a final plea in the voice of a "poor bum": "Why have you taken this away from me[?] . . . I'm too tired now of everything else, I've had enough, I give up, I quit, I want to go home, take me home O brother in the night."[50]

By putting such words of desolation into the mouths of homeless men, Kerouac reinforced prevailing stereotypes of skid row pathology. But for Kerouac, the disaffiliation and defeatism associated with skid row was inspirational, rather than threatening. The poor bum's exhaustion and inertia represented merely a precondition for the awakening of a new consciousness liberated from the instrumental rationality and bureaucratic conformism of Cold War America. Far from seeing skid row as an alienating environment bereft of the authentic relations of nuclear family life, the Beats considered skid row's radical disillusionment with the reigning domestic order as a necessary starting point for reaffiliation with the human family. "Take me home, lock me safe," cried Kerouac's bum, "take me to where all is peace and amity, to the family of life, my mother, my father, my sister, my wife, and you my brother and you my friend . . . O Lord save me."[51]

In his search for freedom *and* fraternity, individualism *and* camaraderie, Jack Kerouac headed back to the road himself, seeking to recover
the patrimony denied to the poor bums of skid row. Kerouac's picaresque
adventures of the late 1940s and early 1950s inspired two of the most celebrated Beat novels, *On the Road,* published in 1957, and *The Dharma
Bums,* which came out a year later. In their stories of masculine liberation
from Cold War domesticity, these road novels, both profoundly influ-
enced by Jack London and John Dos Passos as well as by Walt Whitman
and Mark Twain, chart the birth of Beat counterculture.[52] But in both
novels, attaining freedom requires long periods of initiation in which
countercultural mentors instruct the narrators, thinly veiled versions of
Kerouac himself, in the art and mystery of the road.

In *On the Road,* the mentor is Dean Moriarty, a character modeled on
Kerouac's charismatic friend Neal Cassady. As a literary figure, Dean
functions as a trickster, a carnivalesque spirit who inverts established order, turns day into night and night into day, and bedevils and beguiles all
who pass within his reach. As a historical figure, Dean also represents a
road not taken in American life since the 1930s. He is a "wild boy" grown
to maturity, a former "road kid" who had somehow escaped the New
Deal's reclamation efforts.

Like his real-life counterpart, Dean comes of age on the road, hitching
freight cars with his hobo father and living by the code of the jungle. The
only home he ever knows is the string of cheap hotels along Denver's
Larimer Street skid row. Never having enjoyed the benefits of a transient
camp, the Civilian Conservation Corps, or the U.S. Army, Dean remains
in constant motion, embodying the masculine restlessness that the GI Bill
was meant to forestall. By late 1946, when the twenty-year-old Neal Cassady first met Jack Kerouac, he had already slept with countless women
and men, been arrested ten times, and, by his own count, stolen over five
hundred cars. Incapable of holding down a steady job or raising a family,
this latter-day "Happy Tramp" represented the very antithesis of ideal
manhood in the postwar era. But Neal's very homelessness, his rebellion
against breadwinning norms, excited Kerouac's countercultural imagination, inciting a quixotic search for the rugged freedoms of the road.[53]

In *On the Road,* the narrator, Sal Paradise, becomes the focus of this
quest. Unencumbered by marriage (Sal first meets Dean "not long after
my wife and I split up"), Sal quits his college studies under the GI Bill,
cashes in his veterans' benefits, and joins Dean on a series of cross-country
treks.[54] The ostensible purpose of these journeys is to find Dean's father,
an aging skid row wino who still occasionally hops freights and works odd
jobs. The search fails in large part because they ride in automobiles, not

boxcars, and steer past the railroad yards, jungle hideouts, and former main stems of the old wageworkers' frontier. Speeding through Nebraska along the route of the Union Pacific, Dean spots a jungle camp:

> "But hey, look down there in the night thar, hup, hup, a buncha old bums by a fire by the rail, damn me." He almost slowed down. "You see, I never know whether my father's there or not." There were some figures by the tracks, reeling, in front of a woodfire. "I never know whether to ask. He might be anywhere." We drove on. Somewhere behind us or in front of us in the huge night his father lay drunk under a bush, and no doubt about it—spittle on his chin, water on his pants, molasses in his ears, scabs on his nose, maybe blood in his hair and the moon shining down on him.[55]

In the father's irreparably damaged condition, Kerouac condenses the fate of independent white manhood in postwar America, leaving "no doubt" as to Sal and Dean's irretrievable loss. But the father's demise also allows for a new birth of freedom, a new romance that old hobohemian codes had forbidden.

With hobohemia all but buried and white men under the sway of suburban domesticity, Sal and Dean exchange their romance of the road for a romance of the racial Other. Borrowing from old frontier myths, Kerouac racializes breadwinning domesticity, characterizing steady work and family habits as "white ambitions" that inhibit men from partaking in the "really joyous life" known to impoverished and marginalized nonwhites. While Sal and Dean's occasional forays into skid row highlight the faded glory of the main stem, their visits to urban African American neighborhoods and Mexican villages and migrant camps offer hope for salvation from "white sorrows":

> At lilac evening I walked with every muscle aching among the lights of 27th and Welton in the Denver colored section, wishing I were a Negro, feeling that the best the white world had offered was not enough ecstasy for me, not enough life, joy, kicks, darkness, music, not enough night. I stopped at a little shack where a man sold hot red chili in paper containers; I bought some and ate it, strolling in the dark mysterious streets. I wished I were a Denver Mexican, or even a poor overworked Jap, anything but what I was so drearily, a "white man" disillusioned.[56]

Whereas hoboes on the wageworkers' frontier had cherished the road as both a crucial determinant and privilege of their whiteness, Jack Kerouac imagined whiteness as a prison and the road as an escape from its restrictive bonds. As second-generation ethnics, Kerouac and his alter ego, Sal Paradise, enjoyed the privileges of unambiguous whiteness, a status that had been denied to their immigrant parents' generation. Before they became part of the New Deal coalition, these "white ethnics" were largely seen as inhabiting separate and distinct racial categories—"Slav," "Mediterranean," "Hebrew," and "Alpine," to name a few—that physiologically marked them off from the dominant "Nordic" or "Anglo-Saxon" race. Through their participation in Democratic Party politics, the CIO, and wartime mobilization, the children of the new immigrants achieved full-fledged whiteness as members of a unified "Caucasian" race.[57]

This new racial status allowed white ethnics to take full advantage of such postwar corporate-liberal developments as the GI Bill, programs that collectively redefined whiteness in terms of middle-class suburban domesticity.[58] By the time postwar malcontents like Jack Kerouac began finding their voices in the late 1940s, whiteness itself seemed more monolithic than ever. In escaping the constraints of the feminine home and middle-class job, the Beats embraced the supposedly primitive freedoms of those who lived outside of "white America."

If *On the Road* merges a romance of race with that of the road, *The Dharma Bums, On the Road*'s unofficial sequel, abstracts and distills the countercultural essence of hobohemia even further. Trading the name Sal Paradise for the less proletarian Ray Smith and the Chaplinesque Dean for the more ascetic Japhy Ryder, *The Dharma Bums* depicts the search for masculine liberation as a deliberate and self-conscious quest, rather than a frenzied and unfocused response to "the feeling that everything was dead."[59] The narrator of *The Dharma Bums* is now an accomplished vagabond in his own right, hopping freights up and down the Pacific coast and laying up on skid row. Even though Ray Smith travels the old hobo routes, the jungle fires are now mostly snuffed out and the freight trains are largely empty of passengers, except for an occasional old man who haunts the rails in mystical silence.

In San Francisco Ray meets Japhy, who encourages his protégé to sublimate his wanderlust into a quest for Buddhist enlightenment. If Dean is the son of the last great American hobo, Japhy is a grandchild of the wageworkers' frontier. Growing up in the Pacific Northwest, Japhy ingested a good dose of the "oldfashioned I.W.W. anarchism" and also became a student of hobo folklore, learning "to play the guitar and sing old workers songs."[60]

Shaped by Wobbly lore and Buddhist teachings, Japhy, unlike Dean, is able to articulate his alienation from postwar culture, "all that suburban ideal and sex repression and general dreary newspaper gray censorship of all our real human values."[61] Echoing the *Industrial Worker* and the Colonel in *Meet John Doe*, Japhy denounces living-wage ideals and the postwar family-wage pact. Instead, he celebrates the "Dharma Bums" who refuse

> to subscribe to the general demand that they consume production and therefore have to work for the privilege of consuming, all that crap they really didn't want anyway such as refrigerators, TV sets, cars, at least new fancy cars, certain hair oils and deodorants and general junk you finally always see a week later in the garbage anyway, all of them imprisoned in a system of work, produce, consume, work, produce, consume. . . .

Like the Colonel, Japhy seeks to escape this imprisoning cycle by hitting the road. Like the Wobblies, he leverages his romance of the road into a dream of revolution. "I see a vision of a great rucksack revolution," Japhy exclaims to Ray, "thousands or even millions of young Americans wandering around with rucksacks . . . giving visions of eternal freedom to everybody and to all living creatures."[62] Even as such revolutionary dreams dance in his head, however, Japhy sails off to Japan, exchanging the freedoms of the American road for study in a Buddhist monastery.

When the "rucksack revolution" prophesied by Japhy Ryder in *The Dharma Bums* actually came to pass a decade after the book's publication, the real-life Beat poet Gary Snyder, upon whom Kerouac modeled Japhy, returned from Japan to offer his spiritual guidance. At first glance, the counterculture Snyder found in America in the 1960s bore resemblance to that of his Wobbly forebearers and to the Beats. Like hoboes and Beats, hippies chafed against stifling domestic conventions. Inspired by Kerouac's vision of perfect freedom, many of them hit the road in search of authentic experience.

The "rucksack revolution" also created a whole new generation of "tramp ethnographers" and participant observers who began to search out the aging hoboes lauded by Kerouac—real-life versions of Dean Moriarty's mythic father—in order, as anthropologist James Spradley puts it, "to discover the native point of view." Challenging reigning interpretations of skid row as a zone of "disaffiliation," Spradley's *You Owe Yourself a Drunk* (1971) confirmed the continued vibrancy of a freight-based hobo subculture, using homeless men's countercultural point of view to critique dominant institutions. While Spradley's formal study represented a response to the urban crisis of the 1960s, subsequent ethnographies— such as Michael Mather's photo-essay, *Riding the Rails* (1973), Douglas Harper's *Good Company* (1982), and Ted Conover's journalistic *Rolling Nowhere* (1984)—derived from youthful rail-riding adventures in the 1960s and 1970s, before the crisis of "homelessness" overwhelmed the world of the old-time hobo and bum.[63]

Drawing not only from the Beats but also from a tradition of tramp ethnography that stretched back to the work of Josiah Flynt Willard in the 1890s, Douglas Harper's *Good Company* represented the first sociological study of hobo subculture since Nels Anderson's *The Hobo*. Basing his book on freight-riding journeys he made in the early 1970s, Harper echoes Kerouac in lamenting the passing of a way of life that had once offered American men an alternative to the dull conformism of middle-class whiteness.

Harper's mentor while on the road, a veteran hobo named Carl, represented in extreme form both the alienation from dominant institutions that many Americans were experiencing and the desire for freedom that fueled the counterculture. Like his contemporary Neal Cassady, Carl had come of age during the depression when his father abandoned his family. A stint in the army during World War II turned him "into a tramp." "You learn to live out of a pack," Carl explained, "pretty soon your bedroll's your home." Having escaped the nuclear family imperative and the larger corporate-liberal order that reclaimed so many Forgotten Men, Carl emerged as something of a countercultural hero at a time when the corporate-liberal order was beginning to falter.[64]

The flames of discontent that erupted in the counterculture of the 1960s and 1970s, however, differed greatly from the old hobo campfire, of which Carl represented a dying ember. Unlike their hobo and Beat predecessors, the countercultural rebels of the 1960s and 1970s had never been "wage slaves" or "road kids" alienated from the comforts of home and family life. Rather, they were the children of the postwar settlement, beneficiaries of the privileges that had been bestowed upon white men after World War II. Whereas their parents had come of age in CCC camps and army barracks, these "rucksack revolutionaries" had grown up with the suburbs and now demanded release from the family-wage pact.

The call for deliverance from the middle-class conventions of home and work resonated throughout much of America in the 1960s and 1970s. Indeed, the counterculture's greatest successes and its most profound failures derived from the extent to which its goals of individual self-expression and personal liberation were absorbed by the culture at large. Almost as soon as the counterculture arose to public consciousness, some of its proponents worried that their rebellion might degenerate into hedonism and materialism. In 1969 Hollywood's first counterculture movie, *Easy Rider*, gave expression to these fears. After making easy money on a drug delivery, "Captain America," a laconic motorcycle-hero played by Peter Fonda, stares into a campfire and tells his sidekick: "We blew it." In *Easy Rider*, as in John Dos Passos's *U.S.A.* trilogy, drifting had turned into desiring, floating into striving.[65]

In blowing it, and in getting blown away while riding their motorcycles at the end of the film, the heroes of *Easy Rider* cast doubt not only upon the utopian promise of the counterculture, but also upon the masculine romance of the road. Indeed, the counterculture of the 1960s did as much to undermine this romance as it did to revive it. The postwar cult of masculine breadwinning, which compelled the Beats to invoke memories of hobohemian fraternity, inspired the hippies to "discard masculinity as a useful category for expression."[66] With their legendary long hair, beads, and flowing clothes, hippies exhibited an androgynous, rather than a masculine, ideal of freedom. This affront to masculine identity offended Jack Kerouac, whose raging indignation toward the counterculture was fueled by a desperate addiction to skid row muscatel.

A steady march of events, culminating in an inglorious war in Vietnam, had discredited the Beat vision of heroic masculinity, driving hippie counterculture away from Kerouac's romance of the road. Whereas World War II had created a generation of veterans receptive to masculine rebellions against domestic "conformity," Vietnam gave rise to a wholesale critique of the "battle of the sexes," as young men grew disillusioned with both the reigning domestic order and the customary rebellions against it. Kerouac and others had tried to revive the spirit of the bivouac in order to gain respite from middle-class conventions. But to the counterculture, this spirit amounted to "damned-up sadism," a hypermasculinity that licensed brutality and war crimes.[67] Thus while the postwar domestic revival had attempted to contain errant masculinity, the hippie uprising sought to eradicate traditional notions of manhood altogether.

With the counterculture, men once again "dropped out" and hit the road in protest against settled domesticity. But this time they invited women to join them, thus shattering the binary system of feminine home and masculine homelessness. Whereas the Beats had imagined liberation as a masculine escape from an unchanging feminine domain, hippie counterculture, or at least elements of it, sought to dissolve the boundaries that separated men and women, road and home.

That the counterculture failed to achieve sexual equality and, in fact, spawned its own feminist "revolution within the revolution" did not diminish the impact of the androgynous ideal. By the 1970s, as the feminist movement and the sexual revolution took hold, the domestic order established by the postwar settlement had already begun to collapse. Falling marriage and birth rates, the rise in the number of women entering traditionally male occupations, and the expansion of consumer activities outside the domestic sphere undermined seemingly stable definitions of home. The "hotel spirit," almost legislated out of existence after World

War II, came to life once more, this time in the guise of the "swinging singles scene."[68]

With the experience and meaning of home once again in flux, a variety of social scientists, community activists, and even housing officials revisited the problem of skid row and called into question long-standing definitions of "homelessness." Critics of urban renewal and advocates of hotel housing declared that the men of skid row were not homeless at all, but rather members of a legitimate community with its own "comfortable, even productive life-style."[69] In 1970 the United States Congress responded to these criticisms by passing the Uniform Relocation Act, which for the first time recognized hotel dwellers as bona fide city residents. While the new law required redevelopment agencies to compensate displaced hotel tenants, it did little to stop the ongoing demolition of skid row. Indeed, between 1970 and 1980, an estimated 1 million residential hotel rooms were converted or destroyed by redevelopment.[70] But the counterculture and the various "liberation" movements that accompanied it prompted a critical reassessment of the old main stem. Even though activists largely failed to save the dwindling supply of SROs from the wrecking ball, they did promote a pluralistic vision of housing, one that challenged the assumptions of the suburban ideal.

If the hotel housing advocates of the 1960s and 1970s blurred shopworn distinctions between home and homelessness, the shelter crisis that followed on the heels of skid row's demise clarified matters considerably. By the early 1980s, deindustrialization, economic recession, welfare state retrenchment, and the decline of low-cost housing had conspired to create a new homeless population that neither the Beats, the counterculture, nor postwar "disaffiliation" experts had anticipated. If the culture-at-large, via the counterculture, inherited the road as one-half of hobohemia's legacy, the urban poor, disproportionately nonwhite and female, inherited homelessness as the other half. The very success of the postwar settlement, which recovered the Forgotten Man and eradicated the remnants of the main stem, ensured that homelessness would no longer be equated with "disaffiliated" white manhood. Largely bereft of the romance, the housing, and the racial and gender privileges of their forebearers, the "new homeless" nonetheless sparked a crisis at the very heart of the nation's social life. Conditioned by cultural concerns with gender and racial order, the rediscovery of homelessness in the early 1980s refocused attention on the failed family-wage pact and the waning of nuclear family ideals.

# PART IV

## THE ENDURING LEGACY

*Homelessness and*

*American Culture*

*since 1980*

# R EDISCOVERING
# H OMELESSNESS

I n the wee hours of April 25, 1982, two journalists from the *Sacra-mento Bee* climbed aboard a northbound freight train in search of "the new class of hobo and street person" created by the worst economic recession since the 1930s. Sensing that "something big was happening to America," reporter Dale Maharidge and photographer Michael Williamson spent the next several months crisscrossing the nation's industrial heartland as participant observers of the "new underclass." They traveled by rail, by bus, and by foot. They ate in soup kitchens and, on occasion, from Dumpsters. Like hoboes of old, they took shelter in missions and abandoned buildings, improvising jungle camps when caught between cities. All along the road, they heard hard-luck stories of lost jobs, broken families, and dashed dreams. "The next decade or more seems to be the time of the Out Generation," the journalists concluded. "It's the era of the disenfranchised worker, left out of jobs, left out of the system, forgotten."[1]

Their homes repossessed and workplaces shuttered, the forgotten men and women that Maharidge and Williamson encountered on their journey bore living witness to the betrayals and broken promises of corporate liberalism. The great class bargain of the 1940s, which delivered homeownership and job security to the white working class, lay shattered amidst the declining wages, plant closings, and capital flight of the 1970s and 1980s.

While Maharidge and Williamson were gathering their first impressions of a darkening job front, America awoke to a crisis of homelessness unparalleled since the days of the Great Depression. Old skid row refugees, displaced by urban renewal and gentrification, suddenly found themselves outnumbered by legions of newcomers: men, women, and even children pushed to the streets by the lack of affordable housing. By the time the two hoboing journalists landed back home and began collecting their notes, the word "homelessness" had once again entered the nation's lexicon, signifying a problem separate and distinct from that of poverty in general. Indeed, the rediscovery of homelessness in the 1980s did not simply reflect the stunning growth of poverty and the declining fortunes of the American working class since the heyday of the family-wage pact. Rather, the discourse of homelessness was itself part of a larger struggle to represent the new economic and social realities of the era, to cast such abstract problems as faltering economic growth, labor market restructuring, and increased class stratification as the dramatic loss of home.

Not surprisingly, much of the new reporting and commentary on homelessness—and on the alarming developments for which homelessness served as a compelling metonym—drew heavily upon the symbols, icons, rhetoric, and conventions of depression-era social documentary. Maharidge and Williamson's own *Journey to Nowhere*, a gripping account of their time on the road, expressly acknowledges its debt "to all the Farm Security Administration photographers who documented the last depression so well." Recalling Dorothea Lange's portraits of western migrants and the proletarian memoirs of Edward Dahlberg, Tom Kromer, and Woody Guthrie, *Journey to Nowhere* makes frequent allusions to the 1930s in order to highlight the severity of the contemporary crisis, referred to in the book as "the 1980s Depression." The revival of the documentarian idiom also allows Maharidge and Williamson to depict their subjects as faultless victims of economic disaster. Driven to the road by the Rust Bowl of deindustrialization, the forgotten men and women of *Journey to Nowhere* virtually cry out for the kind of state activism that had granted secure jobs, stable homes, and family wages to a previous generation of depression survivors.[2]

To reinforce this message, the book opens in Youngstown, Ohio, where the collapse of the steel industry has transformed a once-vibrant and prosperous community into a combination ghost town and ghetto. Their local host, Joe Marshall, epitomizes the kind of Forgotten Man whom the New Deal order successfully recovered from poverty. Having entered the steel mills at age fifteen, Marshall survived perilous working conditions, bloody labor battles, and combat on the beaches of Normandy in 1944. Upon his discharge from the army, he returned to the mills and built a good life for himself and his family in Youngstown.

The good life, however, eludes Joe Marshall's son, Joe Jr., who followed his father into the mill after graduating from high school. Unemployed since the plant closed three years earlier, young Joe tours the rubble of his former workplace as if in a daze. When Dale Maharidge asks Joe Jr. if he

someday wants a home and family like his father had at his age, the disenfranchised son responds with barely suppressed anger:

> "*Hell yeah!*" he says sharply, leaning forward on a mound of bricks that he
> punches with his fist, his muscular frame outlined by the jagged Brier Hill
> Works. "I *want* that."[3]

In this passage Joe Jr.'s desire for a normative home life, along with his
rugged muscularity, testify to his membership among the entitled poor.
Unlike the "common tramps," "hobohemians," and "disaffiliated bums"
of previous eras, the "new poor" of the 1980s, Maharidge and Williamson
suggest, are not wayward, deviant, or subversive. Rather, they merely
want to go home.

Like the *National Labor Tribune* of the 1870s and the *Survey Graphic* of
the 1930s, *Journey to Nowhere* depicts the experience of becoming homeless in terms of dramatic downward mobility. The book promises to explore "what causes formerly middle-class people to wind up living on the
streets."[4] In this case, "middle class" largely means white and male, precisely those people historically empowered to claim the entitlements of
full citizenship.

Despite its subtitle, *Journey to Nowhere* offers not so much "a saga of
the new underclass" as a narrative of white male betrayal, a glimpse into
an emerging crisis of white working-class manhood. Women and nonwhites play only supporting roles in the book, appearing as companions to
the native-born white men whose struggles command the authors' primary attention. While almost always present in the missions, boxcars, and
bunkhouses depicted in the book, Mexican and African Americans, for
example, largely go unnamed and rarely give voice to their experiences of
poverty and deprivation. Indeed, the spectacle of white men from the
heartland working the fields of California's Central Valley alongside illegal
immigrants only serves to augment *Journey to Nowhere*'s sense of crisis.
Echoing the racial populism that informed coverage of the Okie migrations in the 1930s and 1940s, Maharidge describes his subjects as "a
strong breed, survivors, unchristened heroes" who are "too proud for welfare" and cling tenaciously to family breadwinning values even in their
destitution (fig. 9.1).[5]

As *Journey to Nowhere*'s familiar saga of Forgotten Manhood and entitled whiteness suggests, homelessness in the late twentieth century involved not only an economic crisis of shelter and housing, but also a
cultural crisis of race, family, and gender. Like much of the commentary
surrounding the "great army of tramps" in the 1870s, exposés of homelessness in the 1980s revealed as much about middle-class social anxieties

Figure 9.1: Dramatizing the economic crisis of the 1970s and 1980s in the liberal populist terms of depression-era documentary, Dale Maharidge and Michael Williamson's *Journey to Nowhere* revived the notion of the noble "Citizen Hobo" entitled to the dignities of a family wage. The drawbacks of such a strategy are apparent in this photograph, which foregrounds the plight of two native-born white men thrust into conditions of poverty and exploitation normally reserved for nonwhites, such as the Mexican laborers, not depicted, with whom these men shared their bunkhouse. By the time the book came into print in 1985, a far more severe crisis of homelessness had eclipsed the drama of the jobless hobo, bringing to the foreground those poor women, children, African Americans, and Hispanic Americans largely ignored in *Journey to Nowhere*. Ten years later Bruce Springsteen retold Maharidge and Williamson's story in *The Ghost of Tom Joad*, an album that, like Woody Guthrie's *Dust Bowl Ballads* and *Bound for Glory*, stripped the hobo romance of its racial populism. Just as Guthrie refashioned John Steinbeck's *Grapes of Wrath* narrative to include the diverse array of poor migrants on the road during the depression, so, too, did Springsteen broaden *Journey to Nowhere*'s vision by foregrounding in his songs the plight of dispossessed Mexican and Vietnamese immigrants. (Used by permission of Michael Williamson.)

as they did about the actual experiences of the poor. Dramatic stories of downward mobility and failed breadwinning arrested the attention of a middle class gripped by the "fear of falling" and grappling with the breakdown of nuclear family life. By casting the experience of becoming poor as a tragic loss of home and a disruption of traditional gender roles, stories of homelessness reaffirmed nuclear family and breadwinning ideals and, in so doing, often won the sympathy of an anxious public.

*Journey to Nowhere*'s latter-day narrative of Forgotten Manhood, however, became harder to sustain when the economic recovery that began in 1983 reclaimed millions of laid-off workers from the unemployment rolls. Despite the recovery, the unsheltered population continued to grow through the 1980s, attracting such widespread concern that homelessness rose rapidly to the top of the nation's social agenda. As reams of new sociological data began to pour in from streets and shelters across the nation, a new profile of the homeless emerged that differed dramatically from the one supplied by Maharidge and Williamson. Those most devastated by the deindustrialization and job migrations of the 1970s and 1980s were not, as it turns out, skilled white workers who had been propelled to affluence by the postwar family-wage pact. Rather, the hardest hit were peripheral low-wage employees and the chronically unemployed who had never enjoyed the protections of collectively bargained contracts or the privileges of suburban homeownership. Those most likely to become homeless were precisely those excluded from *Journey to Nowhere,* namely, women and nonwhites.

With their ability to arouse pity and inspire protectionist intervention, homeless women, especially those with dependent children, soon replaced Maharidge and Williamson's Forgotten Men as the most recognizable emblems of homeless victimization. By contrast, homeless black and Hispanic men, who tended to remain on the streets far longer than their female counterparts, raised the specter of an undomesticated and "savage" masculinity in need of stern control. This dual face of homelessness—"worthy" mothers on the one hand and "unworthy" men of color on the other—governed the most common responses to the crisis: calls for charity and government shelters and demands for police action against panhandlers and squatters.

As in previous eras, homelessness in the late twentieth century marked the limits of the reigning domestic order at the same time that it challenged Americans to redefine and reaffirm the values of home, family, and community. Although the contemporary homeless differ in many respects from their hobohemian and skid row predecessors, they still largely defy the label of "disaffiliation" and, in fact, continue to forge communities even in the absence of permanent shelter. Like hoboes of old, many contemporary street people embrace a counterculture opposed to ideologies of nuclear family life, masculine breadwinning, and the bourgeois work ethic. With these ideals failing to meet the needs or describe the aspirations of many nonhomeless Americans as well, it is clear that the inequalities embodied in homelessness extend far beyond the streets. Imprecise and ideologically loaded as it is, the category of homelessness therefore persists not only as the most visible symptom of larger racial, gender, and class inequalities, but also as an immanent frame of reference for their critical analysis.

## THE NEW HOMELESS

Throughout *Journey to Nowhere*'s picaresque adventures through the "new underclass," Dale Maharidge and Michael Williamson make little reference to "homelessness," instead identifying their subjects as "hoboes" whose main plight is "joblessness." Indeed, at the time the two journalists hit the road, "homeless" remained merely one of many adjectives used to describe the new poverty. It was not yet a keyword in its own right, signifying a distinct condition, status, or social problem. Throughout the 1970s, for example, the *New York Times Index* did not even list homelessness as a category and instead indexed relevant articles under "vagrancy" and "housing." It was not until after the recession lifted in 1983 when "homeless" displaced "vagrancy" as a classification. Two years later the *Index* dispensed with "vagrancy" altogether. In the realm of electronic media, homelessness made its first appearance in December 1982 when ABC, CBS, and NBC each aired news packages featuring the plight of the "homeless," rather than "street people," during the holidays.[6]

The retrieval of this quaint-sounding Progressive Era term in the early 1980s was largely the work of advocacy groups seeking to call attention to the new experiences of poverty that had emerged during the first term of President Ronald Reagan. While not responsible for the recession that, in fact, helped to seal his election, Reagan vigorously pursued a "supply-side" economic agenda that included a massive defunding of federal social welfare and housing programs at precisely the time when poverty rates were soaring. The issue of homelessness allowed activists to focus their opposition to "Reaganomics" by challenging Reagan's narrative of self-reliant entrepreneurial success with one of declining middle- and working-class fortunes.

*Journey to Nowhere,* itself a savage indictment of Reagan's economic and social agenda, depicts the emergence of this new homeless counternarrative in its final captioned photograph. Absent throughout the rest of the book, the homeless suddenly appear in the form of three protesters lying in sleeping bags in front of a Sacramento federal building. A sign next to them declares: "2 MILLION AMERICANS HAVE BECOME LITTER ON THE STREETS.—HOMELESSNESS—A NATIONAL DISGRACE."[7] As recession-related stories of middle-class job loss and home foreclosure dwindled after 1983, such demonstrations thrust the burgeoning homelessness crisis into public view, giving a new frame to social anxieties resistant to sanguine forecasts of economic recovery.

Spearheading this consciousness-raising effort was the National Coalition for the Homeless (NCH), a group of anti-poverty activists and service providers that banded together in the very same month that Dale Maharidge and Michael Williamson embarked on their "journey to nowhere." Reminiscent of the National Committee on the Care of the Transient and Homeless, an umbrella organization formed in the 1930s to publicize the transient crisis and lobby for federal action, the NCH sought to prod federal agencies into assuming some of the burdens of relief. Through high-profile demonstrations, loosely organized publicity campaigns, and hearings before Democratic-led congressional subcommittees, NCH members succeeded in propelling homelessness to the fore of public consciousness.

Challenging both old stereotypes about skid row and emerging ones about the urban "underclass," the NCH countered conservative depictions of the urban poor as "unworthy" agents of a "culture of poverty." The underclass, conservatives contended, was itself to blame for its own condition, promoting countercultural habits and values such as laziness, irresponsibility, criminality, and the rejection of family life. By contrast, homeless activists such as the famous Mitch Snyder emphasized the dignity, moral worth, and essential blamelessness of the new poor. Through a "politics of compassion," they transformed the image of deviant "street people" into that of the "homeless," ordinary people down on their luck and therefore deserving of public attention.[8]

In 1983 homeless activists won their first major concession from the Reagan administration, securing $100 million from the Federal Emergency Management Agency (FEMA) to fund temporary shelters and services for the homeless. Prompted by the spate of publicity surrounding the issue, the Department of Housing and Urban Development (HUD) embarked upon a study of homelessness, releasing a controversial report in May 1984 that downplayed both the severity and size of the problem. Its hastily organized nationwide census counted only 250,000 to 350,000 persons as without shelter on any given night. Instead of laying the issue to rest, the HUD report provoked a whole new "numbers" debate that, in turn, inspired another round of congressional testimony and a new wave of publicity.[9]

As public awareness of homelessness grew, the issue attracted a broader range of attention, from media commentators and politicians to celebrities and even corporate public relations officers. In May 1986 show business manager and promoter Ken Kragen launched "Hands Across America," a corporate-sponsored event designed to galvanize the volunteerist spirit on behalf of the homeless.[10] Six months later the Democratic opposition won control of the United States Senate after campaigning strongly on the homelessness issue.

Using the homeless as a wedge against Reagan's juggernaut of social spending cuts, the new Democratic Congress immediately began to draft comprehensive legislation to deal with the crisis. Republicans disapproved but dared not publicly challenge a bill that vastly increased funding for emergency shelters and services. In July 1987, when a chastened President Reagan quietly signed the McKinney Homeless Assistance Act into law, the 1980s crusade on behalf of the homeless reached its highwater mark.[11] In an age of federal retrenchment, the McKinney Act represented the most important piece of anti-poverty legislation since Lyndon Johnson's Great Society.

If homelessness inspired new activism and legislation, it also prompted an entirely new generation of scholarly research. While conservatives aligned with the Reagan White House continued to view homelessness in the terms of skid row pathology—Reagan himself making reference to those who were homeless "as you might say, by their own choice"—the social scientists who tackled the issue in the 1980s focused squarely on structural causes.[12] That is, they tended to define the problem as a shelter condition, *house*lessness," rather than in terms of undomesticated manhood.[13]

But because homelessness is always a cultural category, an ascribed condition that does not necessarily define or dominate the experiences of the very poor, the new scholarship failed to reach definitive conclusions about what exactly homelessness was and what made people susceptible to it. Indeed, the complex host of factors identified by researchers as contributing to homelessness suggests that the very category was itself an ideological attempt to reduce a series of intractable, long-term social and economic developments to a specialized and discrete social problem.[14]

Most analysts linked the new homelessness of the 1980s to the "gathering storm" that began to rock the U.S. economy a decade earlier. After a remarkable period of rising family incomes and spectacular growth, the nation's economy stagnated in the early 1970s. A sharp decline in manufacturing, spurred by vigorous overseas competition, had an especially devastating effect on income and employment levels. Real wages fell by 7.4 percent during the 1970s, a decline attributable not only to inflation but also to the overall labor market shift away from high-wage manufacturing jobs.[15] As the low-paid retail and service sectors claimed larger proportions of the workforce, corporations increasingly demanded more "flexibility" with its payrolls, seeking to erode the benefits and job security that had been hallmarks of the corporate-liberal era.

This shift in occupational structure and the terms of employment gave rise to a new two-tiered labor system. The top tier featured a core of full-time, permanent employees and highly educated managers and professionals. At the bottom of the low-wage tier lay a growing pool of part-time, contingent, and temporary workers reminiscent of the "casual laborers" who had so vexed the industrial relations experts of Carleton Parker's generation. From this reserve army of casual and chronically unemployed workers emerged the new class of homeless person.[16]

In addition to long-term economic and labor market changes, experts also identified the contraction of the government "safety net" as playing a central role in homelessness. A decade before the budget cuts of the Reagan era, rising inflation steadily eroded the value of various means-tested income-maintenance benefits collectively known as "welfare." The 3.3 million households who received relief under Aid to Families with Dependent Children (AFDC), for example, saw the real value of their benefits decline by 28 percent over the course of the 1970s. During that same time period, the real value of state General Assistance (GA) benefits, the only cash relief available to unattached adults, fell by 32 percent.[17] As part of its supply-side agenda, the Reagan administration further reduced the value of federal anti-poverty programs in order to offset massive tax cuts. Over the course of eight years, the administration altered the eligibility requirements and payment standards for AFDC three times, cutting benefits and eliminating the program's national caseload by almost a half-million people.[18] Similar cutbacks in disability and unemployment benefits, as well as food stamps, compounded the insecurities of the very poor.[19]

The general reduction of government benefits for the poor extended into the realm of public housing. As the number of poor people rose in the 1980s, the availability of low-cost housing declined by 30 percent in absolute terms. Much of this loss was attributable to drastic cuts in federal housing programs. The overall funding for HUD, for example, fell from $35.7 billion in 1980 to $7 billion in 1989, a reduction of just over 80 percent. Over roughly that same time period, the number of housing units assisted by the federal government fell by 70 percent.[20] Rather than fill the gap left by this massive defunding, private developers and landlords virtually abandoned the low-cost market, seeking to "gentrify" and improve urban housing stock to capture higher rents. The result was a rapid loss of affordable housing at the low end of the market, increasing the likelihood that some of the very poor would go without shelter.[21]

The gentrification and abandonment of urban housing during the 1970s and 1980s contributed directly to the most visible and controversial segment of the homeless population, the mentally ill. While many Americans, including President Reagan, attributed homelessness to the "choice" of those who refused confinement in psychiatric hospitals, scholarly observers identified a major cause of the crisis in the "deinstitutionalization" of the mentally ill. As early as the 1950s, state hospitals began releasing their long-term mental patients, a process that accelerated over the next three decades in response to cost-cutting demands, patients-rights lawsuits, and the general recognition of the deleterious effects of long-term hospitalization. By the mid-1980s the nation's institutionalized population had shrunk to a bare 20 percent of its 1950s peak.[22]

The success of deinstitutionalization as a health-care measure depended on a proposed network of community mental health centers strategically located near cheap housing and other support services. The housing of choice, due to its affordability and central location, was the cheap hotel stock of skid row. In one year alone, for example, the Illinois Department of Mental Health placed seven thousand discharged patients in residential hotels on Chicago's Near North Side.[23] As developers began to purchase, demolish, and renovate cheap hotels in the 1970s, poor tenants suffering from mental illness soon found themselves unable to keep pace with rising rents or maintain contact with scarce mental health facilities. By the 1980s mentally disturbed "street people" had become a common spectacle in Chicago and elsewhere.[24] Although fierce debates raged over just how prevalent mental illness was among the homeless, a combined average of studies conducted during the 1980s identified roughly one-quarter of America's homeless population as having a history of mental illness.[25]

While the homeless mentally ill attracted a great deal of attention, the most striking feature of the new homelessness was the unprecedented proportions of women, children, and nonwhites living in shelters and on the streets. For over a century, homelessness had been defined almost exclusively in terms of single white manhood. With the destruction of skid row and the collapse of the corporate-liberal order, the racial and gendered meanings of homelessness changed utterly. Depending on the methods and definitions used, researchers in the 1980s counted one-fifth to one-half of America's adult homeless population as female. Many, perhaps most, of these women were caring for dependent children while in shelters. All told, persons living in families, virtually all of which were headed by women, accounted for one-third to one-half of America's homeless population. On any given night, according to the estimates of the National Academy of Sciences, one out of every seven persons seeking shelter was a child.[26]

Along with the massive influx of women and children into emergency shelters was a dramatic rise in the number of homeless African Americans and members of other putative nonwhite racial groups, such as American Indians and Hispanics. While racial distributions of the homeless differed greatly according to region and city, in no place were African Americans underrepresented among the street and shelter populations. Nationally, racialized minorities comprised well over one-half of the homeless, while in large urban centers like New York, Chicago, Washington, D.C., and Los Angeles, black homelessness in particular reached epidemic proportions. In some of these cities, African Americans accounted for two-thirds or even three-quarters of the local homeless.[27]

As they took their places in public shelters, bus stations, vestibules, parks, or simply on the sidewalks, the new homeless testified to the changes that had transformed the face of American poverty. While feminism's assault on sexual discrimination in the early 1970s opened up a new world of female professional employment, the path to liberation and upward mobility remained closed to most working women. Indeed, millions of women spiraled downward into poverty during the 1970s, suffering disproportionately from the overall decline in wages experienced by all American workers in these years. New labor market pressures, coupled with old patterns of discrimination, funneled most women into low-paying occupations. Meanwhile, rising rates of divorce, separation, and desertion severed millions of women's claims on men's wages.

As American women became increasingly dependent on low-wage jobs and welfare assistance, sociologists identified a new trend, the "feminization of poverty." The soaring numbers of children growing up in poor female-headed households severely compounded the pernicious effects of poverty's feminization. By 1980 two out of every three poor adults in America was a woman, and one out of every five children was poor.[28] It was inevitable that some of these poor women and children would at some point find themselves without shelter.

Likewise, millions of African Americans sank deeper into poverty during the 1970s, despite the stunning gains in education, economic status, and political clout won through decades of struggle in the civil rights movement. Black America, like America generally, evolved into a two-tiered society, with a skilled and credentialed upper tier entering the professional and managerial class and an undereducated lower tier becoming increasingly trapped in a world of crime, ill health, rampant drug addiction, and endemic unemployment. By the 1970s the residential segregation that had helped to create a white middle-class identity in the suburbs after World War II had increasingly isolated the poorest African Americans in urban "hyperghettoes," where the most basic institutions and social structures—schools, jobs, houses, families—were beginning to collapse.

As social supports and networks disappeared, job loss, eviction, drug addiction, mental health problems, and domestic violence forced many of the urban poor to the streets, rather than to the homes of others.[29] By 1980 the African American ghetto dweller had replaced the elderly white man of skid row as the most visible face of homelessness. The age of the tramp, the hobo, and the bum had shuddered to a close.

More isolated, powerless, and physically imperiled than their predecessors, the new homeless of the 1980s bore the most visible costs of the postwar settlement. Indeed, to some extent, they owed their desperate condition to the very measures that rendered the tramp, the hobo, and the bum anachronistic. Like a curse upon the land, homelessness had plagued the American body politic for a century, massing white men in roving armies of labor and alienating them from the privileges of patriarchy, breadwinning, and citizenship. As part of a larger corporate-liberal order that arose with the New Deal, the GI Bill successfully rebivouacked millions of white wage earners in the suburbs and equipped them with the skills needed for professional, managerial, and technical careers. By excluding women and nonwhites from its full range of benefits, the GI Bill augmented the rewards and privileges of white manhood and rendered skid row an embarrassing reminder of past grievances. The failure of the postwar settlement to extend the full social benefits of citizenship to those who had historically been barred from hobohemia ensured that when the corporate-liberal order faltered in the 1970s, a new homeless army would emerge bearing the marks not of white manhood, but of a feminized and racialized "underclass."

If new economic and social conditions created the homelessness crisis of the 1980s, responses to that crisis in many ways replicated and reinforced the gender and racial ideologies that gave rise to the postwar settlement. Indeed, the very choice of the term "*home*lessness," as opposed to the more accurate "*house*lessness," revealed the ideological assumptions at work in the national debate over the new poverty. Deeply entrenched fears, desires, and prejudices about normative housing arrangements, family life, and the racial and gendered distinctions between the deserving and undeserving poor shaped the public and private meanings of the crisis from its inception. "A problem with the concept of homelessness," remark Sophie Watson and Helen Austerberry in their feminist analysis of housing, "is the notion of 'home.'" "A 'house,'" they explain, "is generally taken to be synonymous with a dwelling or physical structure, whereas 'home' is not. A 'home' implies particular social relations, or activities within a physical structure, whereas a 'house' does not."[30] The very concept of homelessness, then, entails a concern not just with housing but with the particular social relations of nuclear family life and their accompanying ideals of manhood and womanhood.

Homelessness emerged as a distinct social problem at precisely the time when increasing numbers of Americans at every economic strata were rejecting the embrace of nuclear families and choosing to live either alone or in the unmarried company of others. Measuring the new poverty in terms of its shattering effects on traditional gender arrangements, the homelessness debate provided an occasion for airing middle-class concerns about the breakdown of nuclear family life. The very terms of this debate stacked the ideological deck by presupposing the legitimacy of the nuclear family and masculine breadwinning imperatives. In other words, both liberals and conservatives agreed on the desirability of restoring the homeless to their "homes," that is, back to the normative gender roles associated with the nuclear family. They disagreed merely over the location of blame, with liberals seeing the homeless largely as dislocated victims in need of aid and conservatives characterizing them as deviants who came to their homelessness through pathological choices of their own.

Liberals largely won this debate in the 1980s by dramatizing homelessness as a widespread crisis of dependent womanhood. In defining the problem, liberal activists, scholars, and politicians emphasized the large numbers of women and children found in emergency shelters, welfare hotels, overcrowded apartments, and other intolerable dwelling conditions. Accompanying this "broad constructionist" approach to homelessness were images of "worthy" dependents, mothers and children, struggling to maintain family units in the absence of male breadwinners (fig. 9.2).[31]

On the flip side of this ideological coin, the conservative interpretation of homelessness sought to limit the scope of the crisis's definition by focusing narrowly on those actually found on the streets, virtually all of whom were young single men. This "strict constructionist" strategy

Figure 9.2: A half-century after Dorothea Lange encountered the "Migrant Mother" in a California pea-pickers' camp, photographer Melchior DiGiacomo took this picture of the destitute Reynolds family along a highway near Galveston, Texas. Appearing on the cover of *Newsweek* magazine's "Homeless in America" issue of 1984, DiGiacomo's photograph embodied the liberal vision of homelessness, which privileged the plight of "worthy dependents" over that of single men and women on the streets. Like Lange's famous image, this *Newsweek* cover sought to publicize a crisis of homelessness while also subtly reassuring readers that "homes"—defined in terms of white motherhood—indeed still existed among the poor, even if adequate houses did not. Such books as Jonathan Kozol's award-winning *Rachel and Her Children* and television dramas as *God Bless the Child* similarly presented the crisis in terms of aggrieved motherhood, helping to galvanize public support for emergency family shelters. (© 1984 Newsweek, Inc. All Rights Reserved. Reprinted by permission. Used by permission of Melchior DiGiacomo.)

allowed conservatives to depict the homeless as "unworthy" men who had exchanged the responsibilities of breadwinning for the "savage" dangers and freedoms of the streets.

Reinforcing nuclear family ideology at its moment of greatest peril, the racialized and gendered terms of the homelessness debate shaped public policy in a way that systematically denied, and continues to deny, homeless men, most of whom are black and Hispanic, access to permanent public housing. Single men of color remain homeless far longer than do single women. Homeless women with children immediately move into shelters and then pass through the shelter system to transitional and apartment housing, a progression impossible for single men. The American provision of housing to the homeless, as Joanne Passaro compellingly argues, depends almost entirely on evaluations of the recipients' gender performances. "The only homeless adults who will be housed," she states bluntly, "are those who return to or recreate normative 'homes'—and the gender roles they imply—in order to survive."[32]

Men who are failed or unwilling breadwinners generally gain only limited access to bare temporary shelters unless they can somehow father a child and form a family unit. Homeless women remain comparatively "hidden" precisely because they have more available housing options, especially if they have children in tow. In the 1990s over two-thirds of New York City's emergency shelter space and virtually all of its subsidized housing and transitional apartments were reserved for homeless families.[33] Viewed on the one hand as dependent, and therefore emasculated, and on the other as hypermasculinized, and therefore dangerous, homeless men are generally expected either to take care of themselves on the streets or face incarceration. "Simply by being in need of help," Peter Marin notes, "men forfeit their right to it."[34] Possessing neither the Forgotten Man's claim on the national polity nor the Migrant Mother's claim on the national conscience, homeless men of color appear destined to remain on the streets until they somehow prove themselves worthy of a nuclear family "home."

Neither pitied nor entitled, the homeless men and women who fail to make it through the shelter system are, in one form or another, gender rebels who pay for their transgressions with their "houselessness." The increasing numbers of securely housed Americans who similarly defy nuclear family and breadwinning conventions do not, of course, suffer similar consequences. Indeed, while the demise of hobohemian and skid row institutions has left the new homeless more impoverished and vulnerable than their predecessors, the hobo romance of the road thrives among entitled white men left untouched by the problems of the urban "underclass" and the "feminization of poverty." Old romances die hard, even as they run up daily against the realities of the streets.

## ROMANCING THE ROAD, SURVIVING THE STREETS

Consumed by the duty of reclaiming their jobs, homes, and breadwinning roles, the Forgotten Men of *Journey to Nowhere* spend little time indulging in masculine romances of the road. There are moments while riding the rails, however, when Dale Maharidge, Michael Williamson, and their proud job-seeking subjects succumb to the siren song of "steel meshing against steel," a lonely tune that exalts "the men who made the metal and the men who now ride it."[35] One of the profiled hoboes who draws from "the power of the train" is Don, a college-educated small businessman who left his wife and children in order to find work. A failed breadwinner who is rapidly shedding his middle-class identity, Don recovers a certain manly strength by hopping a westbound Missouri Pacific freight in St. Louis. "If I can ride one of those suckers across the country," Don asserts while fingering photographs of his young children, "I can do anything." Although he previously had the look of a "soft guy," the hoboing experience has hardened him, making him a "stronger man" than the one the authors found days before in a St. Louis mission.[36]

*Journey to Nowhere*'s brief flirtation with the road notwithstanding, most of the reporting on the "new breed of hobo" that emerged during the recession of 1979–82 emphasized the perils and indignities of homeless migration and the urgent need to restore these "hoboes" to their rightful places as family breadwinners.[37] As the recession lifted in 1983 and the "homeless" replaced the "hobo," however, the road regained its former prominence as an imaginative zone of regeneration for domesticated white men. With homelessness defined as a crisis of aggrieved motherhood on the one hand and of ghetto-dwelling black men on the other, white male hoboing lost its associations with degrading poverty and once more became the subject of romance.

As part of a more general Reagan-era male revolt against the encroachments of feminism, the popular hobo revival of the 1980s largely departed from the countercultural politics of Douglas Harper's *Good Company* and Ted Conover's *Rolling Nowhere*. In an age of homelessness, the hobo vogue celebrated freight hopping as an expression of virile white masculinity even as it propagated a sanitized version of hobo folklore.

In 1986 a small group of "yuppie hoboes" from Beverly Hills began publishing the *Hobo Times* as a guide to recreational rail riding, offering nostalgic reminiscences of the road and a list of mail-order merchandise long on the hobo theme. The National Hobo Association (NHA), claiming several thousand members, sponsored authentic hobo "jungle" gatherings around the nation and, for the hale and hardy, freight-hopping excursions through the desert Southwest. In the tiny town of Britt, Iowa, the annual Hobo Convention, held almost every August since the 1930s, blossomed into a minor media event, attracting over twenty-five thousand visitors to see the coronation of the "Hobo King" and share in the songs and stories of the road. Newspapers, magazines, and television spread word of the hobo revival to male audiences seeking imaginative respite from breadwinning routines. "What can I tell you?" one NHA founder mused to an inquiring reporter as he crouched in a Southern Pacific rail yard. "It's all about being on hobo time. Hobo time means every day's a Friday afternoon. There are no watches out here, no schedules to keep. Living for the moment is what it's all about."[38]

At every turn, promoters of this revival took pains to distinguish hoboes from the homeless, whom rail-riding enthusiasts characterized as either victims to be pitied or dependents to be scorned. "It's so sad to see these homeless people today, women and children," remarked perennial "Hobo King" "Steam Train" Maury Graham in 1989. "They can't take care of themselves on the road."[39] While some hobo revivalists embraced this liberal protectionist perspective, many others were far less charitable, measuring the hobo's rugged self-reliance against the abject dependence of the urban "underclass." "If us hoboes had been exposed to the many amenities that today's 'street people' receive," wrote one former depression-era "road kid" to the editors at the *Hobo Times,* "I might still be a 'bo!"[40] Such racial resentment fed white nostalgia for the road of hobo mythology where the homeless were strong and self-sufficient.

Eschewing the "dharma bums" and "easy riders" of the countercultural Left, the recreational hoboes of the 1980s and early 1990s largely adhered to a conservative populism that folded hoboing into nationalist myths of frontier individualism. "Man, this is America! Man, look at it! That's America," screamed one "yuppie hobo" to a reporter in 1990 as their boxcar hurtled through the Mojave Desert. "No," another shouted, gesturing to his fellow travelers, "*this* is America. *We're* America."[41] Claiming title to the nation on the basis of their rugged individualism and authentic relationship to the landscape, hobo revivalists distilled a bygone counterculture into a homey "Hobo Philosophy" of manly self-reliance and natural living that promised, according to the editors of the *Hobo Times,* to "save America."[42]

Contributors to the NHA newsletter frequently offered critiques of contemporary American culture, especially concerning the "decline in moral values of the American family," the menace of "big government," and the overall lack of "hard work, self-control, and responsibility" among youth and the poor.[43] In 1992 the newsletter went so far as to endorse independent candidate H. Ross Perot for president, on the dubious logic that the diminutive Texas billionaire was a "closet hobo." Explaining that Perot had built a $2.5 billion computer services company from scratch, the editor asserted that "only a person with the self-reliance and perseverance of a hobo could do that."[44]

Such populist romances are, of course, highly unstable, not least because of the contradictions inherent in using the hobo as an emblem of industriousness and family values. The illicit subcultures and hard realities that still governed life on the road also had a way of puncturing the free-floating hobo reverie. Like the "vagabond poets" of the early twentieth century, recreational hoboes of the 1990s discovered that the perils of freight hopping included not only the dangers of boarding and holding down moving trains, but also the hazards of navigating through rough and sometimes violent human terrain.

The "yuppie hoboing" fad was cut short in the late 1990s by revelations of serial murder on the rails. While the investigations that followed cast a pall on recreational train hopping, they also provided a fresh glimpse into the freight-riding subcultures that were still thriving at the turn of the twenty-first century. Apart from his penchant for homicide, there was little that distinguished "Railroad Killer" Angel Maturino Resendez (alias Rafael Ramirez) from the larger floating population of Mexican immigrants who crisscrossed the country by train. Between 1997 and 1999, Resendez, a paranoid schizophrenic, terrorized railroad communities in the Midwest and West, stalking and killing at least nine victims before melting back into the freight-hopping migrant labor stream from which he came. While the Resendez murders further fueled both anti-homeless and anti-immigrant sentiments, they also exposed the shadow network of rail riders that still carried thousands across the old wageworkers' frontier each day.[45]

The case of "Boxcar Killer" Robert Silveria, who admitted in 1996 to murdering a dozen transients, provided even more gruesome insight into the contemporary perils of hoboing. Known by his moniker "Sidetrack," Silveria rode the rails for over fifteen years, allegedly bludgeoning and stabbing to death dozens or even scores of fellow freight hoppers. Silveria's links to a white supremacist brotherhood called the Freight Train Riders of America (FTRA) brought to light a subculture that, in fidelity to the hobo code of yore, jealously guarded the road as the domain of white men. Investigations into the FTRA not only provided leads on hundreds of unsolved assaults and murders, but also unveiled the brutal cultural politics by which some disenfranchised men still used the road to stake their claims to white privilege. Homeless for more than a decade, Robert Silveria wore his claim proudly in the form of the word "Freedom" tattooed around his throat like a necklace, or perhaps a noose.[46]

While right-wing extremists spread terror, the freight-hopping world of the late twentieth century also harbored a growing number of domestic refugees on the Left, prompting a struggle reminiscent of the early-twentieth-century contest over hobohemia. Just as Wobblies sought to recruit the great army of hoboes for revolution, so, too, did anarchist "hobo punks" challenge the FTRA's claims to the road, fusing rail travel with urban counterculture. Committed to living "outside the system" of home and work, hobo punks of the 1990s were largely working-class teenagers, male and female, on the run from abusive or negligent families. Homeless and profoundly alienated from social service institutions, they rejected the bare protections of the shelter system, embracing the unsteady and perilous life of a "crusty."[47]

Searching for a motive behind the hobo punk movement, one journalist reflected that the young travelers were seeking a corner of America untouched by hyper–consumer culture. Like the Wobbly hoboes of the *Industrial Worker* and the Colonel in *Meet John Doe*, hobo punks saw home as a prison where wage earners ransomed their freedom in return for a measure of stability. In a world where the commodity form increasingly dominated everyday life, hobo punks were seeking an "edge" where they might pursue authentic living. "But how do you find that edge," asked one observer of the "crusties," "at a time when every form of youth protest is immediately coopted by MTV? These days even downward mobility is chic."[48]

As if to prove the point, men's magazines responded to the well publicized dangers of the road by refashioning recreational hoboing as a survivalist sport, "the ultimate form of extreme travel," as *GQ* put it in 2000. "Sure, you can pay Amtrak to haul you across the country with a bunch of blue-haired old ladies," asserted the bellicose men's magazine *Maxim* in 1999. "Or you can grow some balls and hop a train." That same year, the *New York Times Magazine*'s men's fall fashion supplement offered a full-color spread of "hobo chic" that effectively quoted the 1933 Warner Brothers' hit *Wild Boys of the Road*. The layout featured sooty teenagers hanging around railroad cars in oversize $1,000 sweaters, jeans, and distressed leather jackets, hair coifed for that "just-slept-in-a-boxcar-of-hay look."[49] Reports of hobo punks and even serial murderers, it seemed, could not suppress courtiers' fantasies of "The Big Rock Candy Mountain," where cutting-edge fashion springs from the masculine proving ground of the road.

While the media lavished attention on the deviant and disreputable subcultures of the rails, scholars of the 1990s revisited the subject of homelessness, reviving ethnographic methods that had been in abeyance since the era of skid row. As homelessness moved from a shocking crisis to an enduring fact of contemporary American life, a new generation of "homeless ethnographers" began to catalog the destitute subcultures that had come of age in the nation's streets, parks, and shelters. No longer pressed with the urgent need of demonstrating the pathos of dislocation or the structural causes of shelter loss ("houselessness"), these scholars emphasized the homeless as agents in their own right, helping to shape and resist the conditions of their existence. Just as the high-profile antics of hobohemia compelled pioneering "tramp ethnographers" of the 1890s to collect data on the nation's great army of wayfarers, so, too, did the increased activism, organization, and collective self-expression of the homeless in the late 1980s and 1990s prompt ethnographers to reconsider the crisis of homelessness from the points of view of the homeless themselves.

Rather than indulge in the patronizing pretense of pure participant observation, in which the observer attempts to perform or "pass" as homeless in order to gain an "insider's view," late-twentieth-century homeless ethnographers almost universally embraced the role of what two scholars termed the "buddy-researcher."[50] Befriending their homeless subjects and supplying them with clothes, transportation, money, and other sorely needed favors, these buddy-researchers won a degree of trust and goodwill. In return, they received intimate knowledge of their subjects' lives.

These scholars also created something of a cross-class alliance with their informants, endeavoring to tell their subjects' stories in ways that vindicated the homeless and indicted the larger society that systematically brutalized them. Turning the tables on the well-publicized studies of the 1980s that had cataloged homeless persons' manifold disabilities, the new ethnographies depicted the homeless as responding rationally to the cruel absurdities of their condition. As Elliot Liebow puts it in his masterful *Tell Them Who I Am* (1993), "there is not nearly so much craziness among homeless persons as there is in the systems ostensibly designed to help them."[51]

But while virtually all of these studies expressed sympathy for their subjects, the same cultural politics that had governed representations of homelessness since the Gilded Age continued to hold sway in the late twentieth century. Following in the footsteps of Gilded Age labor tribunes, New Deal social work journals, and Maharidge and Williamson's

*Journey to Nowhere,* liberal ethnographers of the 1990s downplayed their subjects' deviance, depicting homeless subculture as an expression of the "worthy poor."

In *Down on Their Luck* (1993), David A. Snow and Leon Anderson's landmark ethnography of "unattached homeless street adults" in Austin, Texas, for example, the authors observe that their subjects are "remarkably like most of us in their basic needs, their dreams and desires, their interpersonal strategies, and their proclivity to account for their situation in a fashion that attempts to salvage the self." "Struck far more by their [subjects'] normalcy than by their pathology," Snow and Anderson even argue that the "subculture of street life . . . is not a subculture in a conventional sense . . . in that it is neither anchored in nor embodies a distinctive set of shared values." Rather, the authors continue, "its distinctiveness resides in a patterned set of behaviors, routines, and orientations that are adaptive responses to the predicament of homelessness itself."

Similarly, in his study of homeless women, Elliot Liebow contends that whatever subculture exists in the shelters is "born mainly out of shared homelessness and common needs" rather than out of any shared commitment to living "outside the system."[52] In other words, the objective conditions of "houselessness" themselves create whatever deviation from conventional norms that may appear among the homeless.

While these liberal ethnographies stress homeless persons' normative desires for "home," they also sometimes inadvertently acknowledge their subjects' high degrees of alienation from wage labor, the nuclear family, and the state—three dominant institutions that have largely failed to help the homeless and in many cases have actually damaged them. Snow and Anderson remark that two-thirds of their sample population, for example, blamed their homelessness on family problems, and half of these were veritable "refugees from dysfunctional families." Likewise, Elliot Liebow notes that because "family relationships are almost as likely to be sources of pain and rejection as pleasure and support," many of the homeless women in his study are "desperately trying to run away from them."

Similarly, while Liebow echoes Snow and Anderson in asserting that "the work ethic is alive and well among" the homeless, all the authors provide ample evidence of profound disaffection with "jobs that are dirty and hard and boring and low status and lead nowhere" and, most importantly, that "do not pay enough to live on." The various public and private agencies that service and support the homeless also fare poorly in the estimation of the homeless, who chafe against the impersonal controls, arbitrary treatment, contradictory rules and expectations, and the sheer "brutishness" of the shelter system.[53] Despite the authors' contention that the homeless are "just like you and me," the nation's streets and shelters appear to harbor attitudes and values not too distant from those of the old main stem.

Recognizing these similarities, radical ethnographers of the 1990s explored more thoroughly the deviance and alienation manifest among the homeless, discovering within the practices and ideologies of homeless subculture an immanent and radical critique of the nation's dominant institutions. One of the first authors to revisit the notion of a homeless counterculture was Dale Maharidge, who, along with photographer Michael Williamson, published *The Last Great American Hobo* in 1993 as a critical repost to their own earlier book, *Journey to Nowhere*, as well as to the "long line" of homelessness books that followed it. Invoking the anachronistic term "hobo" in the sense of "hobohemian," Maharidge and Williamson's second book recalls James Spradley's and Douglas Harper's revisionist studies of homeless life during the skid row era.

As they track the fate of a homeless encampment along the banks of the Sacramento River, Maharidge and Williamson record the experiences not of entitled Forgotten Men, nor of dislocated poor people clinging to normative desires for "home," but rather of "non-conformists" who are "trampled by society" for not adhering to the rules of masculine breadwinning.[54] Unlike in liberal ethnographies, where the grotesque conditions of "houselessness" twist and distort their victims' values and attitudes, in Maharidge and Williamson's radical account, "houselessness" itself stands as punishment for deviance.

Characterizing their previous interpretations of homelessness as projections of their own "middle-class reality," Maharidge and Williamson discount those studies that romanticize their subjects, present the homeless as innocent victims of circumstances, or focus only on structural causes. All of these approaches, Maharidge and Williamson argue, impose middle-class norms and expectations about home and work on people for whom the streets serve as a haven from those norms. One must view the homeless, they say, through the lens of "hobo reality" where homelessness is one possible consequence of rejecting "the system," that is, the dominant world of regular jobs and nuclear family life.[55]

This conflict between "middle-class reality" and "hobo [or homeless] reality" animated the radical ethnography of the 1990s. Just as the Wobbly anthem "Hallelujah, I'm a Bum" recognized both the cruel injustices and the marginal glories of hobo life, so, too, do radical ethnographers acknowledge both the brutalities and mean consolations of the contemporary homeless world. In *Checkerboard Square* (1993), a study of homeless "street people" in "North City," David Wagner blames an oppressive "nexus of values"—including "beliefs in the work and family ethics"—for relegating his "unworthy" subjects to the streets, where, by default, they are forced to create their own countercultural community to survive.[56]

Similarly, anthropologist Joanne Passaro's 1996 study of New York City's street and shelter populations, *The Unequal Homeless*, identifies a large number of men and women who view their condition in terms either of their failure to adapt to nuclear family roles or the need to escape familial roles or relationships that had become oppressive. According to Passaro, homelessness represents a "haven from heartless homes" for many poor women, the only sanctuary available from abuse. Other women turn to the shelter system in response to the failure or disappearance of male breadwinners. Those largely unattached women who refuse shelter and remain on the streets join an overwhelmingly male population for whom homelessness "is a space for society's rejects, the transgressors of social identity." Remaining on the streets the longest, explains Passaro, are "men who refuse to be breadwinners, 'non-masculine' men, young men who have been victims of abuse from within nuclear families, and men who are tainted twice, because of poverty and race, and who will most likely never get the chance to be 'men.'"[57] Visible homelessness, in other words, represents an acute crisis of gender and race precipitated in large measure by the categorical force of the nuclear family imperative.

In many ways, this radical interpretation of homelessness as "a space for society's rejects" recalls the "disaffiliation" thesis of the skid row era that characterized homeless men as "not part of the system."[58] John Fiske's contemporary study of shelter residents' reading and television viewing habits, for example, finds homeless men consistently "distancing themselves from the norms of domesticity and family relationships, of work and leisure, of earning and spending money . . . systematically reject[ing] the social values that have rejected them." "Homelessness is not just their material condition," asserts Fiske, echoing Howard Bahr and Theodore Caplow, "it saturates their 'whole way of life.'"[59]

What separates the postwar studies of homeless "disaffiliation" from their contemporary counterparts, however, is the positive valuation that radical ethnographers give to their subjects' "antisocial" behaviors and countercultural ideologies. Sociologists like Bahr and Caplow defined the skid row community as illegitimate because its members did not "go along with the rules" and lived "beyond the reach of organized society."[60] Liberal scholars and journalists of the 1980s and 1990s tried to counter this characterization by emphasizing homeless persons' normative desires for regular work and nuclear family life. Radical ethnographers returned to the basic categories of the skid row studies, but instead of interpreting homeless persons' "disaffiliation" as pathological, attempted to explain their subjects' deviance as rational responses to traditional institutions and ideologies that have failed American society as a whole.

Although radical ethnographies take into account instances of organized resistance among the homeless, they do not necessarily replicate the strategy of Wobbly folklore in depicting their subjects as renegades or members of a countercultural avant-garde. Instead, they view the homeless as both agents and victims; that is, as those who suffer the most for failing to adapt to middle-class-based gender norms that millions of non-homeless people reject as well. Noting that 23 million Americans in the 1990 census reported living alone, Joanne Passaro argues that "what is referred to as a symptom of psychological or social dysfunction among homeless people—their 'disaffiliation' and disaffection with dominant institutions—exists among the rest of us as well, if two of those 'supportive institutions' are marriage and the nuclear family."[61] Similarly, David Wagner links the distinct countercultural community among North City's street people to the larger loss of faith in work, family, and nation that attended the collapse of corporate liberalism. "The crisis of homelessness," he argues, "represents the continued failure of the work and family ethics and of traditional state services to hold much legitimacy."[62]

Dale Maharidge puts the case on a more personal level in *The Last Great American Hobo* when he discusses his realization that "I was just like the people I wanted to write about." Pondering whether he could ever leave behind his comfortable home and corporate job and "choose to become a hobo," Maharidge comes to view the process of becoming homeless as "its own form of death and rebirth."[63]

Joining the nation's most deprived and subordinated caste is indeed a heavy price to pay for transgressing the dominant rules of the postwar settlement. Given their class positions and racial identities, neither Maharidge nor millions of other white middle-class men and women will be forced to make such a choice. While the masculine romance of the road persists among middle-class white men as a means for expressing their disaffection with the family breadwinning imperative, the streets provide the nonconforming homeless with an abject counterculture that is at once part freedom and part prison. For many of America's poor, the horror of this prison's alternatives leaves them with little choice but to live without housing. Until the provision of housing proceeds on the basis of a universal citizenship, the American home will continue to harbor the racial, gender, and class inequalities that inevitably beget the homeless.

As the American age of homelessness stretches into the twenty-first century, the ideal of home as a central place of being seems more urgent and elusive than ever. As in previous eras, Marches on Washington to revive and burnish this ideal have become routine, as groups ranging from the Promise Keepers to the Million Man and Million Mom Marchers dramatize local grievances as crises of home and nationhood. Gathering in the nation's capital to reaffirm the home as the fundamental building block of social order and the wellspring of democratic citizenship, these demonstrators inadvertently testify to the extraordinary diversity of contemporary home ideals. The singular domestic vision that once seemed to command universal allegiance—breadwinning fathers and child-rearing mothers in single-family houses—has fractured, fallen victim to the racial exclusions, gender constraints, and narrow class assumptions that such a vision historically entailed. If postmodernity is defined as the "loss of the center," then the multiplicity of contemporary domestic practices and ideals might serve as the leading hallmark of the postmodern era.

It would be more accurate, however, to consider our age of homelessness not as a dramatic break from previously unified visions of home, but as another phase of a persistent failure to divorce such visions from both the political economies of housing and the entitlements of citizenship. Since the nineteenth century, homeless persons—variously figured as vagrants, tramps, hoboes, transients, migrants, bums, and street people—have sparked successive crises of home and nationhood that fundamentally challenged the narrow domestic visions upon which the privileges of American citizenship have historically been based. By virtue of their social power, dispossessed white men were able to gain access to these privileges, but only after they had created their own threatening homeless world, where privilege was defined in terms of independence from reigning domestic ideals. The recovery of the "Citizen Hobo" after World War II was achieved only through the creation of a political economy and social policy that elevated the nuclear family ideal to a social imperative.

Today the consequences of this achievement continue to weigh heavily upon us. Even in our postmodern era, which ostensibly recognizes the diversity of home ideals, poor people who reject or are rejected by the nuclear family face a gruesome existence where the protections and immunities of citizenship do not include housing. If in America "a man's home is his castle," granting him access to the polity and to social power, then those without homes or those imprisoned in the castle cannot be called citizens. For the homeless, winning citizenship means struggling not only for shelter, but for "home" differently defined. For however it is imagined, the American home remains an essential means for gaining access, belonging, inclusion, and power.

# NOTES

## INTRODUCTION

1. "Home: A Place in the World," a collection of essays published in *Social Research* 58 (spring 1991). On the tyrannies of home, see especially Mary Douglas, "The Idea of Home: A Kind of Space," 303–5.

2. The term "social citizenship" originally derives from T. H. Marshall, "Citizenship and Social Class," in *Class, Citizenship, and Social Development* (New York: Doubleday, 1965), 65–122. Other major historical studies that explore the racialized and gendered meanings of citizenship include Judith Shklar, *American Citizenship: The Quest for Inclusion* (Cambridge: Harvard University Press, 1991); Rogers M. Smith, *Civic Ideals: Conflicting Visions of Citizenship in US History* (New Haven: Yale University Press, 1997); Suzanne Mettler, *Dividing Citizens: Gender and Federalism in New Deal Public Policy* (Ithaca, N.Y.: Cornell University Press, 1998); Linda K. Kerber, *No Constitutional Right to Be Ladies :Women and the Obligations of Citizenship* (New York: Hill and Wang, 1998); and Alice Kessler-Harris, *In Pursuit of Equity: Women, Men, and the Quest for Economic Citizenship in 20th-Century America* (New York: Oxford University Press, 2001).

3. The only comprehensive history of American homelessness is Kenneth L. Kusmer, *Down and Out, on the Road: The Homeless in American History* (New York: Oxford University Press, 2002).

The major and most important policy-oriented studies of homelessness include Paul T. Ringenbach, *Tramps and Reformers, 1873–1916: The Discovery of Unemployment in New York* (Westport, Conn.: Greenwood Press, 1973); Michael B. Katz, *Poverty and Policy in American History* (New York: Academic Press, 1983), esp. 157–81; Sidney L. Harring, *Policing a Class Society: the Experience of American Cities, 1865–1915* (New Brunswick, N.J.: Rutgers University Press, 1983), esp. 201–23; idem, "Class Conflict and the Suppression of Tramps in Buffalo, 1892–1894," *Law and Society Review* 11 (summer 1977): 873–911; Amy Dru Stanley, "Beggars Can't Be Choosers: Compulsion and Contract in Postbellum America," *Journal of American History* 78 (March 1992): 1265–93; John Schneider, "Homeless Men and Housing Policy in Urban America, 1850–1920," *Urban Studies* 26 (February 1989): 90–99; Kim Hopper, "Public Shelter as 'a Hybrid Institution': Homeless Men in Historical Perspective," *Journal of Social Issues* 46 (December 1990): 13–28; and Joan M. Crouse, *The Homeless Transient in the Great Depression: New York State, 1929–1941* (Albany: State University of New York, 1986).

On the social history of tramping, see especially the essays collected in Eric H. Monkkonen, ed., *Walking to Work: Tramps in America, 1790–1935* (Lincoln: University of Nebraska,

1984). See also idem, *The Dangerous Class: Crime and Poverty in Columbus, Ohio, 1860–1885* (Cambridge: Harvard University Press, 1975); and Alexander Keyssar, *Out of Work: The First Century of Unemployment in Massachusetts* (New York: Cambridge University Press, 1986), esp. 111–42.

On hobo labor in the West, see Greg Hall, *Harvest Wobblies: The Industrial Workers of the World and Agricultural Laborers in the American West, 1905–1930* (Corvallis: Oregon State University Press, 2001); Carlos A. Schwantes, *The Pacific Northwest: An Interpretive History* (Lincoln: University of Nebraska Press, 1989), esp. 250–65; Kenneth Allsop, *Hard Travellin': The Hobo and His History* (New York: New American Library, 1967); Roger Bruns, *Knights of the Road: A Hobo History* (New York: Methuen, 1980); Lynne Marie Adrian, "Organizing the Rootless: American Hobo Subculture, 1893–1932," (Ph.D. diss., University of Iowa, 1984); John C. Schneider, "Omaha Vagrants and the Character of Western Hobo Labor, 1887–1913," *Nebraska History* 63 (summer 1982): 255–72; and Clark C. Spence, "Knights of the Fast Freight," *American Heritage* 27 (August 1976): 50–57, 92–97.

On the history of skid row as a built enviornment, see Paul Groth, *Living Downtown: The History of Residential Hotels in the United States* (Berkeley: University of California Press, 1994); Charles Hoch and Robert A. Slayton, *New Homeless and Old: Community and the Skid Row Hotel* (Philadelphia: Temple University Press, 1989); John C. Schneider, "Skid Row as Urban Neighborhood, 1880–1960," in *Housing the Homeless,* ed. Jon Erickson and Charles Wilhelm (New Brunswick: State University of New Jersey Press, 1986), 167–89; and Larry R. Ford, *Cities and Buildings: Skyscrapers, Skid Rows, and Suburbs* (Baltimore: Johns Hopkins University Press, 1994), 64–94.

On the cultural history of the "road" and of the tramp in the American social imagination, see Tim Cresswell, *The Tramp in America* (London: Reaktion Books, 2001); John Seeyle, "The American Tramp: A Version of the Picaresque," *American Quarterly* 15 (winter 1963): 535–53; Frederick Feied, *No Pie in the Sky: The Hobo as American Cultural Hero in the Works of Jack London, John Dos Passos, and Jack Kerouac* (New York: Citadel Press, 1964); William R. Hunt, "'Which Way 'Bo?': Literary Impressions of the Hobos' Golden Age, 1880–1930," *Journal of Popular Culture* 4 (summer 1970): 22–38; William Brevda, *Harry Kemp: The Last Bohemian* (Lewisburg, Penn.: Bucknell University Press, 1986); Michael Denning, *Mechanic Accents: Dime Novels and Working-Class Culture in America* (New York: Verso, 1987), 149–57; and idem, *The Cultural Front: The Laboring of American Culture in the Twentieth Century* (New York: Verso, 1996), esp. 163–99.

The major historical studies of "whiteness" upon which this book draws include David R. Roediger, *The Wages of Whiteness: Race and the Making of the American Working Class* (London: Verso, 1991); idem, *Towards the Abolition of Whiteness: Essays on Race, Politics, and Working-Class History* (London: Verso, 1994); Alexander Saxton, *The Rise and Fall of the White Republic: Class Politics and Mass Culture in Nineteenth-Century America* (London: Verso, 1990); Eric Lott, *Love and Theft: Blackface Minstrelsy and the American Working Class* (New York: Oxford University Press, 1993); Noel Ignatiev, *How the Irish Became White* (New York: Routledge, 1995); Matthew Frye Jacobson, *Whiteness of a Different Color: European Immigrants and the Alchemy of Race* (Cambridge: Harvard University Press, 1998); and Richard Delgado and Jean Stefanic, eds., *Critical White Studies: Looking Behind the Mirror* (Philadelphia: Temple University Press, 1997).

The major works on gender and social policy include Theda Skocpol, *Protecting Soldiers and Mothers: The Political Origins of Social Policy in the United States* (Cambridge: Harvard University Press, 1992); Linda Gordon, *Pitied but Not Entitled: Single Mothers and the History of Welfare, 1890–1935* (New York: Free Press, 1994); Molly Ladd-Taylor, *Mother-Work: Women, Child Welfare, and the State, 1890–1930* (Urbana: University of Illinois Press, 1994); Gwendolyn Mink, *The Wages of Motherhood: Inequality in the Welfare State, 1917–1942* (Ithaca, N.Y.: Cornell University Press, 1995); Joanne L. Goodwin, *Gender and the Politics of Welfare Reform: Mothers' Pensions in Chicago, 1911–1929* (Chicago: University of Chicago Press, 1997); and Kessler-Harris, *In Pursuit of Equity.*

4. Dana D. Nelson, *Capitalist Citizenship and the Imagined Fraternity of White Men* (Durham, N.C.: Duke University Press, 1998).

CHAPTER ONE

1. Jacob Riis, *The Making of an American* (New York: Macmillan, 1947 [1901]), 75, 51, 21. Riis's account of his first three years in America can be found on 21–79.

2. William H. Brewer, "What Shall We Do with Our Tramps?" *New Englander* 37 (July 1878): 521–32.

3. *New York Times*, August 8, 1875.

4. *Chicago Tribune*, July 12, 1877.

5. *Newburyport Herald*, June 14, 1878, quoted in Kenneth Allsop, *Hard Travellin': The Hobo and His History* (New York: New American Library, 1967), 116.

6. Francis Wayland, *Papers on Out-door Relief and Tramps, Read at the Saratoga Meeting of the American Social Science Association, before the Conference of State Charities, September 5th & 6th, 1877* (New Haven, Conn.: Hoggson and Robinson, 1877), 10.

7. Edward E. Hale, "Report on Tramps," *Proceedings of the Conference of Charities and Corrections* (Boston: A. Williams and Co., 1877), 105.

8. Riis, *Making of an American*, 36.

9. Hale, "Report on Tramps," 104.

10. *Oxford English Dictionary* (Oxford: Oxford University Press, 1971 [1888]).

11. On the problem of vagrancy and the figure of the vagabond in Tudor and Stuart England, see A. L. Beier, *Masterless Men: The Vagrancy Problem in England, 1560–1640* (London: Methuen 1986); John Pound, *Poverty and Vagrancy in Tudor England* (London: Harlow, Longman, 1971); Frank Aydelotte, *Elizabethan Rogues and Vagabonds* (Oxford: Clarendon Press, 1913); Norman Berlin, *The Base String: The Underworld in Elizabethan Drama* (Rutherford, N.J.: Fairleigh Dickinson University Press, 1968); and Christopher Hill, *The World Turned Upside Down: Radical Ideas during the English Revolution* (New York: Viking, 1972).

12. Douglas Lamar Jones, "The Strolling Poor: Transiency in Eighteenth-Century Massachusetts," in *Walking to Work: Tramps in America, 1790–1935*, ed. Eric H. Monkkonen (Lincoln: University of Nebraska, 1984), 39; Kenneth L. Kusmer, *Down and Out, on the Road: The Homeless in American History* (New York: Oxford University Press, 2002), 13–22; see also Joan M. Crouse, "Transients, Migrants, and the Homeless," in *The Encyclopedia of American Social History*, vol. 3, ed. Mary Kupiec Cayton, Elliott J. Gorn, and Peter W. Williams (New York: Scribner, 1993), 2143–45.

13. Paul E. Johnson, *A Shopkeeper's Millenium: Society and Revivals in Rochester, New York, 1815–1837* (New York: Hill and Wang, 1978), 38.

14. David J. Rothman, *The Discovery of the Asylum: Social Order and Disorder in the New Republic* (Boston: Little, Brown, 1971); see also idem, "The First Shelters: The Contemporary Relevance of the Almshouse," in *On Being Homeless: Historical Perspectives*, ed. Rick Beard (New York: Museum of the City of New York, 1987), 10–19.

15. Elizabeth Blackmar, *Manhattan for Rent, 1785–1850* (Ithaca, N.Y.: Cornell University Press, 1989), 171–72.

16. Quoted in Alan Trachtenberg, *The Incorporation of America: Culture and Society in the Gilded Age* (New York: Hill and Wang, 1982), 70.

17. Statistics on railroad growth quoted in Edward Chase Kirkland, *Industry Comes of Age: Business, Labor and Public Policy, 1860–1897* (Chicago: Quadrangle Books, 1967), 6; and "Railroads," in *The Reader's Companion to American History*, ed. Eric Foner and John A. Garraty (Boston: Houghton Mifflin, 1991), 907.

18. On the increase in working-class residential mobility in the late nineteenth century, see Stephan Thernstrom and Peter R. Knights, "Men in Motion: Some Data and Speculations about Urban Population Mobility in Nineteenth-Century America," in *Anonymous Americans: Explorations in Nineteenth-Century Social History*, ed. Tamara K. Hareven (Englewood Cliffs, N.J.: Prentice-Hall, 1971); Howard Chudacoff, *Mobile Americans: Residential*

*and Social Mobility in the American Metropolis, 1880–1920* (New York: Oxford University Press, 1972); Stephan Thernstrom, *The Other Bostonians: Poverty and Progress in the American Metropolis, 1880–1970* (Cambridge: Harvard University Press, 1973); Michael B. Katz, Michael J. Doucet, and Mark J. Stern, *The Social Organization of Early Industrial Capitalism* (Cambridge: Harvard University Press, 1982), 102–30; and Alexander Keyssar, *Out of Work: The First Century of Unemployment in Massachusetts* (New York: Cambridge University Press, 1986), 111–42.

On the change in almshouse populations, see Eric H. Monkkonen, *The Dangerous Class: Crime and Poverty in Columbus, Ohio, 1860–1885* (Cambridge: Harvard University Press, 1975), 116–21; and Michael B. Katz, *In the Shadow of the Poorhouse: A Social History of Welfare in America* (New York: Basic Books, 1986).

19. W. L. Bull, "Trampery: Its Causes, Present Aspects, and Some Suggested Remedies," *Proceedings of the National Conference of Charities and Correction*, ed. Isabel C. Barrows (Boston: George H. Ellis, 1886), 196.

20. Riis, *Making of an American*, 41.

21. Keyssar, *Out of Work*, 4.

22. Ibid., 9–38.

23. Katz, *Shadow of the Poorhouse*, 6.

24. Keyssar, *Out of Work*, 50–52. See also Monkkonen, *The Dangerous Class*, 142.

25. On the commodification of housing, see Blackmar, *Manhattan for Rent*, esp. chap. 2.

26. Quoted in Keyssar, *Out of Work*, 162.

27. Michael B. Katz, *Poverty and Policy in American History* (New York: Academic Press, 1983), 171; Eric H. Monkkonen, "Introduction," in *Walking to Work*, 1–17; and idem, "Regional Dimensions of Tramping, North and South, 1880–1910," in *Walking to Work*, 189–211; Keyssar, *Out of Work*, 118–19.

28. Riis, *Making of an American*, 45–49.

29. Katz, *Poverty and Policy*, 172–73; Monkkonen, "Introduction," 12; idem, "Regional Dimensions of Tramping," 195, 205. For the case of carpenters, see Jules Tygiel, "Tramping Artisans: Carpenters in Industrial America, 1880–1890," in *Walking to Work*, ed. Monkkonen, 87–117.

30. Riis, *Making of an American*, 27.

31. Priscilla Ferguson Clement, "The Transformation of the Wandering Poor in Nineteenth-Century Philadelphia," in *Walking to Work*, ed. Monkkonen, 77.

32. Paul Fisher, "A Forgotten Gentry of the Fourth Estate," *Journalism Quarterly* 33 (spring 1956): 167–75; Tygiel, "Tramping Artisans," 87–117; Patricia A. Cooper, "The 'Traveling Fraternity': Union Cigar Makers and Geographic Mobility, 1900–1919," in *Walking to Work*, ed. Monkkonen, 118–38; and Jim Foster, "The Ten Day Tramps," *Labor History* 23 (fall 1982): 608–23. On the British counterparts of this tramping system, see Eric J. Hobsbawm, "The Tramping Artisan," in *Labouring Men: Studies in the History of Labor* (New York: Basic Books, 1964), 34–63.

33. Riis, *Making of an American*, 43.

34. Eric H. Monkkonen, *Police in Urban America, 1860–1920* (New York: Cambridge University Press, 1981), 94–96. Monkonnen's study is the most thorough examination of police station lodging available. See especially 86–109.

35. Stephanie Golden, *The Women Outside: Meanings and Myths of Homelessness* (Berkeley: University of California Press, 1992), see especially 113–30; see also Lynn Weiner, "Sisters of the Road: Women Transients and Tramps," in *Walking to Work*, ed. Monkkonen, 171–88; and Marsha A. Martin, "Homeless Women: An Historical Perspective," in *On Being Homeless*, ed. Beard, 32–41.

36. Katz, *Poverty and Policy*, 166–69; Kusmer, *Down and Out*, 111–13.

37. Clement, "Transformation of the Wandering Poor," 68–69; Kusmer, *Down and Out*, 11. See also Theda Skocpol, *Protecting Soldiers and Mothers: The Political Origins of Social Policy in the United States* (Cambridge: Harvard University Press, 1992).

38. Quoted in Kusmer, *Down and Out*, 138. See also William Cohen, *At Freedom's Edge: Black Mobility and the Southern White Quest for Racial Control* (Baton Rouge: Louisiana State University Press, 1991).

39. Monkkonen, "Regional Dimensions of Tramping," 205, 189–211.

40. Katz, *Poverty and Policy*, 166.

41. Clement, "Transformation of the Wandering Poor," 67; Monkkonen, *The Dangerous Class*, 160; Katz, *Poverty and Policy*, 166, 169; Kusmer, *Down and Out*, 105, 107–8.

42. Clement, "Transformation of the Wandering Poor," 76–77; Monkkonen, *The Dangerous Class*, 160; Katz, *Poverty and Policy*, 166, 168; Tygiel, "Tramping Artisans," 96.

43. William Aspinwall to John James McCook, 26 May 1893 (microfilm: roll 12) *The Social Reform Papers of John James McCook*, ed. Adela Haberski French (Hartford, Conn.: Antiquarian and Landmarks Society, 1977).

44. Katz, *Poverty and Policy*, 171; John J. McCook, "Tramps," *The Charities Review: A Journal of Practical Sociology* 3 (December 1893): 66; Kusmer, *Down and Out*, 106.

45. Terence V. Powderly, "My Painful Experience as a Tramp," *American Federationist* 8 (September 1901): 332. On the various strategies for coping with unemployment in the late nineteenth century, see Keyssar, *Out of Work*, 143–76.

46. Brewer, "What Shall We Do with Our Tramps?," 532.

47. Wayland, *Papers on Out-door Relief and Tramps*, 16.

48. *New York Times*, August 24, 1877.

49. Brewer, "What Shall We Do with Our Tramps?," 523.

50. Allan Pinkerton, *Strikers, Communists, Tramps, and Detectives* (New York: G. W. Carleton, 1878), 47.

51. Police official quoted in John Seeyle, "The American Tramp: A Version of the Picaresque," *American Quarterly* 15 (winter 1963): 543; Hale, "Report on Tramps," 103.

52. Pinkerton, *Strikers*, 47–48.

53. Lee O. Harris, *The Man Who Tramps: A Story of To-day* (Indianapolis: Douglass and Carlson, 1878), 18–19, 28, 35.

54. Kusmer, *Down and Out*, 35–37; Eric T. Dean Jr., *Shook All Over Hell: Post-Traumatic Stress, Vietnam, and the Civil War* (Cambridge: Harvard University Press, 1997), 88.

55. The classic study of antebellum free labor ideology is Eric Foner, *Free Soil, Free Labor, Free Men: The Ideology of the Republican Party before the Civil War* (New York: Oxford University Press, 1970).

56. "Populist Party Platform, July 4, 1892," in *Documents in American History*, vol. 1, ed. Henry Steele Commager (New York: Appleton, Century, Crofts, 1963), 593; see also Trachtenberg, *Incorporation of America*, 70–100.

57. David Montgomery, *Citizen Worker: The Experience of Workers in the United States with Democracy and the Free Market during the Nineteenth Century* (New York: Cambridge University Press, 1993), 83–89.

58. Amy Dru Stanley, "Beggars Can't Be Choosers: Compulsion and Contract in Postbellum America," *Journal of American History* 78 (March 1992): 1265–93.

59. *Report of Committee on Penal Treatment of Inebriates and Vagrants, Made to the General Assembly, May Session 1875* (Hartford, Conn.: Case, Lockwood and Brainard, 1875), 14.

60. *New York Times*, July 9, 1879.

61. On the racialization of nineteenth-century Irish immigrants, see especially David R. Roediger, *The Wages of Whiteness: Race and the Making of the American Working Class* (London: Verso, 1991); Noel Ignatiev, *How the Irish Became White* (New York: Routledge, 1995); and Matthew Frye Jacobson, *Whiteness of a Different Color: European Immigrants and the Alchemy of Race* (Cambridge: Harvard University Press, 1998).

62. Montgomery, *Citizen Worker*, 86–87.

63. Massachusetts statute of 1880 quoted in Keyssar, *Out of Work*, 135.

64. Hale, "Report on Tramps," 103.

65. Montgomery, *Citizen Worker*, 71–83; Paul T. Ringenbach, *Tramps and Reformers*,

*1873–1916:The Discovery of Unemployment in NewYork* (Westport, Conn.: Greenwood Press, 1973), 15–22.

66. Hale, "Report on Tramps," 104.

67. Seventeenth-century English commentator Adam Moore, quoted in Hill, *World Turned Upside Down*, 52.

68. Keyssar, *Out of Work*, 163–65.

69. Harris, *The Man Who Tramps*, 21.

70. Montgomery, *Citizen Worker*, 98–104.

71. Philip S. Foner, *The Great Labor Uprising of 1877* (NewYork: Monad Press, 1977).

72. Wayland, *Papers on Out-door Relief and Tramps*, 15.

73. Harris, *The Man Who Tramps*, 43, 267, 271.

74. Wayland, *Papers on Out-Door Relief and Tramps*, 10.

75. "Tramps," *Unitarian Review* 8 (October 1877): 439.

76. For an overview of the voluminous historical literature on nineteenth-century ideologies of domesticity, see Linda Kerber, "Separate Spheres, Female Worlds, Women's Place: The Rhetoric of Women's History," *Journal of American History* 75 (June 1988): 9–39.

77. Quoted in Ringenbach, *Tramps and Reformers*, 4.

78. Harris, *The Man Who Tramps*, 13.

79. Wayland, *Papers on Out-door Relief and Tramps*, 10–11.

80. John D'Emilio and Estelle B. Freedman, *Intimate Matters: A History of Sexuality in America* (NewYork: Harper and Row, 1988), 57.

81. Wayland, *Papers on Out-door Relief and Tramps*, 11.

82. Harris, *The Man Who Tramps*, 269.

## CHAPTER TWO

1. Walt Whitman, "The Tramp and Strike Questions" (1879), in *Speciman Days and Collect* (NewYork: Dover Publications, 1995 [1883]), 329–30.

2. Quoted in Alan Trachtenberg, *The Incorporation of America: Culture and Society in the Gilded Age* (NewYork: Hill and Wang, 1982), 73.

3. Walt Whitman, "Song of the Open Road" (1856), in *Leaves of Grass and Selected Prose*, ed. John Kouwenhoven (NewYork: Modern Library, 1950), 120. Whitman's remark about tramps "plodding along" is from "The Tramp and Strike Questions," 330.

4. Whitman, "Song of the Open Road," 124.

5. Ibid., 120.

6. Whitman, "Democratic Vistas," in *Speciman Days and Collect*, 221.

7. Quoted in Trachtenberg, *Incorporation of America*, 73.

8. Quoted in Kenneth Allsop, *Hard Travellin': The Hobo and His History* (NewYork: New American Library, 1967), 136.

9. *Journal of United Labor* 4 (December 1883): 604.

10. *National Labor Tribune*, September 25, 1875.

11. Paul T. Ringenbach, *Tramps and Reformers, 1873–1916: The Discovery of Unemployment in NewYork* (Westport, Conn.: Greenwood Press, 1973).

12. *National Labor Tribune*, January 12, 1877.

13. *Workingman's Advocate*, December 30, 1876.

14. *Iron Molders' Journal*, February 10, 1876.

15. For this view see Michael Davis "Forced to Tramp: The Perspective of the Labor Press, 1870–1900," in *Walking to Work: Tramps in America, 1790–1935*, ed. Eric H. Monkkonen (Lincoln: University of Nebraska Press, 1984), 141–70.

16. *National Labor Tribune*, January 13, 1875.

17. *John Swinton's Paper*, July 26, 1885.

18. *Journal of the Knights of Labor*, November 2, 1893.

19. For superb discussions of the meanings of housing to nineteenth-century American workers, see Elizabeth Blackmar, *Manhattan for Rent, 1785–1850* (Ithaca, N.Y.: Cornell Uni-

versity Press, 1989); and David Montgomery, *Citizen Worker: The Experience of Workers in the United States with Democracy and the Free Market during the Nineteenth Century* (New York: Cambridge University Press, 1993), 104–14.

20. *National Labor Tribune*, May 27, 1876.

21. Ibid., November 10, 1877.

22. Henry George, *Social Problems* (New York: Robert Schalkenbach Foundation, 1961 [1883]), 138. See also idem, *Progress and Poverty: An Inquiry into the Cause of Industrial Depression and of Increase of Want with Increase of Wealth* (New York: Robert Schalkenbach Foundation, 1979 [1879]); and Jacob Oser, *Henry George* (New York: Twayne, 1974).

23. Robert H. Cowdrey, *A Tramp in Society* (Chicago: Francis J. Schulte and Company, 1891).

24. *Journal of the Knights of Labor*, November 2, 1893.

25. Ringenbach, *Tramps and Reformers*, 110.

26. Elbert Hubbard, "The Rights of Tramps," *Arena* 9 (April 1894): 593–94.

27. Davis, "Forced to Tramp," 162.

28. Victor Turner, *The Ritual Process: Structure and Anti-Structure* (Ithaca, N.Y.: Cornell University Press, 1977), 95.

29. "Only a Tramp," *Locomotive Engineers Journal* 10 (September 1876): 408.

30. *Iron Molders' Journal*, July 10, 1878.

31. C. W. Noble, "The Border Land of Trampdom," *Popular Science Monthly* 50 (December 1896): 253.

32. *United Mineworkers Journal*, March 29, 1894.

33. William Staats, *A Tight Squeeze; Or, the Adventures of a Gentleman Who on a Wager of Ten Thousand Dollars, Undertook to Go from New York to New Orleans in Three Weeks without Money as a Professional Tramp* (Boston: Lee and Shepard, 1879), 23–26.

34. *National Labor Tribune*, August 14, 1875.

35. Ibid., September 25, 1877.

36. George, *Social Problems*, 129, 130, 6.

37. Herbert Gutman, "Protestantism and the American Labor Movement," in *Work, Culture, and Society in Industrializing America: Essays in American Working-Class and Social History* (New York: Alfred A. Knopf, 1976), 79–117. See also Paul Boyer, *When Time Shall Be No More: Prophecy Belief in Modern American Culture* (Cambridge: Belknap Press of Harvard University Press, 1992).

38. *National Labor Tribune*, December 23, 1876.

39. Gutman, "Protestantism and the American Labor Movement," 90.

40. *Journal of United Labor* 4 (December 1883): 604.

41. *National Labor Tribune*, May 27, 1876.

42. *The Tramp: His Tricks, Tallies and Tell-Tales, with All His Signs, Countersigns, Grips, Pass-Words and Villainies Exposed. By an Ex-Tramp*, ed. Frank Bellew (New York: Dick and Fitzgerald, 1878), 5, 13, 20.

43. Michael Denning, *Mechanic Accents: Dime Novels and Working-Class Culture in America* (New York: Verso, 1987). For a superb discussion of tramps and working-class dime novels, see 65–84.

44. *The Tramp*, ed. Bellew, 5, 32. Subsequent references to *The Tramp* will be cited parenthetically in the text according to page number.

45. See Mary Douglas, *Purity and Danger: An Analysis of Concepts of Pollution and Taboo* (New York: Praeger, 1966).

46. Whitman, "Of the Terrible Doubt of Appearances" (1860), in *Leaves of Grass*, 98–99.

47. The best historical study of the confidence man in antebellum American culture is Karen Halttunen's *Confidence Men and Painted Women: A Study of Middle-Class Culture in Victorian America, 1830–1870* (New Haven: Yale University Press, 1982). For an analysis of the confidence game in relation to the rise of advertising, see Jackson Lears, *Fables of Abundance:*

*A Cultural History of Advertising in America* (NewYork: Basic Books, 1994), esp. 60–74, 99–101. For a discussion of the crisis of confidence in early modern England and America, see Jean-Christophe Agnew, *Worlds Apart:The Market and the Theater in Anglo-American Thought, 1550–1750* (NewYork: Cambridge University Press, 1986).

48. The most brilliant and trenchant contemporary critic of the nineteenth-century cult of sincerity was Herman Melville. His book *The Confidence-Man: His Masquerade,* ed. H. Bruce Franklin (Indianapolis: Bobbs-Merrill, 1967 [1857]), has attracted much critical attention. Studies that discuss Melville's complex novel, as well as other literary depictions of confidence men, include Warwick Wadlington, *The Confidence Game in American Literature* (Princeton: Princeton University Press, 1975); and Gary Lindberg, *The Confidence Man in American Literature* (New York: Oxford University Press, 1982). See also Agnew, *Worlds Apart,* 195–203.

49. Bret Harte's "My Friend the Tramp" was the first story to depict the tramp's confidence game in a humorous and sentimental light. By portraying the tramp's duplicity as utterly transparent, Harte figuratively nullified the confidence game's dangers. Bret Harte, "My Friend the Tramp" (1877), in *The Luck of Roaring Camp and Other Tales* (New York: Dodd, Mead, 1961), 280–92.

50. Jacob A. Riis, *How the Other Half Lives: Studies among the Tenements of NewYork* (New York: Charles Scribner's Sons, 1926 [1890]), 78.

51. Josiah Flynt (Josiah Flynt Willard), *Tramping with Tramps: Studies and Sketches of Vagabond Life* (NewYork: Century Company, 1900 [1899]), 5. On Willard's life and work, see Josiah Flynt, *My Life* (NewYork: Outing Publishing, 1908); Louis Filler, *Crusaders for American Liberalism* (Yellow Springs, Ohio: Antioch Press, 1964 [1939]), 68–72; Rolf Linder, *The Reportage of Urban Culture: Robert Park and the Chicago School,* trans. Adrian Morris (New York: Cambridge University Press, 1996), 115–24; and Tim Cresswell, *The Tramp in America* (London: Reaktion Books, 2001), 60–61.

52. Quoted in *The Social Reform Papers of John James McCook: A Guide to the Microfilm Edition,* ed. Adela Haberski French (Hartford, Conn.: Antiquarian and Landmarks Society, 1977), 31. Biographical information on McCook is drawn from *Social Reform Papers,* 3–31. See also Roger A. Bruns, "Hoboes Told All to 1890s Scholar," *Smithsonian* 8 (November 1977): 141–48; Ralph F. Bogardus and Ferenc M. Szasz, "Reality Captured, Reality Tamed: John James McCook and the Uses of Documentary Photography in Fin-de-Siècle America," *History of Photography* 10 (April–June 1986): 151–67; and Ringenbach, *Tramps and Reformers,* 40. See also Cresswell, *The Tramp in America,* 181–95.

53. William W. Aspinwall to John James McCook, May 18, 1893 (microfilm: roll 12), *Social Reform Papers.* After 1906 Aspinwall's traveling abated considerably as old age frequently forced him to take refuge in veterans' homes. In 1921, at the age of seventy-six, Aspinwall died at the State Soldiers' Home in Erie County, Ohio. Biographical information on Aspinwall is from *Social Reform Papers,* 41–42.

54. John J. McCook, "Leaves from the Diary of a Tramp," part 1, *Independent* 53 (November 21, 1901): 2764.

55. The complete correspondence may be found in (roll 12) *Social Reform Papers.*

56. *Social Reform Papers,* 31. John J. McCook, "Leaves from the Diary of a Tramp," parts 1–9, *Independent* 53 (November 21, 1901): 2760–67; (December 5, 1901): 2880–88; (December 19, 1901): 3009–13; 54 (January 2, 1902): 23–28; (January 16, 1902): 154–60; (February 6, 1902): 332–37; (March 13, 1902): 620–24; (April 10, 1902): 873–74; (June 26, 1902): 1539–44.

57. Aspinwall to McCook, May 18, 1893, *Social Reform Papers.* Subsequent references to this correspondence will be cited parenthetically in the text.

58. McCook, "Leaves from the Diary of a Tramp," part 1, 2761–62.

59. For an excellent discussion of the problems that working-class writers face in establishing the value of their own subjectivity, see Regenia Gagnier, "Social Atoms: Working-Class Autobiography, Subjectivity, and Gender," *Victorian Studies* 30 (spring 1987): 335–63.

60. Quoted in McCook, "Leaves from the Diary of a Tramp," part 6, 337.

61. McCook, "Leaves from the Diary of a Tramp," part 1, 2704. Subsequent references to this series will be cited parenthetically in the text according to part and page number.

62. John J. McCook, "A Tramp Census and Its Revelations," *Forum* 15 (August 1893): 765.

## CHAPTER THREE

1. Jack London, "Tramp Diary" (1894), in *Jack London on the Road: The Tramp Diary and Other Hobo Writings,* ed. Richard W. Etulain (Logan: Utah State University Press, 1979), 41, 54. For a description of London's various hobo journeys and writings, see Etulain's "Introduction," 1–27. On London's experiences with Kelley's Army in Iowa, see "Jack London and Kelly's [*sic*] Army," *Palimpsest* 52 (June 1971): 289–352.

2. The best firsthand account of the Industrial Army movement is Henry Vincent, *The Story of the Commonweal* (New York: Arno Press, 1969 [1894]). The most thorough secondary account of the national movement is Carlos Schwantes, *Coxey's Army: An American Odyssey* (Lincoln: University of Nebraska Press, 1985).

3. W. T. Stead, "Coxeyism: A Character Sketch," *American Review of Reviews* 10 (July 1894): 49.

4. Etulain, "Introduction," *Jack London on the Road,* 4. On Jack London's career in the writer's market, see Christopher P. Wilson, *The Labor of Words: Literary Professionalism in the Progressive Era* (Athens: University of Georgia Press, 1985), 92–112.

5. Wayland, quoted in the *Washington Times,* May 1, 1894.

6. Kelley, quoted in Vincent, *Story of the Commonweal,* 154–55.

7. T. B. Veblen, "The Army of the Commonweal," *Journal of Political Economy* 2 (June 1894): 457. Years after the march, George Speed, leader of the Sacramento Industrial Army, disavowed London's participation in the movement, saying that he "never actually joined the army, but merely traveled around or along." Etulain, "Introduction," *Jack London on the Road,* 3.

8. For information on the social composition of the Industrial Army movement, see H. L. Stetson, "The Industrial Army," *Independent* 46 (May 31, 1894): 681; Stead, "Coxeyism," 47–56; A. Cleveland Hall, "An Observer in Coxey's Camp," *Independent* 46 (May 17, 1894): 615–16; "An Inspection of the Camps," *American Review of Reviews* 10 (July 1894): 4–5; William J. Peterson, "Kelly [*sic*] and His Men," *Palimpsest* 52 (June 1971): 298–303; and Schwantes, *Coxey's Army,* passim.

9. Nels Anderson, *The Hobo: The Sociology of the Homeless Man* (Chicago: Phoenix Books, 1965 [1923]). Anderson used the term "hobohemia" without explanation, giving no account of its provenance. "Hobohemia" first appeared in print in Sinclair Lewis's short story of the same title. This story satirizes fashionable Greenwich Village bohemian life. Sinclair Lewis, "Hobohemia," *Saturday Evening Post* 189 (April 7, 1917): 3–6, 121.

10. London, quoted in Wilson, *Labor of Words,* 96.

11. George Milburn, *The Hobo's Hornbook: A Repertory for a Gutter Jongleur* (New York: Ives Washburn, 1930), 97. See also John Greenway, *American Folksongs of Protest* (Philadelphia: University of Pennsylvania Press, 1953), 201–2.

12. London, "The Tramp" (1904), in *Jack London on the Road,* 133.

13. Frederick Jackson Turner, "The Significance of the Frontier in American History" (1893), in *History, Frontier, and Section: Three Essays by Frederick Jackson Turner,* ed. Martin Ridge (Albuquerque: University of New Mexico Press, 1993), 59–91.

14. Shirley Plumer Austin, "The Downfall of Coxeyism," *Chautauquan* 19 (July 1894): 452.

15. Henry Edward Rood, "The Tramp Problem: A Remedy," *Forum* 25 (March 1898): 91.

16. *Iron Molders' Journal,* September 10, 1877.

17. *John Swinton's Paper,* May 24, 1885.

18. Arthur Vinette, quoted in Jules Tygiel, "Tramping Artisans: Carpenters in Industrial America, 1880–1890," in *Walking to Work: Tramps in America, 1790–1935,* ed. Eric H. Monkkonen (Lincoln: University of Nebraska, 1984), 96.

19. Carlos A. Schwantes, *The Pacific Northwest: An Interpretive History* (Lincoln: University of Nebraska Press, 1989), 250–65.

20. For information on these various migratory groups, see Ronald Takaki, *A Different Mirror: A History of Multicultural America* (Boston: Little, Brown, 1993), 166–90, 191–221, 246–76; Dorothy B. Fujita Rony, "'You've Got to Move Like Hell': Trans-Pacific Colonialism and Filipina/o Seattle" (Ph.D. diss., Yale University, 1996); Michael La Sorte, *La Merica: Images of Italian Greenhorn Experience* (Philadelphia: Temple University Press, 1985), 61–115; David Montgomery, *The Fall of the House of Labor: The Workplace, the State, and American Labor Activism, 1865–1925* (New York: Cambridge University Press, 1987), 65–96; and Zaragosa Vargas, *Proletarians of the North: A History of Mexican Industrial Workers in Detroit and the Midwest, 1917–1933* (Berkeley: University of California Press, 1993).

21. Josiah Flynt, "The American Tramp," *Contemporary Review* 60 (August 1891): 254. On the origins of the word "hobo," see Kenneth Allsop, *Hard Travellin': The Hobo and His History* (New York: New American Library, 1967), 103–5; and *Webster's Dictionary of Word Origins* (New York: Merriam-Webster, 1991).

22. Roger Bruns, *Knights of the Road: A Hobo History* (New York: Methuen, 1980), 205; Anderson, *The Hobo,* 87.

23. Jack London, "Rods and Gunnels" (1902), in *Jack London on the Road,* 89, 94.

24. *New York Times,* February 28, 1876.

25. See London, "Rods and Gunnels," 89–95. Railroad fatality figures from Orlando Lewis, "The American Tramp," *Atlantic Monthly* 101 (June 1908): 745.

26. James J. Davis, *The Iron Puddler: My Life in the Rolling Mills and What Became of It* (Indianapolis: Bobbs-Merrill, 1922), 121.

27. Carleton H. Parker, *The Casual Laborer and Other Essays* (New York: Harcourt, Brace and Howe, 1920), 78.

28. Ernest Poole, "A Clearing-House for Tramps," *Everybody's Magazine* 18 (May 1908): 652. For similar opinions pertaining to Chinese labor, see C. J. Stowell, "Topical Analysis of Public Hearings on the Subject of the Seasonal Labor Problem in Agriculture in California," August 27–29, 1914, reel 5, United States Commission on Industrial Relations.

29. Charles Morgan, journal, April–June 1897, Charles Morgan Papers, box 1, book 1 (Mclean County Historical Society, Bloomington, Ill.).

30. Anderson, *The Hobo,* 74.

31. E. Lamar Bailey, "Tramps and Hoboes," *Forum* 26 (October 1898): 220.

32. Parker, *The Casual Laborer,* 78–79.

33. Peter Speek, "Life Histories: Sam Gray," reel 6, microfilm edition of the United States Commission on Industrial Relations, record group 174 (General Records of the Department of Labor, National Archives, Washington, D.C.).

34. Idem, "Life Histories: Thomas Lee," Commission on Industrial Relations.

35. Alice Willard Solenberger, *One Thousand Homeless Men: A Study of Original Records* (New York: Russell Sage Foundation, 1911), 143–44.

36. Frederick Mills, quoted in Gregory R. Woirol, *In the Floating Army: F. C. Mills on Itinerant Life in California, 1914* (Urbana: University of Illinois Press, 1992), 75.

37. Carl Sandburg, *Always the Young Strangers* (New York: Harcourt, Brace, 1953), 392.

38. Harry Kemp, "The Lure of the Tramp," *Independent* 70 (June 8, 1911): 1270.

39. William W. Aspinwall to John James McCook, June 10, 1893 (microfilm: roll 12), *The Social Reform Papers of John James McCook,* ed. Adela Haberski French (Hartford, Conn.: Antiquarian and Landmarks Society, 1977).

40. Bailey, "Tramps and Hoboes," 220.

41. Nels Anderson, *The American Hobo: An Autobiography* (Leiden, Netherlands: E. J. Brill, 1975), 85. On the evolution of Omaha's main stem, see John C. Schneider, "Skid Row

as Urban Neighborhood, 1880–1960," in *Housing the Homeless*, ed. Jon Erickson and Charles Wilhelm (New Brunswick: State University of New Jersey Press, 1986), 167–89.

42. Anderson, *American Hobo*, 64.

43. Stewart H. Holbrook, *Holy Old Mackinaw: A Natural History of the Lumberjack* (New York: Macmillan, 1956 [1938]), 194.

44. Keith A. Lovald, "From Hobohemia to Skid Row: The Changing Community of the Homeless Man" (Ph.D. diss., University of Minnesota, 1960), 124–25, 106.

45. Parker, *The Casual Laborer*, 80. On the growth of San Francisco's South of Market district, see Alvin Averbach, "San Francisco's South of Market District, 1850–1950: The Emergence of a Skid Row," *California Historical Quarterly* 52 (fall 1973): 197–223; and Paul Groth, *Living Downtown: The History of Residential Hotels in the United States* (Berkeley: University of California Press, 1994), 152–56.

46. Solenberger, *One Thousand Homeless Men*, 9; Anderson, *The Hobo*, 3; "Chicago: Hobo Capital of America," *Survey* 50 (June 1, 1923): 287–90, 303–5.

47. Anderson, *The Hobo*, 12.

48. Chicago Municipal Markets Commission report of 1914, quoted in Charles Hoch and Robert A. Slayton, *New Homeless and Old: Community and the Skid Row Hotel* (Philadelphia: Temple University Press, 1989), 12. For a superb account of the physical and financial infrastructure used to construct Chicago's hinterland, see William Cronon, *Nature's Metropolis: Chicago and the Great West* (New York: W.W. Norton, 1991).

49. Quoted in Lovald, "From Hobohemia to Skid Row," 87.

50. Anderson, *The Hobo*, 110.

51. For descriptions of employment agencies on the main stem, see Frances A. Kellor, *Out of Work: A Study of Unemployment* (New York: Arno Press, 1971 [1915]), 157–93; and Anderson, *The Hobo*, 109–22. See also Perry R. Duis, *The Saloon: Public Drinking in Chicago and Boston, 1880—1920* (Urbana: University of Illinois Press, 1983), 180–81. For a description of employment agency reform efforts, see Paul T. Ringenbach, *Tramps and Reformers, 1873–1916: The Discovery of Unemployment in New York* (Westport, Conn.: Greenwood Press, 1973), 135–60.

52. New York City's Tenement House Act of 1867 established the lodging house as a legal category for the first time. See Robert W. DeForest and Lawrence Veiller, *The Tenement House Problem: Including the Report of the New York State Tenement House Commission of 1900*, vol. 2 (New York: Macmillan, 1903), 331. For a good overview of the Bowery's evolution into a homeless man's district, see Benedict Giamo, *On the Bowery: Confronting Homelessness in American Society* (Iowa City: University of Iowa Press, 1989), 1–30; Kenneth T. Jackson, "The Bowery: From Residential Street to Skid Row," in *On Being Homeless: Historical Perspectives*, ed. Rick Beard (New York: Museum of the City of New York, 1987), 69–79; and I. L. Nascher, *The Wretches of Povertyville: A Sociological Study of the Bowery* (Chicago: Joseph J. Lanzit, 1909).

53. Jacob A. Riis, *How the Other Half Lives: Studies among the Tenements of New York* (New York: Charles Scribner's Sons, 1926 [1890]), 88–89.

54. For further descriptions of cubicles and lodging houses in general, see Groth, *Living Downtown*, 141–48, 168–220; and Hoch and Slayton, *New Homeless and Old*, 44–49. On the growth of purpose-built lodgings in Chicago, see Anderson, *The Hobo*, 27–29. For contemporary descriptions of lodging houses and lodging house life, see Paul Kennaday, "New York's Hundred Lodging Houses," *Charities and the Commons* 13 (February 18, 1905): 486–92; Alexander Irvine, "A Bunk-House and Some Bunk-House Men," *McClure's Magazine* 31 (August 1908): 455–65; William T. Stead, *If Christ Came to Chicago: A Plea for the Union of All Who Love in the Service of All Who Suffer* (London: Review of Reviews, 1894), 147–50; Robert Hunter, *Poverty: Social Conscience in the Progressive Era* (New York: Harper and Row, 1965 [1904]), 114–21; W. P. England, "The Lodging House," *Survey* 27 (December 1911): 1313–17; and Chicago Department of Public Welfare, "Fifty Cheap Lodging Houses," *First Semi-Annual Report of the Department of Public Welfare of Chicago* 1 (March 1915): 66–73.

55. Harry M. Beardsley, "Along the Main Stem with Red: Being an Account of the Hobohemians, Including One Paul of Tarsus and a Guy Named Moses," unpublished paper, March 29, 1917, p. 1, box 126, folder 11, Others' Work, Ernest W. Burgess Papers (Special Collections, Joseph Regenstein Library, University of Chicago).

56. Anderson, *The Hobo*, 7.

57. Solenberger, *One Thousand Homeless Men*, viii.

58. Clifford Shaw, *The Jack-Roller: A Delinquent Boy's Own Story* (Chicago: Phoenix Edition, 1966 [1930]), 80.

59. William Edge, *The Main Stem* (New York: Vanguard, 1927), 19.

60. Beardsley, "Along the Main Stem," 4, Burgess Papers.

61. Anderson, *The Hobo*, 8; see also Hoch and Slayton, *New Homeless and Old*, 24-32; and James Ford, *Slums and Housing*, vol. 1 (Cambridge: Harvard University Press, 1936), 338.

62. On San Francisco's Chinatown as a main stem, see Groth, *Living Downtown*, 156-60; David T. Courtwright, *Violent Land: Single Men and Social Disorder from the Frontier to the Inner City* (Cambridge: Harvard University Press, 1996), 159-68; and Takaki, *A Different Mirror*, 215-21.

63. Anderson, *The Hobo*, 151; Anderson, *American Hobo*, 150-51; Hoch and Slayton, *New Homeless and Old*, 44.

64. Milton B. Hunt, "The Housing of Non-Family Groups of Men in Chicago," *American Journal of Sociology* 16 (September 1910): 147.

65. James Forbes, "The Reverse Side," in *Wage-Earning Pittsburgh*, ed. Paul Underwood Kellog (New York: Arno Press, 1974 [1914]), 339.

66. Gunther Peck, *Reinventing Free Labor: Padrone and Immigrant Workers in the North American West, 1880-1930* (New York: Cambridge University Press, 2000); Montgomery, *Fall of the House of Labor*, 76-77, 94-95; La Sorte, *La Merica*, 69-99.

67. Solenberger, *One Thousand Homeless Men*, 214.

68. Charles Ashleigh, *Rambling Kid* (London: Faber, 1930), 92, 99.

69. Edward Lafot, "Hobo Travels and Hitch-Hiking in 1885-1886," unpublished manuscript, 1935 (Minnesota Historical Society, St. Paul, Minn.); Len DeCaux, *Labor Radical: From Wobblies to CIO, A Personal History* (Boston: Beacon Press, 1970), 56.

70. Powers Hapgood, journal, vol. 2, October 21, 1920, box 2, Powers Hapgood Papers (Minnesota Historical Society, St. Paul, Minn.).

71. DeCaux, *Labor Radical*, 67; idem, *The Living Spirit of the Wobblies* (New York: International, 1978), 14.

72. Sandburg, *Always the Young Strangers*, 391.

73. Mills, quoted in Woirol, *In the Floating Army*, 79.

74. Hapgood, journal, October 16, 1920, Hapgood Papers.

75. Speek, "Life Histories: Sam Gray," Commission on Industrial Relations.

76. See Roy Rosenzweig, *Eight Hours for What We Will: Workers and Leisure in an Industrial City, 1870-1920* (New York: Cambridge University Press, 1983), 35-64; and Duis, *The Saloon*, 113-35, 178-92.

77. Aspinwall to McCook, August 15, 1893 (roll 12), *Social Reform Papers*.

78. Frederick Mills, quoted in Woirol, *In the Floating Army*, 67.

79. Ashleigh, *Rambling Kid*, 92.

80. Cultural analyses of treating, reciprocity, and extravagant expenditure include Marcel Mauss, *The Gift: Forms and Functions of Exchange in Archaic Societies*, trans. Ian Cunnison (New York: W. W. Norton, 1967 [1925]); and George Bataille, "The Notion of Expenditure," in *The Bataille Reader*, ed. Fred Botting and Scott Wilson (Oxford: Blackwell, 1997), 167-81.

81. Edge, *Main Stem*, 39-40, 31, 6; Jim Tully, *Beggars of Life* (Garden City, N.Y.: Garden City Publishing, 1924), 21; Ralph Chaplin, *Wobbly: The Rough-and-Tumble Story of an American Radical* (Chicago: University of Chicago Press, 1948), 180.

82. Anderson, *The Hobo*, 5.

83. "Living Arrangements and Conditions of Industrial Workers," prepared by Frances P. Valiant, September 1, 1914, reel 11, Commission on Industrial Relations. I am indebted to Kristine Stilwell for supplying me with this source. See also Hapgood, journal, October 1, 1920, Hapgood Papers; and Montgomery, *Fall of the House of Labor*, 65.

84. On "whiteness" and racial hierarchy in the early-twentieth-century United States, see Matthew Frye Jacobson, *Whiteness of a Different Color: European Immigrants and the Alchemy of Race* (Cambridge: Harvard University Press, 1998); on the racial identities of early-twentieth-century European immigrants, see David R. Roediger, "Whiteness and Ethnicity in the History of 'White Ethnics' in the United States," in *Towards the Abolition of Whiteness: Essays on Race, Politics, and Working Class History* (New York: Verso, 1994), 181–98. See also Peck, *Reinventing Free Labor*, 166–73.

85. "Living Arrangements and Conditions of Industrial Workers."

86. Paul S. Taylor, *Mexican Labor in the United States*, vol. 2 (Berkeley: University of California Press, 1932), 63ff.

87. See, for example, John J. McCook, "Leaves from the Diary of a Tramp," part 1, *Independent* 53 (November 21, 1901), 2760–61; Jack London, *The Road* (Santa Barbara: Peregrine Press, 1970 [1907]), 69–70; and Peter Speek, "Notes," October 14, 1914, reel 5, Commission on Industrial Relations. For a general discussion of the relations between black and white homeless men in the late nineteenth and early twentieth centuries, see Kenneth L. Kusmer, *Down and Out, on the Road: The Homeless in American History* (New York: Oxford University Press, 2002), 139–40.

88. Anderson, *The Hobo*, 19.

89. McCook, "Leaves from the Diary of a Tramp," part 1, 2760–61.

90. Anderson, *American Hobo*, 71.

91. My thanks to Kristine Stilwell for alerting me to the prevalence of this phenomenon. See also Lynn Weiner, "Sisters of the Road: Women Transients and Tramps," in *Walking to Work*, ed. Monkkonen, 171–88.

92. Charles Ashleigh, "The Floater," *International Socialist Review* 15 (July 1914): 37. See also Joyce L. Kornbluh, ed., *Rebel Voices: An I. W. W. Anthology* (Ann Arbor: University of Michigan Press, 1965), 82.

93. For information on housing for single wage-earning women between 1880 and 1930, see Leslie Woodcock Tentler, *Wage-Earning Women: Industrial Work and Family Life in the United States* (New York: Oxford University Press, 1979), 115–35; Joanne J. Meyerowitz, *Women Adrift: Independent Wage Earners in Chicago, 1880–1930* (Chicago: University of Chicago Press, 1988), 24–27, 70–91; idem, "Sexual Geography and Gender Economy: The Furnished Room Districts of Chicago, 1890–1930," in *Gender and American History since 1890*, ed. Barbara Melosh (New York: Routledge, 1993), 43–71; and Groth, *Living Downtown*, 90–130. For contemporary descriptions of rooming houses for women, see Harriet Fayes, "Housing of Single Women," *Municipal Affairs* 3 (March 1899): 95–105; Eleanor H. Woods, "Social Betterment in a Lodging District," *Charities and the Commons* 19 (November 2, 1907): 964–67; Edith Abbott, *The Tenements of Chicago, 1908–1935* (New York: Arno Press, 1970 [1936]), 306–51; Albert Benedict Wolfe, *The Lodging House Problem in Boston* (Boston: Houghton Mifflin, 1906); and Harvey Warren Zorbaugh, *The Gold Coast and the Slum: A Sociological Study of Chicago's Near North Side* (Chicago: University of Chicago Press, 1929).

94. Will J. Quirke, "A Hobo Deluxe Cruise," *"Hobo" News*, May 1919, 4.

95. Anderson, interview notes, box 126, folder 11, document 44, Burgess Papers; Elizabeth Gurley Flynn, *Rebel Girl* (New York: International Publishers, 1973), 103.

96. Anderson, *The Hobo*, 138–39, 183–84. I am indebted to Kristine Stilwell for calling my attention to hoboes' crucial dependence upon women.

97. Anderson, interview notes, box 126, folder 11, document 73, Burgess Papers.

98. Quoted in Bruns, *Knights of the Road*, 141.

99. Wolfe, *Lodging House Problem*, 140–41.

100. Anderson, *The Hobo*, 144; see also 137–49. For other assessments of homosexuality

among homeless men, see Josiah Flynt, "Homosexuality among Tramps," in *Studies in the Psychology of Sex*, vol. 2, ed. Havelock Ellis (New York: Random House, 1936 [1910]), 359–67; Towne Nylander, "Tramps and Hoboes," *Forum* 74 (August 1925): 230; Frank C. Laubach, *Why There Are Vagrants: A Study Based upon an Examination of One Hundred Men* (New York: Columbia University Press, 1916), 13–14; and Parker, *The Casual Laborer*, 73–74.

101. Howard P. Chudacoff, *The Age of the Bachelor: Creating an American Subculture* (Princeton: Princeton University Press, 1999).

102. On the growth of an urban gay world at the turn of the century, see George Chauncey, *Gay New York: Gender, Urban Culture, and the Making of the Gay Male World, 1890–1940* (New York: Basic Books, 1994), esp. 76–86, 152–63.

103. Anderson, interview notes, box 126, folder 11, document 122, Burgess Papers.

104. John Worby, *The Other Half: The Autobiography of a Tramp* (New York: Lee Furman, 1937), 28.

105. London, *The Road*, 144.

106. DeCaux, *Labor Radical*, 59.

107. Parker, *The Casual Laborer*, 73–74.

108. Sandburg, *Always the Young Strangers*, 383.

109. See, for example, Edge, *Main Stem*, 125–26.

110. Nels Anderson, "The Juvenile and the Tramp," *Journal of Criminology and Criminal Law* 14 (August 1922): 306.

111. Ibid., 301.

112. Greenway, *American Folksongs of Protest*, 203–4. Compare Greenway's version to those tamer ones collected in Irwin Silber, ed., *Songs of the Great American West* (New York: Macmillan, 1967), 292; and Alan Lomax, *The Penguin Book of American Folk Songs* (Baltimore: Penguin Books, 1964), 130.

113. Chauncey, *Gay New York*, 86–91.

114. Anderson, "The Juvenile and the Tramp," 302. See also Flynt, "Homosexuality among Tramps," 364.

115. Tully, *Beggars of Life*, 130–31.

116. Quoted in Greenway, *American Folksongs of Protest*, 201.

117. Ben Reitman, "Following the Monkey," unpublished manuscript, n.d., pp. 80–82, folder 11, Ben Lewis Reitman Papers (Special Collections, University of Illinois-Chicago).

118. Anderson, "The Juvenile and the Tramp," 307, 304, 309.

119. Chauncey, *Gay New York*, 80.

120. See Elliot J. Gorn, *The Manly Art: Bare-Knuckle Prize Fighting in America* (Ithaca, N.Y.: Cornell University Press, 1986), 129–45.

121. Anderson, "The Juvenile and the Tramp," 304.

122. See, for example, Ben Reitman to Emma Goldman, July 27, 1912, box 1, folder 3, Emma Goldman Papers, Papers and Correspondence (Special Collections, Boston University Library).

123. Quoted in Roger Bruns, *The Damndest Radical: The Life and World of Ben Reitman* (Urbana: University of Illinois Press, 1987), 129.

124. Bertha Thompson (Ben Reitman), *Boxcar Bertha: An Autobiography as Told to Dr. Ben L. Reitman* (New York: Amok Press, 1988 [1937]). Although many scholars assume the biographical authenticity of Bertha Thompson, Reitman's original manuscript and correspondence with publishers proves the book's status as autobiographically informed fiction. See Ben Reitman, "Sister of the Road," manuscript, 1934, folder 39, Reitman Papers.

125. On the "performativity" of gender, see Judith Butler, *Gender Trouble: Feminism and the Subversion of Identity* (New York: Routledge, 1990).

126. Edge, *Main Stem*, 119, 127.

127. Ashleigh, *Rambling Kid*, 212.

128. Anderson, *The Hobo*, 149.

## CHAPTER FOUR

1. For J. H. Walsh's own account of the Overalls Brigade's ride to Chicago, see his reports in the *Industrial Union Bulletin*, September 19, October 4, and October 24, 1908. Walsh's first report, entitled "I.W.W. 'Red Special' Overall Brigade," can also be found in Joyce L. Kornbluh, ed., *Rebel Voices: An I. W. W. Anthology* (Ann Arbor: University of Michigan Press, 1965), 40–42. For an account of the Overalls Brigade and the ouster of the homeguard at the IWW's 1908 convention, see Melvyn Dubofsky, *We Shall Be All: A History of the Industrial Workers of the World* (Chicago: Quadrangle Books, 1969), 137–38.

2. "The 'Simple Life' of the Jungles," *Industrial Worker*, March 18, 1909.

3. Quoted in Kornbluh, *Rebel Voices*, 72. Other versions of this song can be found in George Milburn, *The Hobo's Hornbook: A Repertory for a Gutter Jongleur* (New York: Ives Washburn, 1930), 97–101; and John Greenway, *American Folksongs of Protest* (Philadelphia: University of Pennsylvania Press, 1953), 201–2.

4. *Industrial Union Bulletin*, September 19, 1908.

5. On the history of the *Little Red Songbook*, see Kornbluh, *Rebel Voices*, 65–66. See also David A. Carter, "The Industrial Workers of the World and the Rhetoric of Song," *Quarterly Journal of Speech* 66 (fall 1980): 365–74.

6. Carleton H. Parker, *The Casual Laborer and Other Essays* (New York: Harcourt, Brace and Howe, 1920), 115–16.

7. Walker C. Smith, "The Floater an Iconoclast," *Industrial Worker*, June 4, 1910.

8. Kornbluh, *Rebel Voices*, 71. See Dubofsky, *We Shall Be All*, 176–77.

9. *Industrial Worker*, September 10, 1910. See Kornbluh, *Rebel Voices*, 94–126; and Dubofsky, *We Shall Be All*, 173–97.

10. Parker, *The Casual Laborer*, 115–16.

11. Ralph Chaplin, *Wobbly: The Rough-and-Tumble Story of an American Radical* (Chicago: University of Chicago Press, 1948), 172–73.

12. "'The Slum Proletariat,'" *Industrial Worker*, September 23, 1909.

13. "Why I Am a Member of the I.W.W.," in Kornbluh, *Rebel Voices*, 288.

14. William Edge, *The Main Stem* (New York: Vanguard, 1927), 87.

15. Nels Anderson, *The Hobo: The Sociology of the Homeless Man* (Chicago: Phoenix Books, 1965 [1923]), 185.

16. Chaplin, *Wobbly*, 170.

17. Report on Arthur Proctor, November 9, 1919, Military Intelligence Correspondence Division Files, box 2785, file 10110-853-680, Record Group 165, War Department Files (National Archives, Washington, D.C.).

18. Anderson, *The Hobo*, 38, 175–77.

19. Quoted in Frank O. Beck, *Hobohemia* (Rindge, N.H.: Richard R. Smith, 1956), 78.

20. Ibid., 80. See also Roger A. Bruns, *The Damndest Radical: The Life and World of Ben Reitman* (Urbana: University of Illinois Press, 1987), 230–45.

21. Anderson, *The Hobo*, 219.

22. Kenneth Rexroth, quoted in Bruns, *Damndest Radical*, 247; Beck, *Hobohemia*, 67.

23. Anderson, *The Hobo*, 9, 219.

24. Ibid., 229.

25. "The 'Simple Life' of the Jungles."

26. "Out in the Jungles," *Industrial Worker*, April 1, 1909.

27. Dubofsky, *We Shall Be All*, 294–300; Kornbluh, *Rebel Voices*, 227–28. See also Cletus E. Daniel, *Bitter Harvest: A History of California Farmworkers, 1870–1941* (Berkeley: University of California Press, 1981), 81–96.

28. Quoted in Harry M. Beardsley, "Along the Main Stem with Red: Being an Account of the Hobohemians, Including One Paul of Tarsus and a Guy Named Moses," unpublished paper, March 29, 1917, p. 8, box 126, folder 11, Others' Work, Ernest W. Burgess Papers (Special Collections, Joseph Regenstein Library, University of Chicago).

29. Dubofsky, *We Shall Be All*, 313-18; Kornbluh, *Rebel Voices*, 227-33.

30. Chaplin, *Wobbly*, 198-99.

31. Parker, *The Casual Laborer*, 71-72.

32. Frederick Mills, quoted in Gregory R. Woirol, *In the Floating Army: F. C. Mills on Itinerant Life in California, 1914* (Urbana: University of Illinois Press, 1992), 116.

33. Ben Reitman, "The Evolution of the Hobo," n.d., pp. 2, 5, supplement 2, folder 9, Ben Lewis Reitman Papers (Special Collections, University of Illinois-Chicago).

34. Dubofsky, *We Shall Be All*, 376-468; Kornbluh, *Rebel Voices*, 316-50.

35. John A. Fitch, "Class Fighters and a Hobo Who Solved a Problem," *Survey* 32 (September 5, 1914): 558-60. See also Walter V. Woehlke, "Porterhouse Heaven and the Hobo," *Technical World Magazine* 21 (August 1914): 808-13, 938; and Bronson Batchelor, "The Hotel de Gink," *Independent* 81 (January 25, 1915): 127-29.

36. See E. Guy Talbott, "The Armies of the Unemployed in California," *Survey* 32 (August 22, 1914): 523-24; and "Co-operative Movements among Hobos, Experiences of John X. Kelly, Now in Chicago," document 61, n.d., box 127, folder 1, Others' Work, Burgess Papers.

37. *New York Times*, August 19, 1923.

38. Anderson, *The Hobo*, 172. Anderson's notes on How are in "Character Sketch of J. E. How, 'Millionaire Hobo,' also Correspondence with Nels Anderson," document 126, box 127, folder 2, Others' Work, Burgess Papers. See also *New York Times*, July 23 and 24, 1930; "'Millionaire Hobo' Is Dead," *Christian Century* 47 (August 20, 1930): 1020; and "James Eads How: Portrait," *Collier's* (June 26, 1926): 16.

39. Henry A. White, "What of the 'Hobo,'" *"Hobo" News*, July 1921, 10.

40. R. W. Irwin, "The Advance Guide and the International Brotherhood Welfare Association: An Answer," *"Hobo" News*, July 1919, 10.

41. "The Editor on a Rambling Tour," *"Hobo" News*, July 1920, 8; "To Our Readers, Contributors, and Subscribers," *"Hobo" News*, August 1917, 15. For the publication history of the *"Hobo" News*, see Lynne M. Adrian, "Social History Update: An American Studies Contribution to Social History," *Journal of Social History* 23 (winter 1990): 878; and idem, "'The World We Shall Win for Labor': Early Twentieth-Century Hobo Self-Publication," in *Print Culture in a Diverse America*, ed. James P. Danky and Wayne A. Wiegand (Urbana: University of Illinois Press, 1998), 101-28.

42. Beardsley, "Along the Main Stem with Red," 12, Burgess Papers.

43. Anderson, *The Hobo*, 238.

44. Bruns, *Damndest Radical*, 202-14. See also Helen Bryant, "The Hobo College," term paper, History of Education, School of the Art Institute, 1926, 6-12, Reitman Papers; miscellaneous clippings file, Irwin St. John Tucker Papers (Special Collections, University of Illinois-Chicago); and Dorothy Walton, "A Hobo College," *"Hobo" News*, January 1921. For Reitman's original plans, see Reitman, "Following the Monkey," unpublished manuscript, n.d., p. 210, folder 11, Reitman Papers.

45. *"Hobo" News*, August 1917, 19.

46. For examples of IWW attempts to seize IBWA locals, see *New York Times*, March 9, 1914; ibid., July 27, 1914; and Anderson, *The Hobo*, 237.

47. Report on Eric Anderson, October 12, 1917, Military Intelligence Correspondence Division Files, 1917-1941, box 2103.

48. C. E. Arbright, "Alleged I.W.W.s Held at Police Station," March 6, 1919, Investigative Case Files, 1908-1922, reel 743, file 321901, Record Group 65, Federal Bureau of Investigation (National Archives, Washington, D.C.).

49. Mathew C. Smith to L. J. Baley, April 7, 1921, Military Intelligence Correspondence Division Files.

50. "James Eads How," November 10, 1919, Military Intelligence Correspondence Division Files.

51. Lynn D. Copeland to Henry G. Pratt, July 21, 1919, Military Intelligence Correspondence Division Files.

52. *"Hobo" News*, May 1919, 15.

53. Ibid., July 1919, 6; ibid., May 1919, 15.

54. "Songs for the Hobo College—Care of the International Brotherhood Welfare Association," Military Intelligence Correspondence Division Files, box 2802; and *The "Hobo" in Song and Poetry: The Most Complete Hobo Song Book Ever Issued, Containing All the Old Favorites* (International Brotherhood Welfare Association, n.d.).

55. For further discussion of the complicated relations between the IWW and IBWA, see Lynne M. Adrian, "Organizing the Rootless: American Hobo Subculture, 1893–1932" (Ph.D. diss., University of Iowa, 1984), 74–137; and idem, "'The World We Shall Win for Labor,'" 115–20.

56. George W. Fenton, "The Migratory Workers' Union," *"Hobo" News*, April 1919, 13.

57. Anderson, *The Hobo*, 241. See also "Leaflet No. 3 Issued by the Migratory Workers Union," *"Hobo" News*, May 1919, 11.

58. Anderson, *The Hobo*, 174; "Co-operative Movements among Hobos, Experiences of John X. Kelly, Now in Chicago," Burgess Papers.

59. Cleveland Red, "Hobo Session Is Upset—Factions in a Row—Break over Delegates," *"Hobo" News*, November 1922, 9–10; James Eads How, "Solidarity and the May-Day Conference," *"Hobo" News*, May 1922, 13; Adrian, "'The World We Shall Win for Labor,'" 124–26.

60. Adrian, "Organizing the Rootless," 113–14.

61. *Solidarity*, November 21, 1914, quoted in Kornbluh, *Rebel Voices*, 66–67.

62. See, for example, "The Working Stiff," *"Hobo" News*, January 1919, 15. See also "The Migratory I.W.W.," published in the *Industrial Worker* in 1916, reprinted in Kornbluh, *Rebel Voices*, 84.

63. Anderson, *The Hobo*, 188, 190.

64. Adrian, "Organizing the Rootless," 74–137.

65. Harry A. Gordon, "A Criticism," *"Hobo" News*, July 1921, 11; "A 'Hobo' Paper," *"Hobo" News*, July 1921, 9.

66. "'The Slum Proletariat'"; "The 'Simple Life' of the Jungles."

67. Quoted in Anderson, *The Hobo*, 88.

68. Quoted in Woirol, *In the Floating Army*, 125.

69. Ralph Winstead, "Tightline Johnson Goes to Heaven," *Industrial Pioneer* (July 1923), in Kornbluh, *Rebel Voices*, 93.

70. "Why I Am a Member of the I.W.W.," in Kornbluh, *Rebel Voices*, 288.

71. Charles H. Forster, "Despised and Rejected Men: Hoboes of the Pacific Coast," *Survey* 33 (March 20, 1915): 671.

72. Parker, *The Casual Laborer*, 86, 88.

73. *Songs of the Workers: On the Road, in the Jungles, and in the Shops* (Cleveland: I.W.W. Publishing Bureau, 1916), 7. See also Kornbluh, *Rebel Voices*, 84.

74. "The Jungle—An Idyl of Springtime," *Industrial Worker*, September 10, 1910.

75. Richard Brazier, "The Suckers Sadly Gather," in Kornbluh, *Rebel Voices*, 73.

76. Idem, "Meet Me in the Jungles, Louie," in Kornbluh, *Rebel Voices*, 72.

77. Joe Hill, "Constitutional Guarantee:—Life? Liberty? And the Pursuit of—a Job!" *Industrial Worker*, April 24, 1913. See also Kornbluh, *Rebel Voices*, 129.

78. Jack London, "How I Became a Socialist" (1903), in *Jack London on the Road: The Tramp Diary and Other Hobo Writings*, ed. Richard W. Etulain (Logan: Utah State University Press, 1979), 99.

79. Duffield Osborn, quoted in E. Anthony Rotundo, *American Manhood: Transformations in Masculinity from the Revolution to the Modern Era* (New York: Basic Books, 1993), 253. For a superb discussion of the various racial, class, and gendered meanings of "civilization" at the turn of the century, see Gail Bederman, *Manliness and Civilization: A Cultural History of Gender and Race in the United States, 1880–1917* (Chicago: University of Chicago Press, 1995). See also T. J. Jackson Lears, *No Place of Grace: Antimodernism and the Transformation of*

*American Culture, 1880–1920* (New York: Pantheon, 1981); and George Chauncey, *Gay New York: Gender, Urban Culture, and the Making of the Gay Male World, 1890–1940* (New York: Basic Books, 1994), 111–27.

80. On the frontier myth, see Richard Slotkin's trilogy: *Regeneration through Violence: The Mythology of the American Frontier, 1600–1860* (Middletown, Conn.: Wesleyan University Press, 1978); *The Fatal Environment: The Myth of the Frontier in the Age of Industrialization, 1800–1890* (New York: Atheneum, 1985); and *Gunfighter Nation: The Myth of the Frontier in Twentieth-Century America* (New York: Atheneum, 1992).

81. IBWA, *Legal Robbery of the Workers,* cover page, Investigative Case Files.

82. Edge, *The Main Stem,* 202.

83. "'The Slum Proletariat'"; "The 'Slum Proletariat,'" *Industrial Union Bulletin,* February 27, 1909.

84. Quoted in Dubofsky, *We Shall Be All,* 25.

85. "The Floater an Iconoclast."

86. *Solidarity,* November 21, 1914, quoted in Kornbluh, *Rebel Voices,* 66–67.

87. Charles Ashleigh, "The Floater," *International Socialist Review* 15 (July 1914), 34–35; Kornbluh, *Rebel Voices,* 80.

88. Ashleigh, "The Floater," 34–38. See also Kornbluh, *Rebel Voices,* 80–82.

89. Dubofsky, *We Shall Be All,* 186–87, 391–93.

90. "Bingo," "Now for the Eastern Invasion!" *Solidarity,* October 14, 1916. See also Kornbluh, *Rebel Voices,* 242.

91. "Bingo," "Somebody Has Got to Get Out of the Way!" *Solidarity,* August 19, 1916. See also Kornbluh, *Rebel Voices,* 293.

92. Untitled illustration, *Solidarity,* April 28, 1917. See also Kornbluh, *Rebel Voices,* 8.

93. See Eric J. Hobsbawm, "Man and Woman: Images on the Left," in *Workers: Worlds of Labor* (New York: Pantheon, 1984), 83–102; and Elizabeth Faue, *Community of Suffering and Struggle: Women, Men, and the Labor Movement in Minneapolis, 1915–1945* (Chapel Hill: University of North Carolina Press, 1991), chap. 3, esp. 93–95.

94. Elliot J. Gorn, *The Manly Art: Bare-Knuckle Prize Fighting in America* (Ithaca, N.Y.: Cornell University Press, 1986), 187; Chauncey, *Gay New York,* 114.

95. For a fine analysis of the gender politics of such representations, see Melissa Dabakis, "Douglas Tilden's Mechanics Fountain: Labor and the 'Crisis of Masculinity' in the 1890s," *American Quarterly* 47 (June 1995): 204–35.

96. Dubofsky, *We Shall Be All,* 319–33.

97. John L. Ingham, "A Strike in the Progressive Era," *Pennsylvania History* 90 (July 1966): 353–77. See also Dubofsky, *We Shall Be All,* 199–209.

98. This point is well made in Faue, *Community of Suffering and Struggle,* 10–11. See also Michael Ebner, "The Passaic Strike of 1912 and the Two IWW's," *Labor History* 11 (fall 1970): 452–66; Steve Golin, "Defeat Becomes Disaster: The Paterson Strike of 1913 and the Decline of the IWW," *Labor History* 24 (spring 1983): 223–48; and Salvatore Salerno, *Red November, Black November: Culture and Community in the Industrial Workers of the World* (Albany: SUNY Press, 1989), esp. 8–17, 28–30.

99. Ronald Takaki, *A Different Mirror: A History of Multicultural America* (Boston: Little, Brown, 1993), 191–221, 246–76; Dorothy B. Fujita Rony, "'You've Got to Move Like Hell': Trans-Pacific Colonialism and Filipina/o Seattle" (Ph.D. diss., Yale University, 1996); Camille Guerin-Gonzales, *Mexican Workers and American Dreams: Immigration, Repatriation, and California Farm Labor, 1900–1939* (New Brunswick, N.J.: Rutgers University Press, 1994); Daniel, *Bitter Harvest;* David Montgomery, *The Fall of the House of Labor: The Workplace, the State, and American Labor Activism, 1865–1925* (New York: Cambridge University Press, 1987), 65–96; Gunther Peck, *Reinventing Free Labor: Padrone and Immigrant Workers in the North American West, 1880–1930* (New York: Cambridge University Press, 2000), 117–90.

100. Both quotations are taken from Daniel, *Bitter Harvest,* 83.

101. Charles W. Allen, "Hobo College," seminar paper, University of Chicago, March

18, 1923, pp. 20–21, box 149, folder 1, Others' Work, Burgess Papers; Beardsley, "Along the Main Stem with Red," 17, Burgess Papers; Nels Anderson, interview notes, document 25, box 126, folder 11, Others' Work, Burgess Papers.

## CHAPTER FIVE

1. Nels Anderson, *The American Hobo: An Autobiography* (Leiden, Netherlands: E. J. Brill, 1975), 157–61. Anderson had periodically attended high school and college while living and working on a ranch in Utah. He earned money like he always had, through regular stints of migratory labor. See Nels Anderson, "Introduction to the Phoenix Edition" (1961), in *The Hobo: The Sociology of the Homeless Man* (Chicago: Phoenix Books, 1965 [1923]), xi; idem, "A Stranger at the Gate: Reflections on the Chicago School of Sociology," *Urban Life* 11 (January 1983): 396–406; Raffaele Rauty, "Introduction," in Nels Anderson, *On Hobos and Homelessness*, ed. Raffaele Rauty (Chicago: University of Chicago Press, 1998), 2; and Rolf Linder, *The Reportage of Urban Culture: Robert Park and the Chicago School*, trans. Adrian Morris (New York: Cambridge University Press, 1996), 125.

2. Robert E. Park, "The City as a Social Laboratory" (1929), in *On Social Control and Collective Behavior*, ed. Ralph A. Turner (Chicago: Phoenix Books, 1967), 3–18; Park, quoted in Carla Cappetti, *Writing Chicago: Modernism, Ethnography, and the Novel* (New York: Columbia University Press, 1993), 24.

3. Anderson, "Introduction to the Phoenix Edition," xiii.

4. Ibid.

5. Anderson, *American Hobo*, 165.

6. Rauty, "Introduction," 13.

7. Anderson, "Introduction to the Phoenix Edition," xi–xiii; Anderson, *American Hobo*, 170; Rauty, "Introduction," 3; Linder, *The Reportage of Urban Culture*, 125–31.

8. Anderson, *American Hobo*, 170; Rauty, "Introduction," 1. On the Chicago school's impact on American culture, see Linder, *The Reportage of Urban Culture*; and Cappetti, *Writing Chicago*.

9. Robert E. Park, "The Mind of the Hobo: Reflections upon the Relation between Mentality and Locomotion," in *The City*, ed. Robert E. Park, Ernest W. Burgess, and Roderick D. McKenzie (Chicago: University of Chicago Press, 1967 [1925]), 158–60.

10. Park, "Editor's Preface," in Anderson, *The Hobo*, xxiii–xxvi.

11. Alice Willard Solenberger, *One Thousand Homeless Men: A Study of Original Records* (New York: Russell Sage Foundation, 1911), 3.

12. Park, "Editor's Preface," xxv.

13. John J. McCook, "Tramps," *The Charities Review: A Journal of Practical Sociology* 3 (December 1893): 67.

14. Arthur W. Calhoun Jr., *A Social History of the American Family: From Colonial Times to the Present*, vol. 3 (New York: Arno Press, 1973 [1919]), 75.

15. Robert E. Park, "The City: Suggestions for the Investigation of Human Behavior in the Urban Environment," in *The City*, 40.

16. Edmond Kelly, *The Elimination of the Tramp* (New York: G. P. Putnam's Sons, 1908), 71. For Anderson's recommendations, see Anderson, *The Hobo*, 263–77. Other proposals for addressing homelessness included Benjamin C. Marsh, "Causes of Vagrancy and Methods of Eradication," *Annals of the American Academy of Social and Political Science* 23 (May 1904): 445–56; Orlando F. Lewis, "Vagrancy in the United States," *Proceedings of the National Conference of Charities and Correction* (Indianapolis: William B. Burford, 1907), 52–77; idem, "Report of the Committee on Vagrancy and Homelessness," *Proceedings of the New York State Conference of Charities and Correction* (Albany: J. B. Lyon Co., 1908), 237–67; Ernest Poole, "A Clearing-House for Tramps," *Everybody's Magazine* 18 (May 1908): 649–59; Charles K. Blatchly, "A State Farm for Tramps and Vagrants," *Survey* 24 (April 9, 1910): 87–89; Solenberger, *One Thousand Homeless Men;* and Frank C. Laubach, *Why There Are Vagrants: A Study Based upon an Examination of One Hundred Men* (New York: Columbia University Press,

1916). For fuller discussions of reform proposals, see Paul T. Ringenbach, *Tramps and Reformers, 1873–1916: The Discovery of Unemployment in New York* (New York: Greenwood Press, 1973), 82–134; Kim Hopper, "The Public Responses to Homelessness in New York City—the Last Hundred Years," in *On Being Homeless: Historical Perspectives,* ed. Rick Beard (New York: Museum of New York, 1987), 88–101; and Kenneth L. Kusmer, *Down and Out, on the Road: The Homeless in American History* (New York: Oxford University Press, 2002), 73–97.

17. Quoted in Stuart Rice, "The Failure of the Municipal Lodging House," *National Municipal Review* 11 (November 1922): 361.

18. John Schneider, "Homeless Men and Housing Policy in Urban America, 1850–1920," *Urban Studies* 26 (February 1989): 90–99; Kusmer, *Down and Out,* 74–78, 94–95.

19. See Alvin F. Sanborne, "Study of Beggars and Their Lodgings," *Forum* 19 (April 1895): 207; and E. L. R. Gould, "How Baltimore Banished Tramps and Helped the Idle," *Forum* 17 (August 1894): 497–504.

20. Schneider, "Homeless Men and Housing Policy," 93.

21. Hopper, "The Public Responses to Homelessness," 93.

22. Associated Charities of Pittsburgh, *Report for the Third Year* (Pittsburgh: Associated Charities, 1912), 35; James Forbes, "The Reverse Side," in *Wage-Earning Pittsburgh,* ed. Paul Underwood Kellog (New York: Arno Press, 1974 [1914]), 347–48; Kusmer, *Down and Out,* 94–95.

23. William T. Stead, *If Christ Came to Chicago: A Plea for the Union of All Who Love in the Service of All Who Suffer* (London: Review of Reviews, 1894), 17.

24. Jesse Walter Dees Jr. *Flophouse* (Francestown, N.H.: Marshall Jones, 1948), 40.

25. Theodore Waters, "Six Weeks in Beggardom," *Everybody's Magazine* 11 (December 1904): 789–97.

26. Anderson, *The Hobo,* 269–74; Charles Hoch and Robert A. Slayton, *New Homeless and Old: Community and the Skid Row Hotel* (Philadelphia: Temple University Press, 1989), 55–56; Dees, *Flophouse,* 40–44; Arnold M. Rose, "Interest in the Living Arrangements of the Urban Unattached," *American Journal of Sociology* 53 (May 1948): 490.

27. Stuart A. Rice, "The Homeless," *Annals of the American Academy of Political and Social Science* 77 (May 1918): 143.

28. Alice L. Higgins, "Comparative Advantages of Municipal and C.O.S. Lodging Houses," *Proceedings of the National Conference of Charities and Correction* (Fort Wayne, Ind.: Fort Wayne Printing, 1904), 151.

29. "Lodging House Reform," *Charities and the Commons* (March 23, 1907): 1120.

30. On the enforcement of new moral codes, see Paul Groth, *Living Downtown: The History of Residential Hotels in the United States* (Berkeley: University of California Press, 1994), 239–41.

31. Lawrence Veiller, *Housing Reform: A Handbook for Practical Use in American Cities* (New York: Charities Publication Committee, 1910), 5.

32. Edward T. Devine, "The Shiftless and Floating City Population," *Annals of the American Academy of Social and Political Science* 10 (September 1897): 160.

33. Edith Abbott, *The Tenements of Chicago, 1908–1935* (Chicago: University of Chicago Press, 1936), 53–54.

34. Groth, *Living Downtown,* 242.

35. Solenberger, *One Thousand Homeless Men,* 335–41; see also Charles Kettleborough, "Inspection of Hotels and Public Lodging Houses," *American Political Science Review* 7 (February 1913): 93–96.

36. "Lodging House Reform," 1119.

37. Lewis, "Vagrancy in the United States," 62–63.

38. Frances Maule Bjorkman, "The New Anti-Vagrancy Campaign," *American Review of Reviews* 37 (February 1908): 208.

39. T. Alexander Hyde, "A Paying Philanthropy: The Mills Hotel," *Arena* 20 (July 1898): 84.

40. Quoted in John Lloyd Thomas, "Workingmen's Hotels," *Municipal Affairs* 3 (March 1899): 86.

41. "Decent Lodging for Poor Men," *Independent* 75 (September 11, 1913): 638.

42. "A Place for Men on the City's Threshold," *Survey* 36 (June 17, 1916): 303.

43. Anderson, *The Hobo*, 27–28.

44. "Model Lodging Houses for New York," *Review of Reviews* 15 (January 1897): 59–60.

45. Hyde, "A Paying Philanthropy," 81.

46. Paul Kennaday, "New York's Hundred Lodging Houses," *Charities and the Commons* 13 (February 18, 1905): 491.

47. George Chauncey, *Gay New York: Gender, Urban Culture, and the Making of the Gay Male World, 1890–1940* (New York: Basic Books, 1994), 152–63.

48. "Model Lodging Houses for New York," 61.

49. Hyde, "A Paying Philanthropy," 85.

50. Thomas, "Workingmen's Hotels," 90.

51. On increased investment and other changes in the early-twentieth-century lodging-house market, see Groth, *Living Downtown*, esp. 168–200.

52. Solenberger, *One Thousand Homeless Men*, 3.

53. Quoted in Anderson, *The Hobo*, 29.

54. Abbott, *The Tenements of Chicago*, 100.

55. Albert Benedict Wolfe, *The Lodging House Problem in Boston* (Boston: Houghton Mifflin, 1906), 173.

56. John J. McCook, "The Tramp Problem," *Lend a Hand: A Record of Progress* 15 (September 1895): 171–72.

57. Wolfe, *The Lodging House Problem*, 150, 167.

58. Henry James, *The American Scene* (Bloomington: Indiana University Press, 1968 [1907]), 99–107, 438–43. For an analysis of *The American Scene*'s cultural critique, see Ross Posnick, *The Trial of Curiosity: Henry James, William James, and the Challenge of Modernity* (New York: Oxford University Press, 1991).

59. James, *The American Scene*, 102.

60. Park, "The City," 40. Park originally wrote this essay in 1915 and then revised it for republication in 1925.

61. Quoted in Groth, *Living Downtown*, 20.

62. Quoted in ibid., 201.

63. For an excellent study of the various levels of hotel living in the early twentieth century, see ibid., 26–167.

64. "Apartment Hotels in New York City," *Architectural Record* 13 (January 1903): 85–91.

65. Harvey Warren Zorbaugh, *The Gold Coast and the Slum: A Sociological Study of Chicago's Near North Side* (Chicago: University of Chicago Press, 1929), 109, 126.

66. Simon N. Patten, "The Crisis in America Home Life," *Independent* 68 (May 1910): 344–45.

67. Quoted in Gail Bederman, *Manliness and Civilization: A Cultural History of Gender and Race in the United States, 1880–1917* (Chicago: University of Chicago Press, 1995), 201. For a discussion of the "race suicide" controversy, see 200–6.

68. Delos F. Wilcox, *The American City: A Problem in Democracy* (New York: Macmillan, 1906).

69. Wolfe, *The Lodging House Problem*, 161, 164–65.

70. Max Weber, *The Protestant Ethic and the Spirit of Capitalism*, trans. Talcott Parsons (New York: Charles Scribner's Sons, 1958 [1905]), 182.

71. Zorbaugh, *The Gold Coast and the Slum*, 126.

72. Norman Haynor, *Hotel Life* (Chapel Hill: University of North Carolina Press, 1936), 53, 180–82.

73. Ferdinand Tönnies, *Community and Society (Gemeinschaft und Gesellschaft)*, trans. and ed. Charles P. Loomis (New York: Harper and Row, 1957 [1887]).

74. Calhoun, *A Social History of the American Family*, 170–71.

75. See John Modell and Tamara K. Hareven, "Urbanization and the Malleable Household: An Examination of Boarding and Lodging in American Families," *Journal of Marriage and the Family* 35 (August 1973): 467–79; and Richard Harris, "The End Justified the Means: Boarding and Rooming in a City of Homes, 1890–1951," *Journal of Social History* 26 (winter 1992): 331–58.

76. Robert H. Woods, "The Myriad Tenantry of Furnished Rooms," *Charities and the Commons* 19 (November 2, 1907): 956.

77. Wolfe, *The Lodging House Problem*, 46.

78. On the shift from boarding to lodging in Boston, see Mark Peel, "On the Margins: Lodgers and Boarder in Boston, 1860–1900," *Journal of American History* 72 (March 1986): 813–34; Albert Wolfe, "The Problem of the Roomer," *Charities and the Commons* 19 (November 2, 1907): 959; and idem, *The Lodging House Problem*, 38. On San Francisco, see Groth, *Living Downtown*, 93. On Chicago, see Hoch and Slayton, *New Homeless and Old*, 16.

79. Wolfe, *The Lodging House Problem*, 110, 64.

80. Zorbaugh, *The Gold Coast and the Slum*, 74.

81. Wolfe, *The Lodging House Problem*, 47.

82. Ann Taylor Allen, "Feminism, Social Science, and the Meanings of Modernity: The Debate on the Origin of the Family in Europe and the United States, 1860–1914," *American Historical Review* 104 (October 1999): 1098–99.

83. "Apartment Hotels in New York City," 90–91.

84. Margaret Marsh, *Suburban Lives* (New Brunswick, N.J.: Rutgers University Press, 1990), 71–74.

85. On Gilman's career and influence, see Dolores Hayden, *The Grand Domestic Revolution: A History of Feminist Designs for American Homes, Neighborhoods, and Cities* (Cambridge: MIT Press, 1981), 183–277. On the informal practices of cooperative housekeeping among urban women, see Groth, *Living Downtown*, 62–64.

86. On Sinclair's Helicon Hall experiment, see Upton Sinclair, "A Home Colony," *Independent* 58 (June 14, 1906): 1401–8; Leon Harris, *Upton Sinclair: American Rebel* (New York: Thomas W. Crowell, 1975), 93–98; and Ivan Scott, *Upton Sinclair: The Forgotten Socialist* (Lewiston, N.Y.: Edwin Mellen Press, 1997), 67–73.

87. Upton Sinclair, *The Jungle* (New York: New American Library, 1960 [1906]), 314, 318. On Sinclair's struggle to conclude the novel, see Harris, *Upton Sinclair*, 75–77.

88. Quoted in Hayden, *The Grand Domestic Revolution*, 204.

89. Robert Hunter, *Poverty: Social Conscience in the Progressive Era* (New York: Harper and Row, 1965 [1904]), 116–17.

90. Calhoun, *A Social History of the American Family*, 181, 326–27. Other socialist commentators on the lodging house include Kennaday, "New York's Hundred Lodging Houses"; Laubach, *Why There Are Vagrants;* and Robert W. Bruere, "Reanchoring the Home," *Harper's Monthly Magazine* 124 (May 1912): 918–24.

91. Quoted in David Montgomery, *Citizen Worker: The Experience of Workers in the United States with Democracy and the Free Market during the Nineteenth Century* (New York: Cambridge University Press, 1993), 113.

92. Mary Corbin Sies, "The City Transformed: Nature, Technology, and the Suburban Ideal, 1877–1917," *Journal of Urban History* 14 (November 1987): 81–111. See also Marsh, *Suburban Lives;* Kenneth T. Jackson, *Crabgrass Frontier: The Suburbanization of the United States* (New York: Oxford University Press, 1985); Robert Fishman, *Bourgeois Utopias: The Rise and Fall of Suburbia* (New York: Basic Books, 1987), 103–81; and Larry R. Ford, *Cities and Buildings: Skyscrapers, Skid Rows, and Suburbs* (Baltimore: Johns Hopkins University Press, 1994), 126–61.

93. Grosvenor Atterbury, *The Economic Production of Workingmen's Homes: An Outline of*

a *Scientific Solution of the Housing Problem and Its Relation to the Development of the City, with Illustrations of Actual Results Obtained from Researches and Demonstrations, 1904–1925,* n.d., p. 10, Sage Foundation Homes Company, box 19, folder 155, Russell Sage Foundation Collection (Rockefeller Archives Center, Pocantico Hills, N.Y.).

94. Calhoun, *A Social History of the American Family,* 327.

95. Annie L. Diggs, "Garden City Movement," *Arena* 28 (June 1902): 631–32.

96. In 1917 one scholar counted forty-five model working-class suburbs created since the turn of the century. See Robert Leavitt Davison, "Checklist of the Principle Housing Developments in the United States," *Architectural Review* 5 (April 1917): 83–91; this entire volume of *Architectural Review* 5 (January and April 1917) is devoted to working-class housing.

97. Ernest W. Burgess, "The Growth of the City: An Introduction to a Research Project," in *The City,* 47–62.

98. "Apartment Hotels in New York City," 88–89.

99. Charles Musser, *Before the Nickelodeon: Edwin S. Porter and the Edison Manufacturing Company* (Berkeley: University of California Press, 1991), 311.

100. Douglas Gilbert, *Vaudeville: Its Life and Times* (New York: McGraw-Hill, 1940), 269.

101. For information on early comic tramps, see ibid., 269–78; John H. Jowson, *Clowns* (New York: Hawthorn Books, 1976), 282–305; Caroline Caffin and Marious De Zayas, *Vaudeville* (New York: Mitchell Kennerley, 1914), 205–7; Kenneth Allsop, *Hard Travellin':
The Hobo and His History* (New York: New American Library, 1967), 146–48; "Zimmerman, Eugene," in *The World Encyclopedia of Cartoons,* ed. Maurice Horn (New York: Chelsea House, 1980), 599–600; Frederick Burr Opper, *Happy Hooligan: A Complete Compilation: 1904–1905* (Westport, Conn.: Hyperion Press, 1977); Richard Marschall, *America's Great Comic Strip Artists* (New York: Abbeville Press, 1989), 58–73; Charles J. Maland, *Chaplin and American Culture: The Evolution of a Star Image* (Princeton: Princeton University Press, 1989), 3–20; and Kusmer, *Down and Out,* 185–91.

102. Bjorkman, "The New Anti-Vagrancy Campaign," 206.

103. Caffin and De Zayas, *Vaudeville,* 205–6.

104. The literature on carnival and the politics of popular festivity is vast, spanning the disciplines of English literature, critical theory, psychology, anthropology, and history. Most take Mikhail Bakhtin's study as a starting point. See Mikhail Bakhtin, *Rabelais and His World,* trans. Helene Iswolsky (Bloomington: Indiana University Press, 1984 [1968]). The best-known historical studies of carnival and popular festivals include Natalie Z. Davis, *Society and Culture in Early Modern France* (Stanford: Stanford University Press, 1975); Emmanuel Le Roy Ladurie, *Carnival in Romans,* trans. Mary Feeney (New York: G. Braziller, 1979); and Susan G. Davis, *Parades and Power: Street Theater in Nineteenth-Century Philadelphia* (Berkeley: University of California Press, 1986). For a multidisciplinary analysis of carnival, see Peter Stallybrass and Allon White, *The Politics and Poetics of Transgression* (Ithaca, N.Y.: Cornell University Press, 1986), esp. 6–20, 171–90.

105. Robert C. Allen, *Horrible Prettiness: Burlesque and American Culture* (Chapel Hill: University of North Carolina Press, 1991), 174; see also 26–27, 174–76. "Nat Wills, 'The Happy Tramp,'" Billy Rose Theatre Collection (New York Public Library for the Performing Arts, New York City, N.Y.).

106. Bakhtin, *Rabelais and His World,* 317; see also 303–67.

107. Gilbert, *Vaudeville,* 278.

108. Studies of blackface minstrelsy's role in creating working-class identity in the antebellum period include Eric Lott, *Love and Theft: Blackface Minstrelsy and the American Working Class* (New York: Oxford University Press, 1993); David R. Roediger, *The Wages of Whiteness: Race and the Making of the American Working Class* (London: Verso, 1991), 95–131; and Alexander Saxton, *The Rise and Fall of the White Republic: Class Politics and Mass Culture in Nineteenth-Century America* (London: Verso, 1990), esp. chaps. 5 and 7. For a general his-

tory of blackface minstrelsy, see Robert C. Toll, *Blacking Up: The Minstrel Show in Nineteenth-Century America* (New York: Oxford University Press, 1974).

109. For information on the class rhetoric of early variety performances, see Robert W. Snyder, *The Voice of the City* (New York: Oxford University Press, 1989), 12–19. On the early stage tramp, see John H. Towsen, *Clowns* (New York: Hawthorne Books, 1976), 284.

110. Quoted in Allen, *Horrible Prettiness*, 183.

111. Kathryn J. Oberdeck, *The Evangelist and the Impresario: Religion, Entertainment, and Cultural Politics in America, 1884–1914* (Baltimore: Johns Hopkins University Press, 1999), 71–108. See also Snyder, *Voice of the City*. While Oberdeck and Snyder emphasize vaudeville's need to balance refinement and ribaldry, Robert C. Allen focuses mainly on what he calls the "excorporation" from vaudeville of vulgar entertainments like burlesque. See Allen, *Horrible Prettiness*, 178–93.

112. *New York Telegraph*, June 23, 1917. Clippings, Lew Bloom, Billy Rose Theatre Collection.

113. "The Stage," *Munsey's Magazine* 11 (May 1894): 196–98.

114. Quoted in Robert Payne, *The Great God Pan: A Biography of the Tramp Played by Charles Chaplin* (New York: Hermitage House, 1952), 121.

115. *Pittsburg Leader*, June 23, 1907; ibid., April 19, 1908; from Nat M. Wills, clippings, Robinson Locke Collection, envelope 2611, Billy Rose Theatre Collection.

116. *Pittsburg Leader*, February 19, 1910; clipping, n.t., n.d., Nat M. Wills, clippings, Robinson Locke Collection.

117. *Cleveland Plain Dealer*, February 20, 1909; *Pittsburg Leader*, June 21, 1907, Nat M. Wills, clippings, Robinson Locke Collection. For further biographical information on Wills, see Gilbert, *Vaudeville*, 274–77; and Joe Franklin, *Encyclopedia of Comedians* (Secaucus, N.J.: Citadel Press, 1979), 337–38.

118. Snyder, *Voice of the City*, 58–60.

119. Nat M. Wills, *A Son of Rest* (Chicago: M. A. Donohue and Co., 1915), 47.

120. On early comic film, see Charles Musser, *The Emergence of Cinema: The American Scene to 1907* (New York: Charles Scribner's Sons, 1990); and Steven J. Ross, *Working-Class Hollywood: Silent Film and the Shaping of Class in America* (Princeton: Princeton University Press, 1998).

121. Irv. Ott, ed., *The New Tramp Joke Book: Containing a Select Collection of Monologues, Jokes, Funny Stories, etc., as Told by Leading Footlight Artists* (Baltimore: I. & M. Ottenheimer, 1915 [1907]), 50.

122. *New York American*, February 25, 1904, Nat M. Wills, clippings, Billy Rose Theatre Collection; *New York Times*, August 18, 1903.

123. Snyder, *Voice of the City*, 105. See also Howard P. Chudacoff, *The Age of the Bachelor: Creating an American Subculture* (Princeton: Princeton University Press, 1999), 134.

124. Joyce L. Kornbluh, ed., *Rebel Voices: An I. W. W. Anthology* (Ann Arbor: University of Michigan Press, 1965), 72; John Greenway, *American Folksongs of Protest* (New York: Octagon Books, 1970), 174–76; Ott, *The New Tramp Joke Book*.

125. Untitled clipping, 1903, Nat M. Wills, clippings, Billy Rose Theatre Collection; *New York Times*, August 18, 1903.

126. Park, "The City," 40. Although Herbert Blumer first coined the term "symbolic interactionism" in 1937, the concept was, according to Blumer, "implicit in what was being done under Park's direction at Chicago" from the beginning. Quoted in Barbara Ballis Lal, *The Romance of Culture in an Urban Civilization: Robert E. Park on Race and Ethnic Relations in Cities* (New York: Routledge, 1990), 30. See Herbert Blumer, *Symbolic Interactionism: Perspective and Method* (Englewood Cliffs, N.J.: Prentice-Hall, 1969); and Erving Goffman, *The Presentation of Self in Everyday Life* (Garden City, N.Y.: Doubleday, 1959).

127. On the decline of the confidence man's potency as a symbol in American culture, see Karen Halttunen's *Confidence Men and Painted Women: A Study of Middle-Class Culture in Victorian America, 1830–1870* (New Haven: Yale University Press, 1982), epilogue. On the

shift from "character" to "personality," see Warren I. Susman, "'Personality' and the Making of Twentieth-Century Culture," in *Culture as History: The Transformation of American Society in the Twentieth Century* (New York: Pantheon, 1984), 271–85.

128. Susan A. Glenn has argued convincingly that both vaudeville and formal social theory in the early twentieth century were engaged in a critical dialogue about the role of mimesis in the constitution of the self. See Susan A. Glenn, "'Give an Imitation of Me': Vaudeville Mimics and the Play of the Self," *American Quarterly* 50 (March 1998): 47–76.

129. Hutchins Hapgood, *Types from City Streets* (New York: Funk and Wagnalls, 1910), 75.

130. Jack London, "Confession," in *The Road* (Santa Barbara, Calif.: Peregrine, 1970 [1907]), 9.

131. See Josiah Flynt (Josiah Flynt Willard), *Tramping with Tramps: Studies and Sketches of Vagabond Life* (New York: Century Company, 1900 [1899]), 113–36; and Anderson, *The Hobo*, 40–57.

132. Anderson, *American Hobo*, 165.

133. See Jack London, *The People of the Abyss* (New York: Lawrence Hill, 1995 [1903]); idem, "South of the Slot" (1909), in *The Strength of the Strong* (New York: Macmillan, 1914), 34–70; and Anderson, *American Hobo*, 160–70.

134. On the early-twentieth-century genre of tramp ethnography and cross-class undercover investigation generally, see Toby Higbie, "Crossing Class Boundaries: Tramp Ethnographies and Narratives of Class in Progressive Era America," *Social Science History* 21 (winter 1997): 559–92; Mark Pittenger, "A World of Difference: Constructing the 'Underclass' in Progressive America," *American Quarterly* 49 (March 1997): 26–65; and Oberdeck, *The Evangelist and the Impresario*, 228–37.

135. Josiah Flynt, *My Life* (New York: Outing Publishing, 1908), 44.

136. Alfred Hodder, "Josiah Flynt—An Appreciation," in *My Life*, 344. Willard published under the name Josiah Flynt in deference to his famous aunt, who considered her nephew "a common vagabond and a drunkard." Linder, *The Reportage of Urban Culture*, 115. The use of a pseudonym might also have been a part of Willard's penchant for disguise and anonymity. Biographical information is from Linder, *The Reportage of Urban Culture*, 115–24; *The Dictionary of American Biography*, vol. 11, supplement 1, ed. Harris E. Starr (New York: Charles Scribner's Sons, 1946); and Louis Filler, *Crusaders for American Liberalism* (Yellow Springs, Ohio: Antioch Press, 1964 [1939]), 68–72.

137. Other book-length examples of this genre include Walter A. Wyckoff, *The Workers: An Experiment in Reality: The East* (New York: Charles Scribner's Sons, 1897); idem, *The Workers: An Experiment in Reality: The West* (New York: Charles Scribner's Sons, 1898); Edwin Brown, *'Broke': The Man without the Dime* (Chicago: Browne and Howell, 1913); and Frederick Mills's ethnographic account collected in Gregory R. Woirol, *In the Floating Army: F. C. Mills on Itinerant Life in California, 1914* (Urbana: University of Illinois Press, 1992).

138. *Literary Digest* obituary of Willard quoted in Linder, *The Reportage of Urban Culture*, 117.

139. Arthur Symons, "Introduction," in Flynt, *My Life*, xi–xxi.

140. Hodder, "Josiah Flynt—An Appreciation," 349.

141. Allen, *Horrible Prettiness*, 189.

142. Snyder, *Voice of the City*, 34.

143. On the gentrification of popular theater in the late nineteenth and early twentieth century, see Allen, *Horrible Prettiness*, 178–93; Oberdeck, *The Evangelist and the Impresario*, 71–108, 179–213; and Lawrence W. Levine, *Highbrow/Lowbrow: The Emergence of Cultural Hierarchy in America* (Cambridge: Harvard University Press, 1988), 13–81, 177–200.

144. Albert F. McLean Jr., *American Vaudeville as Ritual* (Lexington: University of Kentucky Press, 1965), 110.

145. Nat M. Wills, obituary, *Variety*, December 14, 1917; Gilbert, *Vaudeville*, 174–75.

146. Maland, *Chaplin and American Culture*, 3–35.

147. Emmett Kelly and F. Beverly Kelley, *Clown* (New York: Prentice-Hall, 1954), 49. See also Emmett Kelly, clippings file, Billy Rose Theatre Collection.

148. Opper, *Happy Hooligan;* Marion Kinnaird and Frederick Burr Opper, *The Story of the Happy Hooligan* (Springfield, Mass.: McLoughlin Brothers, 1932), n.p. See also Marschall, *America's Great Comic Strip Artists,* 58–73.

149. See Norman Rockwell, "Hobo and Dog," *Saturday Evening Post,* October 18, 1924, cover; "Man Hugging Dog," ibid., September 27, 1924, cover; and "Dog Biting Man in Seat of Pants (Tenacious Hold)," ibid., August 18, 1928, cover. See also Rockwell's hobo illustrations used in advertisements. Laurie Norton Moffatt, ed., *Norman Rockwell:A Definitive Catalogue,* vol. 1 (Stockbridge: Norman Rockwell Museum, 1986), 381, 433.

## CHAPTER SIX

1. John Dos Passos, *The Best Times:An Informal Memoir* (New York: New American Library, 1966), 170.

2. Ibid., 172; Virginia Spencer Carr, *Dos Passos:A Life* (Garden City, N.Y.: Doubleday, 1984), 301.

3. John Dos Passos, *The 42nd Parallel,* in *U.S.A.* (Boston: Houghton Mifflin, 1960 [1930]), 33, 81, 93, 105, 111, 112.

4. Donald Pizer, *Dos Passos' U.S.A.:A Critical Study* (Charlottesville: University Press of Virginia, 1988), 89–91; Michael Denning, *The Cultural Front:The Laboring of American Culture in the Twentieth Century* (New York: Verso, 1996), 187–88. My interpretation of *U.S.A.* owes much to Denning's wonderful analysis of the trilogy, 163–99.

5. Robert H. Zeiger, *American Workers, American Unions, 1920–1985* (Baltimore: Johns Hopkins University Press, 1986), 4.

6. John Dos Passos, *1919,* in *U.S.A.,* 149, 205.

7. Idem, *The Big Money,* in *U.S.A.,* 493–94.

8. Thomas F. Healy, "The Hobo Hits the Highroad," *American Mercury* 8 (July 1926): 334.

9. Clark C. Spence, "Knights of the Fast Freight," *American Heritage* 27 (August 1976): 97.

10. "That Vanishing American, the Hobo," *New York Times Magazine* (August 18, 1940): 11.

11. Nels Anderson, *The Hobo: The Sociology of the Homeless Man* (Chicago: Phoenix Books, 1965 [1923]), xxi; idem, *Men on the Move* (Chicago: University of Chicago Press, 1940), 3. See also his comments in the preface of *The American Hobo:An Autobiography* (Leiden, Netherlands: E. J. Brill, 1975).

12. Stewart H. Holbrook, *Holy Old Mackinaw:A Natural History of the Lumberjack* (New York: Macmillan, 1956 [1938]), 247–48.

13. Anderson, *Men on the Move,* 170–76. See also Gerald D. Nash, *The American West in the Twentieth Century: A Short History of an Urban Oasis* (Englewood Cliffs, N.J.: Prentice-Hall, 1973).

14. Carey McWilliams, *Ills Fares the Land: Migrants and Migratory Labor in the United States* (Boston: Little, Brown, 1942), 102–3.

15. Carlos Schwantes, *Hard Traveling:A Portrait of Work Life in the New Northwest* (Lincoln: University of Nebraska Press, 1994), 37, 64–65; Howard P. Chudacoff, *The Age of the Bachelor:Creating an American Subculture* (Princeton: Princeton University Press, 1999), 56–61.

16. Henry J. Allen, "The New Harvest Hand," *American Review of Reviews* 76 (September 1927): 279. See also Thomas D. Isern, *Bull Threshers and Bindlestiffs: Harvesting and Threshing on the North American Plains* (Lawrence: University Press of Kansas, 1990), 174–205; and Ted Grossardt, "Harvest(ing) Hoboes: The Production of Labor Organization through the Wheat Harvest," *Agricultural History* 70 (spring 1996): 283–301.

17. McWilliams, *Ill Fares the Land,* 102–3.

18. John J. Hader, "Honk Honk Hobo," *Survey* 60 (August 1, 1928): 455. For commentary on the automobile's effect on hobo labor, see McWilliams, *Ills Fares the Land,* 100–1; Cedric Worth, "The Brotherhood of Man," *North American Review* 227 (April 1929): 487–92; Healy, "The Hobo Hits the Highroad," 334–38; and Adaline A. Buffington, "Automobile Migrants," *Family* 6 (July 1925): 149–53.

19. Anderson, *American Hobo,* 159.

20. McWilliams, *Ill Fares the Land,* 99. On the work of labor investigator Don D. Lescohier, see Don D. Lescohier, *Harvest Problems in the Wheat Belt,* U.S. Department of Agriculture Bulletin 1020 (Washington, D.C.: Government Printing Office, 1922); idem, *Conditions Affecting the Demand for Harvest Labor in the Wheat Belt,* U.S. Department of Agriculture Bulletin 1230 (Washington, D.C.: Government Printing Office, 1924); idem, *Sources of Supply and Conditions of Employment of Harvest Labor in the Wheat Belt,* U.S. Department of Agriculture Bulletin 1211 (Washington, D.C:. Government Printing Office, 1924); idem, "Conditions of Harvest Labor in the Wheat Belt, 1920 and 1921," *Monthly Labor Review* 16 (February 1923): 44–50; idem, "Hands and Tools of the Wheat Harvest," *Survey* 50 (July 1923): 376–82, 409–12; and idem, "Harvesters and Hoboes in the Wheat Fields," *Survey* 50 (August 1, 1923), 482–87, 503–4.

21. Len DeCaux, *The Living Spirit of the Wobblies* (New York: International, 1978), 5–6.

22. Buffington, "Automobile Migrants," 152, 149; McWilliams, *Ill Fares the Land,* 71–90, 156.

23. Marion Hathway, *The Migratory Worker and Family Life* (Chicago: University of Illinois Press, 1934), 104–42. See also McWilliams, *Ills Fares the Land,* 59; and Schwantes, *Hard Traveling,* 67. Those who recommended that labor camps recruit migratory families include Charles H. Forster, "Despised and Rejected of Men: Hoboes of the Pacific Coast," *Survey* 33 (March 20, 1915): 671–72; and Towne Nylander, "The Migratory Population of the United States," *American Journal of Sociology* 30 (September 1924): 129–53.

24. Quoted in Richard Wormser, *Hoboes: Wandering in America, 1870–1940* (New York: Walker, 1994), 107.

25. William T. Cross and Dorothy E. Cross, *Newcomers and Nomads in California* (Stanford: Stanford University Press, 1937), 103–4. See also Cletus E. Daniel, *Bitter Harvest: A History of California Farmworkers, 1870–1941* (Berkeley: University of California Press, 1981), 60–62.

26. McWilliams, *Ills Fares the Land,* 5–7.

27. On California's great agricultural strikes of 1933–34, see Daniel, *Bitter Harvest,* 141–257; Vicki L. Ruiz, *Cannery Women, Cannery Lives: Mexican Women, Unionization, and the California Food Processing Industry, 1930–1950* (Albuquerque: University of New Mexico Press, 1987), 49–51; and Devra Weber, *Dark Sweat, White Gold: California Farm Workers, Cotton, and the New Deal* (Berkeley: University of California Press, 1994), 79–111.

28. See Camille Guerin-Gonzales, *Mexican Workers and American Dreams: Immigration, Repatriation, and California Farm Labor, 1900–1939* (New Brunswick, N.J.: Rutgers University Press, 1994).

29. Daniel, *Bitter Harvest,* 105–6.

30. James N. Gregory, *American Exodus: The Dustbowl Migration and Okie Culture in California* (New York: Oxford University Press, 1989); Weber, *Dark Sweat, White Gold,* 137–61.

31. Quoted in Paul S. Taylor, *Mexican Labor in the United States,* vol. 2 (Berkeley: University of California Press, 1932), 82–83.

32. Quoted in ibid., 84–85.

33. Dorothy B. Fujita Rony, "'You've Got to Move Like Hell': Trans-Pacific Colonialism and Filipina/o Seattle" (Ph.D. diss., Yale University, 1996).

34. Carleton H. Parker, *The Casual Laborer and Other Essays* (Harcourt, Brace and Howe, 1920), 85, 88.

35. Ibid., 123.

36. Ibid., 100, 53, 124. Parker's report on Wheatland can be found on 169–99. For a fine

analysis of Parker's work, see Toby Higbie, "Crossing Class Boundaries: Tramp Ethnographers and Narratives of Class in Progressive Era America," *Social Science History* 21 (winter 1997): 574–79.

37. Lawrence B. Glickman, *A Living Wage: American Workers and the Making of Consumer Society* (Ithaca, N.Y.: Cornell University Press, 1997), 7. On the racial and gender dimensions of the ideology of the American Standard, see 85–91.

38. Ibid., 131–56.

39. Robert E. Park, "The Mind of the Hobo: Reflections upon the Relation between Mentality and Locomotion," in *The City*, ed. Robert E. Park, Ernest W. Burgess, and Roderick D. McKenzie (Chicago: University of Chicago Press, 1967 [1925]), 160; David Montgomery, *The Fall of the House of Labor: The Workplace, the State, and American Labor Activism, 1865–1925* (New York: Cambridge University Press, 1987), 239.

40. Don D. Lescohier, *The Labor Market* (New York: Macmillan, 1919), 267. On the problem of turnover, see Andrea Graziosi, "Common Laborers, Unskilled Workers, 1880–1915," *Labor History* 22 (fall 1981): 512–44. Key primary sources on turnover include Magnus Alexander, "Hiring and Firing: Its Economic Waste and How to Avoid It," *Annals of the American Academy of Political and Social Science* 65 (May 1916): 128–44; Sumner Slichter, *The Turnover of Factory Labor* (New York: D. Appleton, 1919); and Paul F. Brissenden and Emil Frankel, *Labor Turnover in Industry* (New York: Macmillan, 1922).

Studies and commentaries that specifically emphasized the role of casual labor in creating hoboes include Peter A. Speek, "Conclusions and Reform Projects in Regard to Floating Laborers in the Country," pp. 5–16, reel 14, microfilm edition of the United States Commission on Industrial Relations, record group 174 (General Records of the Department of Labor, National Archives, Washington, D.C.); idem, "The Psychology of the Floating Workers," *Annals of the American Academy of Political and Social Science* 69 (January 1917): 72–78; Stuart Rice, "Vagrancy," *Proceedings of the National Conference of Charities and Correction* (Fort Wayne, Ind.: Fort Wayne Printing, 1914), 462–65; C. Luther Fry, "Migratory Workers of Our Industries," *The World's Work* 40 (October 1920): 600–11; and Arthur Pound, "The Casual's Contribution to America: Thoughts on Unemployment, Suggested by Reading the Report of the Russell Sage Foundation," *Independent* 113 (October 18, 1924): 295.

41. Montgomery, *Fall of the House of Labor*, 240–42, 454–57; Lizabeth Cohen, *Making a New Deal: Industrial Workers in Chicago, 1919–1939* (New York: Cambridge University Press, 1990), 159–211; Stuart D. Brandes, *American Welfare Capitalism, 1880–1940* (Chicago: University of Chicago Press, 1976); Alexander Keyssar, *Out of Work: The First Century of Unemployment in Massachusetts* (New York: Cambridge University Press, 1986), 262–98. On advertising and the creation of mass markets, see Richard M. Ohmann, *Selling Culture: Magazines, Markets, and Class at the Turn of the Century* (New York: Verso, 1996); and Susan Strasser, *Satisfaction Guaranteed: The Making of the American Mass Market* (New York: Pantheon, 1989). For an analysis and overview of these macroeconomic changes, see Martin J. Sklar, *The Corporate Reconstruction of American Capitalism, 1890–1916: The Market, the Law, and Politics* (New York: Cambridge University Press, 1988).

42. Melvyn Dubofsky, *We Shall Be All: A History of the Industrial Workers of the World* (Chicago: Quadrangle Books, 1969), 445–46; Joyce L. Kornbluh, ed., *Rebel Voices: An I. W. W. Anthology* (Ann Arbor: University of Michigan Press, 1965), 251–57. On the decline of turnover, see Montgomery, *Fall of the House of Labor*, 459–60.

43. Cohen, *Making a New Deal*, 183–211.

44. *Industrial Worker*, May 1, 1912; *Industrial Unionist*, April 18, 1925; May 9, 1925.

45. Floyd Dell, "Hallelujah, I'm a Bum," *Century Magazine* 110 (June 1925): 137–51.

46. Denning, *The Cultural Front*, 167. Upton Sinclair, *Jimmie Higgins: A Story* (New York: Boni and Liveright, 1919); Hart Crane, "The River" (1930), in *The Complete Poems and Selected Letters and Prose of Hart Crane*, ed. Brom Weber (Garden City, N.Y.: Anchor Books, 1966), 62–69; Edward Dahlberg, *Bottom Dogs* (1930), in *Bottom Dogs, from Flushing to Calvary, Those Who Perish, and Hitherto Unpublished and Uncollected Works* (New York: Thomas Y.

Crowell, 1976), 137–318. See also Charles Ashleigh, *Rambling Kid* (London: Faber, 1930); and William Edge, *The Main Stem* (New York: Vanguard, 1927).

47. Dell, "Hallelujah, I'm a Bum," 142; Malcolm Cowley, *Exile's Return: A Literary Odyssey of the 1920s* (New York: Penguin Books, 1979 [1934]), 58; Floyd Dell, *Intellectual Vagabondia: An Apology for the Intelligentsia* (New York: George H. Doran, 1926). On Dell's life and influence, see Christine Stansell, *American Moderns: Bohemian New York and the Creation of a New Century* (New York: Metropolitan Books, 2000), 48–52, 335–36.

48. John Burroughs, "The Exhilarations of the Road," *Galaxy* 15 (June 1873): 809.

49. William DeVere, *Tramp Poems of the West* (Tacoma: Cromwell Printing, 1891); Bliss Carman and Richard Hovey, *Songs from Vagabondia* (Boston: Copeland and Day, 1894); Henry Herbert Knibbs, *Songs of the Outlands: Ballads of the Hoboes and Other Verse* (New York: Houghton Mifflin, 1914).

50. Harry Kemp, *Tramping on Life: An Autobiographical Narrative* (Garden City, N.Y.: Garden City Publishing, 1922), 389. See also Kemp's collection of poems, *The Cry of Youth* (New York: M. Kennerly, 1914). William Brevda discusses the tensions between the realities of the road and the romances of vagabond poets in his fine biography, *Harry Kemp: The Last Bohemian* (Lewisburg, Penn.: Bucknell University Press, 1986), 114–20.

51. Vachel Lindsay, *A Handy Guide for Beggars* (New York: Macmillan, 1916), viii; idem, *Adventures While Preaching the Gospel of Beauty* (New York: Macmillan, 1914).

52. Roger O. Bruns, *The Damndest Radical: The Life and World of Ben Reitman* (Urbana: University of Illinois Press, 1987), 242; see also 230–45; Frank O. Beck, *Hobohemia* (Rindge, N.H.: Richard R. Smith, 1956), 78–83; and Albert Parry, *Garrets and Pretenders: A History of Bohemianism in America* (New York: Dover, 1960 [1933]), 200–11.

53. Bruns, *Damndest Radical,* 213. Ben Reitman, *The Second Oldest Profession* (New York: Vanguard Press, 1931). See also Stansell, *American Moderns,* 135–37, 294–97; Nels Anderson, "Introduction to the Phoenix Edition" (1961), in *The Hobo: The Sociology of the Homeless Man* (Chicago: Phoenix Books, 1965 [1923]), xi; idem, "A Stranger at the Gate: Reflections on the Chicago School of Sociology," *Urban Life* 11 (January 1983): 400–1; and idem, "Sociology Has Many Faces, Part II," *Journal of the History of Sociology* 3 (spring 1981): 4–5.

54. Anderson, "Stranger at the Gate," 400. See also idem, *American Hobo,* 128, 162–63, 170.

55. Park, quoted in Carla Cappetti, *Writing Chicago: Modernism, Ethnography, and the Novel* (New York: Columbia University Press, 1993), 24.

56. Park, "The Mind of the Hobo," 160.

57. Rolf Linder, *The Reportage of Urban Culture: Robert Park and the Chicago School,* trans. Adrian Morris (New York: Cambridge University Press, 1996), 131; Sinclair Lewis, "Hobohemia," *Saturday Evening Post* 189 (April 7, 1917): 3–6, 121; *New York Times,* February 9, 1919.

58. On the city as a "state of mind," see Robert E. Park, "The City: Suggestions for the Investigation of Human Behavior in the Urban Environment," in *The City,* 1–46; and Harvey Warren Zorbaugh, *The Gold Coast and the Slum: A Sociological Study of Chicago's Near North Side* (Chicago: University of Chicago Press, 1929), 104.

59. Rolf Linder's wonderful analysis of *The Hobo* in particular and Chicago sociology in general clarified much of my own thought about hobohemia's transformation in this postwar period. See Linder, *The Reportage of Urban Culture,* 131–34.

60. Dell, "Hallelujah, I'm a Bum," 146.

61. James Stevens, "The Hobo's Apology," *Century Magazine* 109 (February 1925): 470. On the larger role of folklore in 1920s American culture, see Benjamin Filene, *Romancing the Folk: Public Memory and American Roots Music* (Chapel Hill: University of North Carolina Press, 2000); Richard M. Dorson, *American Folklore and the Historian* (Chicago: University of Chicago Press, 1971); and Michael A. Kammen, *Mystic Chords of Memory: The Transformation of Tradition in American Culture* (New York: Alfred A. Knopf, 1991). See also Ruth Suckow, "The Folk Idea in American Life," *Scribner's Magazine* 88 (September 1930): 245–56.

62. Carl Sandburg, *The American Songbag* (New York: Harcourt, Brace, and World, 1927), 183–92; Johnny Bond, *The Recordings of Jimmie Rodgers: An Annotated Discography* (Los Angeles: John Edwards Memorial Foundation, at the Folklore and Mythology Center, University of California, 1978); Norm Cohen, *Long Steel Rail: The Railroad in American Folksong* (Urbana: University of Illinois Press, 1981), 344–99. See also Godfrey Irwin, ed., *American Tramp and Underworld Slang* (London: Eric Partridge, 1931); F. H. Sidney, "Hobo Cant," *Dialect Notes* 5, part 2 (1919): 41–42; Elisha K. Kane, "The Jargon of the Underworld," *Dialect Notes* 5, part 10 (1927): 433–67; Stewart H. Holbrook, "Wobbly Talk," *American Mercury* 7 (January 1926): 62–65; Nicholas Klein, "Hobo Lingo," *American Speech* 1 (September 1926): 650–53; Charlie Samolar, "The Argot of the Vagabond," *American Speech* 2 (June 1927): 385–92; Vernon W. Saul, "The Vocabulary of Bums," *American Speech* 4 (June 1929): 337–46; David W. Maurer, "The Argot of the Underworld," *American Speech* 7 (December 1931): 99–118; Mamie Meredith, "'Waddies' and 'Hoboes' of the Old West," *American Speech* 7 (April 1932): 257–60; and Robert T. Oliver, "Junglese," *American Speech* 7 (June 1932): 339–41.

63. George Milburn, *The Hobo's Hornbook: A Repertory for a Gutter Jongleur* (New York: Ives Washburn, 1930), xi–xviii. See also idem, "Poesy in the Jungles," *American Mercury* 20 (May 1930): 80–86.

Collections and interpretations of hobo folk songs and lore that rely on *The Hobo's Hornbook* as their sole or primary source of material include B. A. Botkin and Alvin F. Harlow, *A Treasury of Railroad Folklore* (New York: Bonanza Books, 1953), 221–40, 459–62; Alan Lomax, *The Folk Songs of North America* (Garden City, N.Y.: Doubleday, 1960), 406–25; Irwin Silber, ed., *Songs of the Great American West* (New York: Macmillan, 1967), 287–317; and Richard Phelps, "Songs of the American Hobo," *Journal of Popular Culture* 17 (fall 1983): 1–21. Contemporary studies of hobo lore include Al Grierson, "The Great Historical Bum: An Introduction to Hobo Folklore," *Journal of the Vancouver Folksong Society* 4 (October–December 1975): 189–201, 230–42; Cohen, *Long Steel Rail;* and Thomas E. Murray, "A New Look at the Folk Speech of American Tramps," *Western Folklore* 51 (July 1992): 287–302.

64. Jim Tully, *Beggars of Life* (Garden City, N.Y. Garden City Publishing, 1924). See also William H. Davies, *Autobiography of a Supertramp* (New York: Alfred Knopf, 1917); idem, *The Adventures of Johnny Walker, Tramp* (London: J. Cape, 1926); Glen H. Mullin, *Adventures of a Scholar Tramp* (New York: Century, 1925); George Witten, *Outlaw Trails* (New York: Minton, Balch, 1929); idem, "The Open Road: The Autobiography of a Hobo," *Century Magazine* 115 (January 1928): 351–61; and Lennox Kerr, *Back Door Guest* (Indianapolis: Bobbs-Merrill, 1930). For a review of this literature, see John D. Seeyle, "The American Tramp: A Version of the Picaresque," *American Quarterly* 15 (winter 1963): 535–53; and William R. Hunt, "'Which Way 'Bo?': Literary Impressions of the Hobos' Golden Age, 1880–1930," *Journal of Popular Culture* 4 (summer 1970): 22–38.

65. Dean Stiff (Nels Anderson), *The Milk and Honey Route: A Handbook for Hobos* (New York: Vanguard Press, 1930), vi, vii.

66. Stevens, "The Hobo's Apology," 472.

## CHAPTER SEVEN

1. Franklin D. Roosevelt, *The Public Papers and Addresses of Franklin D. Roosevelt*, vol. 1 (New York: Russell and Russell, 1969), 624–27. For discussions of FDR's use of the "analogue of war" to describe the Great Depression, see William E. Leuchtenburg, *The FDR Years: On Roosevelt and His Legacy* (New York: Columbia University Press, 1995), 35–75; and Michael S. Sherry, *In the Shadow of War: The United States since the 1930s* (New Haven: Yale University Press, 1995), 15–29.

2. My account of the Bonus Army is based largely on Roger Daniels, *The Bonus March: An Episode of the Great Depression* (Westport, Conn.: Greenwood Publishing, 1971); Donald J. Lisio, *The President and Protest: Hoover, Conspiracy, and the Bonus Riot* (Columbia: University of Missouri Press, 1974); R. Jackson Wilson et al., *The Pursuit of Liberty: A History of the*

*American People,* vol. 2 (NewYork: Alfred A. Knopf, 1984), 749–64; Jack Douglas, *Veterans on the March* (NewYork: Workers Library, 1934); and W. W. Waters, *B.E.F.:The Whole Story of the Bonus Army* (NewYork: Arno Press, 1969 [1933]).

3. Waters, *B.E.F.,* 4–6; Daniels, *The Bonus March,* 77–78.

4. Quoted in Virginia Spencer Carr, *Dos Passos: A Life* (Garden City, N.Y.: Doubleday, 1984), 301.

5. Daniels, *The Bonus March,* 160, 174, 172.

6. Quoted in Carr, *Dos Passos,* 301.

7. John Dos Passos, "Foreword," in Douglas, *Veterans on the March,* vi. See also Dos Passos, "The Veterans Come Home to Roost," *New Republic* 70 (June 29, 1932): 177–78.

8. Daniels, *The Bonus March,* 104.

9. Ibid., 100.

10. Quoted in Douglas, *Veterans on the March,* 225; Daniels, *The Bonus March,* 105–7.

11. Dos Passos, "Foreword," vi. Dos Passos seems to have come close to titling *U.S.A.*'s concluding "Vag" vignette the "Forgotten Man," in cutting reference to FDR's populist rhetoric and piecemeal reforms. See Donald Pizer, *Dos Passos' U.S.A.: A Critical Study* (Charlottesville: University Press of Virginia, 1988), 101.

12. Nels Anderson, "Sociology Has Many Faces: Part II," *Journal of the History of Sociology* 3 (spring 1981): 14; Daniels, *The Bonus March,* 324n; Lisio, *The President and Protest,* 84.

13. Quoted in Daniels, *The Bonus March,* 122.

14. Quoted in ibid., 218.

15. Ellen C. Potter, "The Problem of the Transient," *Annals of the American Academy of Political and Social Science* 176 (November 1934): 66–73; Nels Anderson, *Men on the Move* (Chicago: University of Chicago Press, 1940), 66; Joan M. Crouse, *The Homeless Transient in the Great Depression: NewYork State, 1929–1941* (Albany: State University of NewYork, 1986), 48.

16. See Crouse, *Homeless Transient,* 76–77.

17. Alvin Roseman, *Shelter Care and the Local Homeless Man* (Chicago: Public Administration Service, 1935), 34. For shelter care in the 1930s, see Kim Hopper, "Public Shelter as 'a Hybrid Institution': Homeless Men in Historical Perspective," *Journal of Social Issues* 46 (December 1990): 13–28.

18. Edwin H. Sutherland and Harvey J. Locke, *Twenty Thousand Homeless Men: A Study of Unemployed Men in the Chicago Shelters* (New York: Arno Press, 1971 [1936]), 195–98; Roseman, *Shelter Care,* 4–5.

19. California, which received more migrants than any state, provided relief for nonresidents through its state transient program between 1931 and 1933. This program would become a model for the federal Transient Bureau. William T. Cross and Dorothy E. Cross, *Newcomers and Nomads in California* (Stanford: Stanford University Press, 1937), 30.

20. Crouse, *Homeless Transient,* 85–86, 179–80.

21. See Sutherland and Locke, *Twenty Thousand Homeless Men,* 35–44, 47; Roseman, *Shelter Care,* 11, 52; "Special Census of the Bowery," *Literary Digest* 107 (November 29, 1930): 20–21; Nels Anderson, *The Homeless in NewYork City* (NewYork: Welfare Council of NewYork City, 1934), 165–66; Alvin Averbach, "San Francisco's South of Market District, 1850–1950: The Emergence of a Skid Row," *California Historical Quarterly* 52 (fall 1973): 215–19; and Benjamin F. Culver, "Transient Unemployed Men," *Sociology and Social Research* 17 (July–August 1933): 522.

22. "Pioneers without a frontier" is quoted in Joan M. Crouse, "Transients, Migrants, and the Homeless," in *The Encyclopedia of American Social History,* vol. 3, ed. Mary Kupiec Cayton, Elliott J. Gorn, and Peter W. Williams (NewYork: Scribner, 1993), 2147. The most complete profile of transients can be found in John N. Webb, *The Transient Unemployed: A Description and Analysis of the Transient Relief Population* (Washington, D.C.: Works Progress Administration, 1935), 1–2, 33–35, 101. See also Culver, "Transient Unemployed Men," 519–34; Herman J. P. Schubert, *Twenty Thousand Transients: A One Year's Sample of Those Who Ap-*

*ply for Aid in a Northern City* (Buffalo: Emergency Relief Bureau, 1935); Cross and Cross, *Newcomers and Nomads*, 30; Freda P. Segner, "Migrant Minnesota: An Analysis of Minnesota Transient Cases," unpublished report for the Transient Division, Minnesota State Relief Agency, November 1936 (Minnesota Historical Society, St. Paul, Minnesota); and Theodore Caplow, "Transiency as a Cultural Pattern," *American Sociological Review* 5 (October 1940): 734.

23. David Scheyer, "Flop-House," *The Nation* 139 (August 22, 1934): 217.

24. Webb, *Transient Unemployed*, 32. On female homelessness in the 1930s, see Stephanie Golden, *The Women Outside: Meanings and Myths of Homelessness* (Berkeley: University of California Press, 1992), 143–49; Lynn Weiner, "Sisters of the Road: Women Transients and Tramps," in *Walking to Work: Tramps in America, 1790–1935*, ed. Eric H. Monkkonen (Lincoln: University of Nebraska, 1984), 171–88; and Marsha A. Martin, "Homeless Women: An Historical Perspective," in *On Being Homeless: Historical Perspectives*, ed. Rick Beard (New York: Museum of the City of New York, 1987), 32–41.

25. Cliff Maxwell, "Lady Vagabonds," *Scribner's Magazine* 85 (March 1929): 292. See also Samuel Elam, "Lady Hoboes," *New Republic* 61 (January 1, 1930): 164–69; "Ladies of the Road," *Literary Digest* 114 (August 13, 1932): 33; and Kathryn Close, "Women Alone," *Survey* 74 (September 1938): 281.

26. Walter C. Reckless, "Why Women Become Hoboes," *American Mercury* 31 (February 1934): 175–80.

27. Owen R. Lovejoy, "Uncle Sam's Runaway Boys," *Survey* 69 (March 1933): 100.

28. Crouse, *Homeless Transient*, 117; Webb, *Transient Unemployed*, 16–17; George E. Outland, *Boy Transiency in America: A Compilation of Articles Dealing with Youth Wandering in the United States* (Santa Barbara: Santa Barbara State College Press, 1938), 103–5.

29. Quoted in Errol Lincoln Uys, *Riding the Rails: Teenagers on the Move during the Great Depression* (New York: TV Books, 1999), 29.

30. Webb, *Transient Unemployed*, 31.

31. *Wild Boys of the Road*, dir. William A. Wellman (Warner Brothers, 1933). The movie inspired at least one teenage hobo to hit the road. "It put ideas in your head," recalled one former wild boy. Quoted in Uys, *Riding the Rails*, 265. See also Thomas Minehan, *Boy and Girl Tramps of America* (New York: Farrar and Rinehart, 1934); and Robert Carter, "Boys Going Nowhere: Notes from the Diary of an American 'Wild Boy,'" *New Republic* 74 (March 8, 1933): 92–95. On representations of youth in the Great Depression, see Barbara Melosh, *Engendering Culture: Manhood and Womanhood in New Deal Public Art and Theater* (Washington, D.C.: Smithsonian Institution Press, 1991), 157–80.

32. Pauline V. Young, "The New Poor," *Sociology and Social Research* 17 (January–February 1933): 239–40. See also F. L. Kellog, "New Faces on the Bowery," *Survey* 64 (April 1, 1930): 15–17; Matthew Josephson, "The Other Nation," *New Republic* 75 (March 17, 1933): 14–16; and Cross and Cross, *Newcomers and Nomads*, 57–58. For similar references to youth, see Lowell Ames Norris, "America's Homeless Army," *Scribner's Monthly* 93 (May 1933): 316–18; and Towne Nylander, "Wandering Youth," *Sociology and Social Research* 17 (July–August 1933): 560–68.

33. Frank Bunce, "I've Got to Take a Chance," *Forum* 89 (February 1933): 108.

34. Tom Kromer, *Waiting for Nothing* (New York: Hill and Wang, 1968 [1935]), 186.

35. Elam, "Lady Hoboes," 164.

36. Potter, "The Problem of the Transient," 71–72.

37. Sutherland and Locke, *Twenty Thousand Homeless Men*, 66–68. See also Roseman, *Shelter Care*, 10–11.

38. A. Wayne McMillen, "An Army of Boys on the Loose," *Survey* 78 (September 1932): 392. See also Outland, *Boy Transiency in America*, 64.

39. Nylander, "Wandering Youth," 562–63.

40. Crouse, *Homeless Transient*, 153–72.

41. Daniels, *The Bonus March*, 222–33. Contrary to legend, few of the Bonus Marchers

who accepted relief positions died in the hurricane that struck the Florida Keys in September 1935. See ibid., 260.

42. Holly Marie Allen, "Fallen Women and Forgotten Men: Gendered Concepts of Community, Home, and Nation, 1932–1945" (Ph.D. diss.,Yale University, 1996), 113. On the history of the CCC, see Leslie Alexander Lacy, *The Soil Soldiers:The Civilian Conservation Corps in the Great Depression* (Radnor, Penn.: Chilton Book Company, 1976); and Olen Cole Jr., *The African-American Experience in the Civilian Conservation Corps* (Gainesville: University of Florida Press, 1999).

43. Gertrude Springer, "Men off the Road," *Survey Graphic* 23 (September 1934): 426–27.

44. John Benton, "Rest for Weary Willie," *Saturday Evening Post* 209 (September 5, 1936): 5; James P. Mitchell, "Coddling the Bums," *The Nation* 139 (August 22, 1934): 216; Robert S.Wilson, *Individualized Service forTransients* (NewYork: National Association of Travelers' Aid Societies, 1935), 70, quoted in Crouse, *Homeless Transient*, 161. For a discussion of sexual fear in the Great Depression, see George Chauncey, *Gay NewYork: Gender, Urban Culture, and the Making of the Gay MaleWorld, 1890–1940* (NewYork: Basic Books, 1994), 352–60.

45. Sutherland and Locke, *TwentyThousand Homeless Men*, 77.

46. ElizabethWickenden, "Transiency-Mobility inTrouble," *Survey* 93 (October 1937): 308–9.

47. Quoted in Crouse, *Homeless Transient*, 169.

48. Allen, "FallenWomen and Forgotten Men," 16, 49–76. See also Melosh, *Engendering Culture*.

49. *Hallelujah, I'm a Bum*, dir. Lewis Milestone (United Artists, 1933).

50. See, for example, John Worby, *The Other Half: The Autobiography of a Tramp* (New York: Lee Furman, 1937); and Carl S. Schockman, *We Turned Hobo* (Columbus: F. J. Heer Printing, 1937).

51. George Pager, "The Hobo News," *New York Folklore Quarterly* 5 (autumn 1949): 228–320; "For Hoboes: Hobo News," *Time* (May 17, 1937): 67–69.

52. *Recollections of Britt, Iowa, 1878–1978* (Lake Mills, Iowa: Graphic Publishing, 1978), 201–5; George A. Horton, "Britt's First Convention," *Palimpsest* 70 (summer 1989): 87–92.

53. "Walter Winchell: On Broadway," *New York Mirror*, January 5, 1935; "Hobo Hegemony: Convention to Decide among Rival Kings of the Road," *Literary Digest* 123 (April 10, 1937): 10–12; "Hoboes of America, Incorporated," *1939 Year Book, Encyclopedia, and Reference Manual*, vol. 1 (n.p.: Printed by the Executive Board, 1938), Ben Lewis Reitman Papers (Special Collections, University of Illinois-Chicago).The knotty history of the various hobo organizations and rival "Hobo Kings" who emerged in the 1930s is untangled in Roger O. Bruns, *The Damndest Radical:The Life andWorld of Ben Reitman* (Urbana: University of Illinois Press, 1987), 255–65. See also Anderson, *Men on the Move*, 19–21.

54. See Ben Reitman to Jeff Davis, March 25, 1939; idem, "Weekly Report No. 6: Report on Visit to Hobo Convention," Chicago Board of Health, April 12, 1939; idem to King of Hoboes and Delegates, August 11, 1939, supplement II, folder 154, Reitman Papers.

55. John E. O'Donnell, "Hobo Lore," unpublished typescript,Works Progress Administration, 1938 (Archive of Folksong, Library of Congress,Washington, D.C.).

56. *Sullivan's Travels*, dir. Preston Sturges (Paramount, 1941).

57. The term "populist outsider" comes from Benjamin Filene, "'Our Singing Country': John and Alan Lomax, Leadbelly, and the Construction of an American Past," *American Quarterly* 43 (December 1991): 611–12. For various perspectives on the 1930s folk revival, see idem, *Romancing the Folk: Public Memory and American Roots Music* (Chapel Hill: University of North Carolina Press, 2000); Robert Cantwell, *When We Were Good:The Folk Revival* (Cambridge: Harvard University Press, 1996); Neil V. Rosenberg, ed., *Transforming Tradition: Folk Music Revivals Examined* (Urbana: University of Illinois Press, 1993); and Michael Denning, *The Cultural Front:The Laboring ofAmerican Culture in the Twentieth Century* (NewYork:Verso, 1996), 133–34, 348–61.

58. Worby, *The Other Half*, inside cover.

59. "Overheard at the Water Tanks," *Hobo News Review* 23 (May 1936).

60. Denning, *Cultural Front*, 127–28.

61. *Meet John Doe*, dir. Frank Capra (Paramount, 1941).

62. Joseph McBride, *Frank Capra: The Catastrophe of Success* (New York: Simon and Schuster, 1992), 429–37.

63. For an analysis of the Popular Front social movement's profound impact upon American culture, see Michael Denning's *Cultural Front*. See especially Denning's analysis of the competing populist rhetorics at work in the 1930s, ibid., 125–36.

64. Daniel J. Leab, "'United We Eat': The Creation and Organization of the Unemployed Councils in 1930," *Labor History* 8 (fall 1967): 300–15; Roy Rosenzweig, "Organizing the Unemployed: The Early Years of the Great Depression," *Radical America* 10 (July–August 1976): 37–60; Lizabeth Cohen, *Making a New Deal: Industrial Workers in Chicago, 1919–1939* (New York: Cambridge University Press, 1990), 262–67.

65. Robert H. Zeiger, *The CIO, 1935–1955* (Chapel Hill: University of North Carolina Press, 1995); Denning, *Cultural Front*, 6–10; Cohen, *Making a New Deal*, 323–60; Devra Weber, *Dark Sweat, White Gold: California Farm Workers, Cotton, and the New Deal* (Berkeley: University of California Press, 1994), 162–99; Cletus E. Daniel, *Bitter Harvest: A History of California Farmworkers, 1870–1941* (Berkeley: University of California Press, 1981), 258–85; James N. Gregory, *American Exodus: The Dust Bowl Migration and Okie Culture in California* (New York: Oxford University Press, 1989), 154–64.

66. For critiques of this proletarian imagery, see Eric J. Hobsbawm, "Man and Woman: Images on the Left," in *Workers' Worlds of Labor* (New York: Pantheon, 1984), 83–102; and Elizabeth Faue, *Community of Suffering and Struggle: Women, Men, and the Labor Movement in Minneapolis, 1915–1945* (Chapel Hill: University of North Carolina Press, 1991), chap. 3.

67. Denning, *Cultural Front*, 269–72; Joe Klein, *Woody Guthrie: A Life* (New York: Alfred A. Knopf, 1980).

68. Woody Guthrie, *Bound for Glory* (New York: Plume, 1983 [1943]), 235, 243.

69. Ibid., 19–36, 263–69.

70. Ibid., 245–55.

71. Denning, *Cultural Front*, 259–69; Gregory, *American Exodus*.

72. John N. Webb and Malcolm Brown, *Migrant Families* (Washington, D.C.: Works Progress Administration, 1938), xiv. See also Marion Hathway, *The Migratory Worker and Family Life* (Chicago: University of Illinois Press, 1934); Victor Weybright, "Rolling Stones Gather No Sympathy," *Survey Graphic* 28 (January 1939): 29–30; and "Interstate Migration of Destitute Citizens," *Monthly Labor Review* 52 (February 1941): 338–49.

73. Crouse, *Homeless Transient*, 8.

74. Wickenden, "Transiency-Mobility in Trouble," 307–8.

75. Denning, *Cultural Front*, 137–38. For other discussions of Lange's "Migrant Mother" and the "icon of motherhood" in depression culture, see Paula Rabinowitz, *Labor and Desire: Women's Revolutionary Fiction in Depression America* (Chapel Hill: University of North Carolina Press, 1991), 97–136; Wendy Kozol, "Madonnas of the Fields: Photography, Gender and 1930s Farm Relief," *Genders* 2 (summer 1988): 1–23; William Stott, *Documentary Expression and Thirties America* (New York: Oxford University Press, 1971), 224–31; and James Curtis, *Mind's Eye, Mind's Truth: FSA Photography Reconsidered* (Philadelphia: Temple University Press, 1989), 45–67.

76. Bertha Thompson (Ben Reitman), *Boxcar Bertha: An Autobiography as Told to Dr. Ben L. Reitman* (New York: Amok Press, 1988 [1937]), 278.

77. On the gender politics and inequities of relief and welfare in the New Deal, see Linda Gordon, *Pitied but Not Entitled: Single Mothers and the History of Welfare, 1890–1935* (New York: Free Press, 1994), 183–306.

78. On the "comradely ideal" in New Deal public art and theater, see Melosh, *Engendering Culture*.

79. Robert Cooley Angell, *The Family Encounters the Depression* (Gloucester, Mass.: Peter Smith, 1965 [1936]), 17, 52. See also Ruth Shonle Cavan and Katherine Howland Ranke, *The Family and the Depression* (Freeport, N.Y.: Books for Libraries Press, 1938); Mirra Komarovsky, *The Unemployed Man and His Family: The Effect of Unemployment upon the Status of the Man in Fifty-nine Families* (New York: Octagon Books, 1971 [1940]); and E. Wright Bakke, *Citizens without Work* (New Haven: Yale University Press, 1940).

80. On the fate of alternative housing designs in the New Deal, see Gail Radford, *Modern Housing for America: Policy Struggles in the New Deal Era* (Chicago: University of Chicago Press, 1996).

81. On suburban expansion and federal housing policy in the depression and postwar eras, see Gwendolyn Wright, *Building the Dream: A Social History of Housing in America* (New York: Pantheon, 1981), 240–61; Kenneth T. Jackson, *Crabgrass Frontier: The Suburbanization of the United States* (New York: Oxford University Press, 1985), 190–245; and Paul Groth, *Living Downtown: The History of Residential Hotels in the United States* (Berkeley: University of California Press, 1994), 253–84.

## CHAPTER EIGHT

1. Bill Mauldin, *Back Home* (New York: William Sloane Associates, 1947), 1–39.

2. Ibid., 108, 48–49.

3. Robert H. Zeiger, *The CIO, 1935–1955* (Chapel Hill: University of North Carolina Press, 1995), 181–87.

4. Michael J. Bennett, *When Dreams Came True: The GI Bill and the Making of Modern America* (Washington, D.C.: Brassey's, 1996), 88.

5. Ibid., 76–180; Keith W. Olson, *The G.I. Bill, the Veterans, and the Colleges* (Lexington: University Press of Kentucky, 1974), 3–39; Milton Greenburg, *The GI Bill: The Law that Changed America* (New York: Lickle Publishing, 1997), 9–22.

6. Mauldin, *Back Home*, 60.

7. Quoted in David T. Courtwright, *Violent Land: Single Men and Social Disorder from the Frontier to the Inner City* (Cambridge: Harvard University Press, 1996), 204.

8. On the GI Bill's education provisions, see Bennett, *When Dreams Came True*, 237–76; and Greenburg, *The GI Bill*, 35–72.

9. On the dramatic drop after World War II in the nation's historically high rates of residential mobility, see Ronald Tobey, Charles Wetherell, and Jay Brigham, "Moving Out and Settling In: Residential Mobility, Home Owning, and the Public Enframing of Citizenship, 1921–1950," *American Historical Review* 95 (December 1990): 1395–422. On the GI Bill's housing provisions, see Bennett, *When Dreams Came True*, 194–236; and Greenburg, *The GI Bill*, 73–86.

10. Brett Harvey, *The Fifties: A Women's Oral History* (New York: HarperCollins, 1993), 69; Elaine Tyler May, *Homeward Bound: American Families in the Cold War Era* (New York: Basic Books, 1988), 6–7.

11. George Lipsitz, *Rainbow at Midnight: Labor and Culture in the 1940s* (Urbana: University of Illinois Press, 1994), 69–154.

12. On the emergence of postwar "corporate liberalism," see ibid., 57–65, 157–81. See also Nelson Lichtenstein, "From Corporatism to Collective Bargaining: Organized Labor and the Eclipse of Social Democracy in the Postwar Era," in *The Rise and Fall of the New Deal Order, 1930–1980*, ed. Steve Fraser and Gary Gerstle (Princeton: Princeton University Press, 1989), 122–52.

13. Kenneth T. Jackson, *Crabgrass Frontier: The Suburbanization of the United States* (New York: Oxford University Press, 1985), 197–203.

14. Charles Hoch and Robert A. Slayton, *New Homeless and Old: Community and the Skid Row Hotel* (Philadelphia: Temple University Press, 1989), 88–89.

15. Chicago Tenants Relocation Bureau, *The Homeless Man on Skid Row* (Chicago: Tenants Relocation Bureau, 1961), 6.

16. Barrett A. Lee, "The Disappearance of Skid Row: Some Ecological Evidence," *Urban Affairs Quarterly* 16 (September 1980): 90. For similar findings, see Donald J. Bogue, *Skid Row in American Cities* (Chicago: University of Chicago Press, 1963), 8–12; Earl Rubington, "The Changing Skid Row Scene," *Quarterly Journal of Studies on Alcohol* 32 (June 1971): 123–35; Howard M. Bahr and Theodore Caplow, *Old Men, Drunk and Sober* (New York: New York University Press, 1974), 49; and John C. Schneider, "Skid Row as Urban Neighborhood, 1880–1960," in *Housing the Homeless*, ed. Jon Erickson and Charles Wilhelm (Brunswick: State University of New Jersey, 1986), 180.

17. Samuel E. Wallace, *Skid Row as a Way of Life* (Totowa, N.J.: Bedminster Press, 1965), 25. See also Relocation Bureau, *The Homeless Man on Skid Row*, 15.

18. "Chicago's Misery Mile," *Commonweal* 50 (September 30, 1949): 598; Schneider, "Skid Row as Urban Neighborhood," 180. Other sensational exposés of skid row include William Slocum, "Skid Row U.S.A.," *Collier's* 27 (August 1949): 26–27, 61–64; and Jerome Ellison, "The Shame of Skid Row," *Saturday Evening Post* 224 (December 20, 1952): 13–16, 48, 51.

19. Bahr and Caplow, *Old Men, Drunk and Sober*, 3, 11.

20. May, *Homeward Bound*, 168; Jackson, *Crabgrass Frontier*, 232.

21. Paul Groth, *Living Downtown: The History of Residential Hotels in the United States* (Berkeley: University of California Press, 1994), 265–67.

22. "Eisenhower's Farewell Address, January 17, 1961," in *Documents in American History*, ed. Henry Steele Commager (New York: Appleton, Century, Crofts, 1963), 687.

23. May, *Homeward Bound*, 3–15.

24. Greenburg, *The GI Bill*, 76. See also Jackson, *Crabgrass Frontier*, 231–45; and Gwendolyn Wright, *Building the Dream: A Social History of Housing in America* (New York: Pantheon, 1981), 240–61.

25. May, *Homeward Bound*, 3–15.

26. Barbara Ehrenreich, *The Hearts of Men: American Dreams and the Flight from Commitment* (New York: Anchor Books, 1983), 1–28.

27. May, *Homeward Bound*.

28. Howard M. Bahr, "Homelessness, Disaffiliation, and Retreatism," in *Disaffiliated Man: Essays and Bibliography on Skid Row, Vagrancy, and Outsiders*, ed. Howard M. Bahr (Toronto: University of Toronto Press, 1970), 46.

29. Bahr and Caplow, *Old Men, Drunk and Sober*, 7.

30. Boris M. Levinson, "The Homeless Man: A Psychological Enigma," *Mental Hygiene* 47 (October 1963): 597, 599.

31. Peter Berger, Brigitte Berger, and Hansfried Kellner, *The Homeless Mind: Modernization and Consciousness* (New York: Vintage Books, 1973).

32. Bahr and Caplow, *Old Men, Drunk and Sober*, 5, 58.

33. Hoch and Slayton, *New Homeless and Old*, 93–114.

34. Bogue, *Skid Row in American Cities*, 106–8; Howard M. Bahr, *Skid Row: An Introduction to Disaffiliation* (New York: Oxford University Press, 1973), 104–5.

35. Rubington, "The Changing Skid Row Scene," 133.

36. James E. Vance Jr., "Human Mobility and the Shaping of Cities," in *Our Changing Cities*, ed. John Fraser Hurt (Baltimore: Johns Hopkins University Press, 1991), 75.

37. Jackson, *Crabgrass Frontier*, 197–203.

38. Federal Housing Administration, *Property Standards: Requirements for Mortgage Insurance under Title II of the National Housing Act, June 1, 1936*, circular no. 2 (Washington, D.C.: Government Printing Office, 1936), 4–5, 14–15. See also Groth, *Living Downtown*, 255–56. For an extended screed on rooming-house blight from the postwar period, see American Society of Planning Officials, *Rooming Houses*, Information Report No. 105 (Chicago: Planning Advisory Service, 1957).

39. Arnold M. Rose, "Living Arrangements of Unattached Persons," *American Sociological Review* 12 (August 1947): 431.

40. Quoted in Mark I. Gelfand, *A Nation of Cities: The Federal Government and Urban America, 1933–1965* (New York: Oxford University Press, 1975), 137.

41. Gelfand, *Nation of Cities*, 105–97. See also Lawrence M. Friedman, *Government and Slum Housing: A Century of Frustration* (Chicago: Rand McNally, 1968).

42. Lee, "The Disappearance of Skid Row," 100.

43. Groth, *Living Downtown*, 268–84; Alvin Averbach, "San Francisco's South of Market District, 1850–1950: The Emergence of a Skid Row," *California Historical Quarterly* 52 (fall 1973): 215–19; Dorothy Gazzolo, "Skid Row Gives Renewalists Rough, Tough Relocation Problems," *Journal of Housing* 18 (August–September 1961): 330–31.

44. Hoch and Slayton, *New Homeless and Old*, 117–22; Melvyn Dubofsky, *We Shall Be All: A History of the Industrial Workers of the World* (Chicago: Quadrangle Books, 1969), 471.

45. Betty Friedan, *The Feminine Mystique* (New York: W. W. Norton, 1983 [1963]), 15–32.

46. Sloane Wilson, *The Man in the Gray Flannel Suit* (New York: Simon and Schuster, 1955); William H. Whyte, *The Organization Man* (New York: Anchor Books, 1956); David Riesman, *The Lonely Crowd: A Study of the Changing American Character* (New Haven: Yale University Press, 1967 [1950]). For an analysis of the problem of "conformity" in postwar America and the role of *Playboy* magazine in advancing male rebellion, see Ehrenreich, *The Hearts of Men*, 29–51; and Michael Kimmel, *Manhood in America: A Cultural History* (New York: Free Press, 1996), 223–58.

47. Slocum, "Skid Row U.S.A.," 64.

48. James P. Spradley, *You Owe Yourself a Drunk: An Ethnography of Urban Nomads* (Boston: Little, Brown, 1970); Douglas A. Harper, *Good Company* (Chicago: University of Chicago Press, 1982). Other revisionist studies of skid row include Wallace, *Skid Row as a Way of Life;* Ronald Vander Kooi, "The Main Stem: Skid Row Revisited," *Society* 10 (September–October 1973): 64–71; and William McSheehy, *Skid Row* (Cambridge: Harvard University Press, 1979).

49. Ann Charters, ed., *The Portable Beat Reader* (New York: Viking, 1992), xv–xxxvi, 1–7.

50. Jack Kerouac, "The Vanishing Hobo," *Holiday* 27 (March 1960): 60–61, 112–13.

51. Ibid., 113.

52. Gerald Nicosia, *Memory Babe: A Critical Biography of Jack Kerouac* (Berkeley: University of California Press, 1994 [1983]), 345.

53. Nicosia, *Memory Babe*, 172–79; Charters, *Portable Beat Reader*, 187–90.

54. Jack Kerouac, *On the Road* (New York: Penguin, 1976 [1955]), 3.

55. Ibid., 232.

56. Ibid., 180–81.

57. On the shift from "race" to "ethnicity" among European immigrants, see especially Matthew Frye Jacobson, *Whiteness of a Different Color: European Immigrants and the Alchemy of Race* (Cambridge: Harvard University Press, 1998), 39–135; David Roediger, "Whiteness and Ethnicity in the History of 'White Ethnics' in the United States," in *Towards the Abolition of Whiteness: Essays on Race, Politics, and Working Class History* (New York: Verso, 1994), 181–98.

58. On the redefinition of whiteness in the postwar era, see George Lipsitz, *The Possessive Investment in Whiteness: How White People Profit from Identity Politics* (Philadelphia: Temple University Press, 1998), 1–23. For information on how the GI Bill disproportionately benefited white males, see Karen Brodkin Sacks, "The GI Bill: Whites Only Need Apply," in *Critical White Studies: Looking Behind the Mirror*, ed. Richard Delgado and Jean Stefanic (Philadelphia: Temple University Press, 1997), 310–13.

59. Kerouac, *On the Road*, 3.

60. Jack Kerouac, *The Dharma Bums* (New York: Signet, 1959 [1958]), 10.

61. Ibid., 27.

62. Ibid., 78.

63. Spradley, *You Owe Yourself a Drunk*, 6; Michael Mathers, *Riding the Rails* (Boston:

Gambit, 1973);Ted Conover, *Rolling Nowhere* (NewYork:Viking, 1984); Harper, *Good Company.*

64. Harper, *Good Company,* 68.

65. *Easy Rider,* dir. Dennis Hopper (Columbia, 1969); Michael Denning, *The Cultural Front:The Laboring of American Culture in the Twentieth Century* (NewYork:Verso, 1996), 189.

66. Ehrenreich, *The Hearts of Men,* 107.

67. Tuli Kupferberg, quoted in ibid.

68. Ibid., 119–21; Howard P. Chudacoff, *The Age of the Bachelor: Creating an American Subculture* (Princeton: Princeton University Press, 1999), 264–67.

69. Vander Kooi, "The Main Stem," 64.

70. Groth, *Living Downtown,* 284–86.

## CHAPTER NINE

1. Dale Maharidge and MichaelWilliamson, *Journey to Nowhere:The Saga of the New Underclass* (Garden City, N.Y.: Dial Press, 1985), 7–8.

2. Ibid., 4, 52.

3. Ibid., 20.

4. Ibid., 9.

5. Ibid., 7.

6. Richard Campbell and Jimmie L. Reeves, "Covering the Homeless:The Joyce Brown Story," in *Reading the Homeless: The Media's Image of Homeless Culture,* ed. Eungjun Min (Westport, Conn.: Praeger, 1999), 23; Jimmie L. Reeves, "Re-Covering the Homeless: Hindsights on the Joyce Brown Story," in *Reading the Homeless,* 54.

7. Maharidge andWilliamson, *Journey to Nowhere,* 189.

8. Joan M. Crouse, "Transients, Migrants, and the Homeless," in *The Encyclopedia of American Social History,* vol. 3, ed. Mary Kupiec Cayton, Elliott J. Gorn, and Peter W. Williams (NewYork: Scribner, 1993), 2152–53. On "the politics of compassion" with reference to homelessness, see Charles Hoch and Robert A. Slayton, *New Homeless and Old: Community and the Skid Row Hotel* (Philadelphia: Temple University Press, 1989), 203–17. See also Mary Ellen Hombs and Mitch Snyder, *Homeless in America: A Forced March to Nowhere* (Washington, D.C.: Community for Creative Non-Violence, 1982).

9. U.S. Department of Housing and Urban Development, *Report to the Secretary on the Homeless and Emergency Housing* (Washington, D.C.: Office of Policy Development and Research, U.S. Department of Housing and Urban Development, 1984). For the congressional hearings on the HUD report's findings, see U.S. Congress, Joint Hearing before the Subcommittee on Housing and Urban Development of the Committee on Banking, Finance, and Urban Affairs and the Subcommittee on Manpower and Housing of the Committee of Government Operations, *HUD Report on Homelessness,* 98th Cong. 2d sess. May 24, 1984.

10. On the politics of Hands Across America, see Reeves, "Re-Covering the Homeless," 56–58.

11. Hoch and Slayton, *New Homeless and Old,* 209. See also Joel Blau, *The Visible Poor: Homelessness in the United States* (NewYork: Oxford University Press, 1992), 111–14.

12. Quoted in John Fiske, "For Cultural Interpretation: A Study of the Culture of Homelessness," in *Reading the Homeless,* ed. Min, 5.

13. On the critical distinction between homelessness and houselessness in scholarly studies, see Joanne Passaro, *The Unequal Homeless: Men on the Streets,Women in Their Place* (NewYork: Routledge, 1996), 21–25.

14. The scholarship on homelessness produced in the 1980s and 1990s is vast, ranging from community-level case studies to national and even global surveys.The first major general studies of contemporary homelessness include Carol L. M. Caton, *Homeless in America* (NewYork: Oxford University Press, 1990); Hoch and Slayton, *New Homeless and Old;* Marjorie Hope and James Young, *The Faces of Homelessness* (Lexington, Mass.: Lexington Books, 1986); Jonathan Kozol, *Rachel and Her Children: Homeless Families in America* (New York:

Crown, 1988); F. Stevens Redburn and Terry F. Buss, *Responding to America's Homeless: Public Policy Alternatives* (New York: Praeger, 1986); Peter H. Rossi, *Down and Out in America: The Origins of Homelessness* (Chicago: University of Chicago Press, 1989); E. Fuller Torrey, *Nowhere to Go: The Tragic Odyssey of the Homeless Mentally Ill* (New York: Harper and Row, 1988); Gregg Barak, *Gimme Shelter: A Social History of Homelessness in Contemporary America* (New York: Praeger, 1991); Michael H. Lang, *Homelessness amid Affluence: Structure and Paradox in the American Political Economy* (New York: Praeger, 1989); Jon Erikson and Charles Wilhelm, eds., *Housing the Homeless* (New Brunswick, N.J.: Center for Urban Policy Research, 1986); Rachel G. Bratt, Chester Hartman, and Ann Meyerson, eds., *Critical Perspectives on Housing* (Philadelphia: Temple University Press, 1986); Blau, *Visible Poor;* Martha Burt, *Over the Edge: The Growth of Homelessness in the 1980s* (New York: Russell Sage Foundation, 1992); Christopher Jencks, *The Homeless* (Cambridge: Harvard University Press, 1994); and Michael Dear and Jennifer Wolch, *Landscapes of Despair: From Deinstitutionalization to Homelessness* (Princeton: Princeton University Press, 1987).

15. Kim Hopper and Jill Hamberg, "The Making of America's Homeless: From Skid Row to New Poor, 1945–1984," in *Critical Perspectives on Housing,* ed. Bratt, Hartman, and Meyerson, 17.

16. See especially ibid., 17–18, 25–26; Blau, *Visible Poor,* 33–47; Rossi, *Down and Out in America,* 186–89; and Barak, *Gimme Shelter,* 63–68. The emerging two-tiered labor system is discussed extensively in David Harvey, *The Condition of Postmodernity: An Enquiry into the Origins of Cultural Change* (London: Blackwell, 1989), 141–72.

17. Hopper and Hamberg, "The Making of America's Homeless," 20.

18. Blau, *Visible Poor,* 52.

19. See ibid., 48–59; Hopper and Hamberg, "The Making of America's Homeless," 19–20, 27–28; Rossi, *Down and Out in America,* 186–89.

20. Fiske, "For Cultural Interpretation," 6.

21. See Hopper and Hamberg, "The Making of America's Homeless," 20–23, 28–32; Blau, *Visible Poor,* 60–76; Rossi, *Down and Out in America,* 181–86; Barak, *Gimme Shelter,* 68–71; Jencks, *The Homeless,* 81–102; Hoch and Slayton, *New Homeless and Old,* 175–81, 211; and Lang, *Homelessness amid Affluence,* 16–19.

22. Blau, *Visible Poor,* 80.

23. Hoch and Slayton, *New Homeless and Old,* 207.

24. See Hopper and Hamberg, "The Making of America's Homeless," 23–24, 31–32; Blau, *Visible Poor,* 77–90; Rossi, *Down and Out in America,* 145–56; Barak, *Gimme Shelter,* 39–43; Jencks, *The Homeless,* 21–40; Hoch and Slayton, *New Homeless and Old,* 203–8; H. Richard Lamb, "Deinstitutionalization and the Homeless Mentally Ill," in *Housing the Homeless,* ed. Erikson and Wilhelm, 262–78; Torrey, *Nowhere to Go;* and Dear and Wolch, *Landscapes of Despair.*

25. Rossi, *Down and Out in America,* 147.

26. Blau, *Visible Poor,* 25–6; Rossi, *Down and Out in America,* 117–20, 132–34.

27. Blau, *Visible Poor,* 26; Rossi, *Down and Out in America,* 122–26.

28. Karin Stallard, Barbara Ehrenreich, and Holly Sklar, *Poverty and the American Dream: Women and Children First* (Boston: South End Press, 1983), 6. See also William H. Chafe, *The Unfinished Journey: America since World War II,* 4th ed. (New York: Oxford University Press, 1999), 439–41.

29. Chafe, *The Unfinished Journey,* 442–45. See also William Julius Wilson, *The Truly Disadvantaged* (Chicago: University of Chicago Press, 1987); and Jacqueline Jones, *The Dispossessed: America's Underclass from the Civil War to the Present* (New York: Basic Books, 1992), 269–92.

30. Sophie Watson and Helen Austerberry, *Housing and Homelessness: A Feminist Perspective* (London: Routledge and Kegan Paul, 1986), 8.

31. For discussions of liberal and conservative depictions of homelessness in the 1980s, see Hoch and Slayton, *New Homeless and Old,* 199–217; and David Wagner, *Checkerboard*

*Square: Culture and Resistance in a Homeless Community* (Boulder: Westview Press, 1993), 1–5.

32. Passaro, *Unequal Homeless*, 3. My discussion of the differential treatment of homeless men and women is heavily indebted to Passaro's analysis, especially 1–34.

33. Ibid., 20.

34. Peter Marin, "Homelessness Mostly Affects Single Men," in *The Homeless: Opposing Viewpoints*, ed. Tamara L. Roleff (San Diego: Greenhaven Press, 1996), 51. See also Hoch and Slayton, *New Homeless and Old*, 223–26.

35. Maharidge and Williamson, *Journey to Nowhere*, 171.

36. Ibid., 67, 68, 75.

37. "A New Breed of Hobo," *Newsweek* (August 16, 1982): 30–31.

38. David Weedle, "Living on Hobo Time," *California* 15 (February 1990): 68.

39. "American Album," *Los Angeles Times*, June 12, 1989.

40. Letters to the Editor, *Hobo Times* 4 (May/June 1990): 2.

41. Weedle, "Living on Hobo Time," 70.

42. "Hobo Philosophy Can Save America," *Hobo Times* 4 (November/December 1990): 1.

43. Letters to the Editor, *Hobo Times* 8 (August/September 1994): 35–36.

44. "Hobo Alumni [*sic*] for President," *Hobo Times* 6 (January/February 1992): 1.

45. *Los Angeles Times*, July 13, 1999; *Houston Chronicle*, May 19, 2000.

46. *Los Angeles Times*, September 17, 1997; Bruce Rubenstein, "Last Train Out," *City Pages* (December 12, 1997), <http://citypages.com/databank/18/887/article3839.asp>.

47. Sarah Ferguson, "Meet the Crusties," *Esquire* 121 (January 1994): 69–75.

48. Ibid., 75.

49. Mary A. Fischer, "Weekend Hoboes," *Gentleman's Quarterly* 70 (November 2000): 262; Steven Kotler, "Damn Track," *Maxim* 19 (June 1999): 109; "Wild Boys," *New York Times Magazine* (September 12, 1999): 112–22.

50. David A. Snow and Leon Anderson, *Down on Their Luck* (Berkeley: University of California Press, 1993), 24–26. See also Elliot Liebow, *Tell Them Who I Am: The Lives of Homeless Women* (New York: Free Press, 1993), x–xii.

51. Liebow, *Tell Them Who I Am*, 3.

52. Snow and Anderson, *Down on Their Luck*, 9, 76, 314–15; Liebow, *Tell Them Who I Am*, 190.

53. Snow and Anderson, *Down on Their Luck*, 262; Liebow, *Tell Them Who I Am*, 112, 182, 227.

54. Dale Maharidge and Michael Williamson, *The Last Great American Hobo* (Rocklin, Calif.: Prima Publishing, 1993), iii.

55. Ibid., 31–32.

56. Wagner, *Checkerboard Square*, 3.

57. Passaro, *Unequal Homeless*, 63, 36.

58. Howard M. Bahr and Theodore Caplow, *Old Men, Drunk and Sober* (New York: New York University Press, 1974), 58.

59. Fiske, "For Cultural Interpretation," 2–3.

60. Bahr and Caplow, *Old Men, Drunk and Sober*, 58.

61. Passaro, *Unequal Homeless*, 12.

62. Wagner, *Checkerboard Square*, 10.

63. Maharidge and Williamson, *The Last Great American Hobo*, 71–73.

# INDEX

*Page references in italic refer to illustrations.*

short